D1440929

"BE SOBER AND REASONABLE"

BRILL'S STUDIES IN INTELLECTUAL HISTORY

"BE SOBER AND REASONABLE"

The Critique of Enthusiasm in the Seventeenth and Early Eighteenth Centuries

BY

MICHAEL HEYD

E.J. BRILL
LEIDEN · NEW YORK · KÖLN
1995

The paper in this book meets the guidelines for permanence and durability of the Committee on Production Guidelines for Book Longevity of the Council on Library Resources.

BR
112
.H45
1995

Library of Congress Cataloging-in-Publication Data

Heyd, Michael.
    Be sober and reasonable : the critique of enthusiasm in the
seventeenth and early eighteenth centuries / by Michael Heyd.
        p.   cm. — (Brill's studies in intellectual history, ISSN
0920-8607 ; v. 63)
    Includes bibliographical references and index.
    ISBN 9004101187 (cloth : alk. paper)
        1. Enthusiasm—Religious aspects—Christianity. 2. Church
history—17th century.   3. Church history—18th century. I. Title.
II. Series.
BR112.H45   1995
273'.7—dc20
                                                            95-17036
                                                            CIP

Die Deutsche Bibliothek – CIP-Einheitsaufnahme

Heyd, Michael:
"Be sober and reasonable" : the critique of enthusiasm in the
seventeenth and early eighteenth centuries / by Michael Heyd.
– Leiden ; New York ; Köln : Brill, 1995
    (Brill's studies in intellectual history ; Vol. 63)
    ISBN 90-04-10118-7
NE: GT

ISSN   0920-8607
ISBN   90 04 10118 7

PRINTED IN THE NETHERLANDS

To Smadar

TABLE OF CONTENTS

PREFACE

This book ventures on an avowedly ambitious task: to trace some of the reactions to "enthusiasm" in the early modern period. The critique of ecstasy, prophecy, and claims to direct divine inspiration is widespread and highly revealing in the period between the Reformation and the Enlightenment. Yet, whereas the "enthusiasts" themselves, and the radical movements with which they were involved, have been the subject of considerable research in the past generation, the establishment's reaction to enthusiasm has not yet received the attention it deserves, and especially not from the broad inter-disciplinary perspective which will be attempted in this book. Such an attempt, however, can by no means be exhaustive. My aim is only to highlight some of the basic issues which I believe are pertinent to this topic.

I became interested in the subject in the course of my search after the origins and historical circumstances of the emergence of modern secular culture. Influenced by the Weberian concept of the disenchantment of the world, and intrigued by Christianity's contribution to this process, I was drawn to look at the critique of enthusiasm in the Protestant world in the seventeenth century, and the impact such critique might have had on the origins of the Enlightenment. My previous work on Jean-Robert Chouet and the introduction of Cartesian science in the Academy of Geneva raised, on the other hand, persistent questions concerning the role of the new natural philosophy in developments leading up to the Enlightenment. Chouet clearly saw Cartesianism as a *philosophia sobria*, as a response to enthusiasm. Yet one of his students, Nicolas Fatio de Duillier, was later to become a spokesman for the so-called French Prophets. The problem of enthusiasm was thus connected in more complex ways than might immediately appear with the spread of the new philosophy and science in the Protestant world in the late seventeenth and early eighteenth centuries.

Many years later, having immersed myself in the religious, medical and philosophical critique of enthusiasm, I also came to realize the limitations of that critique. While we are all called to be *sober and reasonable*, we can be so, I believe, only by recognizing the legitimacy of our own visions, our urge for inspiration, and indeed, our melancholic moments. The search for a balance between these two conflicting inclinations has characterized western civilization ever since classical times. The need to find such a balance is especially urgent nowadays, in a period of high-tech innovations on the one hand, and religious fundamentalist movements as well as other mystical and "enthusiastic" sects on the other. It is a task facing both the individual and society as a whole.

In the course of the years spent working on this subject, I have incurred innumerable debts from institutions, libraries, and individuals. First thanks are due to my own university, the Hebrew University of Jerusalem, which enabled me to take sabbatical leaves for work on this project. I owe particular gratitude to four institutes in which much of the research and writing of this book has been done: The first is the Institute for Advanced Study in Princeton, in which the initial work was carried out in 1979–1980, and where the combination of tranquility and stimulating intellectual exchange contributed much to the theoretical and historiographic conceptualization of the themes of this book; second, Johns Hopkins University in Baltimore, where I spent another sabbatical year in 1985–86. The history of science department there graciously accepted me as a visiting scholar, and the combination of excellent departments in history, history of science and the Institute for the History of Medicine provided me with the most appropriate setting for work on these dimensions of my subject. Thirdly, as a fellow at the Institute for Advanced Studies at the Hebrew University in Jerusalem in 1986–87, and participating in a research group on the Sepharadic Jews in the post-expulsion period, I became aware of some of the parallel problems of Messianism and the response to it in the Jewish world of the early modern period. Though it is not treated in the present book, I am convinced that the issues of the reaction to enthusiasm and millenarianism in the early modern period should be seen in a comparative Jewish-Christian perspective. Lastly, much of the final writing was done at another wonderful Institute, the Netherlands Institute for Advanced Study in the Humanities and Social Sciences (NIAS), where the quiet and friendly social as well as scholarly atmosphere made the term spent there an unforgettable experience.

Equally important, of course, are the libraries and archives, which for an historian are the real laboratories of his work. I had the privilege and good fortune to make use of many of them around the world, all proving extremely helpful and congenial: First of all, the British Library in London where I spent many summers in research.

Similarly, the Bodleian Library in Oxford and the University Library at Cambridge. In the United States, I benefited especially from the wonderful collections of the Folger Shakespeare Library in Washington, from the very rich historical collection of the National Library of Medicine in Maryland, and particularly, from the library of the Institute for the History of Medicine at Johns Hopkins, Baltimore, whose staff was kind enough to provide me with a room for a couple of months. Other libraries in the United States which proved helpful were the Eisenhower Library at the Homewood campus of Johns Hopkins, particularly its rare book collection, the Firestone Library and Speer Library in Princeton, and the Public Library in New York. In Europe I should mention first and foremost the Bibliothèque publique et universitaire in Geneva, its Salle des Manuscrits, and the helpful librarians there, and above all, the Institut d'histoire de la Réformation where I have always felt very much at home. In Paris I benefited as usual from the Bibliothèque nationale. In the Netherlands, I made much use of the Royal Library at the Hague, the University Library at Utrecht, the University Library of Groningen, and above all the University Library of Leiden, where I enjoyed the cordial help of a colleague and good friend, Dr. Christiane Berkvens-Stevelinck. Special mention should be made of the efficient and amiable inter-library help I always received from Dinny Young and her staff at the NIAS library. Last but not least, at home, the National and University Library in Jerusalem has always proved richer than I expected. Special personal thanks are due to Shelly Benvenisti, a good friend as well as the very competent librarian in charge of the general reading room, who has always been ready to go out of her way to trace material.

Yet a book depends not only on institutes and libraries, but primarily on the advice, help and support of people—colleagues, friends and family. Only a few of them can be mentioned here; some figure in footnotes in the course of the book itself. Among colleagues, I would like to mention my former teachers at Princeton, Theodore K. Rabb and Lawrence Stone, as well as Natalie Z. Davis, who were all helpful with advice during the formative stages of the project. At Johns Hopkins, Owen Hannaway and Robert Kargon provided very warm hospitality and John Pococke was extremely encouraging, as he has been with so many others. In Geneva, Pierre Fraenkel, Olivier Fatio, Irena Backus and Christina Pitassi were always most helpful on the issues of Church history into which I have treaded rather recklessly. In the Netherlands, I have received similar help from Hans Posthumus-Meyjes and Nicolette Mout. In Israel, I would like to mention, among numerous friends and colleagues, the interest, advice and encouragement of Yehoshua Arieli, Myriam Yardeni, Yosef Kaplan, Esther Cohen, Avihu Zakai, Yehuda Elkana, Yaron Ezrahi and Rivka Feldhai.

The preparation of such a book also involves many technical and linguistic chores. In transcribing and translating old German texts I was helped by Larissa Naiditch, as well as by my mother Shoshana Heyd. In the verification of some of the Latin texts, I benefited from the help of Ilana Klutstein, and in deciphering and understanding some of the Greek terms, Hannah Rosén was extremely helpful and friendly. Special thanks are due to Mira Reich who invested much time and professional expertise in improving my English and in editing the manuscript. Finally, my brother, David Heyd, was not only a source of help and encouragement (as well as debate) throughout the years, but has also generously and competently gone over the proofs of the whole book. Needless to say, none of the above mentioned bears any responsibility for the mistakes, mistranslations, misprints and misconceptions which remain, but all of them have done much to cut down such errors significantly.

On a personal level, my daughters Einat and Ronith have always been a source of joy, optimism, and encouragement. The greatest debt, however, I owe Smadar Tirosh. In the vagaries of personal life, in the oscillations between melancholy and enthusiasm as well as in moments of sobriety and reasonableness, Smadar has been a source of constant support. Without her unfailing encouragement, this book would never have been completed. It is wholeheartedly dedicated to her.

Jerusalem
July 1995

ACKNOWLEDGEMENTS

Chapter 2 is a significantly revised version of an article published in *History of European Ideas*, Vol. 5, No. 1 (1984): 17–44, under the title "Robert Burton's Sources on Enthusiasm and Melancholy: From a Medical Tradition to Religious Controversy". Thanks are due to Elsevier Science Ltd, Pergamon Imprint, The Boulevard, Langford Lane, Kidlington OX5, 1GB, UK, for their permission to include this revised version in the present book.

Chapter 4 is a revised version of an article published under the title "Descartes—An Enthusiast *malgré lui?*" in David S. Katz and Jonathan I. Israel, eds., *Sceptics Millenarians and Jews*, published by E.J. Brill, 1990, pp. 35–58. I wish to thank E.J. Brill for permission to republish the article in a slightly revised version in the present book.

Chapter 5 is a revised version of an article published under the title "The New Experimental Philosophy: A Manifestation of 'Enthusiasm' or an Antidote to it?" in *Minerva*, vol. 25, no. 4 (Winter 1987), pp. 423–440. © *Minerva*, 1987. I wish to thank Kluwer Academic Publishers for permission to include the revised version of the article in this book.

Chapter 7 is a revised version of an article published under the title "Medical Discourse in Religious Controversy: The Case of the Critique of 'Enthusiasm' on the Eve of the Enlightenment." *Science in Context*, Vol. 8, No. 1 (Spring 1995): 133–157. Thanks are due to Cambridge University Press for permission to include a revised version in the present book.

INTRODUCTION

In our post-modern age, the emergence of Enlightenment culture can no longer be taken for granted as an inevitable aspect of some process of "modernization", or as an indubitable sign of "progress". Recent critique of the Enlightenment, coming from various quarters, calls for the problematization of the origins of Enlightenment culture.[1] If, indeed, the Enlightenment is no longer seen as an unmixed blessing, the questions concerning its historical causes and the social forces underlying it become all the more pressing. How are we to account for the new type of Enlightenment rationalism which rejected, suppressed, marginalized or transformed important irrational manifestations of human experience and behaviour? What were the motives leading the European elite to adopt an "enlightened" outlook on human and social issues, or a new scientific attitude towards nature? And finally, how should one explain the emergence of a secular world view which—if not altogether sceptical towards traditional religion—disdained supernatural intervention in human affairs?

These questions, relating to the origins of the Enlightenment, also raise the broader problem of secularization and rationalization in the modern period in general. What were the causes underlying the broad process of the "disenchantment of the world" ("die Entzauberung der Welt"), to use Max Weber's famous term?[2] Today, in a period witnessing the effervescence of various movements and sects which seek to "re-enchant" the world, an analysis of the motives lying behind its "dis-enchantment", as well as of the price paid in this process, assumes special urgency.

---

[1] For an early radical view see Max Horkheimer and Theodor W. Adorno, *Dialektik der Aufklärung* (1944), translated into English by John Cumming, *Dialectic of Enlightenment* (New York: Continuum, 1982), see especially chapter 1. I am grateful to my colleague, Dr. Rivka Feldhai, for directing my attention to this important critique. More famous and influential, perhaps, is Michel Foucault, *Histoire de la folie à l'âge classique* (rev. ed., Paris: Gallimard, 1972). In English translation, *Madness and Civilization: A History of Insanity in the Age of Reason* (New York: Vintage Books, 1965).

[2] On the concept of "Die Entzauberung der Welt" or "The disenchantment of the world" see Max Weber's famous essay "Wissenschaft als Beruf", in English translation "Science as a Vocation", in H.H. Gerth and C. Wright Mills, eds., *From Max Weber: Essays in Sociology* (New York: Oxford University Press, 1946; paperback edition, 1958), pp. 129–156, especially pp. 138–139.

Historical scholarship in the last generation has focused quite a bit
on questions regarding the social and intellectual origins of the Enlightenment.[3] Significant research has also been done on the secularization of European consciousness in the early modern period, and
on the gradual disenchantment of the world in that period, particularly as it is manifested in the decline of magical beliefs and practices, at least within the elite.[4] Nevertheless, not enough attention
has been paid to one of the major manifestations of these tendencies—the critique of "enthusiasm" in the early modern period. That
critique, and the various reactions to the phenomenon of enthusiasm, may provide some important clues to the motives underlying
the turn of the European elite towards an "enlightened", "disenchanted" culture.

The critique of enthusiasm is indeed one of the recurring themes
in seventeenth century discourse. Whether in religious, scientific, literary or political texts, in England, or on the Continent, the debate
with the so-called enthusiasts occupies an important place. The rejection of enthusiasm is well known to anyone studying the intellectual and religious history of the period. The term itself became a
standard label by which to designate individuals or groups who allegedly claimed to have direct divine inspiration, whether millenarians,
radical sectarians or various prophesiers, as well as alchemists,
"empirics" and some contemplative philosophers. In the Catholic
camp, the confrontation with enthusiasm was less prevalent, it seems
to me, since mystical experience, miracles, and spiritualist tendencies
were more easily incorporated within mainstream orthodoxy.[5] In the

---

[3] The classic book on the intellectual origins of the Enlightenment is Paul Hazard, *La crise de la conscience européenne* (Paris, 1935), translated into English by L. Lewis
May under the title *The European Mind* (London: Hollis and Carter, 1953; Penguin
ed. 1964, and subsequent editions). Among numerous studies in the last generation
see: Ira O. Wade, *The Intellectual Origins of the French Enlightenment* (Princeton: Princeton
University Press, 1971); Lionel Rothkrug, *Opposition to Louis XIV: The Political and
Social Origins of the French Enlightenment* (Princeton: Princeton University Press, 1965);
and concerning England and the Netherlands—M.C. Jacob, *The Radical Enlightenment: Pantheists, Freemasons and Republicans* (London: Allen and Unwin, 1981). Finally,
see the collection of articles edited by Alan C. Kors and Paul J. Korshin, *Anticipations of the Enlightenment in England, France, and Germany* (Philadelphia: University of
Pennsylvania Press, 1987).
[4] See especially: Keith Thomas, *Religion and the Decline of Magic* (New York: Scribner's,
1971; Penguin University Books, 1973, and subsequent paperback editions); Peter
Burke, *Popular Culture in Early Modern Europe* (London: Temple Smith, 1978); Jean
Delumeau, *Le Catholicisme entre Luther et Voltaire* ("Nouvelle Clio", Paris: P.U.F., 1971).
[5] One notable exception is the famous case of the Jansenist miracles, convulsions

Protestant camp, in contrast, such claims presented a real challenge to the religious order, based as it had been since the Reformation primarily on Scripture. Indeed, by the late seventeenth century, many of the Protestant intellectuals, scientists and theologians were fighting simultaneously on at least two fronts: against the spread of deistic and atheistic views on the one hand, and against "enthusiasm", prophe-sying, divinations and other "superstitions" on the other. However, whereas the polemics against deism and atheism have been dealt with quite extensively, less attention has been paid to the parallel confrontation with the "enthusiasts". All in all, historians have been more interested in the enthusiasts themselves and in the radical movements with which they were connected, than in the reaction of the political, intellectual, and ecclesiastical "establishment" to them.[6] This reaction, however, may be at least as interesting and significant as the phenomenon of "enthusiasm" itself, if indeed there is such a clear-cut phenomenon. The argument of the present book will be that the critique of enthusiasm may provide us with important clues towards understanding many of the changes in the religious, scien-tific and cultural attitudes in European society on the eve of the Enlightenment.

Yet, how specific or new was the critique of enthusiasm in the seventeenth and early eighteenth centuries? The conflict between Charisma and established religious institutions, it may be argued, is a recurring phenomenon in the history of religions, surely, in the history of Christianity. Indeed, this is the conceptual framework in which the topic has usually been interpreted by Church historians,

---

and claims of divine inspiration at the tomb of François de Pâris in the cemetery of Saint Médard between 1727 and 1732. The episode should be seen, however, against the very specific political context in France during the years following the papal bull *Unigenitus* of 1713. See B. Robert Kreiser, *Miracles, Convulsions, and Ecclesiastical Politics in Early Eighteenth-Century Paris* (Princeton: Princeton University Press, 1978).

[6] Among numerous studies, see R.A. Knox, *Enthusiasm: A Chapter in the History of Religion* (Oxford: Oxford University Press, 1950), to which I shall return below; George H. Williams, *The Radical Reformation* (Philadelphia: Westminster Press, 1962, revised edition, 1991); Christopher Hill, *The World Turned Upside Down: Radical Ideas During the English Revolution* (New York: Viking Press, 1973); Andrew C. Fix, *Prophecy and Reason: The Dutch Collegiants in the Early Enlightenment* (Princeton: Princeton University Press, 1991); Hillel Schwartz, *The French Prophets: The History of a Millenarian Group in Eighteenth-Century England* (Berkeley, Los Angeles, London: University of California Press, 1980). Schwartz has also published the only book-length study on the oppo-sition to an enthusiastic group: *Knaves, Fools, Madmen and that Subtile Effluvium: A Study of the Opposition to the French Prophets in England, 1706–1710* (Gainsville: University Presses of Florida, 1978), a study which has greatly aided my own research.

particularly those employing a Weberian perspective.[7] With slightly
different emphasis, this is also the approach of R.A. Knox's famous
book *Enthusiasm*.[8] There is much, of course, to be said for such an
approach which regards the reaction against enthusiasm in the seventeenth and early eighteenth centuries as one further chapter in the
perennial conflict between Charismatic movements and established
institutions. Yet, as the present study will try to show, there are specific
characteristics to this confrontation in our period.

First of all, it should be emphasized that enthusiasm was by no
means a unified phenomenon in the early modern period. Rather, it
was a derogatory label, not a neutral designation of one homoge-
neous group. Most frequently it referred to zealous sectarians, millenarians, prophesiers, and other radical groups and individuals
who opposed the existing Church order: they could be the German
and Swiss Anabaptists in the sixteenth century, Fifth Monarchy Men
and Quakers in England in the mid seventeenth century, the
Collegiants and their associates in Holland in the second half of that
century, or the French Huguenot Prophets from the Cévennes around
1700. In Restoration England the term "enthusiast" could even be
ascribed to the Catholics themselves.[9] On another level, the label
could be applied to various Platonist thinkers, to Paracelsian chemists, indeed, to the experimental philosophers of the Royal Society,
and even to philosophers like Descartes. Finally, it was often argued
that there was an affinity between enthusiasm and atheism, and that
these seemingly opposite tendencies actually reinforced each other.[10]

---

[7] Weber's conception of Charisma is developed in the chapters devoted to the
sociology of religion in his *Wirtschaft und Gesellschaft*. For a revised English translation
see Max Weber, *Economy and Society*, ed. Guenther Roth and Claus Wittich (New
York: Bedminster Press, 1968), part 2, chapter 6. See also S.N. Eisenstadt, ed., *Max
Weber on Charisma and Institution Building* (Chicago and London: University of Chicago
Press, 1968), which includes an introductory essay and a useful collection of Weber's
papers on that topic.

[8] R.A. Knox, *Enthusiasm* (see note 6 above). Knox, a Catholic historian, defined
enthusiasm as "ultra supernaturalism" and as "an excess of charity [which] threat-
ens unity". Ibid., pp. 1–2. He was clearly influenced in that view by Bossuet, the
seventeenth century Bishop and Church historian, as he himself admits in the preface (Ibid., p. v).

[9] This was especially true on the eve of the Glorious Revolution. See Henry
Wharton, *The Enthusiasm of the Church of Rome demonstrated in some observations upon the
life of Ignatius Loyola* (London, 1688). Wharton was a protégé of Thomas Tenison, a
principal opponent of James II.

[10] For a classical argument to that effect, see Section I of the second edition of
Henry More's *Enthusiasmus Triumphatus* (1662) to which I shall have occasion to refer
in detail in the following chapters.

For that reason, it is a misguided historical exercise to search for a clear definition of enthusiasm, let alone to look for a well-defined movement. Yet, while enthusiasm as such may be a dubious historical entity, the reaction to it is not. Indeed, the label reflects the attitudes of its users rather than describing any particular group which it purports to designate. Hence, what is needed is a systematic study of the social and intellectual carriers of the term and of its various connotations and denotations. This is an enormous task, and the present study does not claim to be an exhaustive survey and analysis of the topic. Rather, it is an attempt to offer some investigations which will highlight the changing nature of the reaction to enthusiasm in that period, and the significance of these changes in the broader context of the transformation of religious and cultural sensibilities in the seventeenth and early eighteenth centuries.

The denotation of the term "enthusiasm" was indeed very broad in the seventeenth century, and it by no means referred only to religious enthusiasm. This is another characteristic of the term peculiar to that period. As already mentioned, it could also refer to what was called "philosophical enthusiasm" or "contemplative enthusiasm", which characterized certain philosophical, epistemological and scientific methods or systems. Indeed, whereas both Cartesian philosophy and the new experimental science could be viewed by their opponents as types of "enthusiasm", the defenders of the new science saw science as an effective "antidote" to enthusiasm. Enthusiasm and the reaction to it are thus a phenomenon in the history of science no less than in Church history. Equally important, though beyond the confines of the present study, "enthusiasm" had a linguistic connotation in the seventeenth century. It often referred to rhetoric, to the manner of speech, not only to content. The growing suspicion of ornamental style, high-flown language and the tropes and figures of Renaissance rhetoric, together with the stress on "plain style" and on clear and distinct statements, has attracted the attention of many literary scholars in the past two generations. With the "rehabilitation" of rhetoric in recent years, the subject has become even more relevant.[11] However, not enough attention has been given to the links

---

[11] The bibliography on this topic is enormous, of course. For the classic studies on the movement for "plain style" in seventeenth century England see R.F. Jones, "Science in English Prose Style" and "Science and Language in England of the Mid-Seventeenth Century", originally published in the 1930's, and reprinted in *The Seventeenth Century* (Stanford: Stanford University Press, 1951). See also W.S. Howell, *Logic and Rhetoric in England 1500–1700* (Princeton: Princeton University Press, 1956).

between the critique of rhetoric and the critique of enthusiasm in
the second half of the seventeenth century, and the subject should
by no means be confined only to literary historians.[12] Neither should
it be forgotten that the term "enthusiasm" itself has had literary
connotations since classical times, denoting the inspiration of the poet
no less than the prophet or seer.[13] Nevertheless, the linguistic dimension of the reaction to enthusiasm is a subject exceeding the confines
of the present book, and which indeed requires a separate study. At
all events, the term "enthusiasm", had a variety of meanings in the
seventeenth century, whether religious, philosophical, scientific, or
rhetorical. All of these meanings, moreover, had obvious social and
political connotations, as will become clear in what follows.

   No less than the term itself, the reaction to it similarly calls for an
interdisciplinary approach which is not confined to Church history,
literary history or the history of science.[14] The critics of enthusiasm,
even the clerics among them, did not rely only on theological arguments, whether based on ecclesiastical authority, tradition or Scripture. They also had recourse to medical arguments, to a long tradition of medical thought which regarded enthusiasm and claims to
divine inspiration or prophecy as a manifestation of melancholy, of

---

The rehabilitation of rhetoric is most noticeable in the work of Brian Vickers, *In
Defence of Rhetoric* (Oxford: Clarendon Press, 1988). See also his earlier article, "The
Royal Society and English Prose Style: A Reassessment", in *Rhetoric and the Pursuit of
Truth: Language Change in the Seventeenth and Eighteenth Centuries* (Los Angeles: William
Andrews Clark Memorial Library, 1985), pp. 1–76.
   [12] For the most notable exception, see the seminal study by George Williamson,
"The Restoration Revolt against Enthusiasm", *Studies in Philology* 32 (1935): 553–
579, reprinted in Williamson, *Seventeenth Century Contexts* (London: Faber and Faber,
1960), pp. 202–239.
   [13] See A. Delatte, "Les conceptions de l'enthousiasme chez les philosophes
présocratiques", *L'Antiquité Classique* 3 (May, 1934): 5–79. The crucial texts for this
theme of poetic inspiration were the Platonic dialogues "Ion", "Symposium", and
"Phaedrus"; Aristotle's *Rhetorica*, III, 7, and *De Poetica*, 17, 1455a33; and Cicero's *De
Oratore*, II, 46, 194, and *Pro Archia Poeta*, 8, 18. For later periods see R. Wittkower,
"Genius: Individualism in Art and Artists", *Dictionary of the History of Ideas* (New York:
Scribner's, 1973), vol. 1, pp. 297–312. In England, the term "enthusiasm" in the
sense of poetic inspiration was first introduced at the end of the sixteenth and the
beginning of the seventeenth century. See Peter Spoo, "Enthusiasm", in *Europäische
Schlüsselwörter*, Band II: *Kurzmonographien I: Wörter im geistigen und sozialen Raum* (Munich:
Max Huber Verlag, 1964), pp. 50–67.
   [14] For an historiographical survey of the literature on that topic, and for a plea
for such an integrative approach, see my essay "The Reaction to Enthusiasm in the
Seventeenth Century: Towards an Integrative Approach", *Journal of Modern History*
53 (1981): 258–280. The article reflects, of course, the state of research at the time
of publication.

mental illness. Such a medical interpretation of enthusiasm was not in itself new. It had its origins in the medical and philosophical literature of antiquity. What was relatively new in the seventeenth century, however, was the systematic employment of such arguments by ministers and divines, both in England and on the Continent.

The reaction to enthusiasm in the early modern period is thus too specific and at the same time too complex, to be seen simply in terms of a conflict between Establishment and Charisma. Can it be seen alternatively in terms of the conflict between elite and popular culture? This is a perspective which has attracted much historiographical attention in the last generation. Several historians have stressed the growing alienation, even the outright conflict, between the culture of the elite and popular beliefs and practices in the course of the sixteenth and seventeenth centuries.[15] The reaction to enthusiasm may be depicted as one aspect of this general trend. Yet those accused of enthusiasm were not always the illiterate or uneducated. Quite often, they were themselves intellectuals and members of the elite, whether a millenarian such as Comenius, a hermetic poet like the Anglican Thomas Vaughan, a spokesman of the French Prophets such as the Genevan scientist Fatio de Duillier, or their English patrons, Sir Richard Bulkeley and John Lacy. Significantly, the enthusiasts were often accused of deluding and even inciting the popular classes by appeals to their passions, instead of educating them by instruction.[16] The conflict between the enthusiasts and their opponents was, therefore, not necessarily a conflict between representatives of popular culture on the one hand, and the elite on the other. Rather, it could reflect a confrontation between two competing models for the proper relationship between the elite and the populace.

---

[15] Among the numerous studies along these lines, see Jean Delumeau, *Le Catholicisme entre Luther et Voltaire*; Robert Muchembled, *Culture populaire et culture des élites dans la France moderne (XVe–XVIIIe siècles), Essai* (Paris: Flammarion, 1978); and Peter Burke, *Popular Culture in Early Modern Europe*. For a more nuanced view see Natalie Z. Davis, *Society and Culture in Early Modern France* (Stanford: Stanford University Press, 1975), and her many subsequent studies. Indeed, in the past fifteen years, historians have become increasingly sceptical towards this dichotomy between elite and popular culture.

[16] Thus Henry More, with whom I shall deal in Chapter 3 below, accused his enthusiastic opponent Thomas Vaughan of using "sonorous and amazing terms such as might astonish the ignorant [rather] than teach the docible". Quoted by Frederick B. Burnham, "The More-Vaughan Controversy: The Revolt against Philosophical Enthusiasm", *Journal of the History of Ideas* 35 (1974): 42. This question, indeed, also has direct bearing upon the issue of rhetoric and the proper use of language in the seventeenth century.

If not a confrontation between elite and popular culture, the debate with the enthusiasts might reflect the reaction of the traditional professions and the carriers of humanistic and scholastic learning against the various groups, individual intellectuals, and trends of thought which sought to challenge these traditional authorities. It is within this framework that the Paracelsians, the alchemists, the "empirics", and even the experimental philosophers were viewed as "enthusiasts". They were all seen by their opponents as trying to find easy shortcuts to absolute truth, or alternatives to traditional truths. Linked with the "anti-professional" implication, "enthusiasm" was a label often ascribed to innovators, whether in religion, medicine, science, or philosophy. This may be seen most strikingly with respect to a philosopher like Descartes whom his conservative opponents considered an "enthusiast" for precisely these reasons.

The case of Descartes, however, highlights one further connotation of enthusiasm in the seventeenth century. It was a label assigned to individualists who challenged not only traditional authorities, but collective institutions and common beliefs. The enthusiast set his own inspiration, his own thoughts and ideas, against traditional as well as common beliefs, not only in the religious sphere, but in other intellectual, indeed, social and political, spheres as well. In this respect, the challenge of enthusiasm in the seventeenth century was essentially directed against the established social order, religious, political, intellectual and scientific. It is under this broader meaning that groups such as Roman Catholics (viewed from the vantage point of Restoration England), the Socinians, or even the atheists, as well as the alchemists, experimental scientists and Cartesians, besides the various millenarian groups and radical sects, could all be classified under the label of "enthusiasm". Indeed, the phenomenon of enthusiasm was closely linked with a crisis of authority in the seventeenth century, and it is within this context that it gains its historical specificity.[17]

Furthermore—and this is one of the main theses of the present book—the critique of enthusiasm, that which sought to defend the social and intellectual order, itself underwent a certain crisis in the seventeenth century. Indeed, it may be suggested that the "general crisis of the seventeenth century" was primarily a crisis in the ideo-

---

[17] For a discussion of the "crisis of authority" in the seventeenth century and its links with the so-called "general crisis of the seventeenth century", see Theodore K. Rabb, *The Struggle for Stability in Early Modern Europe* (New York: Oxford University Press, 1975). The book is also a systematic survey of the historiographical literature on the "crisis controversy" up to that point.

logical and cultural basis of the social order. Up to the middle of the seventeenth century, the critique of enthusiasm in Protestant societies was based on the traditional foundations of the religious and intellectual order, namely Scripture, humanistic learning, Aristotelian scholasticism and Galenic medicine. The first part of this book (Chapters 1 to 5) is devoted to this type of reaction to enthusiasm. By the second half of the seventeenth century, however, it was becoming increasingly clear that these traditional bulwarks—Aristotelian scholasticism, traditional humanism, Scripture, and the strict orthodoxy of an authoritarian Church—no longer provided a firm enough basis for the social and cultural order. Indeed, these were precisely the traditions attacked by the so-called "enthusiasts". Vis-à-vis such attacks, those who wished to defend the social, religious and cultural order could do so either by resorting repeatedly to the traditional arguments, or by searching for new responses. Chapters 5 to 7 attempt to trace some of these responses to the challenge of enthusiasm, and hence, to delineate some of the foundations of the socio-cultural order in Protestant Europe between 1660 and 1720. What changes can be detected in the responses to enthusiasm in the second half of the seventeenth century? To what extent do these responses incorporate certain characteristics of the so-called "enthusiasts" themselves, such as the openness to innovation, the individualistic orientation, or the empirical method? Behind these general questions lies a more specific query: in what sense do the changes in the response of the establishment to the challenge of enthusiasm indicate a measure of secularization of the ideological basis of that establishment? Can the challenge of enthusiasm be regarded as one of the factors "pushing" both clerics and lay intellectuals not only towards a more "disenchanted" view of the universe, but in the direction of greater emphasis on the natural, scientific and secular basis of the social order? It will be argued that notwithstanding significant nuances and different emphases among churchmen of various theological and ecclesiastical orientations, in England and on the Continent, and in spite of important exceptions that should be noted—a general trend can be detected in the changing characteristics of the critique of enthusiasm at that period. These changes have to do with the "medicalization" of that critique, with the role of the new experimental science, and with the growing emphasis on individual reason in the examination of religious enthusiasm. All these gradual changes amount to a significant transformation in the ideological basis of the social and intellectual order in Protestant Europe.

This transformation can indeed be characterized in terms of "secularization". Secularization, not in the sense of forsaking central Christian or religious tenets, but in the nature of the ideological foundation of the social order. In designating religious eccentrics and non-conformists as "mentally sick", the critics of enthusiasm imperceptibly redefined religious orthodoxy in medical terms of health and mental balance, rather than, or at least, side by side with, theological terms of correct faith. In reaching out for the achievements of the new experimental science, ministers of the late seventeenth and early eighteenth centuries shifted the emphasis from supernatural to natural arguments supporting the social and intellectual order. This shift is also noticeable in the increasing reliance on individual human reason, alongside, if not instead of, Scripture.

The medicalization of the critique of enthusiasm, and the growing reliance of ministers of the Church on individual critical reason, could open the door, however, to more tolerant attitudes towards enthusiasm itself. Indeed, by the early eighteenth century the term "enthusiasm" began to assume its more subjective meaning as sentiment rather as true or false direct divine inspiration. This change is manifest primarily in the work of the third Earl of Shaftesbury to which Chapter 8 is devoted. A similar tolerant, even positive, attitude towards enthusiasm can also be found among certain scientists in the eighteenth century. The last chapter will deal with some of these scientists, primarily Newton's disciple Nicolas Fatio de Duillier, and his Genevan follower, George-Louis Le Sage later in the century. The medicalization and naturalization of the critique of enthusiasm could thus also lead to a certain "rehabilitation" of enthusiasm. It may not be a coincidence that both Shaftesbury and Le Sage are sometimes seen as precursors of a Romantic outlook.

The changing attitudes towards enthusiasm may thus serve as significant indications of broader changes in the religious and cultural attitudes of the Protestant elite in the early modern period, and indeed, of changes in the ideological foundations of the religious and social order. Furthermore, the present book will suggest that the issue of enthusiasm is not only a manifestation of these transformations, but may have been an important motivating force for the adoption of more secular and "rationalist" views by the religious establishment itself on the eve of the Enlightenment. In order to assess these changes, however, one should first turn to the traditional theological critique of enthusiasm since the Reformation.

CHAPTER ONE

THE THEOLOGICAL CRITIQUE OF ENTHUSIASM

In this chapter I shall try to delineate some of the ways in which Protestant theological discourse from the Reformation and up to the middle of the seventeenth century dealt with the phenomenon of enthusiasm. How was the term understood by Lutheran and Reformed theologians? What kind of challenge did enthusiasm constitute to the established Church? What were the responses given to that challenge, and in what ways was enthusiasm de-legitimized? Finally, how did the opponents of enthusiasm account for the prophecies, ecstasies and convulsions of the enthusiasts? The topic of course is vast and here I can only outline some central characteristics of that discourse, by analysing several selected texts. This analysis, which by no means attempts to be exhaustive, may serve as a background against which developments in the reaction to enthusiasm during the seventeenth and early eighteenth century can be appreciated.

The Protestant critique of enthusiasm, of claims to the gift of prophecy and to direct divine inspiration, started almost from the beginning of the Reformation itself, with the appearance of the "Zwickau prophets" in Wittenberg in late December 1521, and with Luther's attack on them in 1522, and his subsequent debates with Andreas Carlstadt and Thomas Müntzer. Luther, however, used the term "Schwärmer" with respect to these prophets, rather than "enthusiasts".[1] While focusing mostly on the erroneous doctrines of the

---

[1] Luther coined the term "Schwärmer" (taken from the designation for swarming, stirred-up bees), for the Zwickau prophets—Nicholas Storch, Thomas Drechsel and Marcus Thomas Stübner, and their followers—as well as Müntzer and Carlstadt. The literature on Luther's debate with the "Schwärmer" is very extensive. For a recent survey see Martin Brecht, *Martin Luther. Shaping and Defining the Reformation 1521–1532*, trans. by James L. Schaaf (Minneapolis: Fortress Press, 1990), chapter III: "Prophets, Enthusiasts, Iconoclasts, Fanatics, and the Peasants' War", pp. 137–195. For an earlier study see John S. Oyer, *Lutheran Reformers against Anabaptists* (The Hague: Martinus Nijhoff, 1964), chapter 1. See also Günther Mühlpfordt, "Luther und die 'Linken': eine Untersuchung seiner Schwärmerterminologie", in Günther Vogler, ed., *Martin Luther: Leben, Werk, Wirkung* (Berlin: Academie-Verlag, 1983), pp. 325–45. Siegfried Braeuer, "Die Vorgeschichte von Luthers 'Ein Brief an die Fürsten zu Sachsen von dem aufrührerischen Geist", *Luthers Jahrbuch* 47 (1980): 40–70. For

"Schwärmer", he also referred to their claims to hear the voice of
God directly, unmediated by Scripture.[2] In the next generation, the
controversy with the various Anabaptists was to increasingly engage
the pens of the "Magisterial Reformers". Whether justifiably or not,
they saw the later Anabaptists as direct successors of the "Schwärmer"
—the Zwickau prophets, Müntzer and Carlstadt.[3] It was in the course
of controversy with the Anabaptists that the label "enthusiasts" began to appear. One of the central texts written against the Anabaptists
in the middle of the sixteenth century was Heinrich Bullinger's *Der
Widertoeufferen Ursprung*, published in 1560.[4] Bullinger, who was Zwingli's
successor at Zurich, summed up in that extensive text his long struggle
against Anabaptists of various types. It was extremely important for
him to show that both he and his former teacher, Zwingli, were
adamantly opposed to the radical doctrines of the Anabaptists.[5] He
counted the "Enthusiastae" and "Extatici", or "Verzückten Brüder",
among the thirteen types of Anabaptists against whom he wrote his
tract, and devoted the first chapter of Book II to them.[6] Yet, as

---

an older article which stresses Luther's own spiritualistic tendencies, see Karl Gerhard
Steck, "Luther und die Schwärmer", *Theologische Studien* 44 (1955). We shall return
to some of Luther's own texts below.

[2] See for example, his "Letter to the Princes of Saxony" of July 1524 in *Martin
Luthers Werke* (Weimar edition, henceforward *WA*), vol. 15, p. 216, lines 12–20, in
English translation, *Luther's Works* (Philadelphia: Fortress Press, henceforward *LW*),
vol. 40, p. 55; and in his "Lectures on Deuteronomy" of the following year, *WA*,
vol. 14, pp. 681, line 14–682, line 15; *LW*, vol. 9, pp. 184–185. For an early use
of the term "Schwärmer", see his sermon on Matt. 15, on March 1, 1523, *WA*, vol.
11, p. 42, lines 24–31. For the use of the term "Schwärmer" in connection also
with Müntzer and Carlstadt, see Luther's letter to Count Johann Friedrich of Saxony
of June 18, 1524 (WA, Briefwechsel, vol. 3, pp. 305–308).

[3] See Oyer, *Lutheran Reformers against Anabaptists*, pp. 246–249. The complex question of the possible relationship between the Zwickau prophets Müntzer and Carlstadt
on the one hand, and the origins of Anabaptism in Switzerland and Southern
Germany on the other, has long been debated by historians, and we cannot go into
it here.

[4] *Der Widertoeufferen ursprung/ fürgang/ Secten/ waesen/ fürnemme vnd gemeine jrer leer
Artickel/... abgeteilt in VI. Buecher/ und beschriben durch Heinrychen Bullingern/ dienern der
kirchen zuo Zürych* (Zurich, 1560; the 1561 edition, which included only slight alter-
ations, has been reproduced by the Zentralantiquariat der DDR, Leipzig, 1975). I
have also used the Latin translation, done by Simler, Bullinger's son-in-law, and
published in Zurich already in the summer of 1560, since that was the version
quoted by later critics of enthusiasm: *Adversus Anabaptistas libri VI nunc primum e Germanico
sermone in Latine conversi, per Iosiam Simlerum* (Zurich: 1560).

[5] On Bullinger's book, its sources, the circumstances surrounding its publication,
and its diffusion, see Heinold Fast, *Heinrich Bullinger und die Täufer* (Weierhof, Pfalz:
Mennonitischen Geschichtsverein, 1959), pp. 64–69, 79–80, 120–121, 128–129.

[6] The chapter was entitled "Von den verzuckten Brüdern/jrem irrthums/und

Bullinger scholars and historians of the Radical Reformation have shown, it is very difficult, and not necessarily fruitful, to identify each of the types of Anabaptists whom Bullinger mentions with a concrete historical group. Bullinger's classification served as a way to arrange, and combat, the various theological principles and traits of the Anabaptists, rather than as an accurate reflection of an historical social reality.[7] This is also true for his chapter on the "enthusiasts". He apparently borrowed the term "Verzückten Brüder" from Sebastian Franck, and relied on two other contemporary sources in his description of them, Johannes Stumpf from Zurich, and the Dutch historian Lambertus Hortensius.[8]

In the second half of the sixteenth century, and in the early seventeenth, the term "enthusiasm" was increasingly used in Protestant theological discourse. To the "Schwärmer", Carlstadt, Müntzer, Schwenckfeld, and the Anabaptists of the Münster episode were added the examples of Paracelsus (1493–1541), David Joris (1501–1556), and later on the German spiritualist Valentin Weigel (1533–1588) and

---

widerlegung oder verwerffung dess selben", and it referred to them also as "Enthusiastae und Extatici"(pp. 30r–32v). In Latin, the title of the chapter was "De enthusiastis, et ipsorum erroribus ac eorum confutatione"(pp. 34r–36v). The "enthusiasts" were counted as the seventh group of Anabaptists with whom Bullinger dealt. Others were the Apostolic Baptizers, the Spiritual Baptizers, the "saintly, sinless Baptizer Brethren", the "Quiet Brethren", the Free Brethren, the Hutterites, the Augustinians, the "Monasterienses" and Anabaptists of Lower Germany, and finally, the "abominable baptizers" among whom Bullinger counted Michel Servetus and Melchior Hofmann.

[7] See Fast, *Heinrich Bullinger und die Taüffer*, pp. 128–131; Claus-Peter Clasen, *Anabaptism. A Social History, 1525–1618. Switzerland, Austria, Moravia, South and Central Germany* (Ithaca, N.Y.: Cornell University Press, 1972), pp. 30–31, and most recently, Aurelio A. Garcia Archilla, *The Theology of History and Apologetic Historiography in Heinrich Bullinger* (San Francisco: Mellen Research University Press, 1992), pp. 218–236, esp. pp. 226–231. Garcia Archilla takes issue with some of Fast's views and regards Bullinger's historical method as more serious. Nevertheless, he too thinks that Bullinger's classification should be seen as based on a combination of theological and historical traits.

[8] Sebastian Franck, *Chronica, Zeyt-büch und geschycht-bibell von anbegyn biss in diss gegenwertig MDXXXI. jar verlengt* (Strasbourg, 1531), pp. 444v–452v, esp. pp. 446r–446v. A facsimile reprint has been published in Darmstadt: Wissenschaftliche Buchgesellschaft, 1969. Johann Stumpf, *Gemeiner loblicher Eydgnoschafft Stetten, Landen und Völckeren Chronickwirdiger thaaten beschreybung*, 2 vols. (Zurich, 1548), vol. II, pp. 465r–465v; Lambertus Hortensius, *Tumultuum Anabaptistarum liber unus* (Basel, 1548), who dealt mostly with the Münster episode. Hortensius did use, however, the term "enthusiasm" in connection with early Anabaptism: "Mox exorti inter ipsos vates (quos prophetas ipsi dixere) ficto enthusiasmo vaticinari stultè credulis, quicquid venit in mentem, coeperunt." Ibid., p. 13. On Bullinger's sources see also Fast, *Bullinger und die Täufer*, pp. 120, 129.

his disciples.[9] Among the critics of Paracelsus and Weigel was the Lutheran theologian Nikolaus Hunnius (1583–1643).[10] Also sometimes mentioned by critics of enthusiasm was Hendrik Niclaes (c. 1502– c. 1580) and his "family of love".[11]

The great effervescence of the enthusiasts, however, and of the polemical literature against them, came in the mid-seventeenth century. The Thirty Years War, the English Revolution, and the "general crisis" all over Europe, were all accompanied by an upsurge of millenarian movements, the spread of radical religious sects, and the frequent occurrence of prophetic visions and pronouncements.[12] I shall discuss some of the English critique of enthusiasm in later chapters. Here, I shall deal mostly with the critique of several theologians in the Netherlands in that generation, who also reacted to developments outside the Low Countries: Friedrich Spanheim (1600–1649),[13] Johannes Hoornbeek (1617–1666),[14] and Samuel Desmarets (Maresius)

---

[9] On David Joris (or David George), see the recent study of Gary K. Waite, *David Joris and Dutch Anabaptism 1524–1543* (Waterloo, Ontario: Wilfrid Laurier University Press, 1990), which includes an extensive bibliography. On Caspar Schwenckfeld and Valentin Weigel see George H. Williams, *The Radical Reformation* (Philadelphia: The Westminster Press, 1962), pp. 810–814, and A. Koyré, *Mystiques, spirituels, alchimistes du XVI siècle allemand* (Paris: Gallimard, 1971).

[10] Nikolaus Hunnius was the son of the famous Lutheran theologian Aegidius Hunnius. Nikolaus himself served as professor of theology in Wittenberg for a few years (1617–1623), and after 1624 was Superintendent of the Lutheran Church in Lübeck. See the article on Nikolaus Hunnius in *Die Religion in Geschichte und Gegenwart*, vol. III, col. 491; and the article on Hunnius in the *Realencyklopädie für protestantische Theologie und Kirche* (3rd ed.), vol. 8, pp. 459–462.

[11] On Niclaes and the Family of Love see Alistair Hamilton, *The Family of Love* (Cambridge: Cambridge University Press, 1981), and idem., ed. with an introduction, *Chronica, Ordo Sacerdotis, Acta HN: Three Texts on the Family of Love* (Leiden: Brill, 1988). On the Familists in England see Jean Dietz Moss, *"Godded with God": Hendrick Niclaes and His Family of Love* (Philadelphia: Transactions of The American Philosophical Society, vol. 71, part 8, 1981), see especially, pp. 30–31.

[12] On the English context see, out of the vast literature, Christopher Hill, *The World Turned Upside Down* (New York: The Viking Press, 1972), and Bernard S. Capp, *The Fifth Monarchy Men* (London: Faber and Faber, 1972). In central Europe, three prominent "prophets" were Christopher Kotter, Christina Pontiatowska and Michael Drabicius (Drabik). The prophecies of all three were promoted by Jan Amos Comenius, himself considered an "enthusiast" by his opponents, as we shall see below.

[13] Friedrich Spanheim the elder (1600–1649), born in Upper Palatinate, was a professor first in Geneva (in philosophy from 1626, in theology from 1631), and from 1642 till his death, occupied the theology chair in Leiden. On Spanheim see *Realencyklopädie für protestantische Theologie und Kirche* (3rd ed.), vol. 18, pp. 572–573.

[14] Johannes Hoornbeek, one of the main Reformed controversialists of his time, was born in Leiden in 1617, taught first at Utrecht, and returned to Leiden in 1654, where he taught till his early death in 1666. See *Realencyklopädie für protestantische Theologie und Kirche* (3rd ed.), vol. 8, p. 350.

(1599–1673).[15] This survey, however, by no means sets out to be exhaustive. Rather, it will attempt to show several of the salient points in the theological critique of enthusiasm from the beginning of the Reformation to the 1660's. In the last part of this book I shall return to the transformations that took place in that critique in the late seventeenth and early eighteenth centuries.

The term—its denotations and connotations in the theological discourse

How did Protestant theologians and ministers understand the term "enthusiasm"? From the beginning, the word was used ambiguously. It could refer to a specific group within the broad spectrum of the "Radical Reformation", or to a specific trait in the doctrine or behaviour of some of the radicals. We find this ambivalence already in Bullinger who gives the following description of the enthusiasts:

> The seventh sect of Anabaptists, is that of the disturbed and enraptured brothers, who are otherwise also called *Enthusiasts* or *Ecstatics*, who, at the beginning of Anabaptism, were not few. They boasted highly of the spirit, which worked in them so strongly that they would come out of themselves and be enraptured, and would be enabled to see extraordinary heavenly revelations and mysteries. When the time of the working of the spirit arrived, they became terrified in their faces, and they assumed horrible gestures, fell down to the ground, as if attacked by an illness, stretched on the ground, laid out like the dead, and that, for a good time: sometimes their whole body trembled in a horrible manner: sometimes they lay stiff like logs of wood. When they awoke from their ecstatic sleep and dream, they started to tell of wonderful visions which the spirit had revealed to them, and of what they had seen in another world ... The common talk of them was: It is the Father's will; the Father has ordered it or said it, etc. The common

---

[15] Desmarets, a Frenchman by origin, was a professor of theology in Groningen, a staunch defender of Calvinist orthodoxy, and, as we shall see in Chapter 5 below, was also a fierce opponent of Descartes. On Desmarets (Maresius) there is a magisterial biography in Dutch by D. Nauta, *Samuel Maresius* (Amsterdam: H.J. Paris, 1935); as well as his short article in *Biografisch lexicon voor de geschiedenis van het Nederlandse protestantisme*, vol. I (1978), pp. 158–160, which includes more recent bibliography. See also P. Dibon, "Lettres de S. Desmarets à Claude Saumaise, 1644–1657", *Lias* 1 (1974): 267–269. Finally, see the famous article by Pierre Bayle in his *Dictionnaire historique et critique* (Geneva: Slatkine, 1969, reprint of the 1820–1824 ed.), vol. X, pp. 243–256. Two other Dutch theologians to whom we shall return in later chapters were Gisbert Voetius, Maresius' chief rival in Utrecht, and his disciple and successor, Martin Schoock, both of them also adamant critics of Descartes.

revelation of all of them, however, or most of them, was that the day
of the Lord was at hand. Some of them were so wanton as to designate already the time and the day itself when the day of the Lord
would come. They then ran around like madmen and shouted in the
streets, the day of the Lord, the day of the Lord, we announce to you
the day of the Lord, etc.[16]

Bullinger was referring mostly to the apocalyptic expectations of the
"enthusiasts", but no less disturbing than the content of their pronouncements was their claim to have direct divine inspiration. He
also describes the enthusiasts' physical ecstasies and convulsions, which
were similar to the symptoms of those suffering from the falling sickness.[17] The enthusiasts were thus characterized by their theological
attitudes (apocalyptic expectations), by their claims to be divinely
authorized in airing their views, and by their external behaviour
(physical ecstasies and convulsions). Bullinger adduced two examples
of such enthusiasts: the first was based on Lambertus Hortensius'
report of an Anabaptist meeting in Amsterdam in February 1535. At
that meeting one Dietrich Schneider went into ecstasy, fell to the
ground and lay there for a while. After getting up, he declared ear-
nestly to those present (seven men and five women) that he had seen
God in his majesty, and in addition, all kinds of things in heaven

---

[16] "Die sibend Sect der Widertoeuffern/ ist die Sect der Stünigen unnd verzuckten
Brüdern/ welche sunst ouch genennt werdend *Enthusiastae* und *Extatici*: deren was in
dem anfang der Toeuffery nit wenig. Sy ruomtend sich hoch dess geists/ der so
krefftig in inen wurckte/ d(a)ss sy von inen selbs kaemind/ verzuckt wurdind/ und
fürtraeffenliche himmelische offnungen und geheimnussen saehind. Wenn dann die
zyt der würckung dess geists vorhanden was/ entsatztend sy sich in irem angesicht/
namend an sich schützliche gebaerden/ fielend darnider zuo der erden/ glych sam
sy waere das boess wee angangen/ stracktend sich uff die erden/ lagend da den
todten glych: und das ein guote zyt lang: etwan erzitteret ir gantzer lyb schützlich/
etwan lagend sy geraget wie die Bloecher. Wenn sy dann erwachetend von irem
verzuckten schlaaff und troum/ huobend sy an zellen wunderbare gesichten/ was
inen der geyst hette geoffenbaret/ unnd was sy gesaehen hettind in yener waelt[. . .]
Ir aller gemeine red was/ Es ist dess vatters will/ Der vatter hats geheissen/ oder
geredt/ etc. Die gemein eroffnung aber irer aller/ oder merteils/ was die/ dass der
tag dess Herren vorhanden waere. Etliche warend so fraefen dass sy fry zyt und tag
bestimptend wenn der tag dess Herren kaeme. Die lüffend dann/ den touben lüten
glych/ herumm/ und schrüwend uff den gassen/ Der tag dess Herren/ Der tag
dess Herren/ Wir verkündend üch den tag dess Herren/ etc." *Der Widertoeufferen
ursprung*, p. 30r. (In German texts quoted in this Chapter, the old Gothic letters ŏ,
å, ŭ, ß respectively.)
[17] The term "das böse" was a term for sickness in general and the falling sickness
in particular in the sixteenth century. The Latin translation of the text indeed uses
the term "comitialis morbus". (*Adversus Anabaptistas*, p. 34r). We shall return to the
medical interpretation of "enthusiasm" in Chapter 2 below.

and hell and announced that the Last Day was coming. With that, he stripped himself naked, ordered his brothers and sisters to do the same, since the children of God must lay aside everything that was taken from the Earth. They then all went out of the house, running like mad, and declaring in a loud voice that the Day of Judgment was approaching.[18] All of them were ultimately arrested, and the men sentenced to death. Bullinger concluded that particular story with a significant moral:

> To that [stage, of roaming around naked] do men arrive when they forsake the written true word of God and heed to their own or, indeed, the Devil's imaginations, and only later dare to ascribe such an impure thing to the Holy Spirit.[19]

This sentence as well as the story preceding it, contains some of the salient points to which we shall return below—the deep feeling that the enthusiasts spell danger to the moral fabric of society, the fear of exposure, both on the concrete-physical level and the symbolic one, the role of Scripture as an antidote to enthusiasm, and the view that the devil was the cause of the enthusiasts' imaginary pretensions.

Bullinger's second example was the story of Thomas Schücker of St. Gallen who in 1526, in a moment of religious ecstasy, cut off his

---

[18] "... [I]n dem jar als man zalt von Christi geburt 1535. dess 10. februarii siben mann unnd fünff wyber Toeuffisch/ in die statt Amsterdamm/ an die Saltzgassen/ in Jann Siberts huss in sinem abwaesen kommen syend. Under denen sye gewesen Dietrych Schnyder/ welcher verzuckt/ zuo der erden gefallen/ unnd da wie er gedachten sinen bruedern unnd schwestern ein guot wyl gelaegen: doch mit der zyt widerumb erwachet sye. Da er nach gethonem gebaett/ mit grossem ernst (das ist/ glyschssnery) angezeigt/ wie er Gott selbs in siner maiestat/ unnd darzuo allerley im himmel und der hell gesaehen habe; und sage dass der Jüngste tag vorhanden sye/ etc. Hiemit zoch er uss alle sine kleider/ so gar/ dass er ouch dass hembd / die scham zuo bedecken/ nit anbehielt. Er gebot ouch sinen bruedern unnd schwestern/ dass sy sich ouch nach sinem byspyl abzugind. Dann es soellind unnd muessind die kinder Gottes abziehen unnd hindan legen alles das von der erden genommen sye ... Unnd als soemlichs beschaehen was/ dass sy alle one scham nackend und bloss da stundend/ spricht Dietrych Schnyder/ was er jnen nun vorthaete/ das soeltind sy alle jm nachtuon. Unnd lüff hiemit also nacket wie er an die waelt erboren was/ zum huss uss uff die gassen/ unnd schrey grusamlich/Wee/ wee/wee/ die raach Gottes/ der tag Gottes/ etc. Dem lüffend die anderen sine bruedern und schwestern nackend hinnach/ wie besaessne lüt/ mit grüssenlichem geschrey/ derglychen man nie gehoert." Bullinger, *Der Widertoeufferen ursprung*, pp. 31r–v.

[19] "Dahin kommend aber die menschen/ wenn sy das geschriben warhafft wort Gottes verlassend/ unn jren selbs/ja des Tüfels ynbildungen losend/ und erst dann soemlich unrein ding gedoerend zuogaeben dem heiligen geist." *Der Widertoeufferen ursprung*, p. 31v.

brother's head.[20] This horrible act was preceded by an excited "anabaptist" sermon which Thomas delivered the night before to all the members of his family. The following morning he required his younger brother Lienhart to kneel before him and asked for a sword. While reassuring the frightened parents and other persons of the household present that he would not do anything but what God the father commanded him—he proceeded to cut off his brother's head. Thomas then ran out naked into the streets "performing horrendous gestures and in kind and measure like those which enthusiasts were used to do."[21] Brought before the Bürgermeister and the town authorities, he shouted furiously, "the Day of God is at hand, the Day of God is coming".[22] When his horrible act was discovered, he was sentenced to death. Once again, for Bullinger, enthusiasm involved apocalyptic pronouncements, immoderate gestures, and above all, patently *immoral* acts. These acts served him as his chief argument in discrediting any arrogation of direct divine inspiration. Indeed, he quotes I John 3:10:

> Per hoc manifesti sunt filij Dei, et filij Diaboli: quisquis non exercet iustitiam, non est ex Deo, et qui non diligit fratrem suum.[23]

It remains unclear whether the labels "ecstatic brothers" and "enthusiasts" in Bullinger refer to a specific group, or designate a cluster of apocalyptic views and antinomian behaviour. However that may

---

[20] Bullinger, *Der Widertoeufferen ursprung*, pp. 31v–32v. Bullinger relied here on Stumpf, *Gemeiner loblicher Eydgenoschafft Stetten*, book 5, chapter 8, in vol. 2, pp. 48r–48v. See also Garcia Archilla, *The Theology of History*, pp. 226–231. The St. Gallen episode has been investigated in John Horsch, "An Inquiry into the Truth of Accusations of Fanaticism and Crime Against the Early Swiss Brethren", *Mennonite Quarterly Review* 8 (1934): 18–31, 73–89.

[21] "Der thaetter aber Thoman Schücker lüff richtigs waegs unnd one verzug hinyn in die Statt/ mit grewlichen gebaerden/ und in wyss und mass wie die verzuckten gern zethuon pflaegend." *Der Widertoeufferen ursprung*, p. 32r.

[22] "Domals was der Statt S. Gallen Burgermeister h. Joachim von Watt/ Doctor/ ein wytuerruempter/ wolgelerter/ fürtraeffenlicher/ eerlicher und gottsfoerchtiger mann. Vor disem huob vilgedachter Thoman an/ mit schützlichen gepaerden schryen/ Der tag dess Herren ist vorhanden/ der tag dess Herren kumpt/ etc." *Der Widertoeufferen ursprung*, p. 32r. The Latin translation read as follows: "Erat autem tum consul S. Galli D. Ioachimus Badianus, doctrinae et pietatis nomine longe celeberrimus, coram hoc horrendis gestibus additis clamaba, Diem domini adesse, Diem domini venire. *Adversus Anabaptisticas*, p. 36v.

[23] *Adversus Anabaptisticas*, p. 36v. In the German original, *Der Widertoeufferen ursprung*, the quotation is on p. 32r. Indeed, Bullinger followed John in citing Cain as an example of a wicked man and his killing of Abel as an example of an extremely wicked act.

be, this profile of the enthusiasts was to recur again and again in the next hundred and fifty years.

The same ambivalence in the designation of the enthusiasts can be detected a century later in the teaching and published work of Friedrich Spanheim. Spanheim devoted much energy, both in his teaching and in his writings, to the controversy with the Anabaptists in general, and the enthusiasts in particular.[24] In the summer of 1646, as the Revolution in England was reaching its most radical stage, Spanheim had five of his students defend disputations on enthusiasm, and indeed made explicit reference to the situation in England.[25] That same year, an English translation of his *Diatriba Historica de Origine, Progressu, et Sectis Anabaptistarum*, appeared under the significant title *Englands Warning by Germanies woe*.[26] Finally, Spanheim referred to the Anabaptists and their assertions of direct divine inspiration in his *Dubiorum Evangelicorum* of 1655.[27]

In the first disputation against enthusiasm Spanheim recognised that the term, in the etymological sense of "divine inspiration", could be both positive and negative; it could refer both to true prophecy and to false claims to such inspiration. Yet, like other polemicists, he restricted the term "enthusiasm" to its negative sense and defined it in the following way:

> [B]y enthusiasts we mean fanatical men, who either feign or presume to have God's breath and inspiration, and whether by diabolical,

---

[24] Many of his students defended theses against the Anabaptists. See Fr. Spanheim, *Disputationes anabaptisticae* (Leyden, 1643–1646; there is a copy of this collection of disputations in the British Library).

[25] These are nos. 16 to 20 of the disputations against the Anabaptists mentioned in the previous note. The reference to the situation in England was made at the beginning of the first disputation: "Quod quidem argumentum eo magis nobis pertractandum est, quia fanaticus iste Spiritus hodieque florentissimas quondam Angliae Ecclesias turbat, et fictis enthusiasmis conscientiarum simul ac Ecclesiarum tranquillitati intercedit." *Disputationum Anti-Anabaptisticarum Decima-Sexta . . . De Enthusiasmo* quam . . . sub praesidio . . . De Friderici Spanhemii . . . Publico examini subjicit Henricus du Rieu . . . 7 Iulii . . . (Leiden, 1646), thesis II.

[26] The *Diatriba Historica de Origine, Progressu, et Sectis Anabaptistarum* was an extended version of the first disputation against the Anabaptists, originally defended in 1643. It was published as an appendix to Johann Cloppenburg's *Gangraena Theologiae Anabaptisticae* (Franeker, 1645). I have used the 1656 edition of that tract, pp. 195–216. The full title of the English translation was: *Englands Warning by Germanies Woe: or An Historicall Narration, of the Originall, Progresse, Tenets, Names and severall Sects of the Anabaptists, in Germany and the Low Countries* (London, 1646).

[27] *Dubiorum Evangelicorum* (Geneva: Chouet, 1655), *Pars Tertia*, Dubium LXXIV, pp. 351–353.

melancholic or voluntary illusions, deceive themselves and others that such inspiration should be assigned to divine revelation.[28]

I shall return later to the threefold explanation Spanheim gave of such presumptions and illusions. The definition itself, however, was quite clear, and so were its denotations. Spanheim explicitly referred to a long line of enthusiasts, from Thomas Müntzer, David George (Joris), John of Leyden and Knipperdoling, as well as Caspar Schwenckfeld and Theophrastus Paracelsus, down to Valentin Weigel and Paul Nagelius.[29]

In his *Diatribe*, Spanheim defined the enthusiasts in a similar way:

> *Enthusiasts* are those, which boasted above the rest, of *divine inspirations, extasies, and secret communication with God*, obtruding their Prophesies for the word of God, and preferring them before the written Word; yea, contended, that that was to be judged by their dreams.[30]

Here too, Spanheim was defining a specific group, with distinctive characteristics, designated by their claims to prophecies which they put before the written word of Scripture. Yet, towards the end of the same chapter, Spanheim returned to the term "enthusiasm", now seeing it rather as one of the general labels given to the Anabaptists:

> ... [I]t is now manifest by what names these Sectaries are called, and for what cause they are given them: and they are either generall or speciall: The generall are *Anabaptists, Catabaptists, Enthusiasts, Fanaticks* and *Libertines* ... It appears likewise that they are called *Enthusiasts*, for the *Enthusiasms, raptures* and other such like things, which they give out for *secret* and *divine inspirations;* and for which, they will not onely have place given to their owne dreames, either in exposition of the Scripture, or determining points of faith, or in direction of the especiall actions of a mans life, but (at leastwise divers of them) ascribe thereunto uncontrollable authority; for which cause also the name of *Fanaticks* was given them.[31]

---

[28] "... [P]er enthusiastas intelligimus homines fanaticos, qui afflatum et inspirationem Dei vel fingunt, vel praesumunt, et vel Diabolicis, vel melancholicis, vel voluntariis illusionibus divinam revelationem tribuendo se aliosque circumducunt." *Disputationum Anti-Anabaptisticarum Decima-Sexta ... De Enthusiasmo*, thesis IV.

[29] *Ibid.*, thesis II.

[30] *Englands Warning by Germanies Woe*, p. 24. The Latin original reads as follows: "*Enthusiastae et Ecstatici* dicti illi, qui prae aliis inspirationes divinas, ecstases, et secreta cum Deo colloquia jactant; prophetias suas pro Dei verbo obtrudunt, et eas scripto verbo praeserunt, immò istud ex somniis suis dijudicandum contendunt". (*Diatriba Historica de Origine, Progressu, et Sectis Anabaptistarum*, p. 215).

[31] Spanheim, *Englands Warning by Germanies Woe*, p. 26. In Latin, the text read as follows: "His in antecessum expensis liquet quibus Sectarii isti insigniantur *Nominibus*,

Here, the term "enthusiasts" does not designate a specific group, but rather, is one of the general names assigned to the Anabaptists. Yet the connotations are the same: the raptures, the claims to direct and secret divine inspiration, and most interesting perhaps—the taking of one's own individual dreams as a source for the interpretation of Scripture and the determination of points of dogma, and the ascription of absolute authority to such dreams.[32] I shall return to these points, which have social and epistemological implications, below.

Another important Dutch Reformed theologian, Johannes Hoornbeek, devoted an extensive discussion to the Enthusiasts and the Libertines in his *Summa Controversiarum Religionis*.[33] Like Spanheim, he understood the term "enthusiasm" in both a positive and a negative sense. In a positive sense, it referred to true divine inspiration, whether ordinary (the effect of the Holy Spirit on the true believers), or extraordinary (the direct inspiration received by the Prophets and the writers of Scripture). Hoornbeek similarly divided negative enthusiasm (which was diabolic in its origin) into an ordinary, common one (the spirit which moved the quiet, sedentary, sectarians against a merely "literal" understanding of Scripture), and an extraordinary, singular type, which was the origin of the false claims to revelation, and to the visions, dreams, and oracles of the enthusiasts.[34] Hoornbeek

---

et quâ de causâ iis insigniti soleant: Sunt verò ea vel *generalia* vel *specialia*: *Generalia* sunt *Catabaptistarum, Anabaptistarum, Enthusiastarum. Fanaticorum* et *Libertinorum* ... Patet etiam eos *Enthusiastas* vocari ob ἐνθουσιασμός, ἐκστάσεις, raptus et alia id genus, quibus et secretas ac divinas inspirationes affingunt, et ob quas somniis istis sive in Scripturae expositione, sive in dogmatum fidei difinitione, sive in specialium vitae actuum directione non locum tantùm, sed et authoritatem ἀνεπεύθυνον esse, aliqui saltem ex iis, voluerunt. Quâ de causâ etiam *fanaticorum* nomen iis haesit."(p. 216).

[32] Spanheim cites the story of Thomas Schücker from St. Gallen which Bullinger, as we have seen above, used in his debate with the Anabaptists. Significantly, he called Thomas "the mad prophet", a term which does not appear in Bullinger's text. Spanheim includes the story in his second chapter, where he deals with the various writers (including Bullinger) who wrote against the Anabaptists, not in the chapter dealing with "enthusiasm" per se. See *Englands Warning by Germanies Woe*, pp. 10–11.

[33] Johannes Hoornbeek, *Summa Controversiarum Religionis* (first edition, Utrecht 1653, amended and enlarged edition, 1658; I have used the Frankfort 1697 edition). Book Six was devoted to the Enthusiasts and the Libertines, and the survey and controversy with the various enthusiasts throughout history took up almost two hundred pages (pp. 378–562).

[34] Hoornbeek, *Summa Controversiarum Religionis*, pp. 378–379. As examples of divine ordinary "enthusiasm" Hoornbeek referred to John 3:8, and to I Corinthians 12:3. For references to divine extraordinary "enthusiasm", he mentioned II Timothy 3:16, and II Peter 1:21. For a warning not to follow bad, diabolic "enthusiasm", he referred to II Thessalonians 2:2: "That ye be not soon shaken in mind, or be troubled,

focused his attention on the latter, seeing in the regular and common enthusiasts a less dangerous type, though both groups were animated by the same (evil) spirit. He therefore defined "feigned enthusiasm" as that in which "one pretends that his own opinions, doctrines or acts, are of the extra-ordinary divine Spirit, and that he is inspired and has celestial revelations."[35]

Under that definition, Hoornbeek proceeded to enumerate and discuss the various enthusiasts throughout history: from the biblical false prophets, through Cerinthus, the Montanists, and the Messalians (or Euchites) in the first centuries of Christianity, to the Zwickau prophets, Thomas Müntzer, Melchior Hofmann, and the Münster Anabaptists in the Reformation period, David Joris, Hendrik Niclaes and Valentin Weigel later in the sixteenth century, and finally some of his own "enthusiast" contemporaries such as the Rosicrucians, Esias Stiefel, and Christian Hoburg (under the pseudonym of Elias Praetorius).[36]

The label "enthusiasm" was thus rather loosely used by Reformed theologians in the sixteenth and seventeenth centuries as far as its specific denotations were concerned. Even when apparently referring to a specific group, as in the case of Bullinger's classification, or that of Spanheim, it is doubtful whether the theologians had a concrete actual collection of people in mind. Rather, they used the term to designate a cluster of claims made by some of their radical opponents (prophecy, apocalyptic prediction, direct divine inspiration unmediated by Scripture), as well as a certain behavioural pattern (ecstasies, convulsions, raptures, shouting). The term, even more than the phenomenon, thus remained quite elusive in the theological discourse of the period. Nevertheless, the label implied a serious challenge to mainstream Reformed theologians—the claim to possess absolute religious truth through direct divine inspiration. Such a claim represented a real threat both to the role and status of the ministers, and, more important, to the principle of *sola scriptura*, to Scripture as the exclusive source of religious truth. Enthusiasm was so dangerous because it challenged the central mediating symbols and institutions

---

neither by spirit, nor by word, nor by letter as from us, as that the day of Christ is at hand".

[35] "Ementitus enthusiasmus est, quando quis suis opinionibus, doctrinae, aut factis extraordinarium divini Spiritus praetendit et mentitur afflatum, coelestesque revelationes." Hoornbeek, *Summa Controversiarum Religionis*, p. 379. See also pp. 381–382.

[36] Ibid., pp. 379–380, and ff.

of Reformed Christianity—Scripture, the Ministry, and as we shall see below, Christological doctrine as well.

Doctrine

How, then, was the challenge of enthusiasm to be met? Protestant ministers and theologians from Luther onwards urged their listeners to heed the call of John and to "try the spirits" (I John 4:1). Down to the early eighteenth century, as we shall see in chapter 6 below, this was the standard battle cry in the struggle against the enthusiasts:

> Beloved, believe not every spirit, but try the spirits whether they are of God: because many false prophets are gone out into the world.

Luther referred to this verse as early as January 13, 1522, in his letters to Nicholas von Amsdorf and to Melanchton concerning the Zwickau prophets.[37] He returned to it in his "Letter to the Princes of Saxony", in the summer of 1524, and more extensively, in a sermon on September 14 of the same year.[38] In that sermon he emphasized the doctrinal criterion referred to in I John 4:2-3:

> Hereby know ye the Spirit of God: Every spirit that confesseth that Jesus Christ is come in the flesh is of God: And every spirit that confesseth not that Jesus Christ is come in the flesh is not of God.[39]

The recognition of Christ's incarnation was thus the doctrinal criterion by which to "try the spirits". Yet, Luther declared that it was not enough to recognize that Jesus Christ came in the flesh, but to understand why he did so—to liberate us from our sins. Indeed, in that sermon Luther principally directed his attack against the Roman Catholics who ignored the real cause of the Incarnation, and consequently put their trust in works, rather than in faith. A few years later he elaborated on this text still further, in his lectures on

---

[37] *WA, Briefwechsel*, vol. 2, Nr. 449, 450, pp. 423, 424–425, *LW*, vol. 48, pp. 364, 366.

[38] *WA*, vol. 15, p. 213, *LW*, vol. 40, p. 52; *WA*, vol. 15, pp. 683–688.

[39] "Sed dicis: per quid cognoscam spiritus dei a malignis? Dicit: dabo tibi signum certum: 'qui confitetur Christum in carnem' etc. oportet ut oculos aperiamus. Qui Iesum Christum non bene cognovit, non potest agnoscere, neque quis spiritus malus vel bonus sit, quia si ratio iudicare debet, tum actum; oportet, ut inditium veniat ex cognitione, quid Iesus Christus sit: si non nosti hunc, frustra iudicas." *WA*, vol. 15, p. 684.

the epistle of St. John, saying that the Incarnated Christ was the
mediator between God and man, as the Word was the incarnated
Holy Spirit.[40] The "Schwärmer" ignored these mediating factors at
their peril. In any case, for Luther, the "trial of spirits" had to focus
first of all on the examination of doctrine, on the content of the
message of those claiming to speak in the name of the "spirits",
whether they were "Schwärmer", enthusiasts, or Roman Catholics.
The critical doctrinal issue was the Christological one, the nature of
Christ and his exact role as Redeemer. As we shall see below, this
would be the doctrinal bone of contention between the enthusiasts
and their critics in the following century as well. No less important,
Luther stressed that the message of the "Schwärmer" and those who
claimed to be divinely inspired had to be judged primarily with reference to the written Word, to Scripture.[41]

A generation later, Heinrich Bullinger similarly emphasized the
content of the enthusiasts' message. Referring to I Corinthians 14,
Bullinger declared that any doctrine preached had to be that of Faith
and Charity. If it claimed to be a divine doctrine, it had to conform
to what was taught in Scripture. The doctrines and alleged "revelations" preached in Anabaptist assemblies, however, did not meet these
criteria. Indeed, Paul does not refer to revelations which

> are not revelations at all, but rather errors undertaken and conceived
> from ourselves, false fantasies out of our [own] trials and out of the
> temptations of others; as, indeed, your Anabaptist revelations are.[42]

---

[40] *WA*, vol. 20, pp. 725–736. See also Christof Windhorst, "Luther and the 'Enthusiasts': Theological Judgements in his Lecture on the First Epistle of St. John
(1527)", *Journal of Religious History* 9 (1977): 339–348.

[41] Zwingli made the same point concerning the "trial of spirits" in his tract against
the Anabaptists: "In catabaptistarum strophas elenchus" of 1527, *Corpus Reformatorum*,
henceforward *CR*, vol. XCIII, I, p. 24. Philipp Melanchton also put the emphasis
on doctrine in his critique of the "fanatici homines" in his *De Orione* of 1553: "Pauci
amant doctrinae studia, et inter eos qui discunt magna dissimilitudo est, multi fanatici
homines horribili furore gignunt impia dogmata, ita crescent tenebrae." *CR*, vol.
XII, p. 52).

[42] "[U]nd nit von offnungen/ die keine offnungen/ sonder uss uns selbs fürge-
nommne und gefasste irrthumb/ uss unsern anfechtungen unn anderer verfuerung
falsche gedicht sind: wie dann üwere Toeuffische eroffnungen sind." *Der Widertoeufferen
ursprung*, p. 98v. In the Latin translation: "non autem de illis revelationibus, quae
non revelationes sunt, sed errores sponte conficti atque concepti ex nostris affectibus,
et aliorum erroneis et falsis figmentis: quales vestrae sunt Anabaptisticae revelationes."
Bullinger, *Adversus anabaptistas*, p. 111v.

We shall return below in this book to the significant reference to temptations and passions as the source of the enthusiast's alleged inspiration. Here we should point out that these inventions were conceived primarily as errors. Bullinger opposed divine revelation to the errors of the will.[43]

As mentioned already, Bullinger was referring mainly to the Apocalyptic pronouncements of the enthusiasts, and he regarded their cries that the Day of Judgment was coming as blasphemous. The doctrine preached by the enthusiasts was considered as innovative, daring and pretentious, contradicting the explicit statements in Scripture. Specifically, such apocalyptic declarations threatened the privileged role of Christ's historical appearance as recorded in Scripture. Once again, the doctrinal challenge of the enthusiasts touched the central mediating symbols linking God and Man in orthodox Christianity.

Almost a century later, we can recognize that same perception in Friedrich Spanheim's critique of the enthusiasts' teaching.[44] The points of doctrine which Spanheim singled out were, on the one hand, those which pertained to the hiatus dividing Heaven from Earth, and, on the other, the doctrine concerning Christ as a central mediating symbol over that hiatus, the doctrine on which Luther also focused, following I John 4:2–3. The enthusiasts, Spanheim argued, conflated Heaven and Hell; viewed matter as co-eternal with God, and taught that God created woman from Himself, begetting His son from her.[45] They also gave a carnal and "epicurean" interpretation of the Kingdom of God (Spanheim probably had the Münster episode in mind), an interpretation which resembled Jewish fables more than Christian doctrine.[46] Thus the transcendental distance between this world and

---

[43] "Nam Paulus de divinis revelationibus loquitur, non de voluntario vestro errore, cui contradicere iubet". Loc. cit.

[44] Spanheim listed the arguments against the content of the preachings of the enthusiasts under the heading of "artificial ostensive" arguments. They were "artificial" in that they were based on reasoning, and they were "ostensive" in the sense of being explicit, in contradistinction to indirect or "apagogical" arguments, to which we shall refer below. *Disputationum Anti-Anabaptisticarum Decima-Octava . . . De Enthusiasmo*, quam . . . sub praesidio . . . D. Friderici Spanhemii . . . Publico examini subjicit Samuel Scherphoff . . . 16 Iulii . . . (Leiden, 1646), esp. theses I, II. The subsequent theses of the disputation presented the arguments of the enthusiasts and the Orthodox responses to them.

[45] "Deum aeternum habere carnem: Deum ex se sibi uxorem fecisse, è qua filium procrearit . . . Infernum esse in caelo, et caelum esse in inferno, caelum *etiam* et infernum unum esse." Ibid., thesis XI.

[46] "Sic regnum Christi carnale et Epicureum in externo splendore et delitiis consistens . . . et sapit fabulas Iudaicas." Ibid., thesis IV.

the divine sphere was obliterated. On the other hand, the enthusiasts rejected orthodox Christological doctrine, the double nature of Christ, and the susceptibility of the Adamite flesh to any remission of sins. The Jesus of orthodox Christianity, they claimed, was a man of sin, and the Virgin Mary, a disgraced woman. The true Christ, according to them, was not born of Mary.[47] Spanheim referred specifically to David Joris, who allegedly denied that Jesus was Christ and most horrendously claimed to be the true Christ and Messiah himself, born of the Holy Spirit, he who will deliver the whole world to salvation or damnation in the approaching Last Judgment.[48] Finally, Spanheim declared, if one tried to collate the various teachings of Müntzer, David Joris, John Mathijs, John of Leyden, Melchior Hofmann, Hendrik Niclaes, Valentin Weigel and others, the enthusiasts' doctrine proved to be incoherent and self-contradictory.[49] Like Bullinger, Spanheim held that the doctrines taught by the enthusiasts were impious and blasphemous, and could not be accepted as Christian.[50] For mid-seventeenth century theologians like Spanheim, then, the controversy with the various enthusiastic sects and individuals was focused to a large extent on issues of doctrine.[51]

Authorization

Nevertheless, the specific problem addressed in the debates with the enthusiasts, as distinct from other Anabaptists and radical sects, was not so much the question of the content of what they said, but that of the authorization for whatever they were saying. Did they, could they, speak by direct divine inspiration? Was it legitimate to expect and wish for such new inspiration? Luther posed some of these questions as early as 1522. In a letter to Melanchton he asked him:

---

[47] "Nostrum Christum esse Anti-Christum, et hominem peccati: Officium Christi concernere solum Novum Testamentum, Mariam Virginem esse foetidam Sambuum, Christum non esse natum ex Maria . . . Adamiticium carnem non esse capacem remissionis peccatorum." Ibid., thesis XI.

[48] Ibid., theses IV, XI.

[49] Ibid., theses II, IV.

[50] Some of the other points of teaching which Spanheim mentions concern the understanding of Scripture, the role of the ministers, and their administration of the sacraments, topics which I shall discuss below.

[51] A detailed refutation of the various enthusiasts and their doctrines in the course of the sixteenth and early seventeenth century may also be found in Hoornbeek, *Summa controversiarum Religionis*, pp. 378–562.

... [F]ind out for me whether they can prove [that they are called by God], for God has never sent anyone, not even the Son himself, unless he was called through men or attested by signs. In the old days the prophets had their authority from the Law and the prophetic order, as we now receive authority through men. I definitely do not want the "prophets" to be accepted if they state that they were called by mere revelation, since God did not even wish to speak to Samuel except through the authority and knowledge of Eli.[52]

Three years later, in his lectures on Deuteronomy, Luther elaborated on some of the signs by which such authorization could be determined. He distinguished between two types of doctrine. The one was "already received and confirmed by divine authority or miracles" and against it, no miracles were to be granted. If any extraordinary acts were performed by the "prophets" who preached against received doctrine, these were acts of the devil. The second kind was doctrine "still to be received":

Here one should not believe unless signs are done, since God never spoke a new Word which He did not confirm with signs ... Therefore when a new doctrine comes, its acceptance is to be suspended until signs occur. If we do this, God is faithful and will not permit them [i.e., the false prophets] to do signs. If, however, we do not suspend our acceptance, He will justly allow signs to be done, that we may be deceived and perish.[53]

Miracles were indeed the signs of authorization, yet they provided such signs only for new doctrine, as had been promulgated by Moses or by the Gospel. Was there any possibility of new doctrine being received in our own days? Luther left this question open, but it was an issue to be discussed frequently in the next two hundred years. Thus, in 1646, Friedrich Spanheim succinctly formulated the same question:

The state of the controversy is therefore [the following]: Whether any precept for beliefs or actions should be desired coming out of individual

---

[52] LW, vol. 48, p. 366. For the German original see WA, Briefwechsel, vol. 2, pp. 424–425.

[53] LW, vol. 9, p. 188. The Latin original reads as follows: "Alterum, quod recipiendum est: hic non debet credi, nisi signa fiant, quia nunquam locutus est Deus novum verbum, quod non signis firmaret ... Igitur differendus est assensus, ubi nova doctrina venerit, donec signa fiant. Quod si fecerimus, fidelis est Deus, qui non permittat eos facere signa. Si autem non fecerimus, recte permittit fieri signa, ut fallamur et pereamus." WA, vol. 14, p. 684, lines 31–37. See also Oyer, Lutheran Reformers against Anabaptism, p. 30.

enthusiasms and private revelations beyond or outside of Holy Scripture.[54]

Did Scripture hint at any future revelations of God? Could those who claimed to prophesy in the sixteenth and seventeenth centuries find the authorization they needed in the Bible? Or, putting it the other way round, if God had often revealed himself in the biblical period, could he not do so again? If prophecy was a recurrent phenomenon in the history of the People of Israel, and in early Christianity, as Scripture indicated, should one not expect such prophecies in the present as well? Numerous chapters and verses in the Bible were called upon in the debate with the enthusiasts concerning these questions.[55] In the Protestant world, up to the late seventeenth century, Scripture was the exclusive public arena in which these issues could be debated. It was the only ultimate source of authorization commonly recognized as of divine origin, and yet open for all to read and have access to. The question, of course, was how to interpret it.

One of the principal sources referred to on the issue of the authorization and legitimacy of contemporary prophecy was I Corinthians 14. It was often cited by the enthusiasts themselves in order to legitimize their claims, and was also frequently commented upon by Reformed and Lutheran theologians in their debates with Anabaptists and enthusiasts. I shall therefore use these commentaries to examine

---

[54] "*Status* itaque *controversiae* est: Utrum praeter vel extra Scripturam S. ex peculiaribus enthusiasmis, et privatis revelationibus petenda sit norma sive credendorum, sive faciendorum?" *Disputationum Anti-Anabatisticarum Decima-sexta . . . De Enthusiasmo*, thesis V.

[55] Spanheim devoted three of the five disputations against enthusiasm to a systematic discussion of these *loci communes*. In the first disputation, *Disputationum Anti-Anabaptisticarum Decima-sexta . . . De Enthusiasmo*, he discussed the various verses which required Christians to "search the Scriptures" and follow only them. In the second disputation—*Disputationum Anti-Anabaptisticarum Decima-septima . . . De Enthusiasmo*, quam . . . sub Praesidio . . . D. Friderici Spanhemii . . . Publico examini subjicit Andreas Winckelius . . . 11 Iulii . . . (Leiden, 1646)—he cited the Scriptural texts, as well as the ecclesiastical authorities which warn against following false prophets. In the fourth disputation—*Disputationum Anti-Anabaptisticarum Decima-nona . . . De Enthusiasmo*, quam . . . sub praesidio . . . D. Friderici Spanhemii . . . Publico examini subjicit Iohannes Haringcarspel . . . 14 Iulii . . . (Leiden, 1646)—he mentioned the various verses the enthusiasts relied on, and systematically refuted their interpretation. These verses were Joel 2:28–29; Hos. 12:11; Psalms 74:9; Luke 2:36; Acts 11:18–27; Acts 13:1; I Cor. 2:15; I Cor. 12:9, 28; I Cor. 14:2, 5, 29, 31, 39 (I shall discuss the commentaries on this chapter in detail below); Eph. 3:5; Eph. 4:11; I Thes. 5:19–20; I Gal. 6:1; Apoc. 11:10; Apoc. 22:9.

the views of the opponents of enthusiasm on the question of the authorization of prophecy and new divine inspiration.

In I Corinthians 14, Paul discussed the spiritual gifts concurrent among the Corinthians, such as prophesying and speaking in tongues. While accepting these "gifts of the spirit" (*spiritualia* in the Vulgate), Paul laid stress on the importance of prophesying for the edification and consolation of the whole community. For that reason, he insisted on clear communication in a known language, rather than on demonstrating the gift of speaking in unknown languages, or the ability of speaking "mysteries".

Even so, the question remained what was meant by "prophesying" in that chapter, and to what extent the practice of the Corinthians could legitimize similar prophesying among later generations of Christians. Sixteenth and seventeenth century theologians tended to interpret the term "prophesying" as *preaching*, or the *exposition* of Scripture, rather than as *predicting* the future or talking under extraordinary divine inspiration. This was, for example, the view of Erasmus in his *Annotationes* on that topic. Discussing the meaning of *prophetia* he says:

> In this passage, Paul does not mean by *prophecy* the ability to predict the future, he means the interpretation of the Holy Scriptures. In like manner Plato distinguished seers (*vates*) from prophets (*prophetae*). Seers, seized by the Godhead, do not understand what they say. Their speech is wisely interpreted by others.[56]

It is interesting to note that Erasmus relied also on Plato in distinguishing between "seers" (*vates*) and "prophets". No less significant is his insistence on the prudent and skilful interpretation of the divine message.

The term "prophesying" was indeed often taken in the sixteenth century as referring to exposition and commentary on Scriptural

---

[56] "Hoc loco Paulus *prophetiam* vocat non praedictionem futurorum, sed interpretationem divinae Scripturae. Quemadmodum et Plato discernit vates a prophetis. Vates arrepti numine, nec ipsi quid loquantur intelligunt, ea prudentes interpretantur caetris." Desiderius Erasmus, *In Annotationes Novi Testamenti*, in *Opera Omnia*, tomus VI (Hildesheim: Georg Holms Verlag, 1962, reproduction of the Leiden, 1705 ed.), p. 728 C–D. See also the recent scholarly edition of the *Annotationes*, edited by Anne Reeve and M.A. Screech, *Erasmus' Annotations on the New Testament: Acts—Romans— I and II Corinthians* ("Studies in the History of Christian Thought", vol. 42; Leiden: Brill, 1990), p. 505. The text quoted above appears already in the 1516 ed. of the *Annotations*. See also M.A. Screech, *Ecstasy and the Praise of Folly* (London: Duckworth, 1980), pp. 214–215, from which the above English translation was taken.

passages, most famously in Zwingli's Zurich where "prophecy" was
that daily exercise in which ministers, canons and students took part
in public readings and interpretations of the Bible in Hebrew, Greek
and Latin, followed by a sermon in German. That type of prophesying later spread to other parts of Europe and became a notable feature of English Puritanism in the Elizabethan period.[57] Yet, with respect to "prophesying" in the Apostolic period, Protestant theologians,
including Bullinger, Zwingli's successor in Zurich, sometimes took a
different approach. Rather than understanding the prophesying of
the Corinthians as merely the interpretation of Scripture, they emphasized the difference between the Church of the Corinthians and
the contemporary Church. Bullinger analysed I Corinthians 14 in
detail in his tract against the Anabaptists, laying the same stress as
Paul had done on the need to edify the whole community, arguing
that in their assemblies the Anabaptists were doing the contrary, sowing
dissension rather than consolation and edification. Yet he went a
step further: the gift of prophesying and speaking in tongues, which
had indeed been prevalent in Apostolic times, was no longer prevalent today, since it was no longer necessary:

> At the beginning of the Church there were indeed several customs and
> many miracles and signs in the Church, which nevertheless, are no
> longer in use, but ceased, such as the gift of languages, as it was once
> given. For after the Christian faith had been sufficiently promulgated
> by the Apostles, and confirmed by miracles, signs ceased. Neither is
> there a cause for us today to complain about that cessation.[58]

The "cessation of miracles" was a crucial concept in Protestant thought
from the late sixteenth century onwards, but it is already found here,

---

[57] On "prophecy" in Zurich see Gottfried W. Locher, *Zwingli's Thought: New Perspectives*, "Studies in the History of Christian Thought" vol. XXV (Leiden: Brill, 1981),
pp. 27–30. On "prophesying" in Elizabethan Puritanism see Patrick Collinson, *The
Elizabethan Puritan Movement* (London: Jonathan Cape, 1967), pp. 126–127, 168–176.

[58] "Es sind zwaren in anfang der kirche etliche bruch unn vil wunder unn zeichen
in der kirchen gewesen/ die aber nit mer im bruch/ sonder abgangen sind/ als
insonders die gaab der spraachen/ wie sy domalen gaeben ward. Dann nach dem
der Christen gloub genügsam durch die Apostel angericht/ und mit vilen zeichen
und wunderen befestnet was/ hortend die zeichen uf. Und koennend wir uns dises
abgangs hüt gar nüt beklagen." Bullinger, *Die Widertoeufferen ursprung*, p. 98r. In the
Latin translation: "Fuerunt equidem olim in ecclesia ritus aliqui, et multa miracula
et signa, quae tamen non amplius in usu sunt, sed cessarunt, veluti donum linguarum,
ea ratione qua tum dabatur. Christiana enim fide ab apostolis promulgata, et signis
atque miraculis confirmata, signa cessarunt. Neque causa nobis est, quod haec hodie
cessasse conqueramur." *Adversus Anabaptistae*, Lib. III, Ch. 10, p. 110v.

in 1560.[59] After the Apostolic period, so the argument ran, there was no longer any need for extraordinary "gifts of the spirit" or the performance of miracles, since Scripture was sufficient to convey the Christian message of salvation. For that reason, there was no need to regret that miracles had ceased.[60]

Bullinger, however, was not content with this theoretical argument, but also pointed out the differences in fact between the assemblies of the Corinthians in Paul's time, and contemporary Anabaptist assemblies. Had the Anabaptists shown any such gifts of the Spirit, Bullinger said, we would have been convinced that their churches were similar to those of the Corinthians:

> If they cannot [do] that, as they [surely] cannot and are not able to— it then follows that this institution [of prophesying and preaching], which is given to those who can speak in tongues, does not regard them [the Anabaptists] as they are ignorant people. If they want, notwithstanding, to continue without the knowledge of tongues, without the gift of interpretation, then, however, they act really like those who anoint the sick without eventual health. When then Paul says "you might all prophesy" he speaks of all those who have the gift of prophecy. You, however, have not [such a gift], as is absolutely clear, so this testimony does not apply to you.[61]

---

[59] See on that topic, D.P. Walker, "The Cessation of Miracles", in Ingrid Merkel and Allen G. Debus, eds., *Hermeticism and the Renaissance* (Washington D.C.: The Folger Shakespeare Library, 1988), pp. 114–124. Walker tends to date to the 1590's the full emergence of this concept in Protestant thought, although he mentions some allusions to it in Calvin.

[60] We find this argument clearly stated by Bullinger earlier in his tract: "Gott unser Herr hat uns sin heilig geschriben wort gaeben/ uss welchem wir alle ding richten/ und alles was uns zuo dem heyl zuo wüssen notwendig ist/ lernen sollend". *Der Widertoeufferen ursprung*, pp. 30r–30v. This was of course a central Protestant principle. For Bucer's view on this issue, see W.P. Stephens, *The Holy Spirit in the Theology of Martin Bucer* (Cambridge: Cambridge University Press, 1970), pp. 133–138. For Zwingli's complex opinion concerning the relationship between Scripture and the Holy Spirit see G.W. Locher, "The Characteristic Features of Zwingli's Theology in Comparison with Luther and Calvin", in his *Zwingli's Thought: New Perspectives*, pp. 142–232, esp. pp. 188–189, and W.P. Stephens, *The Theology of Huldrych Zwingli* (Oxford: The Clarendon Press, 1986), pp. 55–58, 129–138.

[61] "Koennend sy das nit/ als sy es nit koennend noch vermoegend/ so volgt dass sy dise ordnung/ die denen gaeben ist/ die die spraachen koennend/ sy als un wüssende lüt nüt angange. Woellend sy nütdestminder fürfaren one wüssen der spraachen/ und one der gnad der usslegung/ so thuond sy aeben als ordendlich als die thuond/ welche mit oel die krancken salbend one nachvolgende gsundheit. Wenn dann Paulus spricht/ Ir moegend all propheten/ redt er von denen allen die die gnad der prophecy habend. Ir habend sy aber nit/ als klar am tag ligt/ so bewaert üch dise kundtschaft gar nüt." *Der Widertoeufferen ursprung*, p. 98v.

Bullinger thus showed the difference between the Apostolic Churches, where the gift of prophecy still existed, and the churches of his own day. The latter no longer possessed, neither did they need, such gifts of the spirit.

Almost a century later, Friedrich Spanheim offered a similar analysis of I Corinthians 14, first, in his students' disputations of 1646 and more extensively, in his *Dubiorum Evangelicorum*.[62] Like Bullinger, Spanheim refused to see in that chapter of Paul's Epistle any legitimation for the assemblies of the Anabaptists, or for their arrogation of direct divine inspiration. Like Bullinger, he spoke of the distinctions between the Corinthians' churches in the Apostolic period, and the churches of his own time. The gifts of the spirit, Spanheim declared, were characteristic of the church which still needed to be established, not of the church which had already been so:

> The rule of the primitive church is different from the [rule of the] subsequent one, the church which needs to be constituted, from the one [already] established. In the former, the rule of the gifts of languages, prophecies and other kinds of miraculous gifts flourished, as recounted by the Apostle in I Cor. 14. In those ages, it was allowed to everyone to prophesy who was instructed by some kind of divine gift. These gifts were withdrawn, however, and substituted by ordinary means; to introduce the fanatic and insane Anabaptistical confusion is against the explicit precepts of Paul, who distinguished the Pastors from their flock, teachers from their listeners, and wanted the whole Church of the Lord to become orderly and well-arranged.[63]

---

[62] *Disputationum Anti-Anabaptisticarum Decima-nona . . . De Enthusiasmo*, thesis XI, XVI. *Dubiorum Evangelicorum, Pars Tertia*, Dubium LXXIV, pp. 351–353.

[63] "[A]lia enim ratio *Ecclesiae primitivae*, alia *subsequentium*, alia Ecclesiae *constituendae*, alia *constitutae*, in illa vigebant χαρίσματα [Charismata] linguarum, prophetiae, et aliorum id genus donorum miraculosorum, quae recenset Apostolus I *Cor.* XIV. His durantibus licebat omnibus illis prophetare, qui dono ejusmodi divinitus instructi erant. Donis vero illis subductis, et substitutis mediis ordinariis, fanaticum et insanum confusionem Anabaptisticam introducere, contra expressa Pauli praecepta, qui Pastores distinguit a gregibus, Doctores ab Auditoribus, et vult omnia in Ecclesia Domini fieri εὐσχημόνως καὶ κατὰ τάξιν." Spanheim, *Dubiorum Evangelicorum*, p. 353. Spanheim dealt with the same distinction in his disputations on enthusiasm in 1646. See especially, *Disputationum Anti-Anabaptisticarum Vigesima . . . De Enthusiasmo*, quam . . . sub praesidio . . . D. Friderici Spanhemii . . . Publice tueri conabor Jacobus Caroli Zouterius . . . 20. Octobris . . . (Leiden, 1646), thesis V. There he made the distinction between "Ecclesiae Christianae nascentis" or "confirmandae", and "Ecclesiae Christianae adultae" or "confirmatae". In a previous disputation, Spanheim tended to understand "prophesying" as the "interpretation of Scripture"—"donum prophetandi h.e. interpretandi Scripturam". Yet, here too, he sharply distinguished the Apostolic period from the contemporary one. *Disputationum Anti-Anabaptisticarum Decima-nona . . . De Enthusiasmo . . .* thesis XI.

Direct divine inspiration was necessary in the time of the prophets and apostles, when the church was either in need of formation, or of restitution. This was no longer the case in the post-apostolic church. Here, of course, Spanheim was begging the question, since many of the enthusiasts of his day were arguing that the contemporary church was precisely in need of restitution, and hence, of extraordinary gifts of the spirit, and in need of extraordinary callings. In his 1646 disputations against enthusiasm Spanheim addressed the question directly. Among other arguments, he pointed out the difference between the extraordinary Light, Grace, and Zeal with which God inspired those who had already exercised ordinary functions in the church, and the claims of the fanatics for their extraordinary vocation. The former gifts were offered by God in periods which required such extraordinary inspiration, but only to those who had already fulfilled their offices, that is, to the ministers themselves.[64] According to Spanheim, God did not want anyone to act independently of the church already constituted. Divine inspiration, since the apostolic period, did not arrive directly, but was intermediated by means of prayer, reading, meditation, and other suitable preparations.[65] This had been true even of the Reformation itself, on which some of the enthusiasts relied in their calls for a continuous Reformation, and was surely true in his own time, when the Reformed Church was already constituted.[66] Spanheim thus sought to defend the established church of the day, and the established means of divine inspiration, vis-à-vis the extraordinary claims of the enthusiasts.

Indeed, more than Bullinger, Spanheim emphasized the social issue. True, in the times of the Apostles, simple and illiterate fishermen were indeed called to spread the divine message, yet this should by no means provide an example for us to follow today. It could not

---

[64] "Potest enim Deus extraordinarie inspirare singulare lumen, gratiam, zelum iis qui ordinarias vocationes funguntur in Ecclesia . . ." *Disputationum Anti-Anabaptisticarum Vigesima*, thesis IX.

[65] "Inspiratio sane divina utramque paginam facit, sed non enthusiastica vel fanatica, verum sana et sancta, quae non absque mediis, sed per media a Deo instituta et legitimum illorum usum nobis illabitur, quippe quibuscum Deus vult agere ἀμέσως *Ecclesia* iam *constituta*, ut olim cum Prophetis et Apostolis *in Ecclesia* vel *constituenda* vel *restituenda*, sed ἐμμέσως, per preces, lectionem, meditationem, et praeparationem convenientem." *Dubiorum Evangelicorum*, p. 353.

[66] On Spanheim's view of the Reformation, and the reasons why it could not legitimize the contemporary claims of the enthusiasts to an extraordinary calling see *Disputationum Anti-Anabaptisticarum Vigesima*, thesis IX.

justify the mad claims of the Anabaptists that the ruder and less cultivated one was, the more one was like the Apostles, and the fitter to deliver God's message. Not only was it false to assume that God's actions in the time of the Apostles were a legitimate example in our own time. It was also a mistake to assume that God chose only plain and uneducated men to spread his message. While some of the Apostles may have been taken from rude and simple vocations (as prophets like Elisha and Amos were taken from the plough or the herds), they were nevertheless subsequently and systematically instructed by God. One should distinguish, therefore, between the original vocation of the Lord's disciples, and their subsequent mission. In fact, like many of his contemporary colleagues in England, Spanheim came out forcefully in favour of secular knowledge as a helpful tool in preaching the word of God. Although sane theology should not depend on secular learning, especially if it contradicted divine revelation, or claimed to be above it, human learning could nevertheless be useful as an instrument for the better understanding and easier treatment of the divine message.[67]

The dividing line between ordinary and extraordinary inspiration was drawn somewhat differently by two other theologians in the Netherlands, Samuel Desmarets (Maresius) and Johann Hoornbeek. In the late 1660's several of Maresius' students defended theses against the chiliastic views of Labadie, Serrarius, and Comenius.[68] Comenius, who got hold of the theses, wrote a response, to which Maresius answered in his famous *Antirrheticus*.[69] In that text Maresius characterized Comenius as a fanatic, visionary and enthusiast.[70] He too dwelt

[67] *Dubiorum Evangelicorum*, pp. 351–353.

[68] Maresius came out against Serrarius already in 1664 in his *Chiliasmus enervatus, ad D.P. Serarium*. See Nauta, *Samuel Maresius*, pp. 34, 332–334, and E.G.E. van der Wall, *De Mystieke Chiliast Petrus Serrarius (1600–1669) en zijn Wereld* (Leiden: University of Leiden dissertation, 1987), esp. pp. 316–322.

[69] On the controversy between Maresius and Comenius, see Milada Blekastad, *Comenius: Versuch eines Umrisses von Leben, Werk und Schicksal des Jan Amos Komensky* (Oslo: Universitetsforlaget, 1969), pp. 67–74, and W. Rood, *Comenius and the Low Countries* (Amsterdam: A.L. van Gendt and Co., 1970), pp. 198–222. See also Nauta, *Samuel Maresius*, p. 335. The text which Comenius wrote in reaction to the disputations was entitled *De zelo sine scientiae et charitate. Admonitio Fraterna J.A. Comenii ad D. Samuelem Maresium. Pro minuendis odiis et amplicandis favoribus* (1669). The full title of Maresius's response was *Antirrheticus; sive Defensio pii zeli pro retinenda recepta in Ecclesiis Reformatis Doctrina, praesertim adversus Chiliastas et Fanaticos; contra Joh. A. Comenii Fanatici zelum amarum, scientia et conscietia destitutum* (Groningen, 1669).

[70] "Sed praesertim est Comenius Fanaticus, Visionarius et Enthusiasta in folio". *Antirrheticus*, p. 9. See also Bayle's article on "Comenius" Rem. G. in the *Dictionnaire*,

on the theme of the cessation of prophecy and miracles, and the sufficiency of Scripture with which we have dealt above:

> The completion and perfection of the Canonical Scriptures of the Old and New Testament are such that no new Revelations for the fuller instruction of the whole Church are to be added to them or to be expected... We are daily instructed sufficiently in the Holy Scriptures and [are taught] all that is needed to salvation, so that the man of God may become perfect, and thoroughly furnished for all good works. 2 Tim. 3, 15, 16, 17.[71]

Arguing against Comenius' accusation that he regarded the Holy Spirit as redundant in the Church, Maresius emphasized the distinction between the ordinary and the extraordinary works of the Holy Spirit. Only the latter involved new revelations and illuminations of dogma, and those extraordinary works ceased after the period of the Apostles. The regular calls of the Father in our own hearts concerned the offering of prayers, protection against temptation, comfort in tribulation, the preservation of the light of faith, and the zeal for charity.[72] Maresius admitted the affinity between the two types of operation of the Holy Spirit, the light of prophecy and the light of faith. Indeed, for that reason, the terms "prophecy", "visions" and "dreams" could be employed for the ordinary charismatic gifts, as in the famous verse from Joel 2, 28–29, on which both enthusiasts and Catholics mistakenly relied.[73] In a way similar to that of Erasmus and other sixteenth century commentators, Maresius interpreted "prophesying" also in

---

vol. V, p. 266, quoting this sentence. In his article on "Marets", Bayle says approvingly "On ne saurait assez louer notre des Marets de sa vigueur contre les enthousiastes et contre les annonciateurs de grandes révolutions." (*Dictionnaire*, vol. X, p. 246).

[71] "Eam esse plenitudinem et perfectionem Scripturarum Canonicarum V. et N. Test. ut illis nullae novae Revelationes ad pleniorem institutionem totius Ecclesiae, sint adjiciendae vel expectandae... nos quotidiè alloquitur in Sacris Scripturis sufficienter et quantum requiritur ad salutem, et quo perfectus evadat Dei homo, perfectè instructus ad omne bonum opus." *Antirrheticus*, pp. 62–63.

[72] "Non debent restringi operationes Spiritus Sancti ad duo illa capita, illuminationis circa fidei dogmata, et novae revelationis: nam clamat in cordibus nostris Abba Pater, suggerit nobis sanctas preces, nos munit contra tentationes et solatur in nostris tribulationibus, excitat, fovet, conservat lumen fidei, in mentibus nostris et ignem charitatis etc." *Antirrheticus*, p. 64.

[73] "Charismata ordinaria Spiritus Sancti in fidelibus expressit Joël vocabulis *prophetia*, *visionum* et *somniorum*, propter affinitatem quae intercedit inter lumen propheticum et lumen fidei, quod oritur à Spiritu saptientiae et revelationis Eph. 1.17. et per quod sumus omnes edocti à Deo Joh. 6. v. 45 et cujus etiam ductu et beneficio Scripturarum Propheticarum sensum ad salutem assequimur." *Antirrheticus*, p. 64.

I Corinthians 14 as referring to the interpretation of Scripture, rather than to direct divine inspiration.[74] By the time of Paul's mission to the Corinthians, the extraordinary operations of the Holy Spirit were no longer relevant.[75]

A similar dividing line—but with more radical implications—was drawn a few years earlier by Johann Hoornbeek, in discussing the challenge of I Corinthians 14 in his *Summa Controversiarum Religionis*.[76] Like Maresius, he regarded the "prophesying" of the Corinthians as common and ordinary in nature. He started with a linguistic analysis, arguing that "prophesying" in I Corinthians 14 referred to the discussion and explanation of doctrine, rather than to predicting the future (which was not mentioned at all in that chapter), or to "speaking in languages", which was too narrow a meaning of the term.[77] More difficult was the question of the nature of such prophesying, its mode of operation, and by whom it was carried out. Hoornbeek presented three options of interpretation: that such prophesying was to be understood as the office of the ministers and pastors of the church in explaining doctrine; that it was to be understood as the special and extraordinary infusion of the Holy Spirit; and finally, that it was indeed a common and ordinary religious practice in the church of that time, in which the members of the congregation took part for mutual

---

[74] ". . . [E]tiam *prophetare* dicuntur in Scripturis, qui Prophetis et Scripturis explicandis vacant in coetu Ecclesiastico, et illis revelatum dicitur quod ex Scripturis intelligunt I Cor. 14. 29. etc. imò qui et quae intersunt coetibus illis Sacris qui isti Propheticarum Scripturarum interpretationi destinantur, aut illic communibus exercitiis pietatis vacant." *Antirrheticus*, p. 64.

[75] Nicholas Hunnius (1585–1643), a professor of theology at Wittenberg around 1620, pushed the dividing line between the "regime" of extraordinary revelations and that of intermediate inspirations within an established Church further back, to the time of Christ himself. He wrote a short, but highly influential tract against Paracelsus, Valentin Weigel and their disciples entitled *Principia theologiae Fanaticae, quam Paracelsus genuit, atque Weigelius interpolavit*. I have used the 1704 edition (Dresden and Leipzig) done by Johann Heinrich Feustking. Though not referring to Paracelsus and Weigel explicitly as "enthusiasts", Hunnius dealt with the distinction between true divine revelation before Christ's ascension, and false claims to such revelation thereafter, pointing out that such new divine inspiration was nowhere promised, nor did the saints ever expect it, and that it was not commended as a theological principle, indeed, that it was denied to men in the period after the Resurrection. Since then, the will of God is seen revealed in Scripture, and it is clearly and sufficiently comprised therein. Ibid., Cap. IV, pp. 32–37.

[76] *Summa Controversiarum Religionis*, pp. 548–555.

[77] "Existimo, per prophetiam significari *doctrinam*, tractationem, explanationem sacrorum in coetibus Ecclesiasticis, ad mutuam aedificationem et consolationem institutam, ex S. Scriptura, sive alias de articulo aliquo et mysterio religionis." Ibid., p. 549.

edification. Hoornbeek rejected the supernatural, extraordinary interpretation of prophesying, an interpretation which he attributed to the Roman Catholics. He also declined to accept the view that prophesying referred merely to the functions of the ministers. In both cases, it would be improbable that so many prophets, or so many ministers, would be found in one church assembly prophesying, as alluded to by Paul.[78] Hoornbeek therefore tended to accept the third option, and regarded "prophesying" in I Corinthians 14 as referring to a common and ordinary discussion of doctrine and matters of faith by members of the community.[79] In interpreting "prophesying" as referring to the ordinary activity of the Holy Spirit, however, Hoornbeek pushed the dividing line between "extraordinary inspiration" and the "ordinary operations of the holy spirit" further back, before the Apostolic period. At the same time, unlike Maresius, Hoornbeek may have opened up the possibility and legitimacy of free discussion of matters of faith within the community. He thus weakened the monopoly of the clergy on such matters, a monopoly on which previous commentators, who clearly distinguished the practices of the Apostolic church from those of their own, strongly insisted.[80]

Beyond these differences, however, in interpreting I Corinthians 14, or in distinguishing between the practices of the Apostolic churches and the churches of the present day, Protestant theologians were united in insisting that Scripture could not legitimize the enthusiasts' claims to direct divine inspiration. Indeed, they gave a triple answer to the enthusiasts' attempts to authenticate their message by claiming direct divine inspiration: Such direct inspiration was not necessary; it was hardly possible; and it was not legitimate. New divine inspiration

---

[78] Ibid., pp. 550–551.

[79] He emphatically followed Paul, however, in excluding women from such prophesying. Ibid., pp. 551–552. It should be noted that Luther, in his *Open Letter to the Christian Nobility of the German Nation* of 1520 still adhered to the view that any man in the congregation could prophesy, and interpreted I Cor. 14, 30, in that manner. (*WA*, vol. 6, p. 411, lines 21–32, *LW*, vol. 44, p. 134). He was to change his view on the issue in later years. See his treatise of 1532 "Von den Schleichern und Winkelpredigern" (*WA*, vol. 30, 3, pp. 522–23), in English translation, "Infiltrating and Clandestine Preachers" (*LW*, vol. 40, pp. 388–390). Lay prophesying was occasionally practised in the sixteenth century, for example in François Lambert's Church at Hesse, or in John à Lasco's refugee Church in London, but these were definitely the exceptions to the general practice. See Collinson, *The Elizabethan Puritan Movement*, pp. 169–170.

[80] The issue of lay prophesying and "frijsprecherij" was indeed hotly debated in Amsterdam in that generation. I am grateful to Prof. Bietenholz for directing my attention to this highly interesting issue.

was not *necessary*, because Scripture was sufficient for delivering God's message to humanity, and for the achievement of salvation for those who believed in it. For that reason, new divine inspiration was also highly *unlikely* in the Post-Apostolic period (or even in the post-Ascension period, according to some theologians). Miracles, as an attestation of direct divine inspiration, ceased after the times of the Apostles. Therefore, claims to new direct divine inspiration could by no means be *legitimized* on the basis of Scripture. The "sufficiency of Scripture", and the "cessation of miracles" were common themes in Protestant polemics against the Roman Catholics. They were no less relevant against the "enthusiasts" who claimed to perform miracles and to have extraordinary gifts of the spirit like "speaking in tongues".

"By the Fruits you shall know them"

No less important than doctrine, or the legitimacy of the enthusiasts' claims to direct divine inspiration, were the effects of their preaching. At this point, the theological critique bordered on a social and political one. This was particularly true, of course, for Luther's critique of the "Schwärmer" at the time of the Peasants' Revolt. Their spirit was that of rebellion, not of obedience, and, advocating the use of the sword, they arrogated to themselves powers which were the exclusive right of the legitimate secular authorities.[81] In the next generation, in more peaceful circumstances, Bullinger made the same point, though he muted it somewhat. Whereas the message of Christ was that of peace and harmony, the preaching of the enthusiasts was quarrelsome and sowed confusion. Who cannot see where this action and "prophecy" lead, he asked:

> Surely not towards any edification or improvement, but to destruction. Since the rather orderly preaching is withdrawn, impeded, and destroyed, and pure doctrine is complicated and embittered with contentions, dubious questions and muddled trash, and consequently the whole church-service is destroyed and made into nothing.[82]

---

[81] See Luther's "Letter to the Princes of Saxony", *WA*, vol. 15, pp. 212–213, *LW*, vol. 40, pp. 51–52. "Lectures on Deuteronomy", *WA*, vol. 14, p. 682 line 30—p. 683, line 3, *LW*, vol. 9, p. 186.

[82] "Waer kan hie nit saehen wohin dises spyl unnd propheten zuo letst geradten wirdt/ frylich zuo keiner ufbuwung oder verbesserung/ sonder zur zerstoerung. Dann die recht ordenlich predig wirt yngezogen/ verhinderet und zerstoert/ die einfalt

In the seventeenth century, Spanheim and his students repeated and elaborated the same arguments. In Spanheim's own tracts, and in the theses defended by his students, we may find a systematic critique of enthusiasm by the "fruits" it produced. The promotion of Piety and Charity was an a posteriori test for judging whether any inspiration was divine or not. The inspirations and prophecies of the enthusiasts hardly withstood that test.[83] The most flagrant examples for the dreadful religious and moral consequences of their teaching were of course the Münster events of 1533–34. The enthusiasts' declarations that such consequences were the result of the abuses of their teaching, and were due to the frailty of human nature, not to the content of the teaching itself, Spanheim rejected out of hand.[84]

Indeed, Spanheim gave a prominent place in his disputations against enthusiasm to the dangers it entailed for the ecclesiastical order, as well as for the social and political one. He classified most of his critique under the category of "apagogical" arguments against enthusiasm.[85] As a result of the "revelations" of the enthusiasts, Spanheim said, the order of the ministers was displaced, the ecclesiastical hierarchy confounded, the steadfastness of the faithful turned upside down, and the door opened to the errors of heretics and impostors.[86] In fact, he ascribed the victory of Islam over Christianity in the East to the false prophets who sowed divisions within the Church. The license to preach, Spanheim pronounced, was given only to the ministers who were specifically called to that vocation, and no one should preach unless he was sent by God (Romans 10:15), and was so designated by the imposition of hands. He made a clear distinction within the Church between those whose function was to teach and preach,

---

leer mit zancken und zwyfelhafftigem fragen und verwornem gfretz verwicklet unn verbitteret/ und hiemit der gantz kirchgang zerstroeuwt und zuo nüte gemacht." *Der Widertoeufferen ursprung*, p. 99r.

[83] Friedrich Spanheim (praes.) and Samuel Scherphoff, *Disputationum Anti-Anabaptisticarum Decima-octava*, thesis II. This test was one of the "artificial"—i.e. based on reasoning—and "ostensive" arguments which Spanheim adduced against enthusiasm. The other arguments addressed the content of the enthusiasts' doctrine, to which I have referred above, their enticing words rather than their demonstration of the spirit and power of God (I Cor. 2:4), and their ability to predict the future (Isa. 41:22–23).

[84] Friedrich Spanheim (praes.) and Samuel Scherphoff, *Disputationum Anti-Anabaptisticarum Decima-octava*, thesis IX.

[85] *Disputationum Anti-Anabaptisticarum Decima-octava*, theses XV–XXII.

[86] Ibid., thesis XV.

and those who were supposed to listen and learn.[87] No one should arrogate that privilege to himself, Spanheim stressed, quoting Heb. 5:4 ("And no man taketh this honour unto himself, but he that is called of God as *was* Aaron").[88] He thus strongly defended the established Church and the established ministry. To the arguments of the enthusiasts that not only ministers and teachers, but prophets too were called by God (Eph. 4:11: "And he gave some, apostles; and some, prophets; and some, evangelists; and some, pastors and teachers"), Spanheim responded by reiterating the distinction between the period of the *Ecclesia nascentis* and that of the *Ecclesia adultae*.[89] At present, when the Church was constituted and well established, the freedom to prophesy (*libertas prophetandi*) would inevitably lead to licentiousness (*licentia*).[90]

Enthusiasm thus posed a challenge to the ecclesiastical order, as well as to the moral, and indeed, the social and political order. It was not accidental, as I have noted already, that Spanheim had his students defend theses against enthusiasm in the summer of 1646. In the diatribe against the Anabaptists which Spanheim published in that same year, and which was immediately translated into English, he uncompromisingly pointed out the dangers arising from enthusiasm, to both the ecclesiastical and the civil order:

> It is evident moreover, that the enemy of mankind hath laboured by *Anabaptisme*; that the order both of Church and state, being overthrown, or at leastwise disturbed and brought into contempt, the good government of christian Churches and common-wealths might fall to the ground. From hence came it, that the authority of Ecclesiastical order was weakened, by the licentiousnesse of *Enthusiasts*, venting their own dreams and inventions: and the choice of those, who should attend the holy things, committed to the rude multitude; the sacred keyes also, which ought to be born by the representative church, exposed to the pleasure of every one, and so a kind of Anarchy and intollerable disorder brought into the House of God.[91]

---

[87] "Quia ut Deus *Ecclesiarum* aliam vult esse *docentem*, sic etiam vult esse *discentem*, alios praedicare, alios audire, et praedicare quidem eos, quibus impositae manus, et qui ad munus docendi vocati fuere." Ibid. And see also thesis XIX.

[88] Ibid., theses XV, XVI, XIX,

[89] Ibid., theses XVI, XVIII. And see above, p. 33.

[90] "Atqui hac licentia prophetandi data nemo est qui non raptum Spiritus mentiri, revelationes fingere, ordini in Ecclesia instituto obloqui, et dogmata bene constituta solicitare possit . . . alia enim ratio ministerii a Deo instituti omnium confessione, quale olim fuit propheticum et sacerdotale, alia ministerii nec instituti, nec probati, quale sibi arrogant Enthusiastae." Ibid., thesis XXII.

[91] Spanheim, *Englands Warning by Germanies Woe*, p. 45. In the Latin original the

Enthusiasm meant anarchy, disorder and licentiousness. It pitted the whims of the individual against the established clerical authorities ("the representatives of the church"). Moreover, enthusiasm meant that the care of holy matters would be committed to the "rude multitude". It thus involved an appeal to the lower classes. The association which a Reformed professor of theology like Spanheim makes between enthusiasm on the one hand, and the "rude multitude" and individualism, on the other, is of course highly significant. The defence of the ecclesiastical order was closely linked, it was indeed identical, with the defence of the social and political order. Enthusiasm, which was tantamount to individual "inventions", was perceived as a serious threat to that order.

The Demonological Account

The critics of enthusiasm were faced, however, with one further and crucial problem. Even if heretical in content, un-authorized and contrary to Scripture, dangerous to the social, political, ecclesiastical and moral order, the question nonetheless remained—how was one to account for the claims of the enthusiasts, their visions, predictions, and alleged miracles? The most common response up to the middle of the seventeenth century was the demonological one. The devil was the true author of these visions, predictions (especially if fulfilled!) and miracles.

This was clearly the account that Luther gave for the phenomenon of the "Schwärmer". He had already referred to the devil as the cause behind the Zwickau prophets in his letter to Melanchton in 1522.[92] He elaborated on this explanation in his letter to the Princes

---

text reads as follows: "Latâ semel portâ errori per Enthusiasmos aperta; quaevis dogmatum novorum protenta hominibus plebjis et ad novitates prurientibus obtrusa fuêre, et turbulenta ingenia ad novum quendam in Politiâ aequè ac Ecclesiâ statum in orbem Europaeum introducendum erecta fuêre. Et ne vel aliqua conscientiae religione, vel fide Principibus jurejurando obstricta prohiberentur, spargi coeptum, *juramenta* sub Novi Testamenti oeconomiâ illicata esse, adeoque ea sive jam praestita, sive praestanda ipso jure invalida esse. His fundamentis in antecessum jactis, passim tribunitiis concionibus velut ad pileum vocata plebs, coitiones factae, seditiosi armati certatim in Principes suos, et funestis ac civilibus armis vastatae, ac multo sanguine tinctae florentissimae provinciae fuêre." *Diatriba Historica*, pp. 199–200.

[92] *WA, Briefwechsel*, vol. 2, pp. 424–427, *LW*, vol. 48, pp. 366, 371–372. See also Heiko A. Oberman, *Luther: Man between God and the Devil*, trans. by E. Walliser-Schwarzbart (New Haven: Yale University Press, 1989), pp. 227–230, and Oyer, *Lutheran Reformers against Anabaptists*, pp. 30–31, 37–38.

of Saxony in 1524, as well as in the tract "Against the Heavenly Prophets in the Matter of Images and Sacraments" early in 1525.[93] And in his "Lectures on Deuteronomy" later that year, Luther insisted that if we were not careful enough in the "trial of spirits" God could permit Satan to let the false prophets delude the people by false signs and miracles.[94]

Many of Luther's sixteenth century successors continued to adhere to a demonological account of enthusiasm, though not always in the same explicit and outright manner. Caspar Peucer, for example, Melanchton's disciple and successor in Wittenberg, said that the inspirations and predictions of false prophets could only be the work of the devil.[95] In the early seventeenth century, another Lutheran Professor at Wittenberg, Nikolaus Hunnius, similarly referred to the devil in his account of the alleged divine revelations claimed by Paracelsus, Weigel and their disciples:

> That this nonsense of the fanatics, and [their] diabolical deceptions, should be rightly disposed as miserable human [mortal] suffering, covered in the beautiful manner of sanctity—whoever is prudent will easily detect; that is not so easy [however] for the simpler [people].[96]

In the Calvinist world a few years later, Friedrich Spanheim, in disputations defended by his students, viewed the enthusiasts' illusions as caused either by the devil, or by melancholy, or by wilful delusion.[97] Though without elaborating any of these alternative accounts, he clearly entertained the traditional triad explanation: the demonological, the medical and the "political". Besides being possessed by the devil, enthusiasts could simply be cheats wishing to achieve some ulterior aim in their pretences to be divinely inspired. Yet, they might also be sick people, and their claims to inspiration and prophecy could be the symptoms of a melancholic disease. Indeed, as we shall

---

[93] *WA*, vol. 15, pp. 210–221, *LW*, vol. 40, pp. 49–59, 144–149,

[94] "Lectures on Deuteronomy", *LW*, vol. 9, pp. 188–189.

[95] *Commentarius de Praecipuis Generibus Divinationum* (Wittenberg, 1576), fols. 118r–118v, 129v–130r. Peucer, it should be noted, was both a theologian and a physician. We shall return to his views in Chapter 2 below.

[96] "Has Fanaticorum nugas, ac decipulas diabolicas ad miseros mortales fallendum egregie comparatas, et specioso sanctitatis schemate palliatas, cordatus quisque facile deprehendit; non ita facile simpliciores." Nicolai Hunnii, *Principia theologiae Fanaticae*, Proemium, p. 2. See also, Ch. IV, thesis XXI, where the claim of Weigel and his followers to have divine revelations is characterized as based on "fraus et astus Diaboli". Ibid., p. 37.

[97] See above, pp. 19–20.

see below, the demonological account had increasingly to compete with a medical account which explained the characteristics of enthusiasm as the symptoms of melancholy.

More difficult was the problem of the occurrence of successful predictions by the enthusiasts. Here the demonological and "conspiratorial" accounts were especially relevant. Theologians like Spanheim had pointed out that not every prediction which later proved itself correct was necessarily divine prophecy. Had the criterion for prophecy been merely successful prediction, Spanheim, for example, argued, then pagan oracles and divinations would have to be classified as prophecies. Yet, many of these predictions were demonical, many others were natural, many conjectural, and many ambiguous or merely pronounced in an elevated, high-flown style. Such were also the successful predictions of the enthusiasts.[98] In these cases, the enthusiasts were agents of Satan, or wilful cheats, just as the ancient oracles had been. In a later disputation, in response to the enthusiasts' claims to fulfilled predictions, Spanheim contended that, besides the suggestions of an evil spirit, some of these predictions were issued *ex post facto*, others deduced from mere conjecture, and some were based on a knowledge of secondary causes.[99] However, the fact that side by side with the theological account of enthusiasm, there developed in the sixteenth and seventeenth century a medical explanation of enthusiasm, including its successful predictions, is highly significant, and it is to this critique that we shall now turn.

---

[98] "Supponi falsam *hypothesin*, praedictiones omnes futurorum propheticas esse, vel θεοπνεύστους, sunt vero multae etiam δαιμονοπνεύστοι, multae *naturales*, multae *conjecturales*, multae *casuales*, multae *ambigua* et meri cothurni, quales plurimae inter gentiles ab oraculis et vatibus variis Diaboli emanavere, qui in verorum etiam Prophetarum numerum refernendi essent, si ex futurorum quorundam praedictione argumentum ducendum foret." *Disputationum Anti-Anabaptisticarum Decima-octava . . . de Enthusiasmo*, thesis X.

[99] *Disputationum Anti-Anabaptisticarum Vigesima . . . de Enthusiasmo*, thesis XX.

CHAPTER TWO

MELANCHOLY AND ENTHUSIASM: THE SOURCES OF THE MEDICAL CRITIQUE OF ENTHUSIASM

The phenomenon of enthusiasm was not the subject of theological discourse alone in the early modern period. As I remarked in the Introduction, the label could also refer to philosophical contemplation, to empirical and alchemical pursuits, and of course, to poetic and artistic inspiration, even to rhetorical style. Moreover, the debate with the so-called enthusiasts was not conducted solely on theological, philosophical or rhetorical grounds but, increasingly, on medical grounds as well. Enthusiasts who claimed to have direct divine inspiration, to prophesy, or to reveal the hidden truths of nature, were written off as "melancholic", as mentally sick. This "medicalization" of the debate is highly significant. It may present another example of the process of medical marginalization of nonconformists in this period, described by Michel Foucault in his well known book, *Histoire de la folie à l'âge classique.*[1] It also reflects a subtle, but very portentous shift in the ideological basis of the social and cultural order. The link between enthusiasm and melancholy, though perhaps surprising to some modern readers, was by no means new. Its roots go back to classical times. Up to the seventeenth century, however, with a few exceptions to be noted below, this connection was made mostly by physicians for the purpose of diagnosis, and thus had a limited social impact. Transferred to the realm of religious and ideological controversy, the medical interpretation of enthusiasm assumed a different significance altogether. Furthermore, the physiological and psychological analysis of enthusiasm, prophecy and "false" inspiration could easily be applied to Christian inspiration in general, as the deists and other critics of Christianity were to show in the eighteenth century. The medical critique of enthusiasm and the sources for that critique are therefore of major importance for the change that occurred in religious sensibilities in Europe on the eve of the Enlightenment.

---

[1] Michel Foucault, *Histoire de la folie à l'âge classique* (rev. ed., Paris: Gallimard, 1972). In English translation *Madness and Civilization: A History of Insanity in the Age of Reason* (New York: Vintage Books, 1965).

Enthusiasm and Melancholy in the Philosophical and Medical Tradition up to the Seventeenth Century

How did melancholy become associated with enthusiasm, prophecy, and claims to divine inspiration? The history of the conceptions of melancholy since classical times is a fascinating, but highly complicated topic. Melancholy, it should be remembered, was regarded both as one of the four temperaments, and as a specific mental disease, yet the borderline between the two was not always very clear. Here I can provide only a brief survey of the links between enthusiasm and melancholy as they were conceived in the philosophical and medical literature.[2]

The concept of enthusiasm as madness goes back to Plato's notion of frenzy ("furor" or "mania") which was expounded primarily in the *Phaedrus*.[3] There love together with prophecy, ecstasy and poetic inspiration were analysed as various sorts of madness ("mania"). Plato, however, saw the madness which underlay ecstatic and prophetic activities (of the Pythia in Delphi for example) as a divine gift and clearly distinguished it from madness resulting from a disease.[4]

The link between prophecy and melancholy was made in the *Problemata Physica* XXX, I, ascribed to Aristotle, but probably based on a treatise by his disciple Theophrastus. The text opens with a famous question:

> Why is it that all those who have become eminent in philosophy or politics or poetry or the arts are clearly of an atrabilious temperament, and some of them to such an extent as to be affected by diseases caused by black bile . . .?[5]

---

[2] For a general survey of the history of the concept of melancholy as a disease see the recent book by Stanley W. Jackson, *Melancholia and Depression* (New Haven, London: Yale University Press, 1986). On melancholy in ancient times see H. Flashar, *Melancholie und Melancholiker in den Medizinischen Theorien der Antike* (Berlin: De Gruyter, 1966). The classical study on the history of melancholy in philosophy, medicine and art is R. Klibansky, E. Panofsky and F. Saxl, *Saturn and Melancholy: Studies in the History of Natural Philosophy, Religion and Art* (New York: Basic Books, 1964). The following survey is based on these studies, as well as on several of the sources. As will become evident below, I have been led to some of them by the seventeenth century writers on the subject, especially Burton.

[3] *Phaedrus*, 243E–245C, 265A–D.

[4] *Phaedrus*, 265A. It should be noted, however, that scholars differ on the interpretation of Plato's true views in this context, whether he indeed regarded prophecy as a divine gift and a "positive" madness. This question is not relevant to our discussion. The important point is that the Platonic text clearly distinguished between divine "furor" and pathological madness.

[5] *Problemata Physica*, XXX, I 953a 10–13. For the English translation, see W.D.

It proceeds to explain these qualities on the basis of the excess of hot black bile, adding:

> ... [T]hose who possess a large quantity of hot black bile become frenzied or clever or erotic or easily moved to anger and desire, while some become more loquacious. Many too, if this heat approaches the region of the intellect, are affected by diseases of frenzy and possession; and this is the origin of Sibyls and soothsayers and all inspired persons, when they are affected not by disease but by natural temperament.[6]

The *Problemata* thus gave a naturalist account of inspiration, divination, and other outstanding artistic and intellectual qualities. That account was based on an analogy between hot black bile and wine, which had similar effects on human behaviour, and these effects were explained as the result of an excess of air, produced both by wine and black bile. Nevertheless, a clear distinction was still maintained between those who were melancholic by natural constitution, and consequently had the potential of prophecy and excellence in the arts, poetry, politics, or philosophy; and those who were sick with a melancholy disease.[7]

That distinction between "creative" and pathological melancholy tended to be obliterated, or at least overlooked, in the medical tradition after the classical period. Physicians usually saw prophecy and religious ecstasy as symptoms of the disease of melancholy or the result of mania. One of the first representatives of this medical tradition was Aretaeus of Cappadocia in the first century A.D. Aretaeus was an eclectic who combined in his analysis the physiological-humoral doctrine of the Hippocratic texts with the psychological interests of the 'Pneumatic' school. Also characteristic of his approach was the treatment of melancholy and mania as two stages of essentially the same disease, mania being the more acute manifestation of it.[8] The description of religious ecstasy was cited as one special kind of mania:

Ross, ed., *The Works of Aristotle* (Oxford: Clarendon Press, 1927), vol. VII. Another English translation, with slight variations, may be found in Klibansky et al., *Saturn and Melancholy*, pp. 18–29. A scholarly edition with German translation and extensive commentary has been published by H. Flashar in *Aristoteles Werke*, ed. E. Grumach, vol. 19: *Problemata Physica* (Berlin: Akademie-Verlag, 1962).

[6] *Problemata Physica*, XXX, I, 954a 32–38. The Greek term for "inspired" was indeed "entheoi" (ἔνθεοι).

[7] See Klibansky et al., *Saturn and Melancholy*, pp. 15–42. Jackson, *Melancholy and Depression*, pp. 31–33.

[8] On Aretaeus of Cappadocia see Flashar, *Melancholie und Melancholiker*, pp. 75–9, Jackson, *Melancholia and Depression*, pp. 39–41, and Klibansky et al., *Saturn and Mel-*

Some cut their limbs in a holy phantasy, as if thereby propitiating peculiar divinities. This is a madness of the apprehension solely; for in other respects they are sane. They are roused by the flute, and mirth, or by drinking, or by the admonition of those around them. This madness is of divine origin, and if they recover from the madness, they are cheerful and free of care, as if initiated to the god.[9]

This description was clearly influenced by the Platonic notion of "divine furor", particularly its second category as described in the *Phaedrus*, that of ecstasy and purification.[10] Aretaeus's own attitude to this form of mania is not easy to interpret. On the one hand, he equates it with "enthusiasm" in what may be taken as its literal sense, namely as a mania infused by the Gods.[11] On the other hand, he seems to view with some scepticism the claims of these 'enthusiasts' to be initiates of God.[12]

---

ancholy, pp. 44–8. The latter are mistaken, however, in seeing Aretaeus as a writer of the second century who transmitted the thought of Archigenes of Apamea. See Flashar, *Melancholie und Melancholiker*, p. 76, note 6. The most accessible ed. of Aretaeus is by C.G. Kuhn, *Aretaeus, Opera Omnia* (Leipzig, 1828) which includes the Greek text and a Latin translation. The discussion of melancholy is in Part III, Chaps. 5–6 (pp. 75–84). An English translation of Aretaeus was published by F. Adams in 1856, *The Extant Works of Aretaeus, the Cappadocian* (London, 1856).

[9] "Alia reperitur furoris species, qua laborantes propria membra dilacerant, pia cogitatione Diis suis tanquam id postulantibus gratificantes. Id furoris genus a persuasione quadam duntaxat proficiscitur: in caeteris hi temperantes modestique sunt: excitantur autem tibiae cantu, aliove animi oblectamento, aut temulentia, aut praesentium hortatu. Deorum afflatu hic furor provenit: qui cum remittitur, hilares sunt, et curis vacui, tanquam diis initiati." The quotation is taken from a 1763 ed. of Aretaeus which is an amended version of the Latin translation of J.P. Crassus, first published 1552: Aretaeus Cappadocus, *Libri Septem* (Venice, 1763), p. 57. In the English translation of F. Adams, the quotation is on p. 304.

[10] Indeed, in all probability Aretaeus was referring here to the Cybelean rites which originated in Phrygia and were first introduced in Rome in 204 B.C. and officially in the time of Claudius. During those rites some of the worshippers voluntarily wounded themselves and believed that they were uniting with their divinity. Those who castrated themselves became priests of Cybele and were called *Galli*. Similar rites of self-mutilation were practised by the worshippers of Ma of Cappadocia who finally reached prophetic delirium. In Rome they were called *Fanatici*. See on this subject, F. Cumont, *Oriental Religions in Roman Paganism* (New York: Dover, 1956), pp. 46–47.

[11] "Deorum afflatus". ἔνθεος ἥδε ἡ μανίη in the Greek text.

[12] Aretaeus's sceptical attitude is also stressed by A. Rothkopf who sees him, together with Apuleius, as a critic of those religious rituals. Rothkopf, "Manie und Melancholie bei Aretaios von Kappadokien," *Confinia Psychiatrica* 17 (1974): 11. It should also be mentioned that in his chapter on melancholy, Aretaeus included superstitious beliefs among the symptoms, Kuhn, *Aretaeus, Opera Omnia*, p. 75. On the other hand, Professor Owsei Temkin, in a personal communication for which I am grateful, stressed Aretaeus's ambivalent approach to the religious symptoms of the melancholic mania.

The most important writer on melancholy in that period however, was Rufus of Ephesus, whose work *On Melancholy*, now lost, had a profound influence on subsequent writers, and can be partly reconstructed on the basis of later references.[13] Rufus went back to the *Problemata*, but he "medicalized" its thesis, seeing melancholy, with its various psychological effects, as an illness rather than a natural temperament.[14] Whereas Aretaeus focused on ecstasy as one such symptom, Rufus of Ephesus stressed prophetic ability, also mentioned by the *Problemata*, as a religious symptom displayed by melancholics. He was quoted by the Persian physician Al-Razi as saying:

> Et contingit quod quidam istorum narrant et somniant pr(a)eter solitum, et pronosticantur futura, et eveniunt ea quae ipsi pr(a)edicunt.[15]

This quotation suggests that Rufus of Ephesus, like Aretaeus, may have believed in the prophetic capability of melancholics, even though both of them saw it as a pathological symptom. The Byzantine physicians Alexander of Tralles and Paulus of Aegina, on the other hand, were clearly more sceptical concerning the religious claims of those afflicted with melancholy. Alexander of Tralles in the sixth century rendered Rufus's view on this matter in the following way:

> [N]onnulli opinionibus addicti sunt, et se futura praedicere arbitrantur.[16]

---

[13] On Rufus of Ephesus (89–117) see Klibansky et al., *Saturn and Melancholy*, pp. 48–53, and Jackson, *Melancholia and Depression*, pp. 35–39. Rufus was Galen's principal source on melancholy.

[14] Indeed, he regarded the disease of melancholy not as a consequence of an excess of black bile, but rather, as the result either of the cooling down of the blood, or the "burning" of yellow bile, what was to become known as "melancholia adusta". It was with "melancholia adusta" that enthusiasm was usually associated later on.

[15] *Continens Rasis* (Venice, 1509), Lib. I, Tract. IX, Cap. I, fol. VIIr, col. 2. Al-Razi did not translate Rufus's Greek text directly but apparently used other Arabic translations. See Flashar, *Melancholie und Melancholiker*, pp. 84–104; Klibansky et al., *Saturn and Melancholy*, pp. 49–54; and Ch. Daremberg and Ch. E. Ruelle, *Oeuvres de Rufus d'Ephèse* (Paris: l'Imprimerie Nationale, 1879) which is a collection of the fragments of Rufus's *Oeuvre* from various sources, chief among them, Al-Razi. See pp. 454–7 for the text on melancholy, p. 456, lines 1–2 for the sentence quoted above.

[16] A. Trallianus, *De Arte Medica Libri Duodecim*, Book I, Chap. 17, trans., J.G. Andernacus. This translation appeared in many editions in the sixteenth century (the first apparently that of Strasbourg, 1549), and was included in the great edition of H. Estienne, *Medicae Artis Principes post Hippocratem et Galenum* (Paris, 1567), col. 162. Alexander's sceptical attitude is manifest in the connotations of the Greek term *Doxa* (translated by Andernach as *opiniones*) which he uses. Indeed, Liddell and Scott in their *Greek-English Lexicon* use precisely the sentence quoted above as an example of *Doxa* in the sense of hallucination. (Liddell and Scott, *Greek-English Lexicon*, 1948, p. 444b, II, 3.) On Alexander of Tralles, see Flashar, *Melancholie und Melancholiker*,

In the seventh century, Paulus of Aegina explicitly linked melancholy and enthusiasm. Under the chapter 'De Melancolia et Mania et Enteasticis' he mentioned, among various types of melancholics

> [Q]uidam vero et videntur a quibusdam maioribus respici virtutibus et predicere futura quemadmodum divinantes, quos et entheatiscos proprie appellant.[17]

The views of Rufus of Ephesus were also transmitted to later generations by Muslim sources, principally Ishâq Ibn Amrân from Baghdad, and the Persian physician Al-Razi (Rhases or Rhazes in Latin) of the late ninth and early tenth century, to whom I have referred above.[18]

The classical and Arabic tradition on melancholy was brought to the Latin West by Constantinus Africanus who grew up in North Africa in the eleventh century, apparently came to Salerno and spent the last twenty years of his life in Monte Cassino monastery. There he wrote and translated various medical texts, thus transmitting Greek and Muslim medicine to the West. Among his works, one dealt with *Melancholia*.[19] Following Rufus, Constantinus saw excessive meditation as a cause of melancholy, rather than its result. More significantly, he proceeded to apply this insight to the Christian monks and nuns

---

pp. 126–33, and Jackson, *Melancholia and Depression*, pp. 51–54. For more extensive studies see F. Brunet, *Oeuvres médicales d'Alexandre de Tralles*, vol. 1: *Alexandre de Tralles et la Médecine Byzantine* (Paris, 1933); volumes 2–4 include a French translation of his works; and T. Puschmann, *Alexander von Tralles: Original-Text und Übersetzung, Ein Beitrag zur Geschichte der Medizin*, 2 vols. (Vienna, 1878; repr. Amsterdam: Hakkert, 1963) which include an introduction, the original Greek text, and a German translation.

[17] J.L. Heiberg, ed., *Pauli Aeginetae Libri Tertii, Interpretatio Latina Antiqua* (Leipzig: G. Teubner, 1912), p. 33, lines 19–22. For the original Greek text see J.L. Heiberg, ed., *Paulus Aegineta*, in *Corpus Medicorum Graecorum* vol. IX, 1 (Leipzig: G. Teubner, 1921). J.G. Andernach translated also Paulus Aegineta in the sixteenth century. A German translation was published by I. Berendes, *Paulos' von Aegina Des Besten Arztes Sieben Bücher* (Leiden: Brill, 1914). On Paulus see also Klibansky et al., *Saturn and Melancholy*, p. 54, and Jackson, *Melancholia and Depression*, pp. 54–56, who stresses the sceptical attitudes of both Alexander of Tralles and Paulus of Aegina concerning the prophetic abilities of melancholics.

[18] On Ishâq Ibn Amrân see Jackson, *Melancholia and Depression*, pp. 57–59. On Al-Razi, see G. Sarton, *Introduction to the History of Science*, vol. I (Washington: Williams and Wilkins, 1927), pp. 609–10, and *The Encyclopaedia of Islam* (first. ed.), vol. III (1936), pp. 1134–6.

[19] "De Melancholia libri duo" in Constantini Africani *post Hippocratem et Galenum . . . Opera . . .* (Basel, 1536). The precise details concerning Constantinus Africanus, including his original religious convictions, and his exact links with Salerno and Monte Cassino are not altogether clear. See however M. McVaugh, "Constantine the African", *Dictionary of Scientific Biography* (henceforward, *D.S.B.*), vol. III, pp. 393–395. On the question of Constantinus's sources concerning melancholy see Flashar, *Melancholie und Melancholiker*, pp. 89–91, and Klibansky et al., *Saturn and Melancholy*, p. 49, note 129.

of his time, arguing that religious piety and meditation in general, and the monastic way of life in particular, made people especially susceptible to melancholy.[20] It was a view which was to have a long career in the West, down to anti-Catholic polemics in the seventeenth century, as we shall see below.[21]

Whereas Constantinus "Christianized" some of the causes of melancholy, Bernard de Gordon, professor of medicine at Montpellier in the late thirteenth and early fourteenth century, "Christianized" some of its symptoms.[22] In his *Lilium Medicinae*, the traditional symptoms of pagan prophecy and divination were transformed to symptoms of a definite Christian ring:

> It seems to some [of them] that they are prophets, and inspired by the Holy Spirit, and they start to prophesy and predict many future events concerning the state of the World or concerning Antichrist.[23]

Here Bernard was clearly referring to the Beguines, the heretical Spiritual Franciscans active in Provence at that time. In fact, the above quotation strikingly resembles the description of the Beguines by the Council of Béziers in 1299 which Bernard may well have known:

> [I]nter quos nonnulli fuerint qui dicebantur plurimi litterati, quorum aliqui fore noscebantur de religione laudabili, non immerito inter religiones ceteras approbata, ponentium os in caelum, et manus ad vota extendentium, praedicantium multis finem mundi instare, et jam adesse vel quasi tempora Antichristi.[24]

---

[20] Constantinus Africanus, "De Melancholia", Lib. I, pp. 280–284. See also Klibansky et al., *Saturn and Melancholy*, pp. 82–86.

[21] For a discussion of some of the medieval moral and theological texts warning of these dangers in the monastic and contemplative way of life, see Klibansky et al., *Saturn and Melancholy*, pp. 75–81.

[22] On B. de Gordon (Gordonius) and his book *Lilium Medicinae*, see G. Sarton, "Lilium Medicinae", in *Medieval Studies in Honor of J.D.M. Ford*, ed. V.T. Holmes and A.J. Denomy (Cambridge, Mass.: Harvard University Press, 1948), pp. 239–56. Bernard began his book in 1303 but it is not clear when he finished it. See Y. Violé O'Neill, "The History of the Publication of Bernard of Gordon's *Liber de Conservatione Vitae Humanae*," *Sudhoff Archiv für Geschichte der Medizin und der Naturwissenschaften*, vol. 49, no. 3 (September 1965), pp. 269–70, note 3. For a general survey of Bernard's life and works, though dated in its approach, see E. Littré, "Bernard de Gordon, médecin," in *Historie Littéraire de la France*, vol. XXV (1869), pp. 321–37.

[23] My translation. The Latin original reads thus:

> Aliis videtur quod sint prophetae, et quod sint inspirati à spiritu sancto, et incipiunt prophetare, et multa futura praedicere sive de statu mundi aut antichristri.

Bernardi Gordonii *Opus, Lilium Medicinae Inscriptum, de morborum propè omnium curatione, septem particulis distributum* (Lyon, 1574), p. 211.

[24] Mansi, *Sacrorum Conciliorum Nova et Amplissima Collectio*, vol. 24, col. 1216. On

Bernard's identification of the Beguines as melancholics is highly interesting in that here a physician came close to participating in a specific religious controversy, in a manner that was to be developed by Burton in the seventeenth century. However, it is worth stressing that among the theologians who participated in the controversy with the Beguines in the fourteenth century, there was apparently no reference to medical arguments.[25]

A "rehabilitation" of melancholy, linking it with enthusiasm and prophecy in a *positive* sense, came only with the Renaissance.[26] Contrary to most medieval medical writers, Renaissance thinkers tended to take the "supernatural" symptoms of melancholy seriously, and tried to give a systematic account for the ability of melancholics to predict the future or to speak in languages they did not know. Historical scholarship of the last generation has discussed in some detail the rehabilitation of melancholy in the Renaissance and the revived interest in the *Problemata* attributed to Aristotle, which associated melancholy with artistic inspiration and intellectual creativity.[27]

We find such attitudes manifested in the writings of Antonio Guainerio, a Paduan physician of the first half of the fifteenth century, who devoted a whole chapter to the question "How is it that some illiterate [people] who are melancholic become literate, and in what way can some of them predict the future?"[28] In this matter

the Beguines in Provence, see G. Leff, *Heresy in the Later Middle Ages* (New York: Manchester University Press, 1967) vol. I, pp. 195–230.

[25] Thus, the main text of the Inquisition which described and condemned the views of the Beguines—Part 5 of B. Guidonis, *Practica Inquisitionis Heretice Pravitatis*, composed in the 1320s—made no reference to the Beguines as melancholics. I have consulted the French edition and translation by G. Mollat, *Manuel de l'Inquisiteur* (Paris, 1964), vol. I, pp. 108–93.

[26] One exception mentioned by Klibansky et al. was William of Auvergne in the thirteenth century. He argued, however, that the melancholy complexion disposed men to meditation and prepared them for divine inspiration and mystical experience, but such inspiration depended of course on divine grace. *Saturn and Melancholy*, pp. 73–74.

[27] The classical study on this subject is of course *Saturn and Melancholy* by Klibansky, Panofsky and Saxl, especially pp. 241–274. For the sixteenth century see now M.A. Screech, *Montaigne and Melancholy* (London: Duckworth, 1983), especially pp. 10–36, as well as his article "Good Madness in Christendom" in W.F. Bynum, Roy Porter and Michael Shepard, eds., *The Anatomy of Madness: Essays in the History of Psychiatry* (London and New York: Tavistock, 1985), vol. I, pp. 25–39. See also N.L. Brann, "The Renaissance Passion of Melancholy: The Paradox of its Cultivation and Resistance" (unpublished Ph.D. dissertation, Stanford, 1965).

[28] "Quare illiterati quidam melancolici literati facti sunt, et qualiter etiam ex his aliqui futura praedicunt?". A. Guainerius, *Practica* (Venice, 1517), Tract XV, Chapter

Guainerio explicitly relied on the Aristotelian *Problemata*. He did not accept, however, the Aristotelian explanation of these symptoms. Rather, he believed that a melancholic illness, in weakening the bodily chains by which the soul is bound to the senses, freed it to receive astral influences, and recapture knowledge it had had before birth. Guainerio thus combined the Platonic doctrine of *anamnesis* (recollection) with medieval astrological thought in explaining the extraordinary gifts with which melancholic patients were endowed.

As is well known, these ideas were developed systematically by Marsilio Ficino in Florence in the second half of the fifteenth century. Ficino explicitly identified Plato's divine frenzy (*furor*) with "melancholy" as expounded in the *Problemata*. He also combined the neo-Platonic astrological account of divination with the medical tradition which saw excessive meditation as linked with melancholy. Yet for him, not only was the *vita contemplativa* a decidedly positive vocation, but the melancholic or "Saturnine" temperament an essential foundation for that vocation. True, such a temperament was not without its pathological dangers, but they could be avoided by the right mixture of "Jovial" influences.[29]

Ficino was more interested, however, in the creative and contemplative life of the scholar than in the predictions and divinations of prophets. A naturalist interpretation of divination and prophetic ability was developed in the Aristotelian School of Padua at that period. The most prominent and radical representative of that school at the turn of the fifteenth century was Pietro Pomponazzi, who in his *De Incantationibus* (published only long after his death, in 1556) presented a thoroughly naturalist interpretation of prophetic ability, divination and inspiration. Ascribing these phenomena to the effect of the influence of celestial bodies acting as instruments of separate intelligences,

---

IV, fols. 23v–24v. The previous chapter referred to the ability of melancholics to speak in tongues. Ibid., fols. 23r–23v. On Guainerio's rehabilitation of melancholy see also Klibansky et al., *Saturn and Melancholy*, pp. 95–96.

[29] The text in which Ficino expounded his view of melancholy most systematically was *De vita libri tres*, Book I, chapters IV–X. For a new edition with English translation see Carol V. Kaske and John R. Clark, eds., *Marsilio Ficino, Three Books on Life* (Binghamton, New York: The Renaissance Society of America, 1989), pp. 116–137. Another edition with critical apparatus and commentary in German by M. Plessner and F. Klein-Franke was published by Georg Olms Verlag, Hildesheim, New York, 1978. See also Ficino's commentary on Plato's *Phaedrus* in Michael J.B. Allen, *Marsilio Ficino and the Phaedran Charioteer* (Berkeley: University of California Press, 1981), especially pp. 78–82. For a detailed analysis of Ficino's views on this subject see Klibansky et al., *Saturn and Melancholy*, pp. 254–274.

Pomponazzi nevertheless stressed that melancholy was the material cause which made men ecstatic, inspired and enthusiast.[30]

One of Pomponazzi's direct disciples, Girolamo Fracastoro, was a bit more careful and less radical than Pomponazzi.[31] Though his aim was likewise to give a naturalist explanation of all phenomena (he boasted in a letter to Giovan Battista Ramusio that 'I save everything through the movements of our humours'),[32] he was nevertheless circumspect enough to designate the separate intellects as God, angels, or the Devil, stressing that prophecy and divination could not be entirely natural, unless they were successful by accident. Yet, melancholics were the most susceptible to such influences because either they were men of superior intelligence and actions, or, conversely, most liable to fury and insanity and hence of becoming *phanatici*.[33] Only this second type of melancholy was regarded as negative, an opportunity for the devil. Following pseudo-Aristotle, Ficino and Pomponazzi, Fracastoro believed that melancholy could be positive too, serving as the basis for superior intellectual achievement, inspiration and even prophecy.

Still more careful than Fracastoro was Jerome Cardan.[34] Cardan studied in Padua and for most of his life was a professor of medicine in Pavia, but his books (besides those on mathematics where he made

---

[30] P. Pomponatius, *De naturalium effectuum causis sive de Incantationibus* (1567; reprinted Hildesheim, New York: Georg Olms Verlag, 1970), pp. 140–1. The term *enthusiasmus* does not appear in the text itself, but in the margins, and was probably added by Grataroli, the editor of the text. Pomponazzi relied on the *Problemata*, XXX, on Plato, and on the description of the Sibyl of Cumae in the *Aeneid* (Book VI, 47–51, 77–80) which was also quoted by Macrobius in the *Saturnalia* (Book 4, chap. I). Concerning melancholy as the natural origin of demoniacs he referred to the *Conciliator* by Peter of Abano. There is of course an extensive bibliography on Pomponazzi which cannot be quoted here but mention should be made of the very detailed introduction by H. Busson to the French translation of *De Incantationibus: Les Causes des merveilles de la nature ou les enchantements* (Paris, 1930) which analyses the content of the book and traces its sources and later influence.

[31] On Fracastoro, see the article "Fracastoro, Girolamo" by B. Zanobio in *D.S.B.*, vol. 5, pp. 104–7.

[32] Quoted by E. Garin, *Italian Humanism*, trans. P. Munz (New York: Harper and Row, 1965), p. 190.

[33] G. Fracastoro, *Turrius sive de Intellectione*, Lib. II, in *Opera Omnia* (Venice, 1555), p. 203. Christ Church library possesses a 1574 ed. where this text is on p. 146a.

[34] On Girolamo Cardano see Garin, *Italian Humanism*, pp. 188–9, and the article on "Cardano, Girolamo" by M. Gliozzi in *D.S.B.*, vol. 3, pp. 64–7. See also J. Dayre, *Jérôme Cardan (1501–1576) Esquisse biographique* (Grenoble: Allier, 1928), and Cardan's own autobiography *De Vita Propria Liber* written in 1575, but first published in 1643 by Gabriel Naudé. An English translation by Jean Stoner was published in 1930 and reissued in 1962 by Dover.

his most significant scientific contribution) are essentially vast ency-
clopedias of natural philosophy, mostly concerned with curious and
extraordinary phenomena. In the *De Rerum Varietate*, melancholy is
discussed in a chapter on human nature, as a physiological source—
but also as the result—of certain affections, such as fear, meditation,
superstition, hunger and distress. Within this context he mentioned
the special symptoms of melancholy, including visions and the ability
to predict the future. Concerning this point, however, Cardan was
cautious. The supernatural manifestations of melancholics were ultimately the effect not only of physiological factors and daily customs
such as fasting, but also of external influences from above.[35]

Most sixteenth-century physicians, however, who inherited the classical and medieval tradition in discussing the religious symptoms of
melancholy, saw them once again in negative terms, whether pathological or even demonic. Some physicians merely repeated the for-
mulae handed down by the classical and Arabic treatises. Thus,
Leonhard Fuchs, the German Lutheran physician and botanist, was
clearly following Alexander of Tralles when he wrote:

> Quidam se numine afflatos esse existimant, et futura vaticinantur, quos
> ἀνθεαστικοὺς privatim Graeci nominant.[36]

---

[35] G. Cardano, *De Rerum Varietate Libri XVII*, Lib. VIII Chap. XL (Basel, 1557),
p. 293, or the revised edition of Lyon, 1580, pp. 384l–384r. In another work of his,
De Subtilitate, Cardan was more specific. There he mentioned the visions of hermits
among marvellous visions in a waking state, in ecstasy. He explained these visions
as the result of fasting, solitary life and the hermit's mental exertions. All these gave
rise to imaginings typical of the melancholic man. Once again, however, Cardan
allowed for the possibility of true visions of divine, angelic or demonic origin.
G. Cardano, *De Subtilitate Libri XXX*, Lib. XVIII (Nuremberg, 1550), p. 357. A
French translation was published already in 1556 by Richard le Blanc and dedicated to the Duchess of Berry, *Les Livres de Hiérome Cardanus... intitulés de la Subtilité*
(Paris, 1556); see p. 373 for the relevant text.
[36] L. Fuchsius, *De Sanandis Totius Humani Corporis... Malis Libri Quinque* (Lyon,
1546), p. 68r. In the 1547 ed. of that book the quotation is on p. 126. An enlarged
and corrected edition was posthumously published in Frankfurt in 1567, where the
term is spelled correctly ἐνθεαστικοὺς (p. 62). In his reference to enthusiasm as a
symptom of melancholy, Fuchs was probably influenced by Torinus's paraphrase of
Alexander Trallianus, since the translation of Guinther Andernach first appeared
only in 1549, as I noted above. Leonhard Fuchs (1501–66), the famous humanist
physician and botanist, studied medicine in Ingolstadt, converted to Lutheranism
and held the chair of medicine at Tübingen for thirty-one years (1535–66). See
F.H. Garrison, *An Introduction to the History of Medicine* (Philadelphia and London:
Saunders, 1929), p. 229, and *Dictionnaire des sciences médicales* (Paris, 1821), vol. IV,
pp. 282–5. For a recent study of his status in Tübingen and his relations with the
ducal court of Würtemberg based on his correspondence with Camerarius, see

The Dutch physician Pieter von Foreest (Forestus), broke away to some extent from the traditional structure of medical treatises in that he based his discussion on clinical observations, often drawn from his own medical practice.[37] Nevertheless, in analysing his material he relied heavily on traditional authorities and conceptions. Among the symptoms of melancholy, Forestus mentioned claims to inspiration and prediction in a manner clearly influenced by Fuchs or perhaps directly by Alexander of Tralles:

> Nonnulli se numine afflatos existimant, et in illo errore sunt ut omnia futura se vaticinari putent, ἐνθεαστικούς vocant hos Graeci. Et nonnulli credunt se loqui cum angelis.[38]

The German physician Gualther Bruele expressed himself similarly.[39] Fuchs, Foreest and Bruele all mentioned claims to prophecy among the specific signs of melancholy, traditionally enumerated by writers on that topic.

To the extent that sixteenth century physicians took these claims to prophecy, divination, and speaking in tongues seriously, they tended to give them a demonological explanation rather than a naturalist one. In such an interpretation they could rely on Avicenna who already

---

G. Fichtner, "Neues zu Leben und Werk von Leonhart Fuchs aus seinen Briefen an Joachim Camerarius I. und II. in der Trew-Sammlung," *Gesnerus* 25 (1968): 65–82. I have not been able to consult the monograph by E. Stübler, *Leonhart Fuchs—Leben und Werk* (Munich, 1928).

[37] Pieter von Foreest was a Dutch physician born at Alkmaar in 1552. He studied medicine first in Louvain, later in Italy, in Bologna as well as in Padua under Vesalius, and finally in Paris. He returned to his country, inaugurated the chair of medicine in Leiden, but apparently spent most of his time in private practice in Delft. He died in 1597. See *Dictionnaire des sciences médicales*, vol. IV, pp. 190–2, and G.A. Lindeboom, *Dutch Medical Biography. A Biographical Dictionary of Dutch Physicians and Surgeons 1475–1975* (Amsterdam: Editions Rodopi, 1984). For a recent collection of articles on Foreest in Dutch and English see H.L. Houtzager, *Pieter von Foreest: Een Hollands medicus in de zestiende eeuw* (Amsterdam, Atlanta, GA: Rodopi, 1989).

[38] P. Forestus, *Observationum et Curationum Medicinalium, sive Medicinae Theoricae et Practicae Libri XXVIII* (Frankfurt, 1634), bound in his *Observationum et Curationum Medicinalium ac Chirurgicarum Opera Omnia* (Frankfurt, 1660), Lib. X, Observatio XIII, p. 331. Previous editions of the *Opera Omnia* appeared in 1619 and 1623, and of the first 28 books in 1614. Book X of the *Observationes* first appeared in Leiden in 1590.

[39] "Alij vates se augurantes, de rebus futuris multa pollicentur." *Praxis Medicinae Theorica et Empirica Familiarissima* (Leiden, 1589), p. 22. The quotation is in the chapter entitled "Methodus pro cognitione Melancholiae inserviens." A seventeenth-century English translation of this text reads as follows: "... some imagine themselves to be prophets, foretelling much of things to come"; W. Bruele, *Praxis Medicinae, or The Physitians Practise: Wherein are Contained all Inward Diseases from the Head to the Foot*, 3rd ed. (London, 1648), pp. 25–6. Not much is known about the life of Bruele, except for this book. See *Dictionnaire des sciences médicales* vol. III, p. 15.

in the tenth century explained the supernatural abilities of melancholics in demonological terms.[40] Thus Felix Platter, for example, took prophecy and speaking in tongues quite seriously as praeternatural symptoms of melancholy caused by demonical possession (*obsessio*).[41] This was also the view of Jean Fernel.[42] Indeed, in the seventeenth century Daniel Sennert relied on Fernel in making the same point. Sennert did not deny the possibility of speaking in tongues, or the performance of other supernatural feats. But, he insisted on giving such extraordinary abilities a demonological explanation, and explicitly rejected any naturalist or astrological accounting for them, such as that advanced by Guainerio, for example, as we have seen above.[43]

Other physicians were more ambivalent. An Italian, Hercules Saxonia (Ercole Sassonia), who taught medicine in Padua, mentioned claims to prophecy among the symptoms of melancholy, but like his Paduan predecessor, he relied primarily on Plato and on the *Problemata* attributed to Aristotle, rather than on medical authorities.[44] Hercules doubted, however, whether religious zeal at all deserved the name of melancholy, and in a later tract was careful to distinguish such symptoms of melancholy from true prophecy.[45] We thus see in his case

---

[40] See Avicenna, *Liber Canonis, De medicinis cordialibus, et cantica* (Venice, 1555), Lib. III, Fen. I, Tract. 4, Cap. 18–19, esp. fol. 205r.

[41] Felix Platter, *Praxeos Medicai Tomi tres* (Basel, 1625, first ed., 1602), pp. 86, 89–90. For an English translation of some extracts based on the 1656 ed., see O. Diethelm and T.F. Heffernan, "Felix Platter and Psychiatry", *Journal of the History of the Behavioral Sciences* 1 (1965): 10–23, translation of the above mentioned text on p. 16. See also F. Platter's other medical text, *Observationum . . . Libri Tres* (1614), p. 90. On Platter see also the article by P.E. Pilet in *D.S.B.*, vol. XI, p. 33.

[42] See the chapter Fernel devoted to such cases in his *De Abditis Rerum Causis* (Paris, 1560), Lib. II, Ch. XVI, pp. 369–382.

[43] Daniel Sennert, *Medicina Practica*, Lib. I, Part II, Cap. XV, Quaestio I, in Sennert, *Opera Omnia* (Paris, 1641), vol. II, p. 157. On Sennert see the article "Sennert, Daniel" by Hans Kangro in *D.S.B.*, vol. XII, pp. 310–313.

[44] H. Saxonia, *Pantheum Medicinae Selectum, sive Medicinae Practicae Templum, Omnibus Omnium fere Morborum Insultibus Commune, Libris Undecim Distinctum* (Frankfurt, 1603), Cap. XVI, p. 89D. Hercules Saxonia (1551–1606) was born in Padua to a family of doctors, studied there and after a period of successful medical practice in Venice, returned to his home town and taught at the University till his death. See J.A. van der Linden and G.A. Mercklin, *De Scriptis Medicis* (Nuremberg, 1686), pp. 405–6, and *Dictionnaire historique de la médecine* (1756), vol. II, p. 363.

[45] H. Saxonia, *Pantheum Medicinae*, p. 89D. He classified the manifestations of religious melancholy under the category of love-melancholy, the former's object being God, while the other type had women as its object. In his later tract, *De Melancholia Tractatus* (Venice, 1620), Cap. II, pp. 7–8, Hercules analysed the religious symptoms of melancholy in greater detail and explicitly mentioned Plato's four categories of Eros (mistakenly referring to the *Theaetetus* rather than the *Phaedrus*), but stressed the difference between that type of melancholy and true prophecy.

the tensions between the Renaissance interest in a "naturalist" interpretation of prophecy and religious ecstasy, and the Christian care
to separate such phenomena from true divine inspiration.

The same tensions are manifest in the writings of two French
physicians at the turn of the sixteenth century. One of them was
André du Laurens, the famous doctor from Montpellier who later
became physician to Henri IV.[46] Among the symptoms of melancholy Du Laurens mentioned divination, prophetic ability and poetic
inspiration.[47] He referred explicitly to Rhazes and Trallianus as his
sources, taking them as believers in the supernatural abilities of
melancholics.[48] Du Laurens himself remained vague as to the nature
and causes of such phenomena. Yet, he clearly distinguished between
melancholy as a disease and a favourable type of melancholic constitution which gives rise to "a kinde of divine ravishment, commonly
called *Enthousiasma*, which stirreth men up to plaie the Philosophers,
Poets, and also to prophesie".[49] He also mentioned the testimony of
Avicenna "that melancholike persons sometimes doe such strange
things, that the common people imagine them to bee possessed" but
he did not enlarge on this.[50] That he was treading on delicate ground
becomes obvious from his next example of corrupt imaginings which
were sometimes ascribed to melancholy in that period:

> How many famous men be there in this our age, which make scruple
> to condemne these olde witches, thinking it to bee nothing but a
> melancholike humour which corrupteth their imagination, and filleth
> them with all these vaine toyes. I will not cast my selfe any further

---

[46] On Du Laurens, see the article by J.J. Bylebyl in *D.S.B.*, vol. VIII, pp. 53–4,
and Jackson, *Melancholia and Depression*, pp. 86–91. His famous discussion of melancholy was the second part of the *Discours de la conservation de la veue; des maladies
mélancholiques, des catarrhes, et de la vieillesse*, published for the first time in 1594 and
dedicated to the Duchess of Uzès who apparently suffered from all these medical
problems. It became a highly popular book, was reissued in several editions and
soon translated into English, German, Latin and Italian. As we shall see below, it
also had a major impact on Burton's *Anatomy of Melancholy*. I shall use the English
translation by Richard Surphlet, published in 1599 under the title *A Discourse of the
Preservation of the Sight: of Melancholike Diseases; of Rheumes, and of Old Age*. It has been
reproduced by the Shakespeare Association Facsimiles, No. 15 (London: Oxford
University Press, 1938).

[47] *A Discourse of the Preservation of the Sight*, p. 98 (Chapter VI in the Second Discourse.)

[48] Ibid. As we noted above, Rhazes was quoting Rufus of Ephesus on this subject. As for Trallianus, he seems to have been more sceptical than Du Laurens took
him to be as we saw above.

[49] Ibid., p. 86.

[50] Ibid., p. 98.

into the depth of this question, the matter craveth a man of more leisure.[51]

Du Laurens was evidently alluding to the views of the German physician Johann Weyer, who saw witches as innocent victims of melancholy rather than as agents of Satan, but he clearly preferred to refrain from getting involved in this delicate controversy. In late sixteenth century France the question whether to classify certain phenomena as symptoms of melancholy had become highly charged with religious and political connotations.[52]

The same issues also influenced the discussion of melancholy by one of Du Laurens's successors at the French court, the Marrano Jew Elie de Montalto.[53] Montalto was sceptical regarding the supernatural abilities attributed to, or claimed by, melancholics and tended to doubt the veracity of divination.[54] To the extent that such abilities were indeed genuine, he ascribed them solely to the natural effects

---

[51] Ibid., pp. 98–9.

[52] A French translation of Weyer's *De Praestigiis Daemonum* (Basel, 1563), was published already in 1579. To Weyer and his views I shall return below. R. Scott's book *The Discoverie of Witchcraft* which expounded the same view in a more radical fashion was published in 1584 but it is doubtful whether Du Laurens had heard of it, let alone read it, as it was not translated into Latin or French. On the controversies in France at the time regarding the subject of possessions and witchcraft, see D.P. Walker, *Unclean Spirits: Possession and Exorcism in France and England in the Late Sixteenth and Early Seventeenth Centuries* (London: Scolar Press, 1981), as well as Robert Mandrou, *Magistrats et Sorciers en France au XVIIe siècle* (Paris: Seuil, 1968, rpt. 1980), chapters II, III.

[53] Eliahu Montalto (1567–1616) was born in Portugal as a "new Christian" and received his medical education in Salamanca. He left Portugal in 1602, apparently first travelling to Antwerp, then to France, where he treated a companion of Queen Marie de Medicis, and in 1606, to Pisa, where he accepted a position at the university there. In 1610 he moved to Venice and it is there, apparently, that he openly returned to Judaism. In 1611 he returned to France to become a court physician to Marie de Medicis. For a recent interesting discussion of Montalto, which is focused, however, on his anti-Christian polemics, see Bernard Cooperman, "Eliahu Montalto's 'Suitable and Incontrovertible Propositions' A Seventeenth-Century Anti-Christian Polemic", in I. Twersky and B. Septimus, eds., *Jewish Thought in the Seventeenth Century* (Cambridge Mass.: Harvard University Press, 1987), pp. 469–497, esp. pp. 472–73. See also the older study by H. Friedenwald, "Montalto, a Jewish physician at the court of Marie de Medicis and Louis XIII", *Bulletin of the Institute of the History of Medicine* 3 (1935): 129–58.

[54] "Referuntur miranda quaedam et vix credibilia melancholicorum eventa, quod nempe aliqui, dum mente alienarentur, à nemine edocti, evaserint mechanici, philosophi, astronomi, poëtae, et quod maius est, futurorum praesagi, maximè verò ex insomniis. Quae si vera sunt, non in cacodaemonem reducenda, ut quidam faciunt, insaniam talem ab ipsius insultu provenire censentes, sed potiùs in melancholici humoris peculiarem quandam naturam, quantitatem, ac qualitatem unà cum subiecti dispositione." P.E. Montalto, *Archipathologia* (Paris, 1614), p. 297.

of melancholy, not to any influence of the devil, citing the Aristotelian *Problemata* and Aretaeus in support of his view.[55]

The writings of Du Laurens and Montalto indicate that by the late sixteenth century the "religious" symptoms of melancholy such as divination, prophecy and poetic inspiration were being taken seriously even by some physicians. This was clearly the result of the renewed interest in extraordinary phenomena (and in the Aristotelian *Problemata*) during the Renaissance. The question whether to explain such phenomena supernaturally or to give them a naturalist account became a controversial one especially towards the end of the sixteenth century, when it was connected with the debate regarding possessions. Nevertheless, it should be observed that our survey of the religious symptoms of melancholy in the medical literature up to the seventeenth century has shown a remarkable constancy in the principal themes. True, in the specific examples of these symptoms, this literature clearly reflects changing social and religious realities: from pagan Sibyls and soothsayers, through medieval millenarians, to witches' confessions in the sixteenth century. It is a literature which reflects but does not necessarily judge these social and religious phenomena. With few exceptions, like Bernard de Gordon, we found little polemical tone in these medical observations prior to the seventeenth century.

Such a polemical tone concerning visions and prophecy clearly emerges in the humanist, and especially Protestant, literature directed against monasticism and the monastic way of life in the sixteenth century. Some of this literature also relied on medical sources, but its main thrust was that of moral condemnation. One such anti-monastic critic was Polydore Vergil, the Italian humanist who settled in England and became the historiographer of Henry VII and Henry VIII. In the dialogue *De Prodigiis*, written in 1526–1527 but published in 1531, Polydore Vergil set out to give a natural explanation for divinations, visions and prodigies and to distinguish them clearly from true Christian prophecies.[56] He typically dismissed the alleged visions and divinations of monks and nuns as hardly deserving serious consideration. The explanation he provided, however, was psychological rather than physiological, and there was no explicit mention

---

[55] Ibid., p. 298.

[56] On Polydore Vergil, see D. Hay, *Polydore Vergil* (Oxford: Clarendon Press, 1952). The dialogue *De Prodigiis* is discussed on pp. 34–45.

of melancholy, though it may have been implied. Affected as monks were both by the weariness of a life spent without any occupation, and by their vows of penitence, which they had rashly taken as youngsters, they sought to console themselves by giving various counsels and providing predictions on different matters, supposedly based on divine consultation and communication with the heavenly creatures.[57] Whereas the monks, Vergil implied, were in fact impostors, the nuns were blinded by devilish tricks.

Both these themes—that of purposeful imposture, and of diabolic blindness—were picked up and elaborated later in the century by Protestant critics such as Ludwig Lavater, a minister from Zürich, and Johann Weyer, the ducal physician at the court of Jülich-Cleves.[58] In entering the realm of religious controversy, however, this theme was further transformed. Monks and priests were indeed by no means the victims of melancholy and hallucinations, but impostors who deliberately contrived such visions. The melancholic victims were rather the simple laymen who trusted these people. Thus for Lavater, men who falsely believed that they saw ghosts, apparitions and visions, were either melancholic, or possessed madmen, or, alternatively, just fearful, or weak in their senses, or finally drunkards.[59] Priests and monks on the other hand, in spreading credulous beliefs, were deluding the people for the sake of personal profit and even sexual gratification.[60]

---

[57] P. Vergilius, *Dialogarum de Prodigiis Libri Tres* (Basel, 1533), pp. 53–4.

[58] Ludwig Lavater (1527–86) was born to a bourgeois family in Zürich. His father, Hans-Rudolf, was a bailiff of Kiburg and at one point a Bürgermeister of Zürich. Ludwig was Archdeacon and Canon of Grossmünster from 1550, Antistes (Chief Pastor) in 1585. Besides the *De Spectris* to which I shall presently refer, he wrote a biography of Bullinger and a history of the Eucharist controversy in Zürich, *De Ritibus et Institutis Ecclesiae Tigurinae Libellus*. See *Dictionnaire historique et biographique de la Suisse*, vol. 4, p. 482. J. Weyer, or Wier (1518–1588) was born in Grave-sur-Meuse in the Netherlands to a simple family. He was a disciple of Cornelius Agrippa of Nettesheim, studied medicine in Paris and Orleans, and in 1550 became the physician of Duke Wilhelm of Jülich-Cleves-Berg. There is an old biography of Weyer by C. Binz, *Doctor Johann Weyer*, 2nd edition (Berlin, 1896). Weyer is best known nowadays for his views concerning witches, to which I shall refer below.

[59] L. Lavater, *De Spectris, Lemuribus et Magnis atque Insolitis Fragoribus, variisque praesagitionibus, quae plerunque obitum hominum, magnas clades, mutationesque Imperiorum praecedunt. Liber Unus* (Geneva, 1570). A second Latin edition was published in 1580, see especially pp. 8–12. The book was translated into English and published in London as early as 1572 under the title *Of Ghostes and Spirites walking by nyght* and was reissued in 1596.

[60] Lavater substantiated his claim by adducing numerous anecdotes from classical and modern sources (among them Erasmus) in which priests, monks and friars had

The same social distinction between melancholic victims and contriving impostors is even clearer in Weyer's famous book *De Praestigiis Daemonum*, first published in 1563 and significantly enlarged in subsequent editions.[61] Here, the melancholic victims were primarily witches and the possessed, in whose minds the devil put visions and apparitions, using the melancholic humour as both tool and opportunity. On the basis of this diagnosis, Weyer made his well-known critique of witchcraft persecutions.[62] The medical tradition on melancholy was thus introduced into the controversy concerning witchcraft and the role of the devil in it. Indeed, Weyer relied heavily on this medical tradition in enumerating the usual mental symptoms of melancholy, and in citing various anecdotes of melancholics whose imagination had been seriously impaired.[63] Yet all these anecdotes were presented as clinical observations, with no particular polemical edge.

The polemical tone in Weyer's book, besides his criticism of witchcraft persecutions, may be found elsewhere, in the chapters devoted to the direct operations of the devil. It is noteworthy that the enthusiasts, the Sibyls, the Pythias and other false prophets were mentioned

---

abused the trust of their flock, appearing as ghosts and spirits of dead men in order to seduce wives, extort money, obtain a bishopric, or prove a theological point by false miracles. It is in this context that Lavater tied the monastic and clerical way of life to false visions and apparitions, declaring that "Idleness is the nurse and mother of all mischiefe." See chapter VI, pp. 23–8 in the English translation, pp. 21–6 in the Latin edition of 1580.

[61] J. Wierus, *De Praestigiis Daemonum, et Incantationibus, ac Veneficijs, Libri V* (Basel, 1563). In the next twenty years, six editions of the book were published, in the course of which it was materially enlarged and modified. As noted above, a French translation of the 5th (1577) edition appeared in Paris in 1579: *Histoires, disputes et discours des illusions et impostures des diables, des magiciens infames, sorcieres et empoisonneurs.* A reprint of this edition, together with the two dialogues by Thomas Erastus on the subject of witches, was published in Paris in 1885.

[62] Weyer's critique of witchcraft has been the subject of conflicting interpretations. See among others, H.R. Trevor-Roper. "The European Witch-Craze of the Sixteenth and Seventeenth Centuries", in his collection of essays, *The European Witch-Craze* (Harper Torchbooks, 1969), pp. 146–7; H.C. Erik Midelfort, *Witch Hunting in Southwestern Germany, 1562–1684* (Stanford: Stanford University Press, 1972), pp. 25–6; S. Anglo, "Melancholia and witchcraft: the debate between Wier, Bodin and Scot," in *Folie et déraison à la Renaissance* (Travaux de l'Institut pour l'étude de la Renaissance et d'Humanisme, Brussells, 1973), pp. 209–28.

[63] *De Praestigiis Daemonum*, 5th ed. (Basel, 1577), Lib. III, Chap. VII, cols. 255–9. *Histoires, disputes et discours*, pp. 303–8. Among the examples he mentioned were some who claimed to have divine inspiration; one who believed himself to be emperor and ruler of the world, and three men from Friesland, near Groningen, who thought themselves the Father, Son and Holy Spirit. The three were described indeed as seized by enthusiasm (*correptos enthusiasmo*) but the term here has a clear pathological connotation. Most of the anecdotes were added only in this 5th edition.

in the context of an analysis of pagan religions in chapter VIII of
the first book, being presented as agents of Satan, not as his melancholic victims. The argument here was clearly in the tradition of
Christian polemics: before the advent of Christ, the pagan prophets
and Sibyls may have had some power—given to them by the devil—
to predict the future, particularly the coming of Christ, but once
Christ appeared, other predictions, oracles and prophesies were no
longer possible.[64]

For Protestant humanists and physicians of the second half of the
sixteenth century, the medical tradition on melancholy and the theological controversies still existed largely side by side. False prophets,
magicians, enthusiasts, monks and priests, were depicted mostly in
moral and demonological terms, as impostors or agents of Satan.
The melancholics were usually their innocent victims—credulous simple
people, witches, etc., who were prone to fantasy and imaginary visions.

The relative separation between medical critique and ideological
controversy is still more apparent when one looks at the theological
debates with the enthusiasts in the sixteenth century. Theologians
were aware of the medical interpretation which saw visions and claims
to prophecy as symptoms of melancholy.[65] However, they did not
give much prominence to the medical account. Thus, Heinrich
Bullinger mentioned the "melancholic visions" of the enthusiasts almost by the way, in warning his readers not to heed them, in marked
contrast to the need to heed the Word of God in Scripture:

> We were never directed by God towards the raptures of these horrible
> men, [nor were told] that we should learn from them, and from their
> melancholic visions, or [from their] dreams and fantasies which they
> invent, or that we should believe their assumed wilful villainy.[66]

---

[64] *De Praestigiis* (1577), Lib. I, Chap. VIII, cols. 40–2. *Histoires, disputes et discours,*
pp. 32–4.

[65] One fifteenth century example is Jean Gerson, who mentioned melancholy as
a possible cause of alleged revelations. See Gerson, *De Distinctione Verarum Visionum a
Falsis,* in his *Opera Omnia* (Antwerp, 1706), vol. I, cols. 43–59. After coming out
against those who disbelieve in any divine visions and revelations, Gerson says: "Alii
sunt, nec nego, qui ex adverso in oppositum ruunt vitium, qui superstitiosa etiam et
vana et illusoria delirorum hominum facta et somnia, nec non aegrotantium et
melancholicorum portentuosas cogitationes revelationibus ascribunt." Ibid., col. 45.
For an English translation and commentary of that text see Paschal Boland, "The
Concept of *Discretio Spirituum* in John Gerson's 'De Probatione Spirituum' and 'De
Distinctione Verarum Visionum à Falsis'" in *Studies in Sacred Theology* (Second Series
No. 112, pp. 80–81 for a translation of the quotation above (though Boland trans-
lates "neurotic" for "melancholic"). See also pp. 82, 91.

[66] "[U]nd hat uns überal nienan zuo soemlichen verzuckungen/ soemlicher

Bullinger, then, alluded to the medical account, but stressed the wilful, and indeed, the demonic origin of the enthusiasts' claims to visions and prophecy, as we have seen in the previous chapter. A similar attitude is expressed by Bullinger's Lutheran contemporary, the minister and physician Caspar Peucer, already mentioned in Chapter 1 above. In his voluminous treatise *Commentarius de Praecipuis Generibus Divinationum* Peucer's aim was to distinguish between true predictions and false prophecy. He admitted that enthusiasts such as the Sibyls and pagan prophets may all have been melancholic by inclination, but he insisted that their inspirations and predictions could only be the work of the devil.[67] As in the case of witches and the possessed, the fierce debate with the enthusiasts in the sixteenth century tended to demonize them.

Nevertheless, the dichotomy between the physicians' account and the theologians' debate was not completely water-tight, and some intermingling took place. As we have just seen, the demonological interpretation of false prophecy and enthusiasm sometimes included melancholy as an antecedent—though by no means sufficient—disposition. In fact, melancholy was traditionally seen as "balneum diaboli", the devil's bath—both instrument and opportunity for the operation of Satan. On the other hand, a medical explanation of visions and enthusiasm did not necessarily exclude a demonological interpretation of these same phenomena. Except for extreme naturalists like Guainerio and Pomponazzi, Christian physicians and humanists were also obliged to have recourse to a demonological explanation, especially if they took the "supernatural" symptoms of melancholy (successful prediction, speaking in tongues) seriously. Italian humanists such as Fracastoro and Cardan, Protestant divines and physicians like Peucer, Lavater, and Weyer, Catholic physicians like Du Laurens, all maintained an ambivalent stance which criticised popular superstitions on the one hand, and the total scepticism of the "Sadducees" concerning spirits and demons on the other. While

---

grüwlicher und schützlicher lüten gewisen/ dass wir von jnen lernen und jren melancholischen gesichten/ oder selbs erdachten troeumen und fantasien/ oder angenommner schalckheit glouben sollind." *Der Widertoeufferen ursprung*, p. 30v. Bullinger went on to say that "Mahomet", although he indeed suffered from epilepsy, nevertheless wilfully duped his simple listeners.

[67] *Commentarius de Praecipuis Generibus Divinationum*, fols. 118r–118v, 129v–130r. A systematic discussion of melancholy appears in a different section of the book, "De Praesagiis Medicorum", which deals with the skills and predictions of physicians. Ibid., pp. 265r–318v, esp. pp. 295v–308v.

not completely denying phenomena such as prophecy, inspiration and speaking in tongues (as well as magic-and witchcraft for that matter), Protestant and Catholic thinkers of the late sixteenth century were careful to give them a Christian account, ascribing them to either God or the devil, rather than merely to natural causes like humours or astral influences. Moreover, medical arguments were not used as a polemical tool in the religious debate of the time. They would become so only in the course of the seventeenth century.

Robert Burton: From a Medical Tradition to Religious Controversy

The medical and philosophical tradition which linked enthusiasm with melancholy increasingly penetrated the vocabulary and contents of religious and ideological polemics in the seventeenth century, particularly in England. Indeed, the use of naturalist arguments in the controversies with Catholic and Puritan opponents characterised Anglican thought since at least the beginning of the century, and was closely connected with the debates concerning possession to which I have alluded above.[68] One of the key figures in introducing the medical tradition on melancholy into the religious debates with the enthusiasts was Robert Burton.

Robert Burton (1577–1640) and his *Anatomy of Melancholy* have been the subject of numerous studies, most of them made from a literary point of view.[69] Burton, however, was not just a fellow and librarian

---

[68] See the comments by K. Thomas in connection with the Darrel affair and its aftermath, *Religion and the Decline of Magic* (New York: Scribner's Sons, 1971), pp. 484–6, and more extensively, D.P. Walker, *Unclean Spirits*, pp. 13, 33–42. See also Robert Mandrou, *Magistrats et sorciers en France*, pp. 176–178, for parallel developments in France of that time.

[69] L. Babb, *The Elizabethan Malady: A Study of Melancholy in English Literature from 1580 to 1642* (East Lansing: Michigan State College Press, 1951), and his later book, *Sanity in Bedlam: A Study of Robert Burton's Anatomy of Melancholy* (East Lansing: Michigan State College Press, 1959); J.R. Simon, *Robert Burton (1577–1640) et l'Anatomie de la Mélancolie* (Paris: Didier, 1964); B.G. Lyons, *Voices of Melancholy: Studies in Literary Treatments of Melancholy in Renaissance England* (London: Routledge and Kegan Paul, 1971) which deals with some of the European sources of the English conceptions of melancholy; R.A. Fox, *The Tangled Chain: The Structure of Disorder in the Anatomy of Melancholy* (Berkeley: University of California Press, 1976); and J.K. Gardiner, "Elizabethan Psychology and Burton's *Anatomy of Melancholy*" *Journal of the History of Ideas* 38 (1977): 373–388. For an historian's study of Burton and the *Anatomy of Melancholy* see H. Trevor-Roper, "Robert Burton and *The Anatomy of Melancholy*", in his *Renaissance Essays* (Chicago: University of Chicago Press, 1985), pp. 239–274. For bibliog-

of Christ Church College in Oxford, but also a vicar of St. Thomas parish. He was a divine, as well as an academic and amateur of medicine. He devoted a whole section in his *Anatomy of Melancholy* to "religious melancholy", and that section should indeed be read as a sermon, a tract in religious controversy.[70] One Burton scholar, D.G. Donovan, justifiably complained in 1967 that "Burtonian criticism has, strangely enough, paid little attention to Burton the divine".[71] Some attention has since been given to Burton's confusing utterances concerning predestination.[72] Yet the Anglican orientation of his thought may be seen less in his views on specific doctrinal issues, and more in the basic polemical thrust against Catholics on the one hand, and radical Puritans and Sectarians, on the other.[73]

In fighting on this double front, Burton appropriated for his purposes the medical tradition on melancholy, which we have surveyed above. That tradition had the advantage of offering polemical ammunition vis-à-vis enthusiasts and radical Puritans, as well as against Roman Catholics, particularly monks and nuns. Catholics, Puritans, radical sectarians, and enthusiasts, were all gathered together by Burton under the rubric of "religious enthusiasm", and he devoted the fourth and last section in the third part of his book to that topic.[74]

---

raphies of Burton and Burtonian studies see P. Jordan-Smith, *Bibliographia Burtoniana: A Study of Robert Burton's Writings* (Stanford, 1931), and D.G. Donovan, "Robert Burton, 1924–1966" in *Elizabethan Bibliographies Supplements* 10 (1968): 35–46. Finally, see P. Jordan-Smith, *Burton's Anatomy of 'Melancholy' and Burtoniana: A Checklist of a Part of the Collection in Memory of Sarah Bixby Smith (1871–1935)* (Oxford: Printed for the Honnold Library, 1959), which mentions some of Burton's Continental sources.

[70] D.G. Donovan, "Robert Burton, Anglican Minister," in *Renaissance Papers*, ed. G.W. Williams (The South Eastern Renaissance Conference, 1967), pp. 33–9.

[71] Ibid., p. 33.

[72] See D. Renaker, "Robert Burton's Palinodes", *Studies in Philology* 76 (1979): 162–81. I am grateful to J.B. Bamborough for directing my attention to this article.

[73] This broad Anglican dimension of Burton's work is shown, indeed, by Trevor-Roper, though he tends to see Burton's religion as subservient to medical and psychological considerations, rather than the other way round. See Trevor-Roper, "Robert Burton and *The Anatomy of Melancholy*", pp. 267–273.

[74] Robert Burton, *The Anatomy of Melancholy*, Part 3, Section IV. Throughout this chapter we shall refer to the edition by Holbrook Jackson (London: Everyman's University Library, 1932; republished in one volume by Rowman and Littlefield University Library, Totowa, New Jersey; London: Dent, 1975). Section IV is on pp. 311–432, the quotations above are from p. 312. There is also now a new scholarly edition of the *Anatomy*: Robert Burton, *The Anatomy of Melancholy*, edited by Thomas C. Faulkner, Nicolas K. Kiessling, Rhonda L. Blair, Introduction by J.B. Bamborough (Oxford: the Clarendon Press, vol. I, 1989; vol. II, 1990; vol. III, 1994). Since vol. III—which includes the section on "Religious Melancholy"—appeared just before the present book was completed, I have kept the references to the Everyman edition.

"Religious Melancholy" was a category of Burton's own invention,
but was nevertheless conceived as part of a more traditional notion
of "love-melancholy", which was the subject of the whole third part.
Burton himself admitted at the beginning of the section that
". . . whether this subdivision of Religious Melancholy be warrantable, it may be controverted". He added that on this topic, "I have
no pattern to follow as in some of the rest, no man to imitate."[75]
Religious melancholy was itself divided into that of "excess"—the
symptoms of which were blind zeal, superstition, fasting and claims
of inspiration—and that of "defect", which was manifest in religious
despair, blasphemy, scepticism and atheism. Here I shall deal with
the first kind, religious melancholy in excess, under which enthusiasm falls.

Burton mentioned the enthusiasts together with other false prophets, claimers to divine inspiration and men of excessive religious zeal.[76]
He found them among both the sectarians and the Catholic monks
and clergy. They are mentioned several times as examples of "religious melancholy": at the beginning of the section, when the general
notion of "religious melancholy" is introduced; in the second subsection, which deals with the religious causes of melancholy and hence,
of visions and alleged revelations; and at the end of the third subsection, which deals with the various symptoms of religious melancholy
in excess.[77]

Burton clearly saw enthusiasm as a presumption of being inspired,
or of being able to prophesy.[78] Unlike his Renaissance predecessors,
he did not take these presumptions seriously, and regarded the enthusiasts first and foremost as sick people. He therefore relied on the
long medical tradition which saw enthusiasm as a symptom of the
disease of melancholy, and appropriated that tradition for his polemical religious purposes. Burton started with the Platonic notion of
"furor", but gave this concept a clear pathological interpretation.
Referring to the priests in Delphi and Dodona, described in the

[75] *The Anatomy of Melancholy*, III, p. 311. In the note, Burton said that "religious
melancholy" was "called religious because it is still conversant about religion and
such divine objects." Ibid., p. 485, note 2 to p. 311.

[76] Ibid., III, pp. 312, 341–44. They were particularly mentioned as belonging to
contemporary *fatidici dii* ("prophetic gods"), together with "pythonissas, sibyls,
pseudoprophets, heretics and schismatics".

[77] Ibid., III, pp. 311–13, 341–45, 370–372.

[78] Ibid., p. 341.

Phaedrus, he says of Plato: "He makes them all mad, as well he might."[79] Burton typically coupled Plato with Aretaeus of Cappadocia whom I have mentioned above. This pairing was also made by G. Henisch, a contemporary of Burton's who edited and commented on Aretaeus. Henisch gave a clear Platonic interpretation to Aretaeus, but stressed the distinctions between religious mania and pathological mania. Burton, on the contrary, "medicalized" the Platonic notion of "furor" and took Aretaeus to be completely sceptical and negative concerning the religious symptoms of melancholy.[80]

It is not surprising, therefore, that Burton relied mostly on the medieval medical treatises which regarded enthusiasm as a clinical and pathological symptom of melancholy. He listed the Byzantine and Arabic physicians who transmitted Greek medical thought to the West in the Middle Ages: Alexander of Tralles, Al-Razi and Avicenna, then proceeded to "our late writers", Bernard de Gordon, Fuchsius, Bruele, Du Laurens and Montaltus. He specifically quoted Bernard de Gordon, who, as we have seen above, referred to the contemporary Beguines and their apocalyptic prophecies as examples of religious melancholy.[81]

Significantly enough, Burton was very careful not to rely on the Renaissance naturalist account of enthusiasm, which tended to view

---

[79] Ibid., III, p. 312.

[80] Ibid., Part III, p. 312. See also note 7 on p. 485, for the way in which Burton quoted Aretaeus. G. Henisch's edition of Aretaeus was entitled *Aetiologica, Simeiotica et Therapeutica Morborum acutorum et diuturnorum Aretaei Cappadocis* (Augsburg, 1603), see esp. pp. 63–64, for the text, and pp. 327–9, for the commentary. Henisch (1549–1618) was a famous philologist and lexicographer as well as a physician. He was also the Rector of the Gymnasium at Augsburg. (See *Allgemeine Deutsche Biographie*, vol. 11, pp. 750–1).

[81] *Anatomy of Melancholy*, III, p. 312. A copy of Gordon's *Lilium Medicinae* (the 1574 ed. from which I quoted above) was in Burton's own library and was given under his Will to the Bodleian Library (now 8 G 23 Med.) so it is most likely that he used this text. See S. Gibson and F.R.D. Needham, "Lists of Burton's library", in *Oxford Bibliographical Society Proceedings and Papers* ed. F. Madan, I (1922–6), pp. 222–46; p. 229 for reference to Gordon's book. Burton quoted the phrase I have mentioned above (note 23 in this chapter) quite literally, except for minor grammatical variations (note 2 to p. 312 on p. 485), but translated it in the text itself thus: "Some seem to be inspired of the Holy Ghost, some take upon them to be Prophets, some are addicted to new opinions, some foretell strange things, *de statu mundi et Antichristi.*" A copy of the 1546 ed. of Fuchs' *De Sanandis Totius Humani Corporis Malis Libri Quinque* was in Burton's own library and was given under his Will to the Bodleian library. See Gibson and Needham, "Lists of Burton's library", p. 228. A copy of Bruele's 1589 ed. of *Praxis Medicinae* was also in Burton's library and is now in Christ Church library (f. 2.33).

enthusiasm and even melancholy, in positive terms. He rarely referred to Ficino, nor did he mention Pomponazzi in this context, although his own copy of *De Incantationibus*, which is still in Christ Church library, is heavily underlined and annotated in the margins, precisely on the pages on enthusiasm and melancholy.[82] Burton did refer to one of Pomponazzi's direct disciples, Girolamo Fracastoro, but obliterated Fracastoro's distinction between positive and negative melancholy.[83]

What, however, were the causes of religious melancholy? It is a question posed already in Book I:

> Whence it comes to passe that they prophesy, speak several languages, talk of astronomy, and other unknown sciences to them (of which they have been ever ignorant) . . .?[84]

Here, Burton diverged even more from the naturalist account, and his polemical purposes became all the more pronounced. Indeed, he explicitly rejected the views of Plato (the doctrine of *reminiscentia*), Pseudo-Aristotle's *Problemata*, Guainerio, Pomponazzi, Lemnius and Montalto, and inclined towards a demonological explanation, ascribed to Avicenna:

> . . . [B]ut in this I should rather hold with Avicenna and his associates, that such symptoms proceed from evil spirits, which take all opportunities of humours decayed, or otherwise, to pervert the soul of man: and besides, the humour itself is *balneum diaboli*, the devil's bath . . .[85]

Like many of the polemicists who preceded him, Burton saw the devil as the original cause of melancholy in general.[86] He similarly opened his discussion of the causes of religious melancholy with a clear demonological account:

> The *primum mobile*, therefore, and first mover of all superstition, is the devil, that great enemy of mankind, the principal agent, who in a

---

[82] Burton possessed the first edition of *De Incantationibus* Basel, 1556 (Christ Church library, f. 8.45), pp. 152–3.

[83] "Fracastorius, *lib. 2 de intellect.*, will have all your pythonisses, sibyls, and pseudo-prophets to be mere melancholy", *Anatomy of Melancholy*, III, p. 344.

[84] *Anatomy of Melancholy*, I, Sect. 3, Memb. 2, subsect. IV, p. 428. See now also the new scholarly ed. of Part I of the *Anatomy* (1989), p. 427.

[85] *Anatomy of Melancholy*, I, p. 429, (p. 428 in the 1989 edition).

[86] See *Anatomy of Melancholy*, Part I, Sect. 2, Member 1, Subsect. II–III, pp. 202–206 (pp. 174–199 in the new 1989 edition), for a demonological account of witchcraft and magic.

thousand several shapes, after divers fashions, with several engines, illusions, and by several names hath deceived the inhabitants of the earth,
in several places and countries, still rejoicing at their falls.[87]

Nevertheless, the devil acted through secondary causes, and Burton
devoted most of his attention to these causes. On that issue, the
medieval pronouncements on the ascetic way of life as a cause of
melancholy served him as an arsenal for his arguments against Catholic
monks and radical Puritans alike. He argued that melancholy and its
accompanying visions were the result of religious practice, particularly the monastic way of life which involved fasting, solitude and
excessive meditation. Burton made that claim already at the beginning of the first subsection on "religious melancholy", when he discussed certain religious behaviour not only as a symptom, but also
as a cause of melancholy. He returned to this theme in greater detail
in subsection II, where the visions and prophecies of monks, enthusiasts, and other false prophets, were written off as the hallucinations
of desperate melancholics.[88] Here he relied on Guainerio, who in
turn quoted Constantinus Africanus. Constantinus, as we have seen
above, pointed to excessive meditation, fasting, and vigilance, as some
of the causes of melancholy, and Guainerio quoted him on that:

> Qui de die inquit jejunant: et nocte aut[em] vigilant in melancoliam
> faciliter cadunt.[89]

Burton made a note of these sentences in his own copy of Guainerio,
and in his quotation in the *Anatomy*, gave them a sharper polemical twist:

> If you shall at any time see a religious person over-superstitious, too
> solitary, or much given to fasting, that man will certainly be melan-
> choly, thou mayest boldly say it, he will be so.[90]

Burton could rely even more on the humanists and the Protestant
critics of the sixteenth century in castigating monastic asceticism. Yet,
whereas the Protestant critics tended to distinguish between the monks,
who were essentially impostors, and their credulous followers, who

---

[87] Ibid., III, pp. 325–326.
[88] Ibid., III, pp. 312, 341-4.
[89] *Practica*, fol. 41v.
[90] *Anatomy of Melancholy*, III, p. 343. And see note 5 to that page on p. 490.
Burton similarly quoted Cardano in order to make that same point:

> Solitariness, fasting and that melancholy humour, are the causes of all hermits' illusions.
> Ibid., p. 344.

were melancholic, Burton combined these two groups, and saw the monks as melancholics and agents of Satan. In mentioning Weyer, for example, he referred both to Weyer's chapter on the melancholic imagination in book III, and to his analysis of the enthusiasts and other false prophets in the first book.[91] Burton thus implied something that Weyer did not say—that the enthusiasts and pagan prophets were in fact mere melancholics. In this respect, Burton put the anti-monastic critique once again in its medical, if also diabolic, context.[92]

As has been pointed out already, the combination of a demonological and a medical interpretation of false prophecy and enthusiasm was not completely new with Burton. Nevertheless, the concentration on "secondary causes", on melancholy as a natural means by which the devil achieved his ends, meant that the supernatural dimension was pushed backwards. Burton's incorporation of the long medical tradition on melancholy within a polemic with both radical Puritans and Catholic monks, gave an added impetus to the "recession" of the supernatural realm. After all, there was a significant difference whether one saw religious opponents such as monks and radical visionaries primarily as agents of Satan or rather as his victims, needing medical treatment. In this respect, the use which Burton made of the medical tradition for the purpose of religious controversy was momentous. He infused his medical analysis with explicit polemical purposes and incorporated the medical conception of melancholy and its ascetic causes into his controversy with Catholics, radical Puritans and enthusiasts, thus contributing to a profound change in the nature of the critique of enthusiasm itself.[93] In the following chapter, I shall examine the contributions of two other English writers to the "medicalization" of enthusiasm in the middle of the seventeenth century, Meric Casaubon and Henry More.

---

[91] Ibid., III, p. 344.

[92] One typical example was Burton's alleged quotation from Lavater which was indeed an illuminating distortion:

> Solitudo est causa apparitionum; nulli visionibus et hinc delirio magis obnoxii sunt quam qui collegiis et eremo vivunt monachi; tales plerumque melancholici ob victum, solitudinem.

Anatomy of Melancholy, III, p. 491, note 2 to p. 344. Lavater's original text did not mention melancholy and fasting at all in this context and clearly implied that those visions of the monks were fabricated:

> Nulli autem magis rebus illis obnoxij sunt quàm qui in monasterijs et collegiis degunt: nemini igitur novum et inauditum videri debet, si dicamus olim falsas apparitiones multas factas fuisse, et hodie quoque interdum fieri posse. *De Spectris*, p. 44.

[93] From the point of view of Burtonian studies, our findings confirm what the

Burton scholar David Renaker wrote many years ago:

> [T]he *Anatomy* is a highly original work, not only because of the conscious literary art
> with which Burton joined quotations together, but because of the metamorphoses which
> these quotations themselves had undergone in the deep well of unconscious cerebration.

David Renaker, "Robert Burton's tricks of Memory", PMLA 87 (1972): 391. Burton, Renaker argued (ibid., pp. 394–95), relied for his quotations either on memory
or on very sketchy notes, and thus often changed the quotations themselves. Such
changes not only never hurt the point Burton was trying to make, they in fact
served his polemical purposes very well, as we have seen.

CHAPTER THREE

"STRANGE, BUT NATURAL EFFECTS": THE MEDICAL CRITIQUE OF ENTHUSIASM IN THE WORKS OF MERIC CASAUBON AND HENRY MORE

Meric Casaubon

As has often been pointed out, the *Anatomy of Melancholy* was highly influential among a long line of Anglican critics of enthusiasm in the second half of the seventeenth century, from Meric Casaubon to Jonathan Swift.[1] Meric Casaubon is indeed an important critic of enthusiasm in the mid-seventeenth century, and the medical interpretation of enthusiasm was the central theme of his *Treatise Concerning Enthusiasme*.[2] It is thus natural to turn first to him and to the relationship between melancholy and enthusiasm in his work.

The son of the famous humanist scholar Isaac Casaubon, Meric was born in Geneva in 1599, went to school in Sedan, and in 1611, moved with his family to England. He studied first at Eton, and later, after his father's death in 1614, at Christ Church, Oxford, where very probably, he also came to know Robert Burton. Meric Casaubon

---

[1] See C.M. Webster, "Swift and Some Earlier Satirists of Puritan Enthusiasm", *PMLA* 48 (1933): 1141–53; idem., "The Satiric Background of the Attack on the Puritans in Swift's *A Tale of a Tub*", *PMLA* 50 (1935): 210–23; Truman G. Stefan, "The Social Argument against Enthusiasm (1650–1660)", in *Studies in English*, No. 4126 (Austin, University of Texas, 1944), pp. 39–63; George Williamson, "The Restoration Revolt against Enthusiasm", *Studies in Philology* 30 (1933): 571–603; Phillip Harth, *Swift and Anglican Rationalism* (Chicago: Chicago University Press, 1961), pp. 105–116; George Rosen, "Enthusiasm: 'a dark lanthorn of the spirit'", *Bulletin of the History of Medicine* 42 (1968): 393–421; M.V. DePorte, *Nightmares and Hobbyhorses: Swift, Sterne and Augustan ideas of madness* (San Marino, Calif.: The Huntington Library, 1974); John F. Sena, "Melancholic Madness and the Puritans", *Harvard Theological Review* 66 (1973): 293–309; Michael McDonald, *Mystical Bedlam: Madness, Anxiety, and Healing in Seventeenth-Century England* (Cambridge: Cambridge University Press, 1981), pp. 224–226, and note 245 on pp. 296–297.

[2] The subtitle reads "As it is an Effect of *Nature*: but is mistaken by many for either *Divine Inspiration*, or *Diabolicall Possession*". The first edition was published in 1655, the second edition a year later, in 1656. There is a facsimile reproduction of the second edition of the *Treatise Concerning Enthusiasme* with an Introduction by Paul J. Korshin (Gainsville, Florida: Scholars' Facsimiles and Reprints, 1970), and it is to this edition that I shall refer henceforth.

became a protégé of Lancelot Andrewes, then Bishop of Ely, and later of William Laud, by whom he was preferred to a prebend at Canterbury in 1628. From his early years, Casaubon was thus connected with the Arminian party in the Anglican Church. Indeed, during the Revolution he was evicted from two other livings he had held, and with the abolition of episcopacy he lost his prebend as well. In the 1650's he was employed by Sir John Cotton in his library at Westminster, and it was in those years that he wrote and published the *Treatise Concerning Enthusiasme* and later, on Cotton's initiative and perhaps even pressure, the enigmatic *A True and Faithfull Relation of what passed between John Dee and Certain Spirits*. Most of his earlier work was typically humanistic in origin—defending his father's reputation, continuing Isaac's polemics against Baronius' *Annals* and against Catholic historiography in general, and editing and translating various classical texts, chief among them the *Meditations* of Marcus Aurelius. He also composed, in addition, a few religious tracts with a clear anti-Puritan thrust.[3]

In Meric Casaubon we have an instance not just of an Anglican like Burton, nor even a fierce anti-Puritan Laudian, but a characteristic classical scholar who provides an interesting link between Renaissance humanism and late seventeenth-century neo-classicism. Indeed, Casaubon is an upholder of the ideal of "learning" and erudition, and as we shall see in Chapter 5 below, it is from this perspective that he criticised the new experimental science of the Royal Society.[4] Enthusiasm for him was a grave threat primarily to be traditional "bookish" learning which he valued most. For that reason, he characterized as enthusiasts not only those who claimed to predict the future (what he called "Divinatorie Enthusiasme", to which

---

[3] The most up-to-date and detailed survey of Meric Casaubon's life may be found in Michael R.S. Spiller, *"Concerning Natural Experimental Philosophie": Meric Casaubon and the Royal Society* (The Hague: Martinus Nijhoff, 1980), chapter I. A list of his printed works is on p. 218. Earlier discussions of his life are the Introduction by Paul J. Korshin to the facsimile reproduction of *A Treatise Concerning Enthusiasme*; Charles Cotton, "Meric Casaubon, Canon of Canterbury 1628–1671", *Friends of the Canterbury Cathedral* 11 (1938): 51–57; and the article in the *D.N.B.*, vol. III, pp. 1170–71. Two published sources which serve as a basis for these surveys are Anthony Wood, *Athenae Oxonienses*, ed. P. Bliss (1813–1820), vol. III, cols. 934–36, and T.J. ab Almeloveen, ed., *Isaaci Casauboni Epistolae . . .* (Rotterdam, 1709). For a list of manuscript sources see Spiller, pp. 218–219.

[4] On Casaubon as an advocate of "learning" see Michael Hunter's review essay on Spiller's book in *Annals of Science* 39 (1982): 187–192.

he devoted the second chapter of the *Treatise*, after the introductory one), but also contemplative philosophers whom he coupled with mystical theologians and ecstatic monks, all under the category of "Contemplative and philosophicall Enthusiasme" (Chapter III). Chief among these contemplative philosophers was none other than Descartes himself! I shall return to Casaubon's critique of Descartes in Chapter 4 below. This critique highlights the humanistic perspective from which Casaubon viewed the problem of enthusiasm and which also informed his critique of what he called "Rhetoricall Enthusiasme" (Chapter IV), "Poeticall Enthusiasme" (Chapter V), and enthusiasm in praying, "Precatory Enthusiasme", (Chapter VI). This last subject gave him the occasion to take the typical Anglican stance, which we have found in Burton as well, criticizing both Catholics (such as Ignatius Loyola), and the extemporaneous prayers of the Puritans, although in 1655–56 he could only hint at the latter.

Indeed, Casaubon received the very instigation to write the *Treatise* from reading a typical book of Catholic Counter-Reformation spirituality, *The Life of Sister Catherine of Jesus.*[5] The *Life* of Sister Catherine, a young Carmelite nun living in Paris at the beginning of the century, was full of reports of visions, apparitions, and mystical experiences.[6] Significantly enough, the Introduction to the book was written by Cardinal Bérulle, the founder of the Carmelite order and the leader of French Catholic spirituality in that generation. It also

---

[5] *A Treatise Concerning Enthusiasme*, "To the Reader", A3r–A4r. The book to which Casaubon referred was *La vie de soeur Catherine de Jésus* (Paris, 1628). The Bibliothèque nationale has a copy which belonged originally to the Jesuit College in Paris. Its author was Magdeleine de St. Joseph (Madeleine du Bois), the head of the Mère de Dieu monastery in which Catherine lived in her last few years. It was written at the request of Cardinal Bérulle, who was Catherine's patron. Catherine was born in 1589 to a merchant from Bordeaux. At the age of 8 she read a book by Catherine of Sienna, and was deeply influenced by it. She soon began to fast, avoid sleep and dress plainly, and in 1608 decided to enter the monastery of the Incarnation in Paris which belonged to the Carmelite order, headed by Bérulle. In 1617 she was moved, together with Magdeleine de St. Joseph, to the Mère de Dieu monastery. A sickly person, suffering from hydropsy (the accumulation of fluid in the body) which may well have been caused by her frequent fasts and undernourishment, she died in February 1623. See *Vie de Catherine de Jésus*. For other sources on Sister Catherine see Germain Habert, *La Vie du cardinal de Bérulle* (Paris, 1646), pp. 306–309; Hilarion de Coste, *Les Eloges et vies des reynes, princesses, et damoiselles illustres en piété . . .* 1647 ed., tome II, p. 830; Louis Doni d'Attichy [Bishop of Autun], *De Vita et rebus gestis . . . Petri Cardinalis Berulli* (Paris, 1649), pp. 76–81; *Bibliotheca Scriptorum utriusque Congregationis et sexus Carmelitarum ex Calceatorum* (Bordeaux, 1730), p. 76, which is largely a summary of the *Life* of Catherine.

[6] *La Vie de soeur Catherine de Jésus*, pp. 52–80.

received the *approbation* of six high ecclesiastics and theologians.[7] Whereas the present-day historian would hardly be surprised at the official legitimacy, indeed, almost sanctity, accorded by the leaders of the French Catholic Church to the religious experiences of such a nun, the Anglican Meric Casaubon expressed real shock:

> But then that such a judgement should be made, of such an accident, wherein I apprehended so little ground of either doubt or wonder; and this judgement, not the judgement of a woman onely, the Author, as is pretended, of the whole relation; but of men of such worth and eminency: this in very deed troubled me very much.[8]

We have here a clear example of the difference between Catholic and Anglican attitudes towards enthusiasm in the seventeenth century. In the Catholic Church, visions, prophecies, apparitions and mystical experiences could be incorporated within Counter-Reformation spirituality.[9] An Anglican humanist like Casaubon, however, regarded these experiences with deep suspicion and tended to ascribe them to natural causes:

> I found the book to be a long contexture of severall strange raptures and enthusiasmes, that had hapned (sic!) unto a melancholick, or, if you will, a devout Maid. In this I saw no great matter of wonder: Neither could I observe much in the relation of the particulars, but what as I conceived, rationally, probable; so I might believe, charitably, true. I could observe, as I thought, a perpetuall coherence of naturall causes, in every particular: which gave me good satisfaction.[10]

The thrust of Casaubon's book, then, was the claim that all manifestations of enthusiasm and pretended claims to divine inspiration could

---

[7] The six *approbations* were written by Octave de Bellegarde, Archbishop of Sens, Henri E. [de Sponde?], Bishop of Pamiers, Jean Daultruy, a theology professor at the Sorbonne, P. d'Hardivillier, doctor at the Sorbonne and priest of St. Bénoît, M. Grillet, preacher to the Queen, the King's mother, and B. Desprevetz, doctor of theology, priest and canon at Xaintes. See *La Vie de soeur Catherine de Jésus*. See also Casaubon's reference to these *approbations*, *A Treatise Concerning Enthusiasme*, pp. A3v–A4r.

[8] *A Treatise Concerning Enthusiasme*, pp. A3v–A4r.

[9] Indeed, Jean Daultruy even used the term "enthusiasm" in a clearly positive sense in his *approbation*, in reference to "des enthousiasmes de l'Apostre S. Paul". At the same time, it should be stressed, *La Vie de soeur Catherine de Jésus* did not ignore the possibility that some of her visions might have been diabolic illusion rather than divine inspiration. See for example p. 71.

[10] *A Treatise Concerning Enthusiasme*, p. A3v. *La Vie de soeur Catherine de Jésus*, on the contrary, explicitly denied that Catherine was prone to melancholy. As a novice, her Mother Superior says "Elle estoit toujours fort recueillie sans estre aucunement renfermée, ny mélancholique, toujours desireuse de la retraicte, et presté à faire telle action qu'on luy eust voulu ordonner." Ibid., p. 20.

be given a naturalist account, and that these were symptoms of melancholy, not real revelations or manifestations of the Holy Spirit. In this respect, he continued to develop a traditional line in Anglican thought which went back to the turn of the century, and which was clearly expressed, as we have seen in the previous section, in Burton's *Anatomy of Melancholy*. Indeed, like Burton, and possibly under his influence, Casaubon relied on traditional medical sources in making his point, to which he added some classical literary sources as well. However, he took a more pronouncedly naturalist view of enthusiasm, explicitly minimizing, unlike Burton, the demonological interpretation.

In explaining enthusiasm "upon some grounds of nature", Casaubon did not necessarily mean imposture or evil intent, namely the pretension of being inspired for "political" reasons. He referred to "real, though but imaginary, apprehension of it in the parties", that is, to a sincere, even if mistaken, conviction that one was divinely inspired. He thus clearly distinguished between deliberate imposture and a genuine though illusory belief of being inspired, an illusion which was the consequence of ignorance of the natural causes of some extraordinary, though by no means supernatural, effects. Such an illusion was not only mistaken, but had important consequences for the public welfare, and it was for that reason that the uncovering of those natural causes was so important.[11] The crucial distinction for Casaubon, however, was between natural and supernatural enthusiasm. Although outwardly relying on classical sources and on the Platonic tradition in explaining the meaning of the term "enthusiasm", he interjected a clear Christian perspective in insisting on that distinction.[12] By supernatural enthusiasm he understood

> a true and reall possession of some extrinsecal superiour power, whether divine, or diabolical, producing effects and operations altogether supernaturall; as some kind of divination ... speaking of strange languages, temporary learning and the like.

Natural enthusiasm, by contrast, was

> an extraordinary, transcendent, but naturall fervency, or pregnancy of the soul, spirits, or brain, producing strange effects, apt to be mistaken for supernaturall.[13]

---

[11] *A Treatise Concerning Enthusiasme*, pp. 4–5.
[12] For the philological discussion of the meaning of the term and the classification of the various types of enthusiasm see ibid., pp. 15–24.
[13] Ibid., p. 22.

Here, Casaubon was obviously distancing himself not only from the
Platonic tradition, but from some Renaissance authors, who, as we
have seen in the previous chapter, tended to blur the distinction
between the supernatural and the natural. Casaubon, for his part,
explicitly kept religious enthusiasm (that is, true divine inspiration)
out of his discussion.[14] He wished to give a naturalist account of
other types of enthusiasm, precisely in order to distinguish them from
authentic Christian inspiration. Included among these types, however, were sensitive cases such as "divinatory" enthusiasm, mystical
contemplation, ecstatic experiences and extemporaneous praying. In
classifying such phenomena under the category of natural enthusiasm, and in providing a medical account of them, Casaubon was
obviously taking a theological position, especially relevant to the religious scene in England in the 1650's.

The first chapter dealing with a specific type of enthusiasm, that
on "Divinatorie Enthusiasme", clearly reveals the internal tensions in
Casaubon's attitude towards Renaissance views on the subject. On
the one hand, he admitted the possibility of true natural divination,
distinct from imposture, or even from the pretended divination of
deluded people:

> We intend such Enthusiasticall Divination, as by severall Events, and
> by due observation of all Circumstances, hath been observed to be true.[15]

Moreover, like many Renaissance intellectuals, Casaubon was ready
to give a naturalist account for some divinations, thus entertaining
the possibility of true natural divination, as distinct from supernatural prophecies. He disagreed, however, with the naturalist view which
explained all prophecy and divination, including that of Christ, in
naturalist terms. He also rejected the Averroist account of natural
divination, based on the concept of *Intellectus Agens*, an account to
which not only Pomponazzi, but also good Christians, in Casaubon's
eyes, like Bodin, subscribed.[16] The account of divination he relied
upon was based on the concepts of *species* (*idola*) and emanations, a
theory whose origins go back to Democritus and Aristotle, and which

---

[14] "Of Religious *Enthusiasme*, truly and really religious, nothing will be found here".
Ibid., p. 24.

[15] Ibid., p. 36.

[16] Ibid., pp. 50–51. For Casaubon's disagreement with Pomponazzi, especially
with his alleged tendency to explain all prophecy in natural terms, see ibid., p. 35.

was also quite prevalent during the Renaissance.[17] According to that theory, natural objects emit species (somewhat akin, though not identical, to the species of light emitted by objects and conceived by the eyes), which can be received by human beings, especially when their external senses are weak. Not only do objects or natural phenomena emit such species, but their causes do so as well. Thus, people who are sensitive to these emanations can also predict their consequences before they have actually occurred.[18] Indeed, Casaubon referred to "some naturall foregoing signes" that

> may be known, felt or discerned by those men or creatures, that have a naturall disposition or sympathy, whether constant or temporary, to those things or their signes . . .[19]

Casaubon thus shared what may be called a "symbolic" or "emblematic" approach to nature, common to many Renaissance natural philosophers, and interpreted the Atomist and Aristotelian doctrine of species in these terms.[20]

On the other hand, unlike many of his Renaissance predecessors, Casaubon tended to underestimate this type of natural divination, and even to treat it with contempt. He emphasized a point made already by Aristotle, that such natural divination depended on the weakness of reason and the day-time senses, and that it was characteristic of women, weak men, and idiots, indeed, of atrabilious persons,

---

[17] For Renaissance accounts of divination see Lynn Thorndike, *A History of Magic and Experimental Science* (New York and London: Columbia University Press, 1941), vol. VI, chapter XLV.

[18] *A Treatise Concerning Enthusiasme*, pp. 57–58. This was also the account which Aristotle gave for the divinatory power of dreams in his *De Divinatione per Somnum* in the *Parva Naturalia*. See W.D. Ross, ed., *The Works of Aristotle*, vol. III (Oxford: The Clarendon Press, 1931), pp. 462b–464b. Casaubon relied on Aristotle, as well as on the treatise by Synesius from Alexandria, *Liber de Somnis*, which was translated by Marsilio Ficino. It was published by Auger Ferrier in his *Liber de Somnis* (Lyon, 1549), pp. 112–202. See especially pp. 112–116, 164–180. The account of the role of species is on pp. 176–178. Casaubon extended that explanation to account for divination in general, not only by dreams.

[19] Ibid., p. 56.

[20] On the "emblematic" approach to nature in the Renaissance, especially among Jesuit natural philosophers, see William B. Ashworth Jr., "Catholicism and Early Modern Science" in David C. Lindberg and Ronald L. Numbers, eds., *God and Nature: Historical Essays on the Encounter between Christianity and Science* (Berkeley and Los Angeles: University of California Press, 1986), pp. 136–167, esp. pp. 156–157, and his article "Natural History, Antiquarianism, and the Demise of the Emblematic Cosmos", in David C. Lindberg and Robert S. Westman, eds., *Reappraisals of the Scientific Revolution* (Cambridge: Cambridge University Press, 1990), pp. 303–332.

namely melancholics.[21] Precisely for that reason, Casaubon had difficulty with the Pseudo-Aristotelian text of the *Problemata* 30,1, which treated the natural effects of melancholy in a positive way and emphasized the distinction between "natural", and sick, or "distempered" melancholy. For Casaubon, this distinction was hardly intelligible, unless if by the "natural" temper of the *endeoi* (ἔνδεοι) Aristotle was understood to mean the natural preparation for supernatural prophecy.[22] His difficulty with the Pseudo-Aristotelian text may have had a semantic-conceptual reason as well: For Aristotle, "natural" was distinguished primarily from "unnatural" or sick, whereas for the Christian Casaubon, "natural" was distinct from supernatural. In fact a few pages later he said:

> I would not give any occasion of offence, by mixing impertinently and unseasonably things naturall and supernaturall, that is, heaven and earth.[23]

Here, Casaubon clearly diverges from the Renaissance naturalist tradition. For that reason, he also felt easier with the somewhat derogatory Aristotelian account of divination in the *Parva Naturalia* than with the Pseudo-Aristotelian *Problemata*.[24]

Indeed, unlike the author of the *Problemata* and many of his Renaissance followers, Casaubon viewed "natural divination" and enthusiasm with a negative eye, not because he was completely sceptical concerning the possibility of predicting the future (in this, as we have just noted, he agreed with the Renaissance naturalist tradition), but because he tended to see this capabilility in pathological terms. Even more than Burton, Casaubon accepted the Renaissance naturalist

---

[21] *A Treatise Concerning Enthusiasme*, p. 58. On the next page, however, Casaubon seemed to distinguish between emanations, as a natural cause of divination in fools and idiots, and melancholy, as a cause "in a different temper and disposition". Ibid., p. 59. As we shall presently see, Casaubon indeed had some difficulty in reconciling the Aristotelian explanation of divination in *De Divinatione per Somnum*, and the account of prophecy in the Pseudo-Aristotelian *Problemata*. See also Aristotle, *Works*, vol. III, 464a 1.19—464b 1.5.

[22] *A Treatise Concerning Enthusiasme*, pp. 52–53. Casaubon argued that for this reason, Budé in his commentary on the *Pandect* did not quote this Aristotelian distinction in referring to the *Problemata*. Yet, in the 1551 Lyon edition, Budé definitely quoted the part referring to the Sibyls and Bacchic prophecies as attributable to natural, rather than to pathological "distemper". Guillaume Budé, *Annotationes in XXIIII Pandectarum Libros* (Lyon, 1551), p. 654. Budé himself tended, however, to treat enthusiasm apart from melancholy and to give it a demonological interpretation. Ibid., pp. 646–648.

[23] *A Treatise Concerning Enthusiasme*, p. 61.

[24] Ibid., p. 54.

account of enthusiasm, but gave it a pathological twist. It is not accidental that—once again, like Burton—he relied on physicians such as Aretaeus in emphasizing the pathological dimension of the "natural" ability to predict the future.[25] Earlier in the chapter, he referred to Sennert and Peucer who mentioned the ability of sick people to foretell the future, or even to speak in tongues, though concerning this latter talent, Casaubon was more sceptical. Once the disease disappeared, those capabilities vanished with it. Whereas for Renaissance thinkers, raptures and alienation of the mind, even madness, could have a positive sense, Casaubon declared that

> [M]an that can enjoy his naturall wit and reason with sobriety, and doth affect such raptures and alienations of mind, hath attained to a good degree of Madnesse, without rapture, which makes him so much to undervalue the highest gift of God, (Grace excepted, which is but a perfection of Reason, or a reformation of corrupt Reason;) sound Reason.[26]

Finally, Casaubon distanced himself from the naturalist tradition of the Renaissance by not excluding the possibility of a demonological account of true divination, and especially, of speaking in tongues. Like Burton, he disagreed explicitly not only with Pomponazzi, as we have seen above, but also with Levinus Lemnius who gave an exclusive naturalist account of such phenomena.[27]

> ... [T]hat these extraordinary operations do rather proceed from the Devil—Casaubon declared—to me is a great argument, (besides other reasons,) because the very self-same things are known to happen to divers that are immediately possest, without any bodily distemper, other then the very possession, which must needs affect the body more or lesse.[28]

Casaubon regarded the belief in the devil and spirits as a crucial argument against atheism, and thought that at least in the cases of glossolalia (speaking in tongues), the melancholic disease was a natural

---

[25] Ibid., pp. 60–61.

[26] Ibid., p. 62. For the positive attitude towards raptures and even madness in the Renaissance see for example M.A. Screech, *Ecstasy and the Praise of Folly* (London: Duckworth, 1980), chapters 4, 5.

[27] *A Treatise Concerning Enthusiasme*, p. 37. Casaubon was referring to Lemnius's *De Occultis Naturae Miraculis*, Lib. II, Ch. 2. In the 1581 Antwerp edition it is on pp. 140–143. An English translation was published in London in 1658, that is, after the publication of Casaubon's *Treatise*, under the title *The Secret Miracles of Nature in Four Books*. The relevant chapter there is on pp. 92–93. In his debate with Lemnius, Casaubon relied on the Spanish physician Antonio Ponce de Santa Cruz to whom I shall return below. See *Treatise*, p. 39.

[28] *A Treatise Concerning Enthusiasme*, pp. 37–38.

preparation for the intervention of the devil. Here he was relying on medical authorities such as Fernel, Foreest, Langius and Weyer.[29] He also referred to the Jesuit theologian Cornelius à Lapide and the tenth century Byzantine philosopher, Michael Psellus, in stressing the demonological intervention in cases of speaking in tongues.[30] Thus, in spite of the naturalist thrust of his *Treatise*, Casaubon, like many of his predecessors in the sixteenth and early seventeenth century, also had recourse to the devil in order to counter the extreme naturalist claims of some Renaissance thinkers. Nevertheless, the demonological dimension played a relatively minor role in Casaubon's account of enthusiasm. The main ground on which he distanced himself from

---

[29] Ibid., p. 40. Casaubon characterized Fernel as "a man so learned, and religious, and by profession, a Physician" having the name of being "the first and chiefest of his time", and referred to his *De Abditis Rerum Causis Libri Duo*, book II, chapter XVI, pp. 369–381, in the Paris edition of 1560 (pp. 88–91 in the 1577 Frankfurt edition). Fernel mentioned there the case of a patient who was able to speak Greek during fits of possession although he had never learnt that language. Fernel ascribed that ability to the devil, who makes use of humours and other physiological disorders to achieve his purposes, but came out explicitly against any attempt to cure such possession by magical means. Ibid., pp. 373–375 (p. 90 in the 1577 edition). Casaubon went on to adduce Pierre de Foreest (Forestus), *Observationum et Curationum Medicinalium ac Chirurgicarum Opera Omnia*, Lib. X, Observatio XIX, pp. 340–341, a text also used by Burton, as we have seen in the previous chapter. Foreest similarly made use of the demonological account, although he stressed significantly that "Quamvis Daemoniaci semper fere sint melancholici: non tamen omnes melancholici sunt Daemoniaci; quamvis male tales esse à nonnullis putentur." Ibid., p. 341 left. On Weyer and his views concerning the role of the devil in enthusiasm and divination see Chapter 2 above.

[30] *A Treatise Concerning Enthusiasme*, p. 40. Cornelius à Lapide (Cornelis Cornelissen van den Steen) was born in Limburg in 1567 and died in Rome in 1637. He taught Scripture first in Louvain, later at the Collegio Romano. His *Commentaria in Pentateuchum Mosis* was indeed, as Casaubon noted, a popular work among both Catholics and Protestants. See *The New Catholic Encyclopedia*, vol. 8, p. 382. Casaubon referred to his commentary on Genesis 11: 6–7 which is on p. 130 left in the 2nd edition of Antwerp, 1618. Michael Psellus (1010–1078), the famous philosopher and politician in the Byzantine court who re-introduced Platonic philosophy in Byzantium, wrote among other things a demonological treatise in Greek which was translated into Latin first by Ficino, and later by Gilbert Gaulminus, *De Operatione Deaemonum Dialogus* (Paris, 1515). Casaubon referred to a story related by Psellus (ibid., pp. 84–87) of a Greek woman who when possessed, spoke the Arminian tongue which she had never known. That work was also translated into French by Pierre Moreau, *Traicté par dialogue de l'énergie ou opération des diables* (Paris, 1576). The relevant story is in chapter XVI, pp. 35r–37r. It is worth noting that Psellus took an explicitly anti-medical view of enthusiasm, debating with the physicians who wished to see enthusiasm and divination as the effect of physical maladies. Ibid., chapter XIV, pp. 30r–31v. Psellus's Greek text may also be found in Migne, *Patrologiae Patres Graeci*, vol. 122, cols. 857–859. On Psellus see also the article by David Pingree in *Dictionary of Scientific Biography* (henceforward, *D.S.B.*), vol. XI, pp. 182–186.

the sixteenth century naturalist view was not that of demonology, but rather of medicine, namely, giving divination a largely natural explanation, yet seeing it in negative terms, as a disease. Like Burton, then, Casaubon stressed the pathological nature of enthusiasm, relying on a long medical tradition for that purpose, and even more than Burton, emphasized its natural character.

This attitude becomes even clearer in the next chapter of the *Treatise*, Chapter III on "Contemplative and Philosophicall Enthusiasme". Under that label, Casaubon included a whole range of phenomena, beginning with Platonic philosophy, continuing with ecstatic tendencies and mystical theology, and ending up, surprisingly enough, with René Descartes, a point to which I shall return in Chapter 4 below. On the issue of "philosophical enthusiasm" Casaubon was even more hesitant than he had been in the case of divination to grant any measure of authenticity to the claims of the enthusiasts. He could not ignore the contemplative tradition from Plato onwards, nor could he write it off altogether as false. The value of the contemplation of God and the forsaking of worldly matters was too much a part of the Christian tradition. Yet, right from the beginning of the chapter, Casaubon warned against the dangers for Christianity itself inherent in that contemplative orientation:

> And if this Philosophy hath been a great advantage to Christianity, as some ancient Fathers have judged: yet of Christians it hath many Hereticks; and is to this day the common refuge of contemplative men, whether Christians, or others, that have run themselves besides their wits: who also have not wanted Disciples, studious and ambitious to vent and propagate the abortive fruits of such depraved phansies, unto others.[31]

Indeed, said Casaubon, some of Plato's expressions in his sublimest contemplation seem

> to countenance some vices, no lesse brutish and unnaturall, then his best vertues and abilities have exceeded, or have been thought to exceed ordinary nature.[32]

Casaubon was thus clearly suspicious even of philosophical contemplation proper, that is

---

[31] *A Treatise Concerning Enthusiasme*, pp. 69–70.
[32] Ibid., p. 70.

intellectuall pleasures and contentments, proceeding from the elevation of the mind above ordinary worldly objects, and fixed upon the contemplation of things naturall, and supernaturall: which Operation of the mind . . . is by some called *Enthusiasme*.[33]

I shall return in Chapter 4 below to some of the epistemological reasons for his suspicions. Relying on Hippocrates, Casaubon pointed out that one of the effects of such learning and contemplation may be melancholy. That idea, as we have seen, enjoyed a long career in medical thought down to the seventeenth century.

However, in this chapter, Casaubon concentrated on another type of "Contemplative Enthusiasme", not the intellectual one "proceeding from the elevation of the mind above ordinary worldly objects", but rather, that of ecstasy, which claimed to effect an actual separation of the soul from the body, or even the absolute transformation of man into God.[34] True, a partial deprivation of the senses was possible, but that could be naturally accounted for. Insisting on the interdependence of soul and body, and the fact that the power of sense was resident ultimately in the soul itself, Casaubon admitted that man could willingly dissociate himself from certain data coming from the senses. He quoted the Stoic saying that "pain is but *opinion*", and cited the Lacedaemonian boys who could keep their countenances unchanged while their backs were torn by the most unmerciful whips and scourges.[35] It is in this context that he presented the famous example of the alleged possession of Marthe Brossier in 1599.[36] For Casaubon, this indicated that a woman could be immune to pain without any supernatural intervention, simply by will power. Her case was thus one of counterfeit rather than possession. Here Casaubon clearly sided with the naturalist account of many of the physicians who examined Marthe, rather than with the demonological interpretation of the monks, clergy and some other physicians. The Brossier affair also gave Casaubon the opportunity to make some anti-Catholic remarks.[37] No less important, it provided an example

---

[33] Ibid., p. 71. Casaubon was referring here not only to Plato himself, but also to Philo of Alexandria.

[34] Ibid., p. 71.

[35] Ibid., pp. 71–74.

[36] On the affair of Marthe Brossier, see D.P. Walker, *Unclean Spirits* (London: Scolar Press, 1981), pp. 33–42, and Robert Mandrou, *Magistrats et Sorciers en France au XVIIe siècle* (Paris: Plon, 1968), pp. 163–179.

[37] "The Monks and Friers (sic!) were very zealous that she might be accounted possest, as thinking thereby to get great honour to their Exorcisms, and to give a

of the dangers to public peace accruing from a misunderstanding of
such phenomena:

> I am very well pleased with the occasion that offers it self, that the
> Reader may the better be satisfied, how necessary the knowledge of
> these things is, not for the satisfaction of curiosity only, but even for
> the maintenance of publick peace.[38]

A naturalist account of "enthusiasm" was thus crucial for the main-
tenance of the social, political and cultural order. In this respect, the
Anglican, French-born Casaubon, sided with the *politique* party in
France at the turn of the century.[39]

Whereas Casaubon could accept the possibility of a partial deprivation of the senses, as in the case of Marthe Brossier, and gave only
a naturalist account of such abilities, he was entirely sceptical as regards
claims for a total separation of body from soul, that is, with respect
to trances and ecstasies. It is to this subject that he devoted the major
part of his chapter on "contemplative enthusiasme", and it is here
that the medical interpretation of enthusiasm became most prominent. Right from the start, however, Casaubon was careful to exclude from his account supernatural ecstasy based on the authority
of Holy Scripture. He even enlarged "supernatural ecstasy" to include "many others, which either good, though not infallible authority, or sound reason, upon due examination of circumstances, hath
commended unto us for such."[40] Moreover, Casaubon did not rule
out entirely the possible role of the devil. Yet, he pushed such intervention "backwards", drawing an analogy between the general will
of God, and the general will of the Devil—

> who, for ought I know, may have a hand in all, or most diseases, to
> which mortall man (through sin) is naturally liable. . . . However, we
> make a difference between personall immediate possession, or operation,

---

great blow (their own profession: I have a good Author for it) to the Hereticks, who
despised them." *A Treatise Concerning Enthusiasme*, p. 76. Casaubon clearly relied here
on Jacques De Thou, *Historiarum sui temporis*, Tome V (Geneva, 1620), to whom he
referred explicitly on the following page. Indeed, as De Thou himself stressed, the
affair broke out a few days after the Edict of Nantes was reluctantly ratified by the
Parlement of Paris, and it should be seen in this context. See also Walker, *Unclean
Spirits*, p. 34.

[38] *A Treatise Concerning Enthusiasme*, p. 75.

[39] In fact, 1599, by coincidence, was also the year of Meric Casaubon's birth! On
the ideological context surrounding the Brossier affair see Walker, *Unclean Spirits, loc.
cit.*, and note 37 above.

[40] *A Treatise Concerning Enthusiasme*, p. 80.

which we oppose to naturall causes; and that generall concurrence, or intervention of the Devil, which may be supposed in all that is evil, whether in a morall or naturall sense.[41]

Within these limits, Casaubon emphasized the pathological character of ecstasy. Following Scaliger and Sennert, he defined pathological ecstasy as "Privatio officiorum animae sentientis, moventis et intelligentis", clearly distinguishing it from true, supernatural ecstasy, which was "Animae abstractionem à potentiis sensitivis, et aliquando etiam intellectualibus."[42] Indeed, unlike the case of divination, Casaubon did not see any element of truth in the pathological ecstatic experience. In this respect, he diverged explicitly from Aristotle, who coupled ecstasy (like that of the Pythia) with dreams and divination.[43] No emanations operated in the case of ecstasies, unlike that of divinations. The visions and sights reported by ecstatic persons were purely the concommitant of natural diseases such as epilepsy. Even after the patient was cured from his original disease, those illusions left impressions in the brain which the person believed to be the impressions of real visions and to which he might often relapse (a phenomenon which Casaubon called "extraordinary ecstasie"). Side by side with epilepsy and similar diseases, a man could become ecstatic "through mere melancholy . . . without any direct ecstasie, yet liable to the effects of it, ecstaticall impressions, and illusions in the brain."[44] Casaubon proceeded to distinguish, following Fyens, between melancholy as a bodily disease (*vitio corporis*), and melancholy caused by psychological factors such as study or love-melancholy, a distinction we have found already in Burton. Both types of melancholy could cause ecstatical impressions similar to those caused by epilepsy.[45] Casaubon did not enlarge upon the physiological mechanisms causing such illusions (I shall return to some of them in a later chapter),

[41] Ibid., p. 81.
[42] Ibid., pp. 86–87. For Sennert's discussion of ecstasy see his *Institutionum Medicinae Libri V*, Lib. II, Part III, Sect. II, Cap. IV (chapter under the title "De Symptomatum Sensuum internorum"), in Daniel Sennert, *Opera Omnia* (Paris: 1641), vol. I, p. 401.
[43] *A Treatise Concerning Enthusiasme*, pp. 82–83.
[44] Ibid., p. 87.
[45] Ibid., pp. 87–88. Casaubon relied on Thomas Fienus, *De viribus imaginationis tractatus*. In the 1635 Leiden edition of that work the phrase Casaubon quoted is on p. 200. The first edition appeared in Louvain in 1608. Fienus, or Fyens (1567–1631), was a native of Antwerp who studied medicine in Italy, became professor of medicine in Louvain and was also private physician to Maximilian, the Duke of Bavaria, and to Archduke Albert at Brussels. On Fienus and his treatise, see Thorndike, *The History of Magic and Experimental Science*, vol. 6, pp. 235–237.

but he clearly relied on the medical tradition in explaining this type of enthusiasm, and in offering a naturalist, though completely "negative" account.[46]

This becomes clearer in the many examples and illustrations adduced concerning the medical causes of ecstasy.[47] Casaubon began with a case mentioned by Tertullian, of a woman who went into fits during church services, and claimed to converse with angels, as well as with the Lord himself. He continued with a certain Galinducha in the time of the Emperor Mauritius, and then skipped to more recent instances of a baker's boy in Oldenburgh in 1581, an ecstatic maid in Fribourg who had visions in 1560, and a case he had witnessed in his own parish, of one John Carpenter, "between a Yeoman and a Labourer", who related his visions of Heaven, Paradise, and Hell, and who claimed soon to convert many thousands of people by his ministry and revelations.[48]

The purpose of all these examples, ancient as well as contemporary, was to show that ecstatics who claimed to have supernatural visions were in fact sick with epilepsy or melancholy. Casaubon indeed advised Carpenter's wife "to repair to some Physician: for that her husband, I thought, though little sign of it yet, would be very sick." Yet, some of the good women of the Parish, "of the inferior sort", concluded that the poor man was possessed, and that the woman who was called to treat him was in fact a witch. They drove her out of the house and the man consequently died that same night.[49]

Casaubon was obviously criticizing popular beliefs and customs, yet his main thrust in this section was anti-Catholic. He expressed amazement at the fact that not only the populace, but intellectuals and learned men have given credit to the pretensions of these ecstatic individuals:

> But for ignorant people to be bold and confident, and in their confidence to deceive themselves and others, is no wonder at all, a man needs but open his eyes, to see such sights at every door. That which

[46] For this reason, Casaubon devoted an extensive discussion (pp. 83–86) to a somewhat forced interpretation of Mark: 3, 21—"And when his friends heard of it, they went out to lay hold on him: for they said, He is beside himself"—a verse which refers to Jesus and commonly interpreted as a case of ecstasy. For Casaubon it was important to understand the Greek term παρ' αὐτοῦ as meaning fainting rather than "in ecstasy".
[47] Ibid., pp. 88–119.
[48] Ibid., pp. 88–100. Quotation from p. 97.
[49] Ibid., p. 99.

I (not without some indignation sometimes) have wondred [sic!] at, is; that even learned men, yea men of great fame and credit in the world for their parts and performances in other kinds, have in this particular of Ecstasies and Raptures, been so apt in all ages to be gulled.[50]

Typically, these "men of great fame" were Catholic, whereas the sceptics and naturalists on whom Casaubon relied were Protestant, whether the Huguenot theologian Franz Junius, the Swiss physician Paul Lentulus, or the Lutheran theologian Paulus Eber.[51] Casaubon devoted the most detailed discussion to the case of a Doctor of Divinity in Peru who became a disciple of a plain woman who regularly fell into trances and raptures. The Doctor himself soon began to make prophecies, perform miracles, and claim to be King, Pope, and indeed, Redeemer of the whole world. He was ultimately burned at the stake by the Inquisition. Casaubon's source for this story was the Jesuit Joseph Acosta.[52] While relying on his testimony, Casaubon nevertheless seriously criticised Acosta's view of the case, as well as the Inquisition's handling of the matter. Whereas Acosta and the Inquisition saw the Doctor as an heretic who was probably possessed by the devil, Casaubon regarded him as a typical melancholic. The fact that the Doctor was perfectly "normal" on all other issues, except for his claims to supernatural revelations, did not mean that he was not sick. Casaubon pointed out "that there is a sober kind of distraction or melancholy . . . where the distemper is confined to some *one* object or other", a fact that Acosta and the other "grave men and Judges" were apparently not aware of.[53] Casaubon relied on a long line of medical authorities in making this point, beginning with Aristotle and Aretaeus, and ending up with his contemporaries, Fyens, Du Laurens, and Sennert, as well as citing some examples from his own experience.[54]

---

[50] Ibid., p. 101.

[51] Franciscus Junius (François du Jon) (1545–1602) taught theology at Heidelberg. Paul Lentulus (c. 1560–1613) was a physician from Bern who also served for a while as physician to Queen Elisabeth. Paulus Eberus (1511–1569), was a close associate of Melanchton and a professor of Old Testament in Wittenberg.

[52] Ibid., pp. 102–106. Joseph Acosta, *De temporibus novissimis libri quatuor*, lib. 2, c. 11 (Rome, 1590), pp. 54 ff. José de Acosta (1539\40–1599\1600) was a Jesuit missionary in Peru, served as the second provincial of the order there, and towards the end of his life became Rector of the Jesuit College in Salamanca. His best known book, soon translated into several European languages, was *Historia natural y moral de las Indias* (Seville, 1590). On Acosta see the biographical and bibliographical article in C. Sommervogel, S.J., *Bibliothèque de la Compagnie de Jésus*, vol. 1 (1890), cols. 31–38.

[53] *A Treatise Concerning Enthusiasme*, p. 106. My italics.

[54] Ibid., pp. 106–109.

The anti-Catholic thrust of Casaubon's critique of trances and ecstasies is most notable, however, in his discussion of the case of Sister Catherine of Jesus, which prompted him, as we have seen above, to write the *Treatise* in the first place. He returned to an analysis of *The Life of Sister Catherine* towards the end of his third chapter, in the context of his treatment of ecstasies and "mystical theology", to which women especially were susceptible, "whom all men know to be naturally weaker of brain, and easiest to be infatuated and deluded."[55] After describing and analysing some of her experiences, Casaubon concluded:

> Truely I do not see any cause to believe that in any of these many Visions or Ecstasies, there was any thing at all supernaturall, either divine or diabolicall, more then is in every common disease . . . I conceive them all, both Visions and Ecstasies, to have been the effect of pure melancholy; very agreeable to what hath happened unto other melancholick persons, in other places.[56]

"Pure melancholy" led the patient to inflict immoderate castigations and vexations upon him- or herself, bodily penances to which Sister Catherine was "strangely addicted" from early youth. Such voluntary chastisements seemed outwardly a mark of piety, but in fact, were the symptoms of a melancholic disease. They in turn led to the trances and ecstasies which Sister Catherine experienced.[57] Like Burton, Casaubon linked monastic asceticism and its consequent mystical experiences with melancholy, rather than with true religious piety, and it is here that his anti-Catholic outlook came to the fore.

The medical, rather than judicial perspective on ecstasies, led Casaubon to a different attitude towards such poor men who were

> . . . no dangerous men, nor liable, if they meet not with very severe Judges, to any other judgement, then to be laughed at by some, (which is uncharitable enough, since it is a common chance,) and to be pitied by others.[58]

The question indeed was that of deliberate will and responsible action:

> . . . [I]f a man, neither factious in his life, nor abettor of strange Opinions, when himself, in a fit of burning fever, or through some proper

---

[55] Ibid., p. 157. The discussion of Catherine's case is on pp. 158–165.
[56] Ibid., p. 164.
[57] Ibid., pp. 158–164.
[58] Ibid., p. 113.

distemper of the brain, occasioned by a melancholick constitution of
body or otherwise, should fall into a conceit, and speak accordingly,
that he is Christ, or God or the like; I think he should have hard
measure, if he should be punished as a Blasphemer.[59]

Much of the debate hinged on the question whether the understanding of such pretenders and enthusiasts was sound or not. Casaubon
devoted a few pages to arguing that, *pace* Galen, the understanding
of these melancholics was indeed impaired, even though the source
of the disturbance was in the imagination.[60]

Casaubon thus clearly subscribed to a naturalist understanding of
ecstasies, and saw them as the result of the melancholic distemper.
(Significantly enough, however, like Du Laurens a generation before
him, he was careful to view the issue of witches "to be a quite different case"!)[61]

Nevertheless, a naturalist account of ecstasies and raptures did not
necessarily mean that the ecstatic persons in question were passive
patients. Indeed, Casaubon proceeded to ask whether "it may be
thought possible in nature, without the concurrence of any supernaturall cause, for any one man or woman to put themselves into a
Trance, or Ecstasie, when they will", that is, whether trances and
ecstasies could be deliberately induced.[62] He devoted a long discussion to this question, and cited various cases from the medical and
religious literature, beginning with the example of the African priest
Restitutus mentioned by St. Augustine. He proceeded to refute systematically the view of the physician Thomas Fyens, who denied the
possibility of inducing such ecstasies deliberately.[63] The issue was really
that of the power of the imagination, and Casaubon argued that the
imagination could stir the passions in such a way as to ultimately
cause raptures and trances. He phrased his final conclusion cautiously
but nevertheless clearly:

> . . . [G]ranting what must be granted, and doth often happen in the
> world, besides the ordinary course of nature, yet by causes that are
> naturall . . . a voluntary ecstasie is not a thing impossible to nature.[64]

---

[59] Ibid., p. 114.
[60] Ibid., pp. 115–117.
[61] Ibid., p. 118.
[62] Ibid., p. 119.
[63] Ibid., pp. 120–122, for the discussion of St. Augustine's story; pp. 123–126, for
a critique of Fienus's view.
[64] Ibid., p. 129. Among the medical authorities on whom Casaubon relied in

Casaubon went on to deal briefly with another question which, as we shall see in a later chapter, was to preoccupy also the next generation of critics of enthusiasm:

> Whether it be probable or possible, that naturall Ecstasies and Enthusiasms, such as proceed from naturall causes merely, should be *contagious*?[65]

Casaubon did not give a definite answer to that question, but he pointed out that contagion could be of different sorts.[66]

As for contagious ecstasies, he mainly had the Messaliani or Euchites in mind, who by praying got themselves into collective raptures which gradually spread in monasteries, towns, and indeed almost to whole countries. The only cure for such contagion, said Casaubon, was absolute destruction.[67] He concluded with a significant statement:

> Which may seem strange, that that [namely, prayer] wherein the happinesse and perfection of a Christian, being well used, doth chiefly consist; as being that which bringeth man nearest unto God; through abuse and excesse, should become liable to the punishment of highest crimes.[68]

---

reaching that conclusion were: Daniel Sennert, *Medicina Practica*, Lib. VI, Pars IX, "De Morbis a fascino et incantatione, ac veneficijs inductis", in Sennert, *Opera Omnia*, vol. III, pp. 1126–1162; Henricus ab Heer, *Observationes Medicae* (Liège, 1630), Observat. XXVII: "Melancolicorum casus rari"; Guilhelmus Fabricius, *Observationum et Curationum Chirurgicarum Centuriae Sex*, Centuria 3, Observationes xiv–xv, in *Opera quae extant omnia* (Frankfurt, 1646), p. 195–197. In the next few pages (pp. 129–133), Casaubon cited further authorities to substantiate his claim that such artificially induced ecstasies were possible. Among them, interestingly enough, was the Spanish physician Antonio Ponce de Sancta Cruz, in his commentary on Hippocrates, *De morbo sacro*. Ponce de Santa Cruz, *Praelectiones Vallisoletanae, in Librum magni Hipp. coi de Morbo Sacro* (Madrid, 1631), pp. 177–181. In fact, Ponce de Santa Cruz aimed in this chapter primarily to distinguish between divine ecstasy and false raptures, and he tended to give a demonological account of the latter, including those of Restitutus, which he discussed in detail. Nevertheless, Casaubon interpreted some of his statements as lending credence to the naturalist interpretation.

[65] *A Treatise Concerning Enthusiasme*, p. 134. My italics.

[66] His analogy is significant: how is a mad dog contagious? by breath or only by its teeth? Casaubon mentioned in that connection the view of Aretaeus, "a Physician of great note, and greater antiquity" that the very breath of a mad dog was enough to infect. (Ibid., p. 134).

[67] Ibid., p. 135. The Messaliani or Euchites were a monastic sect of the 4th and 5th century in Syria and Asia Minor. They practised incessant prayer as a way to salvation and redemption from the demon who, since Adam's fall, was united with the soul of every man. Such constant prayer also led them to visions and ecstasies. They were denounced as heretics by the Council of Ephesus in 451. See *Oxford Dictionary of the Christian Church*, p. 906.

[68] *A Treatise Concerning Enthusiasme*, p. 135. Casaubon took up the issue of Prayer in chapter VI, the last chapter of his book, entitled "Of Precatory Enthusiasme". He also returned there in greater detail to a discussion of the Messalians or Euchites

This was indeed the main dilemma of the critics of enthusiasm, who found themselves reproving an excess of religious piety, which in a moderate measure they considered an eminent virtue.

Casaubon finally discussed the possibility of the soul quitting the body, and later returning to it. We shall return to his views on the soul-body relationship in Chapter 4 below. He was extremely sceptical about any such claims, emphasizing that even St. Paul himself did not describe his own divine raptures in terms of a separation of his soul from his body.[69] As for the numerous testimonies of the experience of a body which for some three days seemed to be dead, with the soul departing it, and then coming back to life—Casaubon relied once again on the medical literature, saying that

> Physicians are agreed upon it; and they ground it upon certain experience, that a man in *ecstasi melancholica*, or a woman, *in hysterica passione*, may be gone three dayes, and come to themselves again.[70]

Mystical experiences, trances, and ecstasies, were thus pathological symptoms, rather than signs of religious piety. True, Casaubon was careful not to cast doubt on the possibility of a true, supernatural type of enthusiasm, whether of divine or diabolic origin.[71] Yet, the thrust of his whole book was to give a naturalist interpretation to the various types of enthusiasm. Such an understanding was essential, in his view, not only in order to save lives (as in the case of poor Sister Catherine, whose life could have been preserved by proper medical treatment), and not even just for the sake of Truth ("more precious then many lives,")—but for maintaining public peace "which hath often been disturbed by such, whether artifices, or mere mistakes."[72] Even more than Burton, Casaubon gave an explicit naturalist account

---

(ibid., pp. 283–286), stressing that their ecstasies should be seen as the effect of "Naturall Enthusiasme", that is, of a natural distemper. Only with respect to their ability to foretell future things was Casaubon ready to entertain the possibility that the devil took "the advantage of such naturall distemper, to produce supernaturall effects." (p. 286)

[69] Ibid., pp. 142–143. On that issue, Casaubon also debated with Cardan and Bodin who had entertained such a possibility. Ibid., pp. 140–142.

[70] Ibid., p. 137. He quoted Sennert again on this issue.

[71] As he said, for example, of prayer, at the beginning of the chapter on "Precatory Enthusiasme":

> As therefore there is a true, religious, supernaturall *Enthousiasme*, that belongeth unto Prayers; and a false, diabolicall, supernaturall, (directly opposite unto the former;) neither of which we desire to meddle with, more then of necessity, for distinction sake ... Ibid., p. 275.

[72] Ibid., p. 165.

of enthusiasm in order to maintain the social and religious order. And like Burton, he looked backwards, to the long medieval and Renaissance medical tradition, for providing such a naturalist account.

Henry More

A year after Casaubon first published his *Treatise Concerning Enthusiasme*, and in the same year that the second edition was printed, another famous text against enthusiasm, that of Henry More, appeared. Although it similarly presented enthusiasm as a clinical manifestation of melancholy, More's text, later known under the title *Enthusiasmus Triumphatus*, was written from a very different point of view. Indeed, turning from Casaubon to Henry More, we pass from the world of late humanism to the intellectual milieu of Cambridge Platonism in the middle of the seventeenth century. Against this background, the similarities between Casaubon and More, especially in their medical critique of enthusiasm, are all the more significant.

Henry More first published his text in 1656 under the pseudonym of Philophilus Parresiastes, as a preface to two other texts of his, written a few years earlier, against the mystic and "enthusiast" Thomas Vaughan. *Enthusiasmus Triumphatus* was incorporated in a revised version in More's *Several Philosophical Writings* of 1662.[73] These texts were thus written largely during More's "philosophical" period, before the Restoration, prior to the period when theological and religious topics would become increasingly predominant in his writings.[74] In the 1650's

---

[73] The attacks against Thomas Vaughan were *Observations upon Anthroposophia Theomagica and Anima Magica Abscondita*, first published under the pseudonym of Alazonomastix Philalethes in Parrhesia (London), 1650, and *The Second Lash of Alazonomastix*, published anonymously in Cambridge in 1651, which was written in reply to Vaughan's response, *A Man Mouse Taken in a Trap*. Both were re-published in 1655, and in 1656 were joined by *Enthusiasmus Triumphatus, or a Discourse of the Nature, Causes, Kinds, and Cure, of Enthusiasme* published as a preface to these texts. *Enthusiasmus Triumphatus* was re-published with some slight changes in *A Collection of Several Philosophical Writings of Henry More* (London, 1662), vol. I. The main changes were a different version of the first section, two new sections in the middle (sections 59–60), an important addition to section 63 (61 in the 1656 ed.), and an additional last section (section 67). Unless otherwise specified, I shall refer to the 1656 edition. Up to section 59, the numbering of the sections is identical (though not the pagination).

[74] On the turning point in More's thought, at least in terms of emphasis, see Aharon Lichtenstein, *Henry More: The Rational Theology of a Cambridge Platonist* (Cambridge, Mass.: Harvard University Press, 1962), pp. 147–148, and the recent important article by Alan Gabbey, "Philosophia Cartesiana Triumphata: Henry More (1646–

Henry More was constantly preoccupied with the dual threat of enthusiasm on the one hand, and atheism on the other. Indeed, from the very beginning of his controversy with Vaughan, More pointed out the dialectical relationship between these two dangers:

> ... [I]t is too common a disease now adayes to be driven by heedlesse intoxicating imaginations under pretense of higher strains of Religion and supernaturall light, and by bidding adieu to sober reason and a purified mind, to grow first fanaticall, and then Atheisticall and sensuall, even almost to the height of abhorred Gnosticism.[75]

Indeed, More saw enthusiasm as a danger to Christianity no less serious than atheism. In 1660, in *The Great Mystery of Godliness* he said

> ... I dare pronounce with a loud voice aforehand, That if ever *Christianity* be exterminated, it will be by *Enthusiasme*. Of so great consequence is it rightly to oppose so deadly an evil.[76]

More explained that he intended to combat enthusiasm here by pointing out the reasonableness and usefulness of the Christian religion, whereas in *Enthusiasmus Triumphatus* he had combated enthusiasm "by discovering the Natural Causes and imposturous Consequences of Enthusiasme".[77] Even more than Casaubon's *Treatise*, enthusiasm was accounted for by Henry More almost exclusively in terms of melancholy, and clearly as a disease. Though less profuse than Burton or Casaubon in quoting and mentioning his sources, More clearly relied on traditional medical writers in linking enthusiasm with melancholy, chief among them being Burton himself, as we shall presently see. More's recourse to the medical, indeed, the Galenic tradition should raise more questions than it has done so far among students of More.[78] How did his reliance on medical authors,

---

1671)", in Thomas M. Lennon, John M. Nichols, and John W. Davis, eds., *Problems of Cartesianism* (Kingston and Montreal: McGill-Queen's University Press, 1982), pp. 171–250, esp. p. 173.

[75] Henry More, *The Second Lash of Alazonomastix*, p. 12. The same point was made in *An Antidote against Atheisme* (1652), Preface, sig. A5r–A6r, in *Enthusiasmus Triumphatus*, section 64, pp. 60–61, and again in the first section of the revised 1662 edition of *Enthusiasmus Triumphatus*. See also Noel L. Brann, "The Conflict between Reason and Magic in Seventeenth-Century England: A Case Study of the Vaughan-More Debate", *Huntington Library Quarterly* 43 (1980): 103–126, esp. pp. 111–112.

[76] Henry More, *An Explanation of the Great Mystery of Godliness* (London, 1660), "To the Reader", p. vi.

[77] Loc. cit.

[78] Several articles have been published in recent years on More's debate with Vaughan and on his critique of enthusiasm, but none of them deals in detail with

his portrayal of enthusiasm as a physiological disease, fit in with his broader Platonic orientation? Would not one expect the Cambridge Platonist Henry More to view melancholy in positive terms too, as Ficino and many of his Renaissance followers had done? This question points of course to a broader problem: the basic ambivalence in More's attitude towards enthusiasm.[79] Indeed, some historians have suggested that one should see More's debate with Thomas Vaughan and other enthusiasts as "a fraternal rivalry within the same family" rather "than as a combat between spokesmen of radically divergent world views."[80] Henry More himself admitted in 1662 in a highly significant passage that his critique of enthusiasm was part of an internal conflict:

> I must ingenuously confess that I have a natural touch of Enthusiasme in my Complexion, but such as, I thank God, was ever governable

More's medical account and with the problems it raises: Frederick B. Burnham, "The More-Vaughan Controversy: The Revolt against Philosophical Enthusiasm", *Journal of the History of Ideas* 35 (1974): 33–49; Noel L. Brann, "The Conflict between Reason and Magic", pp. 103–126; Arlene M. Guinsburg, "Henry More, Thomas Vaughan and the Late Renaissance Magical Tradition", *Ambix* 27 (1980): 36–58.

[79] Characteristic of More's ambivalence is his relationship with Anne Conway and the circle at Ragley Hall. His *Enthusiasmus Triumphatus* was written largely as a rebuke to the enthusiasm of the Quaker variety rampant at Ragley Hall. See Arlene M. Guinsburg, "Henry More, Thomas Vaughan", pp. 43, 53. See also Marjorie H. Nicolson, *Conway Letters* (New Haven: Yale University Press, 1930), especially pp. 378–381.

[80] See Noel L. Brann, "The Conflict between Reason and Magic", p. 104. For another detailed analysis of More's ambivalent attitude to the Rosicrucian and hermetic tradition see Arlene M. Guinsburg, "Henry More, Thomas Vaughan". Guinsburg analyses the development of More's thought following the debate with Vaughan and *Enthusiasmus Triumphatus*, and shows how he gradually came to adopt some of Vaughan's conceptions (especially concerning the soul, World Spirit, the causes of motion, as well as certain Cabbalistic ideas), though always from a perspective that remained at a distance from the subjective and anti-rational views of the enthusiasts. See especially ibid., pp. 44, 46–47, 49, 53–54. For a similar view see also Aharon Lichtenstein, *Henry More*, pp. 75–80. Lichtenstein rightly points out that More's concern with the personal and spiritual element of religious life should not be confused with a subjective orientation. More saw his "inner light" as that of universal reason, whereas the "inner light" of the Quakers and the enthusiasts he regarded as subjective and indeed, I would add, pathological. Nevertheless, it should be remembered that these distinctions are themselves very much "in the eyes of the beholder". For a Theosophic view of More which stresses his visionary and mystic orientation, and the similarities between More and contemporary "hermeticists" and Cabbalists see also Serge Hutin, *Henry More, Essai sur les doctrines théosophiques chez les Platoniciens de Cambridge* (Hildesheim: Olms, 1966). For a contrary view, stressing the rational character of More's thought, see C.A. Staudenbaur, "Platonism, Theosophy, and Immaterialism: Recent Views of the Cambridge Platonists", *Journal of the History of Ideas* 35 (1974): 157–69.

enough, and I have found at length perfectly subduable. In virtue of which victory I know better what is in Enthusiasts then they themselves, and therefore was able to write what I have wrote with life and judgements, and shall, I hope, contribute not a little to the peace and quiet of this Kingdome thereby.[81]

Indeed, his Cabbalistic and philosophical interests could make More a typical representative of what Casaubon called "contemplative enthusiasm". Yet More took a critical distance from enthusiasm, and like Casaubon and Burton, viewed it as a pathological phenomenon. In this section I shall first examine some of More's pronouncements and sources on melancholy and enthusiasm, and then try to see how this medical critique of enthusiasm might fit into his broader views, particularly those concerning the relationship between mind and body.

The main aim of *Enthusiasmus Triumphatus* was indeed to expose the natural causes of the disease of enthusiasm, clearly distinguishing it (as Casaubon had done) from true divine inspiration. Nor did More make in 1656 any systematic references to the devil as a cause of enthusiasm, although he did not exclude such a possibility.[82] By providing such a "clinical" account of enthusiasm, he did not wish to exonerate the enthusiasts themselves (nor did he want to persecute them), but mainly to deter their potential followers.[83] He clearly located enthusiasm in the faculty of imagination, which was freer than the outward senses, yet not altogether voluntary, as were will, reason and understanding. More saw the imagination in physiological terms, as the result of the inward motion and configuration of the "animal spirits", independent of any external sensation—"our Imagination alters as our Blood and Spirits are altered."[84] When the external senses

---

[81] Henry More, *A Collection of Several Philosophical Writings* (London, 1662), "The Preface General", p. x. This passage was also referred to by Richard Ward, More's early biographer, who discussed in some detail this basic ambivalence in More's thought. Richard Ward, *The Life of the Learned and Pious Dr. Henry More* (London, 1710, ed. with an introduction by M.F. Howard, London, 1911), chapter III, pp. 80–87.

[82] See *Enthusiasmus Triumphatus*, 1656 ed., "To the Reader", and sections 1, 2, 60, 61 (pp. 1–2, 58–59). In the 1662 edition, as we shall see below, More added a section at the end of the treatise in which he explained why in 1656 he had not referred in greater detail to the demonological account of enthusiasm.

[83] The moral responsibility of the enthusiast was also a point on which More would elaborate in the 1662 edition of the text, as we shall see below.

[84] Section 7, p. 7 of the 1656 edition. See also section 3–6, pp. 3–6. "Animal spirits" was a Galenic conception of one of the physiological correlates, or instruments of the soul. The function of the animal spirits was to transmit sensations from the external senses to the soul, and voluntary motion from the soul to the various

and the free faculties of reason and understanding are weak, the imagination can be strong enough to persuade the soul that its images are indeed real. This happens in sleep, when we dream, as well as in the case of mad and melancholic men. The latter could imagine themselves to be prophets, Messiahs, angels, or indeed God himself. Henry More remained pretty vague, however, as to the role of the soul in imagination, whether it was active or passive. On the one hand, he presented the brain and animal spirits as those which "the Soul works upon within, in her imaginative operations" and the imagination, as the figuration or modification "which the Soul necessarily and naturally moulds them into in our sleep".[85] On the other hand, he viewed the strength of imagination as a function of "the Soul's weaknesse or unweildinesse whereby she so farre sinks into Phantasmes, that she cannot recover her self into the use of her more free faculties of Reason and Understanding."[86] What it was "that thus captivates our Imagination and carries it away out of the reach or hearing of that more free and superiour faculty of Reason", More found hard to define, but he was convinced, on the basis of experience, "that there are sundry materiall things that do most certainly change our mind or Fancy."[87] Among the material factors he mentioned were weather, wine, poisonous bites (like that of the tarantula), and nourishment. The most general cause, however—"whose nature notwithstanding is so various and *Vertumnus*-like, that it will supply the place of almost all particulars"—was melancholy.[88] At this point, More went on to list the medical and philosophical sources on the links between melancholy and enthusiasm.

Like Casaubon, More linked the Aristotelian *Problemata* with medical authorities such as Aretaeus, Du Laurens, Sennert, and Burton

members of the body. See Owsei Temkin, "On Galen's Pneumatology", *Gesnerus* 8 (1950): 180–189, and Chapter 7 below, in which this concept is discussed in detail. Henry More clearly saw the "animal spirits" in corpuscular terms. Thus in *An Antidote against Atheism*, first published in 1652, he said: "For these *Animal Spirits* are nothing else but matter very thin and liquid, whose nature consists in this that all the particles of it be in motion, and being loose from one another, fridge and play up and down according to the measure and manner of agitation in them." *An Antidote against Atheism*, Book I, Ch. XI, section 2, p. 33, in the edition published in *A Collection of Several Philosophical Writings* of 1662.

[85] *Enthusiasmus Triumphatus*, section 5, p. 4.
[86] Ibid., section 6, p. 5.
[87] Ibid., section 7, pp. 6–7.
[88] Ibid., section 11, p. 10. Vertumnus was the god of the changing year, and hence, of change and exchange in general.

himself.[89] Indeed, he mentioned in passing the "positive" Aristotelian view of melancholy as the cause of poetic and rhetorical inspiration, but he focused his own attention on melancholy "when it reaches to a disease".[90] More also relied on traditional medical sources in accounting for the fact that melancholics, except for one specific delusion (such as their claims to prophesy or to speak with God and the angels) could be entirely sober. He referred his reader principally to Sennert and to Burton, both of whom in turn quote other medical sources like Du Laurens, Platter, Foreest, and others to illustrate that point.[91] Beyond being the source of delusion in general, More stressed that melancholy was "the most religious complexion that is".[92] Indeed

> [T]he very nature of Melancholy is such, that it may more fairly and plausibly tempt a man into such conceits of inspiration and supernaturall light from God, then it can possibly do into those more extravagant conceits of being Glasse, Butter, a Bird, a Beast or any such thing.[93]

Consequently

> [S]uch a *Melancholist* as this, must be very highly puffed up, and not onely fancy himself inspired, but believe himself such a speciall piece of *Light* and *Holinesse* that God has sent into the world, that he will take upon him to reform, or rather annull the very Law and Religion he is born under, and make himself not at all inferior to either *Moses* or *Christ*, though he have neither any sound Reason nor visible miracle to extort belief.[94]

More interpreted the Aristotelian link between melancholy and zeal (τὸ ζέον), as well as the comparison of the effects of wine to those of melancholy, in clear pathological terms, just as Burton, Casaubon, and most physicans before him had done. He mentioned both Fernel and Sennert as making the same comparison.[95] Sennert had explicitly rejected the Renaissance and Platonic "positive" interpretation of the pseudo-Aristotelian text. Melancholics, though perhaps more ingenious,

---

[89] Ibid., sections 11, 12, pp. 10–12.

[90] Ibid., section 11, p. 10.

[91] Ibid., sections 12–13, pp. 11–14. Sennert discussed this issue in this *Practica Medicina* Lib. I, Par. II, Cap. VIII, see Sennert, *Opera Omnia*, vol. II, pp. 125–129, esp. 125–126.

[92] *Enthusiasmus Triumphatus*, section 15, p. 14.

[93] Ibid., section 14, p. 14.

[94] Ibid., section 15, p. 15.

[95] Ibid., section 17, p. 17. See J. Fernel, *Methodi Medendi Ferneliana, enucleata et controversiarum decisionibus illustrata* (Wittenberg, 1630), Cap. XI, p. 60. For the reference in Sennert, see following note.

could not perform anything above nature (such as predicting the future or speaking in tongues unknown to them), owing to their disease.[96] It is noteworthy that the Cambridge Platonist Henry More was referring here to an explicitly anti-Platonic medical text. He similarly followed the medical interpretations in stressing that the "Spirit" which the enthusiast claimed had inspired him was

> nothing else but that flatulency which is in the melancholy complexion, and rises out of the *Hypochondriacal* humour upon some occasionall heat . . . Which fume mounting into the head, being first actuated and spirited and somewhat refined by the warmth of the heart, fills the mind with variety of imaginations, and so quickens and inlarges invention, that it makes the Enthusiast to admiration fluent and eloquent.[97]

More interpreted such quick fluctuations between excessive joy and hopeless despondency as the result of the tendency of the melancholic humour to become very hot and then quickly cool down. The melancholic saw his "high" moments of ecstasies and raptures as the result of the uplifting hand of God, when in fact it was the result of a paroxysm of melancholy.[98]

Henry More clearly subscribed, then, to the theory of humours. It was the mixture of melancholy and a proportionate dose of the sanguine humour which led to "enthusiasm". He combined this medical view, however, with a pronounced moralistic approach. The licentious way of life of many of the enthusiasts—from Simon Magus, Montanus and Manes, through Mahomet and more recently, David George—was a clear proof that they were hardly God's prophets and agents (let alone God himself as some of them claimed), that their pretensions were the result of "a lower kind of working" of melancholy.[99] This moral critique also had a social and rhetorical dimension: all these mock-prophets and false Messiahs could "show

---

[96] "[T]amen ad id, quod supra hominis vires perficiendum nec melancholia, nec alia morbosa constitutio disponere potest." Daniel Sennert, *Medicina Practica*, Lib. I, Part II, Cap. XV, Quaestio I, in Sennert, *Opera Omnia*, vol. II, p. 157. As we have seen in Chapter 2 above, Sennert, like Fernel, did not deny the possibility of speaking in tongues or the performance of other supernatural feats. He only rejected any naturalist or astrological explanation of such abilities, like the one offered by Guainerio, and insisted on giving such extraordinary abilities a demonological explanation. (Ibid., pp. 156–157.) Henry More, on the other hand, virtually ignored this demonological account.

[97] *Enthusiasmus Triumphatus*, section 17, p. 17.

[98] Ibid., section 18, p. 18, and section 23, p. 24.

[99] Ibid., section 21, pp. 20–23.

no Title but an unsound kind of popular Eloquence, a Rapsodic of sleight and soft words, rowling and streaming Tautologies."[100]

Nevertheless, More quickly returned to the medical perspective. Specifically, he regarded the mystical interpretations of Scripture, the quakings of the Quakers, the arrogated visions and revelations of the enthusiasts and their ecstasies—all as clinical manifestations of melancholy. The Quakers were seen indeed as "the most *Melancholy Sect* that ever was yet in the world". Their tremblings were explained as the result of the strong passions of fear, love, and veneration which were in turn the consequence of melancholy.[101] Their fits, in which they would fall to the ground, were clearly epileptic, the result of gross vapours obstructing the supply of spirits in the *Arteriae Carotides* and the *Plexus Coroides*, and these vapours often arose from black bile. Here More once again referred back to Galen.[102] Visions were similarly the result of a ligation of the outward senses in which "what ever is then represented to the mind is of the nature of a dream".[103] Ecstasies too were just another symptom of melancholy. Like Casaubon, More defined ecstasies as nothing else but "Somnus praeter naturam profundus".[104] Ecstatic enthusiasts simply took their dreams for "true histories and real transactions" after they woke up, because of the extraordinary clearness of these dreams. Owing to "a more perfect privation of all communion with this outward world" in such deep sleep, what the imagination presented to the soul was as clear and vigorous as the perception of the outward senses. Here More took the opportunity to make a broader epistemological point: "But strength of perception is no sure ground of truth."[105]

Like Casaubon, More also raised the question of the possibility of voluntary ecstasies and epilepsies, and like Casaubon, he affirmed such a possibility. Once again he took the example of the contemporary Quakers to show that by solemn silence and earnest meditation, enthusiasts could easily transmute their melancholy into tremblings, convulsions, apoplexies and ecstasies. To the historical example of

---

[100] Ibid., p. 23.

[101] Ibid., section 25, pp. 25–26.

[102] Ibid., section 26, p. 26. On Galen's conception of epilepsy see also Owsei Temkin, *The Falling Sickness; a History of Epilepsy from the Greeks to the Beginning of Modern Neurology* (Baltimore: Johns Hopkins Press, rev. ed., 1971), pp. 60–64, and R.E. Siegel, *Galen's System of Physiology and Medicine* (Karger: Basel, New York, 1968), pp. 308–315.

[103] *Enthusiasmus Triumphatus*, section 27 pp. 26–27.

[104] Ibid., section 28, p. 27.

[105] Loc. cit.

the African minister Restitutus mentioned by Augustine and Casaubon, More added those of Cardano and his father Facius, as well as of the notorious Laplanders.[106] In some cases of the Quakers, More was ready to entertain the possibility of demonic possession, but he quickly returned to "that which is *Natural*".[107]

Finally More dealt with the phenomenon of divination. There was nothing supernatural in the tendency of enthusiasts to foretell the future, he declared. Unlike his Renaissance predecessors, however, and unlike Casaubon, More did not claim that melancholy could provide a natural explanation of successful prophecy. Melancholy only explained the subjective confidence of the pretended prophets—"the vehemency of their own Melancholy adding that confidence to their presage as if God himself had set it upon his Spirit".[108] Successful predictions could be explained either on the basis of "ordinary prudence" which can detect the probable grounds of future events, or as the result of mere chance—out of numerous false predictions, a few might be true. Once again, the Platonist More shared the scepticism of the non-Platonist physicians concerning the possibility of natural prophecy.[109]

How, then, to distinguish between true religious inspiration and the claims of melancholic enthusiasts, between what is divine and what is the consequence of natural complexion? More turned to that question towards the very end of the treatise, and dealt with it more explicitly than Casaubon had done. He put forward three criteria: The first was a moral (and a social) one:

> That that Piety or Goodnesse which is from the Spirit of God is universall, extirpating every vice and omitting nothing that is truely a divine virtue.[110]

---

[106] On the role of Lapland and the Lapps as a nation of "enthusiasts", see also Chapter 4 below. Restitutus, Cardano and Facius, as well as the Lapps, were also mentioned by Sennert as possessed by demons, see Sennert, *Institutionum Medicinae Libri V*, Lib. II, Part III, Sect. II, Cap. IV, in his *Opera Omnia*, vol. I, p. 401.

[107] *Enthusiasmus Triumphatus*, section 29, p. 29.

[108] Ibid., section 30, p. 29.

[109] More made, however, one notable exception concerning those who act in certain public affairs: "For it is not at all improbable but such as act in very publick affairs in which Providence has a more special hand, that these agents driving on her design may have a more special assistance and animation from her." Yet, he was quick to add—"this is Enthusiasme in the better sense, and therefore not so proper for our discourse who speak not of that which is true, but of that which is a mistake." Ibid., section 31, pp. 29–30.

[110] Ibid., section 60, p. 58. In the *Scholia* to the Latin edition of that text pub-

The important point to stress is that it was the universality of Piety which was crucial and which distinguished true piety from false. Whereas the enthusiast was an exclusivist, withdrawing himself from society, and, more important, restricting his "piety" to a select group, the religious concerns of the true Christian were universal. Indeed, More's stress on the universality of divine grace is well known, and lies behind his rejection of the Calvinist doctrine of Predestination.[111]

The second criterion was the traditional one of Scripture—"A belief of those Holy Oracles comprehended in the Old and New Testament". Like sixteenth century theologians, as we have seen in Chapter 1 above, More stressed the belief in Christ as a mediator—as the Son of God and as the Judge in the Last Judgment, in contradistinction to the attempts of the enthusiasts to circumvent Christ's mediatory role by searching direct contact with God.[112] The last and for our purpose, most relevant criterion was that of "universall Prudence, whereby a man admits nor acts nothing, but what is solidly rationall at the bottome." "He that finds himself thus affected—More added—may be sure it is the Spirit of God, not the power of Complexion or Nature that rules in him."[113] Here we have an epistemological and psychological criterion which is typical of More's rational orientation. Prudence and Reason were the best antidotes to enthusiasm or melancholy. More did not go so far as to dispense with the necessity of miracles, however. The "rude and unprepared" might need miracles in order to believe even in rational and prudent men. Yet the enthusiasts were destitute of both reason and the ability to perform miracles, hence their pretences were utterly vain.[114]

True enthusiasm, by contrast, was that of "devout and holy souls . . . modest enough and sober":

> witnessing no other thing to the world then what others may experience in themselves, and what is plainly set down in the holy Scriptures.

---

lished many years later, More emphasized the values of Humility, Charity and Purity as the distinguishing marks of true inspiration. *Henrici Mori Cantabrigiensis Scriptorum philosophicorum tomus alter* (London, 1679), p. 222.

[111] More rejected Calvinist predestination as early as 1630, while he was still at Eton. See Marjorie H. Nicolson, "Christ's College and the Latitude-Men", *Modern Philology* 27 (1929): 36.

[112] *Enthusiasmus Triumphatus*, p. 58. In the *Scholia* to the Latin edition of *Enthusiasmus Triumphatus* of 1679, More developed this point in greater detail, *Scriptorum philosophicorum tomus alter*, p. 225.

[113] *Enthusiasmus Triumphatus*, Section 60, pp. 58–59.

[114] Ibid., section 60, p. 59.

He added that

> in none of these things do they pretend to equallize themselves to Christ,
> whom God has exalted above men and Angels, but to professe the
> efficacie of his Spirit in them to the praise and glory of God, and the
> comfort and incouragement of their drooping Neighbour.[115]

Modesty, sobriety, universality and the reliance on Scripture were
the moral, psychological, social, and religious signs of "warrantable
Enthusiasme", the existence of which More did not deny by any
means. As we shall see in a later chapter, these criteria were also at
the root of the criticism directed by the new experimental scientists
against the enthusiasts.[116]

It is only at this point, toward the very end of his text, that More
hints at a positive role of melancholy, thus linking himself with the
Platonic tradition of the Renaissance:

> ... for these Rapturous and Enthusiasticall affections *even in them that*
> *are truely good and pious, it cannot be denied but that the fuell of them is usually*
> *naturall or contracted Melancholy*, which any man may perceive that is
> religious unless his Soul and Body be blended together, and there be
> a confusion of all; as it is in mistaken *Enthusiasts*, that impute that to
> God which is proper to Nature.[117]

More shifted his emphasis here from the distinction between the
natural and the divine causes of enthusiasm, to a distinction between
body and soul. Melancholy indeed disposed the body to "enthusiastic affections" but true inspiration was brought about only when "the
mind perfects the action through the power of the Spirit."[118] Pretended enthusiasts confused body and soul—not just the natural and
the supernatural—when they claimed to have divine inspirations while
in fact they were merely sick with melancholy. At this point More
drew an analogy between a mathematical disposition and a religious

---

[115] Ibid., section 61, p. 59.

[116] See Chapter 5 below.

[117] Ibid., section 62, pp. 59–60.

[118] Ibid., p. 60. It is worth noting that many years later, in the *Scholia* to the 1679
Latin edition of *Enthusiasmus Triumphatus*, More gave a very different interpretation
to what he had said here. There, he no longer viewed melancholy in its Platonic
connotations of a disposition to inspiration, but rather in traditional Christian terms,
as an expression of moral remorse based on the recognition of the moral law by
natural light. In that sense, melancholy was indeed an important preparation for
divine grace, though by no means for divine inspiration. *Scriptorum philosophicorum*
tomus alter, pp. 225–226.

complexion. Just as a mathematical theorem was not necessarily true simply because it was aired by someone of a "mathematicall complexion", so claims of inspiration were not authentic only because they were made by melancholics. Conversely, the religious message of the truly inspired person could not be written off merely because of his melancholic bodily disposition, just as we would not deny the truth of a mathematical theorem by ascribing it simply to the bodily complexion of the one who put it forward.[119] Being deeply concerned by the problem of atheism, no less than that of enthusiasm, More wished to ascertain the possibility of true religious inspiration, and to prevent the application of his medical interpretation to religious phenomena in general. He did so by insisting on a clear distinction between body and soul, between the natural and the divine.[120] At the same time, he adopted the Platonic and Pseudo-Aristotelian link between melancholy and inspiration in a strictly circumscribed sphere. The melancholic temperament provided at most a pre-disposition for inspiration. The visions and pretended prophecies of the enthusiasts, in contrast, were the consequence of the sickness of melancholy.

In the years following the first publication of *Enthusiasmus Triumphatus*, the Platonic elements in More's thought became more prominent. This is clear, for example, in his conception of the soul as expounded in *The Immortality of the Soul*, published in 1659. There, he still insisted on a clear distinction between body and soul, yet he introduced a certain gradation in the soul's faculties, including in them not only Will and Reason, but the lower faculties of Memory, Imagination, the Sensitive Power, as well as what he called "Plastic Power" (responsible for the heart's motions, for respiration and other involuntary motions). The gap between the corporeal functions and those of the soul was thus bridged. Indeed, More tended to see the union between body and soul as based on some "vital congruity" and ascribed to the "plastic" part of the soul a definite role in this union. The same ambivalence is noticeable in his conception of the "animal spirits" in this text to which I referred at the beginning of the chapter.

---

[119] *Enthusiasmus Triumphatus*, section 63, p. 60.

[120] This was also a major point in More's *An Antidote Against Atheism*, first published in 1652. The sharp distinction between body and soul also enabled him to entertain the possibility of true ecstasy, the temporary separation of the soul from the body. Ibid., Book I, Chapter XI, section 2, Book III, Chapter XI, pp. 32–37, 123–124, and the Appendix, Chapter XIII, p. 184 in the edition published in *A Collection of Several Philosophical Writings* of 1662. On the similarity between atheists and enthusiasts according to More see above.

On the one hand, they were clearly linked with the body, and at this point, More was following the Galenist medical tradition. At the same time, however, the "animal spirits" were not only seen as instruments of the soul, but were compared to light and linked with the celestial substance, in a manner typical of the Platonic tradition.[121]

More's increasingly Platonic orientation is manifest in the passages he added to *Enthusiasmus Triumphatus* when he republished it in 1662, in *A Collection of Several Philosophical Writings*. Most important, perhaps, he added another type of true and positive "enthusiasm":

> And what I have said in behalf of Christians, is in its measure due to those diviner sort of Philosophers, such as *Plato* and *Plotinus* ... To such Enthusiasm as this, which is but the triumph of the Soul of man inebriated, as it were, with the delicious sense of the divine life, that blessed Root and Originall of all holy wisedom and vertue, I must declare my self as much a friend as I am to the vulgar fanatical Enthusiasm a professed enemy.[122]

By 1662, and in marked contrast to the views of Casaubon, More regarded the "philosophical enthusiasm" of the Platonists as a type of true enthusiasm, not as a manifestation of disease.

In 1662 More also added a section at the very end of the treatise in which he answered two major criticisms of the medical approach to enthusiasm:

> ... that I have omitted the activity of the Devil, and the wilfull wickedness of the Mind of man, but resolved all into Complexion, or present temper, or rather distemper, of the body arising from natural causes that necessarily act thereupon. Whence men may judge my Discourse as well an excuse for, as a Discovery of, this disease of *Enthusiasm*.[123]

To the first objection, that he had ignored the demonological account of enthusiasm, More responded first by arguing that the devil "can doe no more than God permits", and that he only makes use

---

[121] See *The Immortality of the Soul* (London, 1659), book II, chapters VII, IX–XI, XIV, pp. 138–143, 209–236, 260. See also Arlene M. Guinsburg, "Henry More, Thomas Vaughan". On light as an incorporeal substance in the Platonic tradition, especially in Kepler, see David C. Lindberg, "The Genesis of Kepler's theory of Light: Light Metaphysics from Plotinus to Kepler", *Osiris* 2 (1986): 5–42. On the celestial substance and the "astral spirit" see below.

[122] "Enthusiasmus Triumphatus", in *A Collection of Several Philosophical Writings of Dr. Henry More* (London, 1662), section 63, p. 45. (The equivalent section in the 1656 edition to which this paragraph was now added had been 61).

[123] Ibid., section 67, p. 47.

of melancholy, which in this respect is indeed *Balneum diaboli*.[124] In
principle, however, More added concerning the devil that

> his *Causality* is more vagrant, more lax and general then to be brought
> in here, where my aim was to indigitate the more proper and constant
> causes of that *Disease*. I might adde also less philosophical for this present
> search which was onely into the *natural* principles of the said Distemper.[125]

More thus stated clearly that a demonological account was not part
of a philosophical and natural explanation of enthusiasm.[126]

More serious was the charge that a medical account relieved men
from any moral responsibility for their fanatical vagaries. Referring
to the medical causes of enthusiasm, More responded

> That though these causes do act necessarily upon the body, and the
> body necessarily upon the Mind, yet they do not act irresistibly, unless
> a man have brought himself to such a weakness by his own fault; as
> he that by his intemperance has cast himself into a Fever, who then
> fatally becomes subject to the laws thereof.[127]

Similarly, the cure of melancholy and enthusiasm was one's own
responsibility:

> For it is his own fault that he is not *temperate, humble,* and *attentive to
> Reason*; without recourse to which indispensable vertues he can never
> be freed from that foulness and uncleanness of his Astral Spirit (which
> is the inmost lodge and Harbour of all imposturous fancyes and
> Enthuisastick dreams) nor can ever arrive to that secure state of the
> Soul, where the importunities of deceitfull Imagination are alwaies
> declined and eluded by the safe Guidance and Conduct of the *Intellec-
> tual Powers*.[128]

---

[124] Ibid., p. 47. For Burton's similar view, see Chapter 2 above.
[125] Ibid., p. 48. Already in 1656, More said concerning a diabolical account of
the spirit of Paracelsus and his disciples: "... I confesse I think too harsh a censure,
well meaning men being lyable to Melancholy and Lunacies as well as to Agues
and burning Feavers." *Enthusiasmus Triumphatus* (1656), section 49, p. 50. By 1679,
however, he tended to go back and ascribe such diabolical influence to Paracelsus.
See *Scholia* to the Latin edition of *Enthusiasmus Triumphatus* in *Scriptorum philosophicorum
tomus alter*, p. 223, and p. 225.
[126] It is worth pointing out that with respect to witchcraft, More tended to accept
the role of the devil, and was reluctant to assign it a natural explanation, thus
agreeing with the views of Bodin rather than with Wier. See *An Antidote against Atheism*, Book III, Ch. XI, pp. 122–124, in *A Collection of Several Philosophical Writings*. See
also Brann, "The Conflict between Reason and Magic in Seventeenth-Century
England", pp. 113–122.
[127] "Enthusiasmus Triumphatus" (1662), section 67, p. 47.
[128] Ibid., p. 48.

Like Burton, Henry More thus closely associated the medical critique of enthusiasm with a moral critique. Ascribing enthusiasm to
melancholy did not mean relieving the enthusiasts from responsibility for their behaviour.

In the above quotation, however, More also introduced a Neo-
Platonic term into the medical account, the concept of the Astral
Spirit. In fact, he had done so two years earlier, in *An Explanation of
The Grand Mystery of Godliness*. At the end of a chapter discussing Henry
Nicolas, the founder of the Family of Love, More wrote:

> But there is also a more subtil Uncleanness, from which who is not
> free, if he knew his own weakness, he would be ashamed to profess
> himself *perfect*; and that is the Impurity of the *Astral Spirit*, in which is
> the Seat and Dominion of unruly Imagination. Hence are our *Sidereal*
> or *Planet-Strucken* Preachers and Prophets, who being first blasted them-
> selves, blast all others that labour with the like impurity, by their *Fanatick*
> Contagion. Those in whom *Mortification* has not had its full work, nor
> refined the *Inmost* of their natural Complexions, are subject to be smit-
> ten and overcome by such *Enthusiastic storms*, till a more perfect Purifi-
> cation commit them to the safe custody of the *Intellectual Powers*.[129]

The *Astral Spirit* or the *Astral Body* was a Platonic term revived in the
Renaissance designating the aetheric vehicle or starlike garment surrounding the soul which descended from heaven and entered the
individual body. Whereas Platonists like Ficino regarded it as the
mean, the link, between the terrestrial body and the incorporeal soul,
sixteenth century physicians like Fernel tended to identify the Astral
Spirit with the medical "animal spirits".[130] Henry More followed this
same tendency. Though using a Neo-Platonic term, with all its astrological connotations, he nevertheless regarded the Astral Spirit as
part of the body, as the seat of impulses, "misguided Phansy" and
"complexionall Imaginations", clearly distinguishing it from "Eternal
Reason", the rational soul.[131]

---

[129] Henry More, *An Explanation of The Grand Mystery of Godliness*, Book VI, Chapter
XIII, p. 254.
[130] See on this whole subject the important article by Daniel P. Walker, "The
Astral Body in Renaissance Medicine", *Journal of the Warburg and Courtauld Institutes*
21 (1958): 119–133, as well as his book *Spiritual and Demonic Magic from Ficino to
Campanella* (London: Warburg Institute, 1958), esp. pp. 38–39.
[131] *The Grand Mystery of Godliness*, p. 254. In the *Immortality of the Soul*, published the
year before, More had already expounded the three types of vehicles of the soul,
the terrestrial, the aerial and the aetherial, the latter being of a celestial substance.
Yet he stressed the corpuscular nature of all these vehicles, and identified the celestial

The Cambridge Platonist Henry More thus combined Platonic concepts which sought to mediate between body and soul with a Cartesian emphasis on the distinction between body and soul; a Renaissance view which saw some positive functions in the melancholic temperament, with the medical tradition which stressed that melancholy was a disease. Like Burton and Casaubon, More employed this medical tradition for the purposes of religious polemics with the so-called enthusiasts. Yet, as with respect to the problem of enthusiasm itself, More's attitude was fraught with internal tensions. He was deeply influenced by the Platonic tradition of the Renaissance and relied on it in order to stress the vital and spiritual principles in nature as against atheism and the perceived materialism of corpuscularian philosophy (including that of Descartes). Yet in order to defend the established Anglican Church vis-à-vis the threat of enthusiasm, he was driven to adopt a stance very similar, not only to that of Descartes, but to that of a Galenist like Burton, or a conservative humanist like Casaubon.[132] No less significant is the fact that in a period when the traditional medical theory of the humours was increasingly criticised and modified, we find Henry More still adhering to it, although it should be emphasized that he already assigned a greater role to the "animal spirits".[133]

More's indebtness to both Descartes and the Platonic tradition, however, sets him apart from Casaubon in several important ways. In this, as well as in his association with the new Royal Society,

---

substance with the watery moisture of the seed referred to by Aristotle in *De Generatione Animalium* on the one hand, and with the "subtile matter" of Descartes on the other. Ibid., Lib. II, Cap. 14, pp. 258–261. On the concept of spirits and souls in the *Immortality of the Soul* see also Michael Boylan, "Henry More's Space and the Spirit of Nature", *Journal of the History of Philosophy* 18 (1980): esp. pp. 395–96.

[132] As late as 1662 More still tried to keep the balance between the Cartesian-Corpuscular and the Platonic strains in his thought, declaring: "It is therefore very evident to me that the ancient *Pythagorick* or *Judaick Cabbala* did consist of what we now call *Platonisme* and *Cartesianisme*, the latter being as it were the *Body*, the other the *Soul* of that Philosophy; the unhappy disjunction of which has been a great evil to both." (*A Collection of Several Philosophical Writings*, "The Preface General", Sect. 16, p. xviii. See also Brann, "The More-Vaughan Debate", p. 121). It is significant that More also used here, as a metaphor, the distinction between body and soul, thus clearly emphasizing his commitment to that distinction.

[133] In this respect he also followed Sennert. See for example *Medicinae Practicae*, Lib. I, part II, Ch. VIII, in *Opera Omnia*, vol. II, p. 126, where the change in "animal spirits" is presented as the proximate cause of melancholy. I shall return in Chapter 7 below to the concept of "animal spirits", to the changes in the medical thought of that time, and to the impact these changes may have had on the critique of enthusiasm.

More's intellectual leanings are very different from those of the conservative humanist Meric Casaubon, in spite of the common medical arsenal on which both of them rely. These differences come to the fore in the phenomena to which the term "enthusiasm" was ascribed by each of them. Whereas Henry More focused on religious enthusiasm which claimed to have direct divine inspiration, for traditional intellectuals like Casaubon, there was also "philosophical enthusiasm", which claimed to reach innovative and absolute truths by means of contemplation. We should therefore turn now from the medical critique of enthusiasm to the objects against which that critique was directed in the mid-seventeenth century. One of its targets was no other than Descartes himself.

CHAPTER FOUR

DESCARTES AND THE CARTESIAN PHILOSOPHY: A MANIFESTATION OF ENTHUSIASM?

I have examined so far the theological critique of enthusiasm and the emergence of a medical critique of enthusiasm. Both referred primarily to religious enthusiasm, especially to claims of prophecy, to apocalyptic announcements concerning the approaching Day of Judgment, and to pretensions of having direct divine inspiration. By the middle of the seventeenth century, however, the term "enthusiasm" assumed other, broader meanings. It could be applied to intellectual and scientific pursuits besides religious experience proper. The various connotations of the label can tell us much about the intellectual orientation of those who use it, and the changes in those connotations reveal a great deal about the transformations in the intellectual climate of the mid-seventeenth century. This chapter and the following one will attempt to trace some of these transformations.

As we have seen already in the previous chapter, Aristotelian and humanist intellectuals like Casaubon viewed "contemplative philosophy" as an important type of enthusiasm. Under that category, surprisingly enough, appeared also the philosopher René Descartes. Usually regarded today as the founder of modern rationalist philosophy, Descartes was seen by some conservative seventeenth century intellectuals as an enthusiast rather than a rationalist. Borrowing the phrase coined by Richard H. Popkin, who has dealt with what is in some ways the parallel issue of Scepticism, one may say that Descartes was "an enthusiast malgré lui" in the eyes of several of his Aristotelian and humanist opponents.[1] Of course, other accusations were directed against Descartes, such as "scepticism", to which I have just

---

[1] Richard H. Popkin, *The History of Scepticism from Erasmus to Spinoza* (Berkeley, Los Angeles: University of California Press, 1979), chapter X. It should be remembered that whereas in the sixteenth century, humanism was an innovative movement, often distinguished from (and even contrary to) traditional scholastic Aristotelianism, by the seventeenth century, the humanists were defending the "ancients" as against the "moderns", and humanism was regularly combined with Aristotelianism in the curriculum of many of the colleges and universities, both Protestant and Catholic. This fusion, and the conservative character which humanism assumed in the seventeenth

alluded, and even more commonly "atheism". Cartesian philosophy was often suspected of "atheistic" implications, both by Protestants (Reformed as well as Anglican) and by Catholics (especially Jesuits).[2] Nevertheless, alongside this charge, the labels "enthusiasm" and "fanaticism" were assigned to Descartes' philosophy by several English and Continental critics. Such a practice not only indicates the broadening of the term "enthusiasm" in that period. More important, it manifests the intellectual and ideological use of that label, and the special cultural role which the concept performed, as well as the social and cultural locus of the phenomenon to which it was applied.

Descartes' Image as "Rosicrucian" and Enthusiast

The first image of Descartes as an enthusiast was linked to his alleged affiliations with the notorious Rosicrucian order in his early years in Germany. The question of the young Descartes' association with "Rosicrucianism" has been reopened recently.[3] Here, I shall focus

---

century is clearly manifest in the work of Meric Casaubon, especially if we compare him to his father Isaac.

[2] On the charges of concealed "atheism" uttered by Reformed theologians against Cartesian philosophy see Ernst Bizer, "Die reformierten Orthodoxie und der Cartesianismus", *Zeitschrift für Theologie und Kirche* 55 (1958): 306–372. On the Anglican critique, especially that of Henry More, see Marjorie Nicolson, "The Early Stages of Cartesianism in England", *Studies in Philology* 26 (1929): 356–74, and the recent article by A. Gabbey, "Philosophia Cartesiana Triumphata: Henry More (1646–1671)", in T.M. Lennon et al., eds., *Problems of Cartesianism* (Kingston: McGill-Queens University Press, 1982), pp. 171–250. Samuel Parker similarly warned against the atheistic implications of Descartes' philosophy in his *Disputationes de Deo et Providentia Divina*, London, 1678. Scottish Presbyterians were also making the same charges. See for example Alexander Pitcarnius, *Compendiaria et perfacilis Physiologiae Idea, Aristotelicae forte conformior . . . Una cum anatome Cartesianismi in qua Cartesii speculationes metaphysicae examini subjiciuntur* (London, 1676), Section I, Art. 1, sect. 1. On the Jesuit critique of Descartes accusing him of atheism see Gaston Sortais, "Le Cartésianisme chez les Jésuites français au XVIIe et au XVIIIe siècle", *Archives de Philosophie*, vol. 6, no. 3 (1929). For one such typical argument concerning the atheistic implications of Cartesian philosophy see [Ant. Rochon], *Lettre d'un Philosophe à un Cartésien de ses Amis* (Paris: Published by le Père Paradies, 1685), pp. 50–62.

[3] See William R. Shea, *The Magic of Numbers and Motion: The Scientific Career of René Descartes* (Canton, MA.: History of Science Publications U.S.A., 1991), chapter 5, as well as his earlier article in *Annali Dell'Istituto E Museo Di Storia Della Scienza di Firenze*, vol. 4, no. 2 (1979), pp. 29–47. Shea argues that there is enough circumstantial evidence to show that young Descartes was seriously interested in the Rosicrucians and was deeply influenced by the hermetic literature. A similar argument was made by Frances A. Yates, *The Rosicrucian Enlightenment* (London: Routledge and Kegan Paul, 1972), pp. 113–117. The sceptical view concerning these links was stated by

my attention not on the actual historical links between Descartes and the Rosicrucians, but on the *image* of Descartes in the eyes of his opponents, his image as a "Rosicrucian", "mystic" and "enthusiast". Such an image, perhaps, is almost as important historically as the real influence which the "hermetic" tradition might have had on the development of Descartes' thought.

According to Adrien Baillet, Descartes' seventeenth century biographer, Descartes was accused of being a member of the Rosicrucian order as early as 1623, when he came back from Germany to Paris.[4] Unfortunately, not much of the evidence concerning this impression of Descartes has survived, but the scanty written records indicate that it may have been quite widespread already during his lifetime. The charges accusing Descartes of "enthusiasm" and of affiliations with the Rosicrucians, seem to have been prevalent in the 1640's and 1650's, re-emerging in the late 1680's and the 1690's. They appeared first in the famous debates held in Utrecht in the early 1640's concerning Descartes' philosophy. These debates were instigated by a series of theses written by Henricus Regius and defended in the period between June 1640 and December 1641. Regius, a professor of medicine in Utrecht, was one of Descartes' early supporters. He was attacked mainly by Gisbert Voet (Voetius), the renowned theologian who was also Rector of the University at that time, as well as by his disciple (then already teaching in Groningen), Martin Schoock (Schoockius).[5] In theses published in December 1641 in response to

Henri Gouhier in his classic book, *Les premières pensées de Descartes* (Paris: Vrin, 1958), pp. 117–141. See also Auguste Georges-Berthier, "Descartes et les Rose-Croix", *Revue de synthèse* 18 (1939): 9–30; Gustave Cohen, *Ecrivains français en Hollande dans la première moitié du XVIIe siècle* (Paris: Champion, 1920), pp. 402–409; C. Louise Thijssen-Schoute, *Nederlands Cartesianisme* (Amsterdam: N.V. Noord-Hollandsche Uitgevers, 1954), pp. 230–232, and pp. 662–663 (of the French summary by Paul Dibon).

[4] Adrien Baillet, *La vie de Monsieur Des-Cartes* (Paris, 1691), book II, chapter II, in vol. I, pp. 87–92, see esp. p. 91. (A modern reprint edition of this text has been published by Garland, New York and London, 1987, in the series "The Philosophy of Descartes" edited by Willis Doney.) In making this point, Baillet relied on the Oratorian Nicholas Poisson to whose work, *Commentaire ou Remarques sur la Méthode de René Descartes* (Vendôme, 1671) I shall return below. See also Charles Adam and Paul Tannery, *Oeuvres de Descartes* (Paris: Vrin, 1957–58), vol. 10, pp. 196–97. Henceforward I shall refer to this edition of Descartes' works as AT.

[5] On this episode see Gustave Cohen, *Ecrivains français en Hollande*, pp. 535–567, and Cornelia Serrurier, *Descartes, L'homme et le penseur* (Paris: P.U.F.; Amsterdam: Editions Français, 1951), pp. 121–137. On Martin Schoock and his philosophy teaching in Groningen see Paul Dibon, *La Philosophie néerlandaise au siècle d'or: L'enseignement philosophique dans les universités à l'époque pré-cartésienne, 1575–1650* (Amsterdam: Elsevier, 1954), pp. 180–88.

those of Regius, Voetius referred, among other things, to the Cartesian programme of the mathematization of physics. As Voetius understood it, Descartes' alleged ascription of motion and physical efficiency to quantities and figures clearly savoured of magic.[6] The only alternative to the traditional physics of substantial forms seemed to him to be the magical and Pythagorean view of nature.[7] Two years later, in *Admiranda Methodus Novae Philosophiae Renati Descartes*, published officially by Voetius but written in fact by his protégé Martin Schoock, the accusations were even more explicit. There, Descartes' claim to find the key to all knowledge in geometry and algebra was likened to the attempts of scientists with a mystical orientation such as Faulhaber to decipher the mysteries of the Scriptures with the help of the mathematical sciences.[8]

---

[6] ". . . Cum quantitati et figurae tribuitur efficientia et motus, qui formis earumque qualitatibus activis tribui solet, videndum ne aliquando adolescentes imprudenter per consequentiam admittant axioma illud Magicum, ab omni theologia et philosophia Christiana hactenus rejectum: *Quantitatis et figurae aliqua est efficacia, eaque aut per se aut cum aliis concurrit tanquam activum transmutationis principium.*" Quoted from the tenth article of the second thesis. These theses were defended by Lambert van den Waterlaet, under the presidency of Voetius (who also added an Appendix and Corrolaria) on December 23rd and 24th, 1641, in response to theses defended under Regius on December 8th. They were ultimately published in *Testimonium Academiae Ultraiectinae, et Narratio Historica qua defensae, qua exterminatae novae Philosophiae* (Utrecht, 1643), pp. 41–42. The whole text is on pp. 36–57. See also AT, vol. III, pp. 459–464, 487–491, 511–519. The above text is quoted on p. 513.

[7] Descartes dismissed this argument with derision. In his letter to Regius of January 1642 he wrote: "Eodem titulo Geometria et Mechanicae omnes essent reijciendae; quod quam ridiculum et a ratione alienum nemo non videt. Nec hoc sine risu possem praetermittere, sed non suadeo." AT, vol. III, p. 504. For a French translation see Geneviève Rodis-Lewis, *Lettres à Regius* ("Bibliothèque des Textes Philosophiques", Paris: Vrin, 1959). The relevant sentences read as follows: "Donc il faudroit rejeter la géométrie et toute la mécanique. On sent le ridicule de cela, et rien n'est plus déraisonnable. Je ne pourrois jamais passer cet article sans rire [un peu à ses depens]; mais je ne vous le conseille pas." Ibid., p. 89.

[8] "Ne quid enim dicam de Faulhabero, aliisque, qui scientiae hujus subsidio, Caballistarum instar, in Prophetis ac Apocalypsi, mysteria uni adhuc Deo nota rimari instituerunt, in circulis passim audire est ex illius Professoribus, eam viam ad omnes alias scientias, judicem reliquarum disciplinarum, cynosuram veritatis, judicii rectricem, humani ingenii perfectricem, et quid non esse? . . .". Martin Schoockius, *Admiranda Methodus Novae Philosophiae Renati Descartes* (Utrecht, 1643), chapter 8, pp. 128–129, quoted also in AT, vol. 8/2 p. 152, note a. On Schoock as the author of the *Admiranda Methodus* see Dibon, *La philosophie néerlandaise*, p. 182. Johann Faulhaber (1580–1635) was a noted mathematician who founded his own mathematical school at Ulm. He also had obvious mystical and alchemical interests: he attempted to calculate the date of the end of the world on the basis of the books of Daniel and Revelation, and was a believer in the Rosicrucian order. The young Descartes was indeed in contact with him and apparently studied with him in 1620. See the article on Faulhaber by Paul A. Kirchvogel in the *D.S.B.*, vol. IV, pp. 549–553.

The chief significance of the *Admiranda Methodus* for our purpose, however, is that it explicitly linked Descartes with "enthusiasm". Already the Preface declared that the book will prove "that this new method in philosophy leads straight not only to scepticism, but also to enthusiasm, atheism and frenzy".[9] The fourth part of the book was indeed devoted to these issues, its first chapter showing that Descartes' new method led to scepticism, the second, that it led to enthusiasm, and the third, that it ended up in atheism.[10] I shall return below to a closer analysis of the arguments of the chapter on enthusiasm, but the way in which "enthusiasm" was coupled with "scepticism", "atheism" and "frenzy" is itself highly telling. Descartes' philosophical method was castigated on all these accounts and labelled with all these epithets simultaneously, contradictory as they may seem to us.

The issue of Descartes' links with Rosicrucianism was also raised by Schoock in the introduction to the *Admiranda Methodus*. True, Schoock rejected the allegations that Descartes was a member of the Rosicrucian order, because, unlike them, he was most ambitious and rather than keep silent as they did, he wished to get himself known in all corners of the earth.[11] The hostile and ironic tone is unmistakable here. Nevertheless, if not one of the Rosicrucians, Descartes was clearly similar to them in his constant wandering from one place to the other, and in his tendency to live in hiding. Whether that tendency could be explained on the basis of misanthropy, bad conscience or some mental delusion, Schoock could not tell, but the image of Descartes is significant: He is the outsider, the "liminal" to use the terminology of the late anthropologist Victor Turner, the one who does not belong to any one place and is not an integral part of any society.[12] No less significant is one possible explanation for Descartes' behaviour which Schoock mentions, that of mental delusion,

---

[9] ". . . novam hanc philosophandi methodum, recta non tantum ad Scepticismum, verum Enthusiasmum quoque, Atheismum ac phrenesim ducere." *Admiranda Methodus*, Praefatio.

[10] Chapter II in Part IV, entitled "Eadem Methodus recta ad Enthusiasmus ducit", is on pp. 255–261 of *Admiranda Methodus*.

[11] "Cui suspicioni—Schoock says concerning the suspicion that Descartes was a member of the Rosicrucian order—et ego non invitus accederem, nisi scirem hominem ambitiosissimum velle nomen suum (quod studiose dicti Fratres silentio premi curabant) apertis tibiis per omnes orbis angulos decantari." *Admiranda Methodus*, Preface, pp. 14–15. Also quoted in AT, vol. 8/2, p. 142, note b.

[12] Victor Turner, *Dreams, Fields, and Metaphors: Symbolic Action in Human Society* (Ithaca, N.Y.: Cornell U.P., 1974), especially chapters 6, 7.

once again, an account typically given of enthusiasts in that period.[13]

Across the Channel, in England, it was even easier to conflate the new ideas of Descartes with the alchemical, Paracelsian and mystical notions of the so-called "enthusiasts", since some of the latter were making precisely that same link themselves, referring almost in the same breath to Paracelsus, Bacon and Descartes.[14] It is hence hardly surprising that an Anglican conservative humanist such as Meric Casaubon regarded Cartesianism as one further manifestation of "enthusiasm." As we have seen above, Casaubon had already mentioned Descartes in 1656 together with mystical theologians and enthusiastic groups such as the Alumbrados in Spain or the Quakers in England.[15] Casaubon did not link Descartes with the Rosicrucians, however, nor did he refer to Descartes' life and personality as Schoock had done. Rather, he focused on the Cartesian method, associating it "with this *Mystical Theologie*, against which I think too much cannot be said."[16] I shall return later to some of the reasons behind this link, but at this stage it is worth noting one significant allusion: "If he would have dealt ingeneously—Casaubon says ironically concerning Descartes' new method—he might in two or three lines, that had contained the names but of three or four herbs, have prescribed a farre shorter way."[17] Whereas for Voetius, Descartes' programme for the mathematization of nature seemed similar to that of the Cabbalists and mystics, for Casaubon, the Cartesian method seemed similar not only to that of the mystics but, in its presumed shortcuts, quite like the herbal medicine practised by quack physicians. Indeed, in a later text, *On Learning*, written apparently in 1667, which remained in manuscript until recently, Casaubon compared Descartes to other reformers of method such as Raymond Lull, Peter Ramus, the mystical theologian Johannes Trithemius, and finally, the educational reformer Comenius, all of them searching for shortcuts to the attainment of knowledge and seeing in method the key to such knowledge.[18]

---

[13] See Chapters 2 and 3 above.
[14] See for example, John Webster, *Academiarum Examen* (London, 1653), pp. 76–78. This text was published by Allen G. Debus in *Science and Education in the Seventeenth Century: The Webster—Ward Debate* (London: Macdonald, New York: Elsevier, 1970).
[15] Meric Casaubon, *A Treatise Concerning Enthusiasme* (Gainsville, Florida: Scholars' Facsimiles and Reprints, 1970), pp. 172–173.
[16] Ibid., p. 173.
[17] Ibid., p. 172.
[18] This text was partly published by Michael R.G. Spiller, *"Concerning Natural Experimental Philosophie." Meric Casaubon and the Royal Society* (Martinus Nijhoff: The Hague, 1980), Appendix II. See esp. pp. 202–203, 209–210. The whole text (which

In the next generation, between 1660 and 1690, the ideological campaign against Descartes focused mostly on his alleged "atheism" rather than his "enthusiasm".[19] This was probably the result of the publication of the works of Hobbes and the *Tractatus Theologico-Politicus* of Spinoza, both considered disciples of Descartes.[20] True, the label "enthusiasm" was sometimes resorted to, but mostly, it seems, under the influence of Schoock's *Admiranda methodus* rather than as an argument developed independently.[21] Similarly, the specific Rosicrucian connection was not seriously taken up by Descartes' critics, although this dubious reputation seems to have been quite widely attached to him. In 1670, one of his defenders, the Oratorian Nicolas-Joseph Poisson, felt the need to refute that charge systematically in his *Remarques sur la méthode de Descartes*, a text to which we shall return.[22]

---

is at the Bodleian library, Ms. Rawlinson, D. 36.1) was printed in Spiller's B. Litt. dissertation, "Conservative Opinion and the New Science, 1630–1680: With Special Reference to the Life and Works of Meric Casaubon" (Oxford, 1968). The treatise was addressed to Francis Turner (1638–1700), later bishop of Ely. It should be stressed, however, that this type of criticism, raised by Casaubon against Descartes, the educational reformers, and—as we shall see in the next chapter—the new scientists, was part of a broader attack on what he saw as the decay of learning and the philistine tendencies of his time in general. See M. Hunter's Essay Review of Spiller's book in *Annals of Science* 39 (1982): 189–190.

[19] It should be emphasized that we are not dealing here with the strictly philosophical controversy raised by Cartesianism in that period, but rather with the labels ascribed to Descartes' philosophy. On the former subject, see among other studies, A. Watson, *The Downfall of Cartesianism, 1673–1712* (The Hague: Martinus Nijhoff, 1966).

[20] On the campaign against Descartes in the 1670's, especially in Holland and France see F. Bouillier, *Histoire de la philosophie cartésienne* (Paris: Delgrave et Cie., 1868; Slatkine Reprints, 1970), vol. I, chapters XXII, XXVI, XXVII, and Edward G. Ruestow, *Physics at Seventeenth and Eighteenth-Century Leiden. Philosophy and the New Science in the University* (The Hague: Martinus Nijhoff, 1973), pp. 73–78. See also H.J. Martin, *Livre, pouvoirs et société à Paris au XVIIe siècle* (Geneva: Droz, 1969), pp. 877–878. For the parallel debates in England, especially Henry More's polemics against Descartes see Marjorie Nicolson, "The Early Stages of Cartesianism in England", and Alan Gabbey, "Philosophia Cartesiana Triumphata: Henry More (1646–1671)".

[21] An example of such an implicit reference is a dissertation defended by Georgius Sebastian Kraus in Altdorff in 1677 under the presidency of Johann Christoph Sturm, *De Cartesianis et Cartesianismo Brevis Dissertatio* (Altdorff, March 31, 1677), pp. 18–19, where Descartes is accused of scepticism, enthusiasm and atheism, in the same manner and order as Schoock had declared. This dissertation may be found in the British Library. Sturm was in fact an experimental scientist, the founder of the *Collegium Curiosum sive Experimentale*, and the teacher of J.G. Doppelmayr. See *D.S.B.*, vol. IV, p. 166, article on Doppelmayr, and *Allgemeine Deutsche Biographie*, vol. 37, pp. 39–40.

[22] Nicolas-Joseph Poisson, *Commentaire, ou Remarques sur la méthode de Descartes* (Vendôme, 1671), pp. 30–33. A modern facsimile edition has been published by Garland, New York and London, 1987, in the series "The Philosophy of Descartes", ed. by W. Doney. The text is also quoted *in extenso* in AT, vol. X, pp. 196–197,

Descartes' alleged "enthusiasm" again became a common theme
of anti-Cartesian polemics in the 1690's. The prevalence of this label
in connection with Descartes is clearly reflected in a satirical work
published anonymously in 1690 by the Jesuit father Gabriel Daniel
and entitled *Voyage du monde de Descartes.*[23] That work, aimed principally at the sharp Cartesian distinction between body and soul, related in a satirical fashion the voyage of the disembodied souls of the
narrator, of Mersenne, and of another old friend of Descartes in the
upper spheres. On their way to visit Descartes in the third heaven,
they meet the souls of other philosophers, among them Aristotle, and
later on Voetius, who serves as Aristotle's secretary. The latter suggests to them a treaty of accommodation and cessation of arms between the followers of Aristotle and the disciples of Descartes (clearly
reflecting here the philosophical opinions of Gabriel Daniel himself).
One of the articles of that treaty stipulates that the Cartesians will
refer to Aristotle with more respect, whereas the Aristotelians will
refrain from calling Descartes "Enthusiast", "Madman", "Heretick"
or "Atheist"—all of these evidently labels commonly used by the
opponents of Descartes at that time.[24]

---

note a. On Poisson see the article in the *Biographie universelle ancienne et moderne*,
vol. 33, pp. 586–587, and the three part article by L'abbé Clément, "Le Cartésianisme
à Vendôme: Le Père Nicolas-Joseph Poisson (1637–1710)", *Bulletin de la Société
Archéologique scientifique et littéraire du Vendômois* 37 (1898): 258–275; 38 (1899): 23–46;
164–175.

[23] The work was translated two years later into English by T. Taylor of Magdalen
College, Oxford, and dedicated to his friend James Ludford of Ansely, *A Voyage to
the World of Cartesius* (London, 1692). Father Daniel (1649–1728) entered the Jesuit
Order in 1667, taught rhetoric, philosophy and theology and was later a librarian in
a Jesuit house in Paris, but became particularly famous as an historian. He received
the title of *historiographe de France* from Louis XIV, and his *Histoire de France* was
highly regarded by Voltaire. See Augustin de Backer and Carlos Sommervogel,
Bibliothèque des écrivains de la Compagnie de Jésus (Liège, 1853–1861), vol. II, cols. 1795–
1816, G. Sortais, "Le Cartésianisme chez les Jésuites français au XVIIe et au XVIII
siècle", *Archives de Philosophie* 6 (1929): 56–62, and Vernon J. Bourke, "An Illustration
of the Attitude of the Early French Jesuits towards Cartesianism" in *Cartesio: nel terzo
centenario del "Discorso del Metodo"*, a special supplement to vol. 19 of *Rivista di Filosofia
Neo-Scolastica*, July 1937, pp. 129–137, which includes a summary of the main arguments of the *Voyage*. As we shall presently see, Daniel was not a committed Aristotelian, but was rather interested in a synthesis of ancient and modern Philosophy
(*Philosophia Nova Antiqua*).

[24] [Gabriel Daniel], *A Voyage to the World of Cartesius*, p. 135, and in general, pp. 119–
155. In the Latin translation of that text, *Iter per mundum Cartesii* (Amsterdam, 1694)
the term for "enthusiast" is *fanaticus* (p. 140). Daniel also hinted at the similarity
between Cartesianism and magic. At a certain point he had Descartes' friend say to
the narrator: "you see the *Cartesian Philosophy* teaches without any Sin, what *Apollonius*

Father Daniel did not know of Descartes' dreams of 1619, and did not refer to his Rosicrucian interests. Just one year later however, Baillet published extracts from Descartes' early writings in his *Vie de Monsieur Descartes*, including the *Cogitationes Privata* and the *Olympica* which contained the description of his dreams of 1619.[25] While Baillet pointedly rejected the notion of Descartes as a member of the Rosicrucian order, his *Vie de Mons. Descartes* included enough material to give new life to the association of Descartes with enthusiasm in general and Rosicrucianism in particular.[26] It was put forward most systematically in the satirical work by Bishop Huet, *Nouveaux Mémoires pour servir à l'histoire du Cartésianisme*, published anonymously in 1692,

---

Thyanaeus and many other *Magicians* could not do, without first giving themselves to the Devil." *A Voyage to the World of Cartesius*, p. 50.

[25] A. Baillet, *La Vie de Monsieur Descartes* (Paris, 1691). An abridged edition appeared in 1692, *La Vie de Mons. Descartes . . . réduite en abrégé* (1692, 2nd ed. 1693) and that edition was translated into English the following year as *The Life of Monsieur Des Cartes containing the History of his Philosophy and Works. As also The Most Remarkable Things that Befell him during the Whole Course of his Life*, tr. from the French by S.R. (London, 1693). The *Olympica* was among Descartes' papers in the possession of Clerselier, who received them from his brother-in-law, the diplomat Chanut. On Clerselier's death in 1684 they were bequeathed to the abbé Jean-Baptiste Legrand who instigated Baillet to write a biography of Descartes, and provided him with Descartes' papers, including the *Olympica*. Extracts from this text, as well as other papers, were also copied by Leibniz when he visited Clerselier in Paris in 1675–76. The original texts (with which Poisson was also acquainted) have unfortunately been lost, but Leibniz's extracts are now among his papers in the Royal Library in Hanover. See also AT, vol. I, p. xlvii; Leonard J. Wang, "The Life and Works of Adrien Baillet", Columbia Ph.D. diss., February, 1955; Gregor Sebba, " Adrien Baillet and the Genesis of His *Vie de M. Des-Cartes*", in Thomas M. Lennon, et al., *Problems of Cartesianism*, pp. 9–60, and most recently, John R. Cole, *The Olympian Dreams and Youthful Rebellion of René Descartes* (Urbana and Chicago: University of Illinois Press, 1992), especially chapters 1 and 2. Cole's book is essentially a psycho-historical analysis of Descartes' dreams, claiming the historicity, validity and significance of the *Olympica* for the development of his personality and thought. Cole is less interested in the image of Descartes in the eyes of his detractors. He refers in passing to Bishop Huet, but not to the historical significance of Descartes' image as an "enthusiast".

[26] Baillet, *Vie de Mons. Descartes*, Livre II, Ch. II, pp. 87–92. Baillet's famous account of Descartes' dreams of 1619 is in the previous chapter, pp. 81–86. There, he quotes Descartes himself from the *Olympica*, referring to his "enthusiasm", clearly using this term in a positive sense: "Il nous apprend que le dixiéme (sic!) de Novembre mil six cent dix-neuf, s'étant couché *tout rempli de son enthousiasme*, et tout occupé de la pensée *d'avoir trouvé ce jour là les fondemens de la science admirable*, il eut trois songes consécutifs en une seule nuit, qu'il s'imagina ne pouvoir être venus que d'en haut." (Ibid., p. 81, see also AT, vol. X, p. 181.) Later on, Baillet quoted Descartes as referring to "le Génie qui excitoit en luy l'enthousiasme dont il se sentoit le cerveau échauffé depuis quelques jours, luy avoit prédit ces songes avant que de se mettre au lit, et que l'esprit humain n'y avoit aucune part." (Ibid., p. 85, and AT, vol. X, p. 186.)

with a second edition in 1711.[27] That work consisted of a piece of
fiction according to which Descartes did not die in Sweden in 1650,
but rather feigned his sickness and death, while in fact he slipped
away to Lapland where a devoted group of disciples were waiting
for him. He also possessed the secret of prolonging his life up to five
hundred years. In Huet's work, Descartes tells his friend Chanut, the
French ambassador to Sweden at whose residence he lived in
Stockholm, the story of his life. Descartes dwells particularly on a
detailed relation of his dreams in 1619, as well as on his relationship
with and admission to the Rosicrucian order. Huet exploited to the
utmost Baillet's account of Descartes' dreams, thus clearly depicting
him as a self-confessed enthusiast who claimed to have had direct
divine inspiration.[28] It is worth noting that Huet let Chanut put forward a physiological explanation of these dreams:

> Monsieur Chanut l'interrompit à ce discours, pour luy demander com-
> ment il avoit reconnu que toutes ces visions étoient des révélations du
> Ciel, et non pas des songes ordinaires, excitez peut-être par les fumées
> du tabac, ou de la bière, ou de la Mélancolie.[29]

In mentioning melancholy, Huet was clearly alluding to the medical
account of enthusiasm commonly given in the seventeenth century
by its opponents. As for tobacco, it also played a major role in Gabriel

---

[27] I shall use the 1711 edition of this text. [P.–D. Huet], *Nouveaux Mémoires pour
servir à l'histoire du Cartésianisme*. The work was written as a sequel to his *Censura
Philosophiae Cartesianae* (1689) and in reaction to P.S. Régis' response to that book,
Réponse au livre qui a pour titre "P.D. Huetti Censura Philosophiae Cartesianae" (Paris, 1691).
The *Nouveaux Mémoires* was indeed addressed to Regis. It is worth noting, however,
that in his youth, while studying at Caen, Huet was quite attracted to Cartesianism.
See *Memoirs of the Life of Peter Daniel Huet, written by himself*, tr. from Latin by John
Aikin, vol. I (London, 1810), pp. 29–30. There Huet says "I long wandered in the
mazes of this reasoning delirium (*ibid.*, p. 30). For a short article on Bishop Huet
(1630–1721), focusing mainly on his scepticism, see Richard H. Popkin, "Huet, Pierre-
Daniel", *The Encyclopedia of Philosophy*, vol. 4, pp. 67–68. See also Bouillier, *Histoire de
la philosophie cartésienne*, vol. I, chapter XXVIII.
[28] *Nouveaux Mémoires*, pp. 28–29.
[29] Ibid., p. 29. It should be noted that Baillet himself mentioned the possibility
that since it was St. Martin's Eve, Descartes "auroit bû le soir avant que de se
coucher". Descartes, however, explicitly denied it. (*Vie de Mons. Descartes*, p. 85.) In
the English translation the text also alluded to the possibility "that he had been a
little Cracked-brain'd", but there is no explicit mention of melancholy, nor of its
effects. (*The life of Monsieur Descartes*, p. 36.) Baillet, on his part, refrained from com-
mitting himself and began the next sentence with "Quoy qu'il en soit . . ." (*Vie de
Mons. Descartes*, p. 85). In the English translation the reservation is even stronger—
"whatever was the matter with him, I cannot tell" (*Life of Monsieur Descartes*, p. 36).

Daniel's satire two years earlier. It was by sniffing tobacco, mixed with a certain type of herb, that Descartes and his friends could dissociate their souls from their bodies.[30]

No less significant and ironic is the response Huet put in Descartes' mouth, a response which vaguely resorts to his method as a means of verifying such outlandish truths: "C'est en quoi cette méthode est admirable, répliqua le Philosophe, de déterrer des veritez si éloignées de la raison humaine."[31] Descartes then proceeds to his encounter with the Rosicrucians. Departing from Baillet's account, Huet's Descartes did indeed succeed in forming contact with the Rosicrucians and climbed fast in the hierarchy of that society, ultimately becoming one of its inspectors. The consequences were clear:

> J'ay renoncé au mariage, j'ay mené une vie errante; j'ay cherché l'obscurité et la retraite; j'ay quitté l'étude de la Géométrie, et des autres sciences, pour m'appliquer uniquement à la Physique, à la Médecine, à la Chymie, à la Cabale et aux autres sciences secrettes.[32]

So far from being the rationalist philosopher, Descartes is depicted by Huet as a typical Paracelsian enthusiast. Of course, he outwardly denied his links with the Rosicrucians throughout his life, as Chanut himself reminds him in reaction to his confession. But Descartes' explanation for this is clear:

> M'eussiez-vous conseillé de l'avoüer, et ne connoissez-vous pas le peuple? Tout le monde m'auroit regardé comme un sorcier; et d'ailleurs ne viens-je pas de vous dire que les Statuts de la Secte défendent aux confrères de se faire connoître?[33]

The theme of disguise in Descartes' life was central to Huet's description. The work was obviously satirical and cannot be taken seriously as historical evidence for Descartes' real links with the Rosicrucians but it is nevertheless significant as an expression of the image of Descartes in the eyes of his opponents. For the sceptical humanist Huet, Descartes' alleged association with the Rosicrucians served to highlight the esoteric nature of his method, the invisible and disguised nature of his career, and indeed, Descartes' own credulity. He also depicted him as a founder of a religious sect, rather

---

[30] Gabriel Daniel, *A Voyage to the World of Cartesius*, especially pp. 21–22.
[31] *Nouveaux Mémoires*, p. 30.
[32] Ibid., p. 32.
[33] Ibid., pp. 32–33.

than of a philosophical school. Thus, he hoped that his disciple Regius would become "le premier martyr du Cartésianisme" but instead, Regius turned out to be its "premier schismatique." Indeed, Huet ironically had Descartes say about Regius "cet insolent me traita à son tour de visionnaire et d'enthousiaste."[34] The term "enthusiasm" once again assumes here a negative connotation. For Huet, Cartesianism was not a public and rational philosophy which could serve as an alternative to enthusiasm, but rather, another version of "enthusiastic" philosophy which was secretive, disguised, individualistic and yet highly authoritarian. In his claims to discover the ultimate truth and the key to all knowledge Descartes was as pretentious as any of the magicians and alchemists.

A few years later, an English Catholic, John Sergeant, expressed a similar view of Descartes, also relying on Baillet's biography. Like Huet, Sergeant did so in the course of a debate with a Cartesian, in his case, the Franciscan Antoine Le Grand.[35] Yet, whereas Huet was a sceptic who held a fideistic position on religious matters, Sergeant was essentially an Aristotelian and believed that an updated Aristotelian philosophy was the best response to the sceptical challenge. Sergeant focused his critique on Descartes' method, and I shall return to the epistemological issues involved in that critique. He mainly rejected Descartes' exclusive reliance on "ideas", but the way he characterized this epistemological approach is significant:

> Now, Sir, This looks like a kind of Rosycrucianism in Philosophy, to build all your Doctrine on *Ideas*, and yet keep the *Secret* among yourselves, and *conceal* from us *what* those same ideas *are*.[36]

It is in this context that Sergeant could refer to Baillet's publication

---

[34] Ibid., p. 18.

[35] J.S. [John Sergeant], *Non Ultra, or a Letter to a Learned Cartesian* (London, 1698). Like Huet, Sergeant was linked for some time with Bossuet and his circle. On Sergeant see the article in the *D.N.B.*, vol. 17, pp. 1189–1191, and John Bossy, *The English Catholic Community, 1570–1850* (London: Darton, Longman and Todd, 1975), pp. 67–69 on his role in the English Catholic church in that generation. Antoine Le Grand (1629–1699) was a Franciscan friar from Douay who was sent to England on the English mission and settled in Oxfordshire. He was an ardent advocate of the Cartesian method and was involved in a long debate with Sergeant to which we shall have occasion to return. Sergeant's *Non Ultra* was just one text in that debate. On Le Grand see *D.N.B.*, vol. 11, pp. 862–863, and John K. Ryan, "Anthony Legrand (1629–1699): Franciscan and Cartesian", *The New Scholasticism* 9 (1935): 226–250, which includes a bibliographical summary of his writings.

[36] Sergeant, *Non Ultra*, p. 6.

of extracts from the *Olympica* to fortify his claim that Descartes was in fact an enthusiast. Looking at the 1619 dreams—as indeed Baillet had done—from the perspective of Descartes' method (published almost twenty years later), Sergeant saw them as the result of Descartes' attempt to free himself from dependence on the senses. In a tract written in 1699 and entitled *Raillery defeated by Calm Reason* he wrote:

> Whence, I took notice of that [method] . . . of *Cartesius* who, (as the Writer of his Life tells us,) by endeavouring to bring himself to question all the Certainty he had receiv'd from his senses, fell into Fits of *Enthusiasm*.[37]

Although in 1698–99, in response to Le Grand's protests, Sergeant tended to restrict his accusation, denying the claim that Descartes was *habitually* a fanatic, his earlier *Method to Science* clearly implied, as we shall see below, that Cartesian epistemology in general savoured of "enthusiasm."[38] For a Catholic Aristotelian like Sergeant, Cartesianism was a manifestation of enthusiasm not so much in its wish to achieve absolute and sure knowledge, as it had been for Huet, but in the way by which it claimed to achieve that knowledge, relying exclusively on innate ideas. Sergeant was less concerned than Huet with Descartes' life and personality, but for both of them, Cartesianism was individualistic, secretive, pretentious and hence, linked with enthusiasm, and indeed with Rosicrucianism. And both relied on Baillet's biography to strengthen their case in depicting Descartes as an "enthusiast."

One final reference to Descartes as an "enthusiast" should be mentioned—that by Jonathan Swift in his famous *A Tale of a Tub*, first published in 1704. I shall return to this text below, but it is worth stressing at this point that Swift was clearly influenced by previous critics of Descartes, especially Casaubon, in regarding him as an enthusiast and moreover, as mentally deranged.[39]

---

[37] John Sergeant, *Raillery defeated by Calm Reason: or the New Cartesian Method of Arguing and Answering Expos'd. In a Letter to all Lovers of Science, Candour and Civility* (London, 1699), p. 14. The text (and the quotation above) was also directed against Malebranche. Sergeant was here defending his *Method to Science* to which I shall presently refer, a work fiercely attacked by Le Grand.

[38] John Sergeant, *The Method to Science* (London, 1696). The limiting of this accusation is most explicit in a letter appended at the end of *Non Ultra* of 1698: "The settling this Later Method . . . (that we must deny all our Knowledge of Natural Truths, had by our senses) had confessedly lost *Cartesius* his Wits, for some time." *Non Ultra*, pp. 108–109.

[39] See Michael R.G. Spiller, "The Idol of the Stove: The Background to Swift's

The Epistemological Critique of Cartesianism as "Enthusiasm"

Up till now I have traced Descartes' image as an "enthusiast" and his alleged links to Rosicrucianism as expressed by his opponents. Whether taken seriously or not (let alone, whether true or not), these allegations indicate that for conservative thinkers in the seventeenth century, Cartesianism, so far from being a response to the challenge of enthusiasm, was in fact one of its manifestations. The term "conservative critics" by which I have designated the opponents of Descartes is very broad, of course, and as such, somewhat hollow. They were a heterogeneous group, from different countries, from various religious camps (Reformed, Anglican, Catholic), spreading over two generations in time. Yet, disparate as the group was, it had important common characteristics. Socially speaking, all of them regarded themselves as defending established institutions, whether the Universities, the Church or religious orders such as the Jesuits. They associated Cartesian philosophy with enthusiasm primarily because they viewed it as a threat to those institutions. Intellectually speaking they were humanists, Aristotelians, and sometimes, as in the case of Gabriel Daniel, eclectics who wished to achieve a synthesis between traditional philosophy and the new one. There were also common themes in their critique of Cartesianism, and it is to these themes, and the specific reasons behind the association of Cartesianism with enthusiam that we should now turn. I shall try and examine what they tell us about the epistemological, social and psychological implications of Cartesianism, and about the connotations of the term "enthusiasm" itself.

The humanist and Aristotelian critics of Descartes were conscious of the fact that the "Cartesian revolution" was—among other things—a consequence of and a response to a crisis of humanistic scholarship and traditional scholasticism in the early seventeenth century. Meric Casaubon interpreted that crisis as the dialectical result of the very flowering of humanistic scholarship which had brought about an "explosion of knowledge." As might be expected, he regarded the generation of Scaliger, Lipsius and his own father, Isaac Casaubon, as that in which humanistic learning reached its peak:

> It is my opinion that learning . . . in this last age, some three or fowre score years agoe, was brought to that perfection, as noe other age of

Criticism of Descartes", *Review of English Studies* 25 (1974): 15–24.

the world ever saw it in . . . But no wonder if it did not hold long. It was come to that height, that for a man to make himselfe considerable (besydes competent witt and judgment, without which nothing can be done, and are not, to that degree, every mans happines) soe much labour, soe much industrie was required, as is enough to fright any whom God hath not endowed with extraordinarie courage, and strength of bodie withall.

Consequently—

Any new project, promising new discoveries of a shorter way, must needs be very acceptable unto most.[40]

As we have seen above, Casaubon mentioned the attempts of Ramus, Lull, Trithemius and Comenius to devise a new method which would provide a short-cut to knowledge. He focused his attention, however, on Descartes' *Discourse on Method* which he clearly put in the context of the mystical and Pansophic reactions to humanism.[41] Indeed, the search for a short-cut, for direct access to knowledge, was a typical enthusiast characteristic and one reason why Casaubon regarded Descartes as an enthusiast.

Towards the end of the century, John Sergeant similarly regarded the "short cut" to learning pretended by Descartes as one indication of his "enthusiasm." Yet, as an Aristotelian, he saw the crisis to which Descartes tried to respond as a crisis of scholastic philosophy, brought about by scepticism, rather than as a crisis of humanism. Sergeant admitted that following the great variety of commentaries on Aristotle, there was a real danger of complete scepticism. In reaction to that danger, thinkers like Thomas White, Sir Kenelm Digby and Descartes came to the fore. "All of them promis'd *Science*, which kept up those Men's drooping Spirits from Despair of Truth."[42] White and Digby were essentially Aristotelian in their principles (as well as Catholics and acquaintances of Sergeant). Descartes, in contrast, "ravell'd all the schemes hitherto woven by others, moulled *all* the World in a

---

[40] Meric Casaubon, "On Learning", p. 21, in Michael R.S. Spiller, *"Concerning Natural Experimental Philosophie": Meric Casaubon and the Royal Society* (The Hague: Martinus Nijhoff, 1980), pp. 202–203.

[41] Ibid., pp. 203, 209–210.

[42] Sergeant, *Non Ultra*, letter dedicatory (addressed to Sir Edward Southcot). On Sir Kenelm Digby (1603–1665) see *D.N.B.*, vol. 5, pp. 965–971, and *D.S.B.*, vol. IV, pp. 95–96; on Thomas White, often referred to as Albius or Blacklo (1593–1676), see *D.N.B.*, vol. 21, pp. 79–81, and *D.S.B.*, vol. XIV, pp. 301–302. On the crisis of scepticism in the late sixteenth and early seventeenth century, though naturally from a different perspective than that of Sergeant, see Popkin, *The History of Scepticism*.

New Frame, and set up for his Single Self, without any Copartner."[43] Like Casaubon, Sergeant viewed the Cartesian response to the intellectual crisis of the early seventeenth century as but another manifestation of enthusiasm. So far from providing a way out of that crisis, a new and firmer foundation for the socio-cultural order, Descartes' philosophy was regarded as subversive of that order. In this respect, there was indeed a clear parallel between the charge of scepticism and that of enthusiasm, as levelled against Descartes.

This parallel was explicit as early as 1643, in Schoock's *Admiranda Methodus*. As in the case of scepticism, Schoock did not argue that Descartes was consciously an enthusiast, only that his philosophy necessarily led to such a stance.[44] The Cartesian recommendation to forsake the senses and to rely exclusively on the mind and on the examination of its ideas seemed to Schoock most dangerous.[45] This was true even for such axioms as "the whole is greater than any of its parts":

> For when one first is taken away from the senses to the contemplation of these axioms, which seem to be engraved in him, one abandons the rule and its norms, and can easily feign to himself forsaken axioms which, had he held to the norm, would be found false and unworthy of faith.[46]

For Schoock and Voetius, the senses were an indispensable source of knowledge and a guarantee that this knowledge was public and well-founded in reality, rather than subjectively feigned. Exclusive reliance on reason, as advocated by Descartes, not only undermined the basis for secure knowledge, thus leading to scepticism, but smacked of enthusiasm as well. It bestowed a prerogative on the individual human mind, with no external control.

This was especially true for Descartes' proof of the existence of

---

[43] Sergeant, *Non Ultra*, ibid. On the role of Sergeant and White in the English Catholic community as leaders of the so-called "Blackloist" faction, see Bossy, *The English Catholic Community*, pp. 62–67.

[44] *Admiranda Methodus*, p. 255.

[45] "Periculosae vero aleae plenissima haec methodus est." Ibid., pp. 255–256.

[46] "Quando primo enim a sensibus abducitur ad contemplationem eorum axiomatum, quae ei insculpta videntur, exuitur amussi ac norma sua, sibique relicta facile axioma quod fingere potest, quod si normae exhibeatur, postea falsum ac sublestae fidei deprehendatur." Ibid., p. 256. In his famous letter to Voetius, which was a response to the *Admiranda Methodus*, Descartes argued that such epistemological maxims made the contemplation of divine matters impossible. See AT, vol. VIII, pp. 171–2. I shall return to this point presently.

God, which seemed to Schoock to be strikingly close to the contemplation of the mystics. Though he substituted the term "mind" for the traditional mystical terms of "internal man", "spirit", or "the talk of God"—in substance, Descartes' argument was very similar to that of the mystics and enthusiasts:

> For indeed, the mind immersed in profound meditation, discovers the existence of God, according to Descartes, without any discourse. God should be discovered in existence either immediately, or by mediation of the idea [of God] ... how easily is it prone to lead him to most profane enthusiasm.[47]

Since God (or the idea of God) was in him, Descartes could conclude with other enthusiasts that *he* was in God, and that everything he did, he did by the existence of God, thus reaching the antinomian conclusion that he could not sin.[48] Once again, Schoock did not argue that this was Descartes' explicit position, only that it was a potential and dangerous conclusion for those who followed his method. For these reasons, Descartes was comparable, according to Schoock, to enthusiasts such as Sebastian Franck, Henry Niclaes, Dirk Coornhert and Jan van Ruysbroeck. Indeed, he saw Descartes' meditations as

---

[47] "Enimvero mens profundae meditationi immersa, Deique existentiam in se absque ullo discursu, hoc expresse enim Renatus vult, inveniens, Deum sibi in existentem aut immediate, aut mediante idea ... invenire debet, quam facile vero sic ad profanissimum Enthusiasmum ei aditus datur." *Admiranda Methodus*, p. 258. Schoock was referring here to Descartes' phrase in the *Postulata* of the *Rationes dei existentiam et animae a corpore distintionem probantes More Geometrico* contained in his response to the Second Objections: "diu multumque in natura Entis summi perfecti contemplanda immorari [in the original—"immorentur ... quo"] absque ullo discursu cognoscat Deum existere." See AT, vol. III, p. 163, l. 23–28. Descartes summarized there in a few sentences (which Schoock did not quote) his ontological proof for the existence of God. Later on Schoock argued that such contemplation of God, relying only on the limited and imperfect human mind, necessarily meant ascribing imperfections to God himself. Ibid., p. 260. Descartes responded to that point by concluding ironically that apparently Schoock and Voetius did not wish to think about God lest they be regarded as enthusiasts, or lest they attribute any imperfection to Him. *Epistola ad Voetium*, AT, vol. VIII, p. 172. Indeed, while clearly distancing himself from enthusiasm, Descartes was obviously influenced by the contemplative tradition and by Catholic spirituality. See also the following two notes.

[48] "Deum sibi in existentem Cartesianus quis deprehendit per ideam, cur non ergo instar Enthusiastae sic etiam concludat: Deus in me est, et ego in Deo, ergo per Deum in existentem omnia ago et consequenter neque pecco neque peccare possum ...". *Admiranda Methodus*, pp. 258–259. In his letter to Voetius, Descartes responded specifically to that argument, saying that such a conclusion could be elicited only by the enthusiasts themselves: "Quas consequentias fateor à solis Enthusiastis, deliris, et vestri similibus elici posse." *Epistola ad G. Voetium*, AT, vol. VIII, p. 172, l. 9–10.

far more effective in leading men to the blasphemous pronounce-
ment "I am God" than any of the traditional mystical meditations.[49]

The critique of Cartesian epistemology as presumptive and excessively contemplative in dissociating human reason from the senses
characterized later opponents of Descartes as well. Thus Casaubon
says of Descartes' method in his tract *On Learning*:

> What a mysterie doth he make of his *Ego sum: ego cogito*, to attaine to
> the excellencie whereof, a man must first strip himselfe of all that he
> hath ever knowne, or beleeved. He must renounce to his natural rea-
> son, and to his senses; nothing but caves and solitudes will serve the
> turne for such deepe meditation, such profound matter: rare inven-
> tions to raise the expectations of the credulous, and in the end to send
> them away pure Quacks, or arrand Quakers.[50]

To understand this seeming paradox—the view of Descartes as an
irrational philosopher—we need to analyze more closely the concept
of "reason" as used by the critics of Descartes.

Casaubon declared himself a rational thinker par excellence:

> I am one, I confesse, that think reason should be highly valued by all
> creatures, that are naturally rationall. Neither do I think we need to
> seek the *Image of God* in man elsewhere, then in perfect Reason; such
> as he was created in. *Holinesse* and *Righteousnesse* were but fruits of it.[51]

Cartesian philosophy, by contrast, was treated by Casaubon, as by
Schoock, as an example of mystical theology, the type of "contemplative and philosophical enthusiasm" to which he devoted the third
and longest chapter in his *Treatise Concerning Enthusiasme*. His objection to that mystical theology was not only its heathenish, pagan
origins, or the fact that it was derogatory to Scripture, but that "it
deprives a man of the use of Reason."[52] For Casaubon, as for Schoock,

---

[49] *Admiranda Methodus*, pp. 259–260. It is worth mentioning that recent scholarship
concerning Descartes has gone some way in a similar direction. Thus, Amos
Funkenstein has shown that seventeenth century philosophers, including Descartes,
tended to equate human knowledge with divine knowledge, in essence if not in
extent. See Funkenstein, *Theology and the Scientific Imagination* (Princeton: Princeton
University Press, 1985), especially p. 291. On a somewhat different level, Gary Hatfield
has pointed out Descartes' debt to the long tradition of spiritual meditations. See
G. Hatfield, "The Senses and the Fleshless Eye: The *Meditations* as Cognitive Exercises", in Amelie O. Rorty (ed.), *Essays on Descartes' Meditations* (Berkeley and Los
Angeles: University of California Press, 1986), pp. 45–79.

[50] "On Learning", pp. 23–24, in Spiller, *"Concerning Natural Experimental Philosophie"*,
p. 205.

[51] *A Treatise Concerning Enthusiasme*, p. 173.

[52] Ibid., p. 171.

Reason was closely linked with the *senses*, and in this respect he was not only a humanist, but a follower of the Aristotelian and Thomistic tradition, rather than the Platonic one. Intense contemplation might stop the influence and hinder the operation of the senses, but by thus alienating itself from the senses, the mind paved the way to ecstasy, trance and enthusiasm.[53] At its extreme, Casaubon regarded this disengagement of the mind from the senses as pathological, a manifestation of melancholy. No wonder then, that he saw Descartes' effort to free himself from the senses as an irrational act of enthusiasm, similar to the ecstasy of the Alumbrados or the Quakers.[54]

A few years later the comparison between Descartes and the Quakers was repeated by Samuel Maresius (Desmarets). Confuting the Cartesian radical separation of soul from body, a separation which denied any spatial location for the spirit, and arguing that such a view contradicted both Scripture and common sense, Maresius proceeded to ask:

> What would indeed these men respond to that? Would they take refuge in their clear and distinct ideas which they claim to have as internal divine revelations (for so in fact they speak), and thus make them equal to the Holy Scriptures? Yet this would introduce Quakerism into Philosophy and they would insolently turn back from the principles of Descartes himself, who acknowledged that even the most active light of reason gives way to the certainty of divine revelation.[55]

Maresius was criticizing here the epistemological claims of the Cartesians (though not of Descartes himself) to have clear and distinct ideas as if by internal divine revelation, thus competing with Scripture. Such claims amounted to the introduction of Quakerism in philosophy. Although he did not use the label "enthusiasm" itself, Maresius clearly regarded Cartesian epistemology as dangerously close to what Casaubon had called "philosophical enthusiasm." Indeed, a major thrust of the critique of Descartes by Maresius and his students was directed at the Cartesian claims to human infallibility,

---

[53] Ibid., pp. 178–79.

[54] Ibid., p. 173, and see also the quotation above from "On Learning".

[55] "Quid vero ad id ista respondent isti homines? An confugient ad suas claras et distinctas perceptiones, quas volunt haberi pro internis revelationibus Divinis (ita enim loquuntur) et sic aequari Sacris Scripturis? Sed hoc foret Quakerismum Philosophicum introducere insolenterque recedere a principiis ipsius Cartesii, qui agnoscebat vel ex actissimum rationis lumen infra revelationis Divinae certitudinem subsidere." Samuel Desmarets, *De abusu philosophiae cartesianae in rebus theologicis et fidei* (Groningen, 1670), p. 77. On Desmarets (Maresius) see also Chapter 1 above.

which the Calvinist Maresius found incompatible with the fallen nature of man.

A similar type of critique can be found twenty years later coming from the satirical pen of the Jesuit Gabriel Daniel. Like the Calvinist Maresius, Daniel criticized the radical Cartesian separation of soul from body, indeed, his whole satire was based on that point. And like Casaubon, Daniel saw the Cartesians as Platonists in their stress on contemplative philosophy. In fact, he had Descartes' old friend say, "*M. Descartes* had often Fits of Extasy."[56] More important, according to Daniel's satire, Descartes received the crucial secret of separating his soul from his body by an extraordinary revelation from God.[57] In the same vein, Father Daniel had Aristotle ask Descartes' disciples how Descartes knew that God did not deceive him, and that what he conceived distinctly was indeed true—"Hath God revealed it to him?"[58] For the Jesuit Daniel as for the Anglican Casaubon and the Reformed theologians Schoock and Maresius, Cartesian epistemology necessarily implied a claim to some divine inspiration, that is, some type of "enthusiasm".[59]

The epistemological issue was dealt with much more extensively and explicitly by John Sergeant a few years later. Indeed, this was the core of his debate with the Cartesian Antoine Le Grand. As I have mentioned already, Sergeant attacked "The Whole way of Ideas" characteristic of Cartesian philosophy. Referring to Descartes' first rule of method, he said:

---

[56] Gabriel Daniel, *A Voyage to the World of Cartesius*, p. 14 and p. 54 for the reference to the Cartesians as Platonists.

[57] "So far *M. Descartes* took Reason along with him for his Guide; and for ought I know he might have stop'd there, had not Fortune, or rather the good Providence of God . . . reveal'd to him in an extraordinary manner the Secret that he was in search of." Ibid., p. 13.

[58] Ibid., p. 84.

[59] One final sentence is worth quoting from a later text by Father Daniel, *Nouvelles difficultés proposées à l'auteur du Voyage du Monde du Descartes* (first published in 1693; see also the 1720 edition of the *Voyage*). There he has one of the protagonists say to the Cartesian: "Je voeux, et de tout mon coeur, estre Cartésien. Aidez-moy à cela. Communiquez-moy vos lumières, ou celles que vous recevez de Monsieur Descartes . . . Il m'est fort indifférent que vous les produisiez du fond de vostre esprit, ou que vous me parliez en homme inspiré." Ibid., p. 3. On the anti-contemplative and empirical orientation of the Jesuits, including Father Daniel, and on their objections to the radical separation between body and soul, see also Bouillier, *Histoire de la philosophie cartésienne*, vol. I, chapter XXVII.

... this is the main Hinge of all the *Cartesian* Hypothesis, which persuades them to place the *Ground of Truth* within their *own Minds*, and its *Productions*; and not in the *Things themselves*.[60]

The Cartesian rule of evidence meant a reliance on subjective reason, on private reason completely severed from the outward world. In *The Method to Science* Sergeant linked Cartesian epistemology in general with enthusiasm and fanaticism. It is a passage worth quoting in full:

> Having thus got rid of the Senses giving us notice of *outward* things, by imprinting Notions in them, which Experience teaches us is the *ordinary* way of knowing any thing, it follows of course, that they must recurr to *Extraordinary* ways by *Inward* means, or to *Inward Light*; which is the method of Fanaticks in Religion, when they have rejected the *ordinary* ways of believing their proper Teachers. And, hence, the *Cartesians* tell us they know there is a *God*, by the Divine *Idea* of himself which he has imprinted in them; which is in other Terms to say, that they have it by *Divine Revelation*; for Knowledge, according to them, being caus'd in them by those *Ideas*, nay, consisting formally in their having the *Ideas* of things in them; and *God* giving them those *Ideas* without the help of *Second* causes, it follows that *God* is the immediate Cause of all our Knowledge; and, so, no thanks at all to the things in Nature, or to Natural Agents...[61]

Sergeant, like Casaubon, identified the *lumière naturelle* of Descartes with the "Inward Light" of the fanatics. Similarly, while Descartes had recourse to God as a *guarantee* of the correspondence between the ideas or objects in our mind and external reality, Sergeant took him to mean that God was the direct *source* of all our knowledge. This interpretation was more suitable to the epistemology of Malebranche, according to whom we see all things in God, and the ideas we immediately perceive are to be identified with the ideas that God used in creating the world. And indeed, Sergeant relied heavily on Malebranche in his criticism of Cartesianism:

> It may seem harsh that I should resemble tho' (sic) *Cartesian* method to *Fanaticism*, or pretend they bring a kind of *Enthusiasm* into Philosophy. Let the so much applauded *Malebranche* be my Compurgator. That very Ingenious and Eloquent Person, who has a peculiar Talent of talking Nonsense as prettily and plausibly as any Man I ever read...[62]

---

[60] Sergeant, *Non Ultra*, p. 13.
[61] Sergeant, *The Method to Science*, Preface, p. C 6 verso.
[62] Ibid., p. C 8 recto.

According to Malebranche, Sergeant continues

> Those that *hear* us do not *learn* the Truths we speak to their *Ears*, unless
> he that discover'd them to us (he *means* GOD the *Giver* of Ideas) do
> *reveal* them at the same time *to the Mind. So that all science* it *seems, comes
> by* Divine Revelation . . . Was ever such Quakerism heard of among
> Philosophers! Or, plain honest Human Reason so subtilized and exhal'd
> into Mystick Theology by Spiritual Alchemy![63]

The comparison to Quakerism, Mystical Theology and Spiritual
Alchemy needs no further comment. For Sergeant, Malebranche only
made explicit the enthusiastic character of Cartesian philosophy.

Against this, Sergeant presented his own, essentially Aristotelian
epistemology as a rational one, that of 'calm reason'. Like Schoock
and Casaubon, Sergeant stressed the close links between Reason and
the senses, and the fact that our mind simply reflects the objects
existing in the external world. Cognition should be grounded in the
nature of things, and Aristotelian epistemology and logic, Sergeant
believed, ensures that grounding:

> I am not conscious to my self, that I have any thing in my Method
> but what is entirely built on the Nature of the thing in hand; I mean,
> Notions, Propositions, and Rational Discourses, found in the Minds of
> all Mankind; which way of Building on the Nature of the Subject of
> which we are speaking, is the only Ground that can give solidity to
> any Discourse.[64]

The Aristotelian method was thus not only based on external reality,
it was also a universal and public method to science. For "the *first
Rule* of our knowledge of all Truths whatever must be *common* to *all*
Knowing Natures in the World."[65] While Descartes clearly believed
that his own method was such, common to all knowing subjects, his
critics denied this, seeing his method as subjective, private and hence—
"enthusiastic." Indeed, its productions could well be a matter of fancy.
The only guarantee against such danger was to guide our thoughts
and judge them by their conformity to things in Nature, and not
vice versa:

> since we are sure Creative Wisdom made *them*, and implanted Truth *in
> them*, whereas 'tis *Uncertain* whether *God* or our whimsical Fancies gave

---

[63] Ibid., pp. D verso—D 1 recto. A similar argument was made a generation
earlier by Desmarets as we have seen above.
[64] *Non Ultra*, p. 11–12.
[65] Ibid., p. 15.

us our *ideas*: and 'tis certain they are the off-spring of the latter, if they be not conformable to the Things without us.[66]

For Sergeant, a realistic epistemology of the Aristotelian type—where Reason was based on sense data—was the only universal epistemology, the only one which avoided the dangers of subjective fancy and enthusiasm, and which thus could serve as the basis of the public social order.[67]

Vis-à-vis Cartesian epistemology and the Cartesian conception of Reason, conservative critics posited either an Aristotelian epistemology or a humanistic view of Reason in terms of human learning. It may be worthwhile to conclude this subject with a quotation from Swift's *Tale of a Tub* which for all its irony encapsulates the humanistic conception of Reason versus the Cartesian view of Reason which is regarded as "enthusiastic", indeed, as mad:

> For, the Brain in its natural Position and State of Serenity, disposeth its Owner to pass his Life in the common Forms, without any Thought of subduing Multitudes to his own *Power*, his *Reasons* or his *Visions*; and the more he shapes his Understanding by the Pattern of Human Learning, the less he is inclined to form Parties after his particular Notions; because that instructs him in his private Infirmities, as well as in the stubborn Ignorance of the People. But when a Man's Fancy gets *astride* on his Reason, when Imagination is at Cuffs with the Senses, and common Understanding, as well as common Sense, is Kickt out of Doors; the first Proselyte he makes, is Himself, and when that is once compass'd, the Difficulty is not so great in bringing over others; A strong Delusion always operating from *without*, as vigorously as from *within*.[68]

For Swift, as for Casaubon, human understanding should be shaped by human learning. The attempts of individual innovators and revolutionaries like Descartes to free themselves from this tradition, or more precisely, to subdue it to their own powers, visions, and alleged

---

[66] *The Method to Science*, Preface, p. C 8 verso.

[67] Sergeant also criticized Locke's theory of knowledge, though much less sharply than that of Descartes. In fact, Locke, like Sergeant, tried to counter the Cartesian epistemology based on "innate ideas" which seemed to him too subjective, and to offer instead a public epistemology, though quite different, of course, from that of Sergeant. On the development of English theories of knowledge in the Restoration period, from the Cambridge Platonists to Locke, focusing, among other things, on the debate with the enthusiasts, there is an interesting unpublished Ph.D. dissertation by Craig Diamond, "Public Identity in Restoration England: From Prophetic to Economic", Johns Hopkins University, Baltimore, 1982.

[68] Jonathan Swift, *A Tale of a Tub*, ed. by A.C. Guthkelch and D. Nichol Smith (Oxford: Clarendon Press, 1958), p. 171.

'Reason' meant that they had in fact forsaken Reason and let fancy, imagination and delusion overwhelm them.

The Social Critique

The epistemological critique of Cartesianism thus involved a social and psychological critique as well. Conservative critics labelled Descartes' philosophy "enthusiasm" not only because of its epistemological presumptions and the rejection of the senses, but also because of its strong individualistic character and innovative nature. The Cartesian method rejected previous authorities and relied exclusively on the natural light of the individual.[69] At the same time, Descartes claimed to achieve absolute certainty and hence projected an air of authoritarianism. This combination of individualism and authoritarianism is what seemed to his critics typical of enthusiasm. Already in 1655 Casaubon compared Descartes to Minos and to Numa Pompilius who wished their laws to be received as oracles, and for that reason tried to persuade their people "that they did not come by them [these laws] as other men did by theirs; but that they were the fruits of caves and darkness."[70] In 1667, in his unpublished treatise On Learning, Casaubon elaborated on that theme and described Descartes' method as a manifestation of pride and self-conceit, causing him to lose his wits:

> But for his *Method*: I tooke him for one, whom excessive pride and self-conceit (which doth happen unto many) had absolutely bereaved of his witts. I could not beleeve that such stuffe, soe ridiculous, soe blasphemous (as I apprehended it, and doe still) could proceed from a sober man. A cracked brain man, an Enthusiast, such a one as Acosta gives us the relation of, and I out of him in a booke of that subject, I tooke him to be.[71]

---

[69] On Descartes' concept of "natural light", its possible sources and the problems it involves see John Morris, "Descartes' Natural Light", *Journal of the History of Philosophy* 11 (1973): 169–187. The Cartesian notion of "natural light" may indeed have influenced an "enthusiast" like the Quaker Robert Barclay and his own conception of "inner light". See Leif Eeg-Olofsson, *The Conception of the Inner Light in Robert Barclay's Theology: A Case Study in Quakerism*, Studia Theologica Lundensia (Lund: CWK Gleerup, 1954), Introduction, especially pp. 14–15, note 2. I am grateful to Gordon Des Brisay of St. Andrews University, Scotland, for directing my attention to this point and to Eeg-Olofsson's book.

[70] Casaubon, *A Treatise Concerning Enthusiasme*, p. 172.

[71] Casaubon, "On Learning", p. 22, in Spiller, *"Concerning Natural Experimental Philosophie"*, p. 203.

Here Casaubon compared Descartes to a priest in Peru whose case (as reported by Joseph Acosta) he described in detail in *A Treatise Concerning Enthusiasme*.[72] That priest pretended to be King, Pope, Lawgiver and Redeemer, and was subsequently burnt at the stake for heresy. As we have seen already in Chapter 3 above, Casaubon tended to give a medical interpretation to such presumptions, also in the case of Descartes, ascribing them to melancholy.

Similar arguments were made by French critics in the same years. Thus, the Aristotelian physician Pierre Petit stressed the individualistic, authoritarian and innovative character of Cartesian philosophy, although he did not use the term "enthusiast" explicitly. He compared Descartes to Paracelsus, Campanella, Van Helmont and other pretentious innovators, and asked ironically:

> What then? how to explain the reputation of Descartes? Why does he have so many [people] dedicated to him? Why do we continue to believe that he is above all doubt concerning his genius? Why do we embrace his opinions as certain dogmas and oracles? Why do we approach his books only with the utmost reverence as if they were sacred records? Why do we venerate and preserve them as if they were the shield or the statue of Pallas fallen from heaven? Should not rather this novelty and ambition render him suspicious to us, who holds a view which is always contrary to the highest authorities whom on this account all scholars throughout the ages have set forth to themselves as examples and guides in philosophizing?[73]

The ironic comparison of Descartes' work not only to the sayings of the Oracle, but also to the venerated shield or statue of Pallas Athene

---

[72] *A Treatise Concerning Enthusiasme*, 1656 ed., pp. 102–106. Casaubon refers to Joseph Acosta, *De temporibus novissimis*, book II, Chapter XI, pp. 54–56. Acosta cites this example in the course of discussing the diabolical pride which led certain people to claim that they were the Messiah or God. See also Chapter 3 above.

[73] "Quid igitur? quia Cartesius famam, quia multos sibi deditos habet, continuo hunc extra omnem ingenii aleam credemus? Ejus opiniones pro certis dogmatis atque oraculis amplectemur? libros velut sacra monumenta non nisi summa cum religione adibimus? tanquam delapsa caelo ancilia aut Palladium quoddam venerabimur ac custodiemus? Ac non potius hunc nobis novitas et ambitio suspectum reddet, quod viam semper contrariam tenuit summis auctoribus, quos ab hinc tot saeculis Eruditi omnes sibi philosophandi duces atque exempla proponunt?", Pierre Petit, *De Nova R. Cartesii Philosophia Dissertationes*, pp. 2–3. The phrase "extra omnem ingenii aleam" is taken from Pliny the elder's preface to his *Natural History*, in the context of a reference to Cicero. See Pliny, *Natural History*, vol. 1, trans. and ed. by H. Rackham, "Loeb Classical Library" (Cambridge, Mass.: Harvard, 1958), pp. 6–7. I am grateful to Dr. Ilana Klotstein who has pointed this reference to me. On the physician Pierre Petit (1617–1687)—who should not be confused with the mathematician and friend of Pascal by the same name—see *Nouvelle biographie générale*, vol. 39, pp. 710–711.

fallen from the sky, is significant, raising the association of enthusiasm even if Petit did not use the term itself. According to Petit, Descartes' ambition and claim to novelty should arouse our suspicion rather than our admiration. Further on, he elaborates on this point:

> Descartes could have been one among other [philosophical authorities] had he followed the right path of studies. Yet his ambition dictated otherwise. For that reason, he saw it necessary to diverge from the common path, to go away wandering alone in paths untrodden before by anyone, if he wanted indeed to rule without competition. Not only that, but [he saw it necessary] to open there an asylum to which all those who have deserted the better studies, a crowd avid of novelties, will hurry as though it was the place of Romulus. Thus one has his wish fulfilled; by such tricks the leader of the sect is being listened to, moderating and tempering the different factions and assemblies of people, dispersed like the diaspora of the Jews in various places, by the shadow of their dreams. He enjoys the plaudits of his own theater.[74]

Petit thus analysed Descartes' search for novelty and authority in terms similar to the *ad hominem* critique we discussed in the first section of this chapter, portraying him as a wanderer, a leader of a sect, a manipulator of the dreams of the multitude. Indeed, Petit employed the classical critique of rhetoric against Descartes himself.

A few years later, the Jesuit father René Rapin made a similar point.[75] Descartes' claims to innovation, coupled with his authoritarianism, put him in line with dubious and extravagant philosophers such as Cardan and Paracelsus:

> ... [T]here are Men of dark, perplex'd Ideas, and of a Genius obscurely profound, who are yet reverenced as Oracles, and acquire a

---

[74] "Fuisset igitur unus e multis Cartesius, si recta studia secutus esset. At aliud dictabat ambitio. Proinde sibi a communi via deflectendum vidit, in avia quaedam loca secedendum nullius ante trita solo, si vellet sine aemulo regnare. Neque id modo, sed et ibi asylum aperiendum, ad quod omnes meliorum studiorum desertores, omnis rerum novarum avida, ceu ad Romuli locum, turba conflueret. Sic voti compos factus est: hisque artibus nunc sectae princeps auditur, variasque hominum variis locis factiones et Synagogas, ceu Judaeorum διασπορὰν, somniorum suorum umbra moderatur, et temperat. Fruatur theatri sui plausibus." Ibid., pp. 206–207.

[75] Le P. Rapin, *Réflexions sur la philosophie ancienne et moderne, et sur l'usage qu'on doit faire pour la Religion*, sections xvii–xxvi (Paris: 1676; subsequent editions in Rapin's *Oeuvres* in Amsterdam, 1709, and in 1725). For an English translation see *The Whole Critical Works of Mons. Rapin, newly done into English by several hands* (London: 1706, 3rd ed., 1731), vol. II, pp. 377–395. On Rapin see *Nouvelle biographie universelle*, vol. 41, pp. 650–653 and Bayle's article "Rapin, René" in his *Dictionnaire historique et critique* (Geneva: Slatkine Reprints, 1969; reprint of the Paris ed., 1820–1824, vol. XVII, pp. 470–474). Bayle does not refer to Rapin's polemic with Descartes.

Sort of an Empire over Mens Judgments, only because they are more peremptory and confident in their Determinations, and owe all their Authority to their Presumption. 'Twas by this means *Paracelsus* advanc'd his Credit in the last Age: He recommended himself by an Affectation of being obscure . . . His Boldness in setting up for a Master, engaged some to be his Scholars, and his Doctrine met with those that embrac'd it, as propos'd under the surprizing Air of a mighty secret ["sous un air de mystère"]. *Descartes* ow'd his Reputation to the like Measures . . . This is an Art by which that Author never fails to take, because 'tis by this he plays the Oracle.[76]

Though he does not use the term "enthusiasm" explicitly, Rapin accuses Descartes both of being too sceptical and of pretending to be an Oracle.[77]

Towards the end of the century, the same point was made not only by Sergeant, but by the much better known Jonathan Swift in *A Tale of a Tub*:

Cartesius reckoned to see before he died, the Sentiments of all Philosophers, like so many lesser Stars in his *Romantick* System, rapt and drawn within his own *Vortex*.[78]

Swift was in all probability influenced directly by Casaubon, and like him, he saw Descartes, together with other innovators in philosophy, as mentally sick in his incredible egocentric pretensions:

For, what Man in the natural State, or Course of Thinking, did ever conceive it in his Power, to reduce the Notions of all Mankind, exactly to the same Length, and Breadth, and Height of his own?[79]

We shall presently return to the psychological interpretation, but we

---

[76] Rapin, *Reflections upon Philosophy in General*, in *The Whole Critical Works*, vol. II, p. 394. For the French text, see pp. 379–380 of the 1709 or 1725 edition mentioned in the previous note.

[77] On the accusation of scepticism, see section xviii, p. 381 in the 1706 English edition. The term "enthusiast" appears in fact in the English translation of Rapin in reference to the emperor Julian who is characterized as "The wildest Enthusiast" (in French, "Le plus visionnaire de tous") and in reference to Cardan's claim to have had communication in Dreams with his Spirit, a claim which "has still more of the Enthusiast, or the Madman." (In French the phrase is "est encore plus extravagant"). See pp. 386, 378, and in the French edition, pp. 343, 350. For a similar critique of Cartesian authoritarianism, though without linking it explicitly to his enthusiasm, see the work of another Jesuit some years later: Gabriel Daniel, *A Voyage to the World of Cartesius*, pp. 6–7. Father Daniel was particularly ironic concerning Descartes' claims to infallible authority, given his own revolt against the authority of Aristotle.

[78] Jonathan Swift, *A Tale of a Tub*, p. 167.

[79] Ibid., p. 166.

should first pay attention to the social significance of Descartes' image as an individualistic innovator. In the eyes of his conservative critics, not only Descartes the man, but also his method, were anti-social and it was for that reason that he was regarded as an enthusiast. The rejection of tradition as implied by the Cartesian method had obvious social implications. Thus, Casaubon made these implications clear by reference both to Descartes and to Hobbes, though mainly the former:

> Certain it is, the designe of both is and hath beene; but of Cartesius particularly; that all other bookes and learning should be layd asyde, as needles, but what came from him, or was grounded upon his principles. And if all other bookes and learning, as he would have it, there would be little use of libraries or Universities, which is that many would have.[80]

To Casaubon, living in England throughout the Interregnum period, when the universities were under fierce attack on the part of the radicals, Descartes was clearly yet another of the enthusiasts who rejected traditional learning and humanistic scholarship. He was no different from the alchemists, Paracelsians and mystics who came out against the scholastic curriculum in the universities, and indeed was mentioned together with Fludd and Paracelsus, not only by Casaubon but by a radical like John Webster in his *Academiarum Examen*.[81] Casaubon similarly associated Descartes with the more moderate advocates of the reform of learning, Samuel Hartlib and John Dury.[82] From his perspective, all critics of traditional learning and traditional institutions of learning were enthusiasts.

The same social argument was still made at the end of the century by John Sergeant. For Sergeant, as we have seen above, Cartesian epistemology (as developed by Malebranche) meant that we received our truths by divine revelation:

> To what end then are Teachers, Professors, Schools and Universities, if, when we have done what we can by all our Teaching and Learning, nothing but Divine Revelation must do the business, or gain us any science.[83]

---

[80] Casaubon, "On Learning", p. 25, in Spiller, *"Concerning Natural Experimental Philosophie"*, p. 206.

[81] See above, note 14. Swift likewise coupled Descartes with Paracelsus to whom he also added Epicurus and Diogenes, all innovators fit for the whips and chains of Bedlam. *A Tale of a Tub*, p. 166.

[82] "On Learning", p. 35, in Spiller, *"Concerning Natural Experimental Philosophie"*, pp. 213–214.

[83] Sergeant, *The Method to Science*, Preface, p. D.

In a broader sense, the Cartesian enterprise, individualistic, egocentric and allegedly secretive, was seen as opposed to the public social order. The accusations levelled against Descartes the person, which I have surveyed above, had their correlate critique directed at his method and epistemology, and their social implications. While traditional learning was public and had served as the basis of the social order, Descartes' method of introversion was completely private, indeed subversive of the social order. This is the significance of terms like "caves" and "darkness" used by Casaubon in his *Treatise Concerning Enthusiasme*.[84]

The Psychological Critique

The epistemological and social critique of Descartes as an "enthusiast" is closely linked with the psychological dimension. In rejecting Reason and tradition, in its highly individualistic, introvert, indeed, anti-social orientation, Cartesian philosophy was in fact a pathological phenomenon, a manifestation of madness. As in the case of religious enthusiasm, "philosophical enthusiasm" was not only a "heresy", it was also an expression of delusion and mental sickness. As we have seen above, Casaubon characterized Descartes as a "cracked brain man".[85] Beyond the rejection of social and intellectual norms, Cartesianism was similar to Melancholy in its oscillation between deep despair and the heights of unlimited confidence. This was also the technique used by Descartes himself to gain disciples, a technique which Casaubon compared to that of the "Jesuited Puritans"—Catholics who allegedly assumed the guise of Puritans and radical sectarians in England:

> ... first to cast them downe to the lowest pitt of despaire, and then, with such engines of persuasion they are commonly well stored with, to rayse them up againe to the highest pitch of confidence; but soe that they leave themselfes a power still to caste downe and to raise againe, when they see cause; which must needs oblige the credulous disciple, as he hath found the horrour of the one, and the comfort (whether reall or imaginarie) of the other, to a great dependencie. Soe Descartes, after he hath obliged his disciples to forgett and forgoe all

---

[84] Casaubon, *A Treatise Concerning Enthusiasme*, p. 172. See also Spiller, "The Idol of the Stove".

[85] See above, p. 132.

former praecognitions and progresses of eyther senses or sciences, then
he thinks he hath them sure; they must adheare to him tooth and
nayle, or acknowledge themselfes to have beene fooled, which of all
things in the world (though nothing more ordinarie in the world) with
most men is of hardest digestion.[86]

The Cartesian method of attaining certainty via the stage of radical
doubt was thus seen by critics like Casaubon in pathological terms.
Forsaking the trodden path of patient accumulative human learning
with the hope of attaining quick and absolute truth meant running
the risk of insanity.

Whereas Casaubon did not know of Descartes' dreams of 1619, a
generation later Bishop Huet and John Sergeant could rely on Baillet's
report in making the same points. We have seen above that Huet, in
words ascribed to Chanut, clearly referred to melancholy as a possible explanation of Descartes' dreams. In his *Non Ultra* of 1698,
Sergeant noted that the attempt to free oneself from knowledge transmitted by the senses "had confessedly lost *Cartesius* his Wits for some
time."[87] In a tract he published the following year, Sergeant was
more explicit:

> I took notice of that [Method] . . . of *Cartesius* who, (as the Writer of
> his Life tells us), by endeavouring to bring himself to question all the
> Certainty he had received from his senses, fell into Fits of *Enthusiasm*.
> I thought it my Duty I owed to Mankind, and to the Subject I was
> writing of, to forewarn studious Men of following such methods as
> might prejudice their Wits.[88]

The theme of madness is of course still more prominent in Swift's
Tale of a Tub. Swift's characterization of the Aeolists, though not
specifically referring to Descartes, is well in line with Casaubon's view
of Cartesianism as one example of enthusiasm in general:

> And, whereas the mind of Man, when he gives the Spur and Bridle to
> his Thoughts, doth never stop, but naturally sallies out into both extreams
> of High and Low, of Good and Evil; His first Flight of Fancy, commonly
> transports Him to Idea's of what is most Perfect, finished, and exalted;
> till having soared out of his own Reach and Sight, not well perceiving
> how near the Frontiers of Height and Depth, border upon each other;

---

[86] Casaubon, "On Learning", p. 24, in Spiller, *"Concerning Natural Experimental Philosophie"*, p. 205.
[87] Sergeant, *Non Ultra*, p. 109.
[88] Sergeant, *Raillery defeated by Cold Reason*, p. 14.

With the same Course and Wing, he falls down plum into the lowest Bottom of Things.[89]

Specifically with respect to Descartes, Swift analyzed his ability to attract disciples in psychological terms not devoid of irony:

For, there is a peculiar *String* in the Harmony of Human Understanding, which in several individuals is exactly of the same Tuning. This, if you can dexterously screw up to its right Key, and then strike gently upon it; Whenever you have the Good Fortune to light among those of the same Pitch, they will by a secret necessary Sympathy, strike exactly at the same time.[90]

It is worth going back, at this point, to Bishop Huet, who similarly explained the diffusion of Cartesianism as a process carried out by irrational—indeed, magical means—though not exactly as a psychological process. Referring to the Lapps, with whom Descartes reputedly lived after 1650, Huet had him declare to his friend Chanut:

Vous sçavez que les Lappons, par le moyen de leurs Tambours magiques, sont portez en esprit par tout où ils veulent, et que dans vingt-quatre heures ils en rapportent des nouvelles certaines, et des marques reconnaissables. J'envoyeray ces gens-là à la découverte; je sçaurai quel sera l'état de ma secte à Paris, à Leide, à Utrecht, et ce qu'on dira de moi à Stockholm, et selon les besoins je m'y transporterai. Je me ferai connoître à mes sages amis, et à mes fidèles disciples. Je leur donnerai les conseils et les préceptes nécessaires pour la propagation de ma secte, et pour l'extirpation du Péripatéticisme.[91]

Thus, not only Descartes but the successful diffusion of his philosophy were viewed by his critics as an irrational phenomenon which called for a psychological or 'magical' account. So far from providing a rational response to the challenge of enthusiasm, Cartesianism was seen by its critics as a manifestation of enthusiasm. That label was ascribed to Descartes with all its seventeenth century connotations of pretension to direct divine inspiration, subversion of the social order, irrational epistemology and psychological madness.

---

[89] *A Tale of a Tub*, pp. 157–58.

[90] Ibid., p. 167. As we shall see in a later chapter, the same metaphor of the musical string was also used by clerical critics against the Quakers and French Prophets in order to explain the rapid spread of enthusiasm.

[91] Huet, *Nouveaux Mémoires*, pp. 34–35. In this respect, Spiller is not entirely correct in seeing Casaubon and Swift as the only ones who viewed the propagation of Cartesianism in terms of "brainwashing". See *"Concerning Natural Experimental Philosophie"*, p. 71.

A Cartesian Response

What were the responses of the Cartesians themselves to such charges? In conclusion, let us analyze one such response, that of the Oratorian Nicolas-Joseph Poisson whom I have had occasion to mention already.[92] In his *Commentaire ou Remarques sur la Méthode de René Descartes*, Poisson stressed the differences between Descartes and the Rosicrucians with whom he was allegedly associated, referring to the various dimensions of the subject which have been discussed in this chapter. The first distinction was epistemological and methodological:

> ... [J]e croy devoir ajoûter encore, qu'il y a peu d'apparence, que M. Desc., qui avoit le goust trop fin pour estre amy de ces sortes des visionnaires qui donnoient tout à l'Empirisme, et peu de chose au raisonnement, eût fait alliance et eût pris lettre de confraternité avec des gens qui estoient entierement opposez à sa maniere d'estudier.[93]

Significantly, Poisson equated Rosicrucianism with empiricism. Whereas Aristotelian critics of Descartes regarded Cartesian rationalism, especially the doctrine of innate ideas, as an indication of enthusiasm, for Poisson, it was precisely his rationalist method which distinguished Descartes from the Rosicrucians. Empiricism, on the contrary, was typical of visionaries and enthusiasts.[94] Once again we see that the ideological connotations of epistemological methods in the seventeenth century were very much "in the eyes of the beholder".

The second distinction Poisson made was ontological and perhaps less surprising:

> Car quel rapport y a-t-il entre ce qu'enseignent ces *Freres*, que tous leurs remedes deviennent specifiques par des qualitez occultes, et ce que promet M. Desc. de n'admettre aucune de ces qualitez?[95]

---

[92] See notes 4, 22 above.

[93] Poisson, *Commentaire ou Remarques sur la Méthode de René Descartes*, p. 32. See also AT, vol. 10, p. 197, note a.

[94] Poisson apparently relied here on Henri de Sponde, Bishop of Pamiers, who depicted the Rosicrucians as using the methods of the "empirics" to cure diseases. Henri de Sponde, *Annalium ... Baronii Continuatio*, vol. II (Paris, 1647), p. 971. On Sponde see the article "Spondanus, Henri" in *The New Catholic Encyclopedia*, vol. 13, pp. 614–615. There is also a full-length study of Sponde by J.M. Vidal, *Henri de Sponde, recteur de Saint-Louis des Français, évêque de Pamiers 1568–1643* (Paris, 1929). On the term "empirics", which was often associated with "enthusiasts" in the seventeenth century, see the next chapter below.

[95] Poisson, *Commentaire*, p. 32, and AT vol. 10, p. 198, note. At this point Poisson relied—as a marginal note indicates—on Gassendi and his critique of Robert Fludd

The rejection of "occult qualities" was of course a hallmark of the new philosophy of nature by which it sought to distinguish itself not only from the alchemical tradition but indeed from the Aristotelian philosophy of nature as well.[96] Poisson also referred to the innovative character of Cartesian philosophy, once again reversing the argument of the critics and seeing in this emancipation from tradition a sign, not of enthusiasm but of the sober character of Descartes' philosophy. The Rosicrucians, by contrast—

> font venir leur science d'un Arabe inconnu, qui vivoit il y a deux cens ans: ce qui convient peu avec ce que M. Desc. a escrit, et qu'il dit n'avoir appris qu'à force de mediter.[97]

Indeed novelty was regarded by the proponents of the new philosophy and science not as subversive but, on the contrary, as supportive of a sane social and intellectual order.[98] It is worth noting, however, that Poisson makes no reference to another social aspect—the esoteric nature of Rosicrucianism and enthusiasm, nor does he defend Cartesianism as a public philosophy. As we shall see in the next chapter, this is a point which will be more emphasized by members of the Royal Society in England.

Finally, Poisson turned to the theological dimension:

> Enfin leurs visions qui les entestent jusqu'à leur faire manquer de respect pour la religion Catholique, dans laquelle ainsi que dans les autres ils promettent ne rien changer, reviennent peu à ce sentiment si pieux et si raisonnable qu'avoit M. Desc., lorsqu'il a soumis ses ouvrages au jugement de l'Eglise.[99]

---

and the Rosicrucians. See Gassendi, *Examen Philosophiae Roberti Fluddi Medici in quo et ad illius libros adversus R.P.F. Marinum Mersennum . . . scriptos, respondetur* (1629), in Gassendi, *Opera Omnia* (Lyon, 1658), pp. 213–268. See especially pp. 260–264 where Gassendi responds to Fludd's defence of the Rosicrucians.

[96] The question of occult qualities during the scientific revolution has been the subject of some revisionist views in recent years. See Keith Hutchinson, "What Happened to Occult Qualities in the Scientific Revolution?", *Isis* 73 (1982): 233–253, and Ron Millen, "The Manifestation of Occult Qualities in the Scientific Revolution", in Margaret J. Osler and Paul L. Farber, eds., *Religion, Science and Worldview: Essays in Honor of Richard S. Westfall* (Cambridge: Cambridge University Press, 1985), pp. 185–216. Nevertheless, as the quotation above indicates, contemporary natural philosophers like Poisson explicitly rejected any reference to "occult qualitities", and interpreted Descartes as taking the same stand.

[97] Poisson, *Commentaire*, p. 32, and AT, vol. 10, p. 198, note.

[98] I shall develop this point in the following chapter.

[99] Poisson, *Commentaire*, pp. 32–33, and AT, vol. 10, p. 198, note.

Whereas the Rosicrucians threatened to subvert the established religious order, whether Catholic or Protestant, Descartes submitted to the authority of the Church. In religion, unlike philosophy, innovation was dangerous. Here, the Rosicrucians—their disavowals to the contrary notwithstanding—were in fact introducing novelty whereas Descartes accepted "piously and reasonably" the traditional order of the Church. We shall see that in this respect, the Catholic Poisson (and indeed, Descartes himself to a large extent) differed profoundly from English Protestant scientists across the channel. Poisson and Descartes sought to countervail the Rosicrucian and Pansophic type of enthusiasm by clearly separating the religious sphere from natural philosophy.[100] Whereas innovation and the autonomy of thought were justified and constructive in the latter, they were dangerous in the former. Indeed, other Continental Cartesians in that generation— including Protestants—made the same point. They presented Descartes' philosophy as a "sober philosophy" (*Philosophia Sobria*), not only because it trained men to control their passions, but because it avoided any involvement in theological issues.[101] English natural philosophers, on the other hand, would seek to counter the danger of enthusiasm by linking the new science with a new type of theology, as we shall see in the following chapter.

The gap separating the Cartesian and Oratorian Poisson from many of the experimental scientists both in England and on the Continent is made even more evident in his concluding remarks concerning the Rosicrucians:

> Je laisse au P. Garasse à examiner si ces sectaires ont esté des Heretiques, ou comme les appelle Sponde *surculus Luteranorum*, ou si ce n'estoit qu'une assemblée de Sçavans, comme estoit l'Académie des *Ardans* à Naples, de la *Crusca* à Florence, la *Société Royale* à Londres, et d'autres semblables qui se tiennent à Paris.[102]

---

[100] As for Descartes, there is an extremely interesting letter of his to an anonymous addressee, written apparently in August 1638, in which he criticizes the pansophic programme of Comenius by insisting on a strict separation of revealed truths— accepted by faith and owing to divine grace—from the truths of natural philosophy acquired by human reason. AT, vol. 2, pp. 345–348. For a satire on this principle of segregation see Gabriel Daniel, *A Voyage to the World of Cartesius*, pp. 27–29.

[101] Such arguments were made, for instance, by Jean-Robert Chouet, the Cartesian professor of philosophy in Calvin's Academy in Geneva in the 1670's. See my book *Between Orthodoxy and the Enlightenment: Jean-Robert Chouet and the Introduction of Cartesian Science in the Academy of Geneva* (The Hague, Jerusalem: Martinus Nijhoff, Magnes Press, 1982), pp. 141–142.

[102] AT, vol. 10, p. 198, note. In mentioning Garasse, Poisson was probably refer-

The passage may be ironic (including the reference to the Jesuit Garasse, no friend of the Oratorians), but the possible comparison of the Rosicrucians with the new scientific societies, and specifically with the Royal Society of London, is highly significant.[103] For the Cartesian Poisson, these societies may not have been that different from the Rosicrucian order, and the experimental scientists quite similar to the "empirics". *They*, not the rationalist Descartes, were suspected of "enthusiasm".[104] It is time now indeed to examine that other version of the new science in the seventeenth century, the experimental science of the Royal Society. Was it another manifestation of "enthusiasm" or perhaps the best antidote to it? Our next chapter will be devoted to this question.

---

ring to his *La doctrine curieuse des beaux esprits de ce temps* (Paris, 1623). On Père Garasse and his role in the Rosicrucian scare of the 1620's see Frances Yates, *The Rosicrucian Enlightenment*, chapter VIII, esp. pp. 103–105, and J.S. Spink, *French Free-Thought from Gassendi to Voltaire* (New York: Greenwood Press, 1960), chapters I, II. As for Sponde, Poisson referred to his characterization of the Rosicrucians in his *Annalium . . . Baronii Continuatio*, vol. II, p. 971a (see note above).

[103] Interestingly enough, Poisson mentioned literary societies like the *Accademia della Crusca* of Florence (founded in 1582 and devoted mainly to the purification of Tuscan Italian) alongside the new scientific academies.

[104] It should be noted that Poisson ignored the experimental tendencies in Descartes' own scientific work. A Jesuit critic like Gabriel Daniel, in contrast, indeed referred satirically to Descartes' wish to prove every tenet by experience. "It was his way (as all know) to endeavour to make good by Experience, the Truths he had discover'd by the meer Light of his Understanding." *A Voyage to the World of Cartesius*, p. 9.

CHAPTER FIVE

THE NEW EXPERIMENTAL PHILOSOPHY: A MANIFESTATION OF "ENTHUSIASM" OR AN ANTIDOTE TO IT?

Descartes was not the only new philosopher labelled "enthusiast" by conservative critics in the second half of the seventeenth century. The new experimental philosophers were similarly characterized as enthusiasts by their opponents. Enthusiasm implied indeed a claim to have access to divine secrets not only through direct divine inspiration but—as in the case of the alchemists—by the study of nature. The term "enthusiasm" was also associated with the "empirics", i.e., quack doctors and practitioners of popular medicine.[1] By the 1660's the term had been broadened by conservative thinkers to include the new experimental scientists as well. Yet, more than in the case of Cartesianism, the nature of the relationship between the new experimental philosophy and enthusiasm was a hotly debated issue. While classified by its detractors as a manifestation of enthusiasm, experimental philosophy was regarded by its proponents as the best *antidote* to enthusiasm. In fact, the ideology of the new science in Restoration England developed to a significant extent against what was seen as the enthusiasm of the sectarians and even Puritans of the Interregnum period.[2] This is especially manifest in Thomas Sprat's *History of the Royal Society*.[3] In his wish to provide legitimacy for the new science, Sprat stressed its "respectable" character and the service

---

[1] For an early association of "empirics" with "enthusiasts" see Thomas Adams, "The Sinners Passing-Bell or Phisicke from Heaven", a sermon published in *The Divells Banket* (London, 1614), esp. pp. 328–329a. On Adams, see *D.N.B.* vol. I, p. 102.

[2] George Williamson, "The Restoration Revolt against Enthusiasm", *Studies in Philology* 32 (1935): 553–579, reprinted in his *Seventeenth Century Contexts* (London: Faber and Faber, 1960), pp. 202–239; Frederick B. Burnham, "The More-Vaughan Controversy: The Revolt Against Philosophical Enthusiasm", *Journal of the History of Ideas* 35 (1974): 33–49; and P.B. Wood, "Methodology and Apologetics: Thomas Sprat's *History of the Royal Society*", *British Journal for the History of Science* 13 (1980): 1–26.

[3] See especially, Wood, "Methodology and Apologetics" referred to in the previous note. A modern edition of Thomas Sprat is *The History of the Royal Society of London, for the Improving of Natural Knowledge*, ed. J.I. Cope and H.W. Jones (St. Louis, Miss.: Washington University Studies, 1958).

science could perform for other established institutions, primarily the Anglican church. Beyond that, he wished to present the new natural philosophy as a firmer intellectual foundation for the social, political and religious order than the old scholastic philosophy had been. To do so, it was crucial to show that the new science was indeed the best response to the challenge of enthusiasm. Sprat's efforts should be seen, however, against the background of the critique of conservative opponents who portrayed the new experimental science as a manifestation of enthusiasm, rather than an antidote to it.

The Critics

The critics of the Royal Society saw the new experimental science as a threat to the social, intellectual and religious order; it is not surprising, therefore, to find that they associated it, among other things, with "fanaticism" and various manifestations of enthusiasm. Unfortunately, not much of this criticism was given written form. Before the publication of Sprat's *History of the Royal Society* in 1667 it was apparently mostly oral, and can be inferred only by studying Sprat's arguments themselves.[4] Published attacks on the Royal Society mostly appeared later—in response to Sprat's *History* as well as to Joseph Glanvill's *Plus Ultra* of 1668.[5] There was one reported attack which does not seem to have been printed; at all events, it is no longer extant. This was the sermon delivered by the preacher Robert South, public orator of Oxford University between 1660 and 1677, at the opening of the Sheldonian Theatre in Oxford on 9 July, 1669.[6] Nevertheless, John Wallis's account of that sermon sent to both Oldenburg and Boyle hints at a possible connection which South may have made between the new science and enthusiasm. To Boyle, Wallis wrote:

---

[4] See R.H. Syfret, "Some Early Reactions to the Royal Society", *Notes and Records of the Royal Society* 7 (1949–50): 207–258, esp. p. 258; and Michael Hunter, *Science and Society in Restoration England* (Cambridge: Cambridge University Press, 1981), pp. 136, 139.

[5] Joseph Glanvill, *Plus Ultra* (London, 1668); facsimile edition and introduction by J.I. Cope, (Gainesville, Florida: Scholars' Facsimiles and Reprints, 1958).

[6] Robert South (1634–1716) was a prominent preacher and churchman of what was to become the High Church party. See *D.N.B.*, vol. XVIII, pp. 683–685.

... Dr. *South*, as university orator, made a long oration. The first part of which consisted of satyrical invectives against *Cromwell*, fanatics, the Royal Society, and new philosophy; the next, of encomiastics, in praise of the archbishop, the theatre, the vice-chancellor, the architect, and the painter; the last, of execrations against fanatics, conventicles, comprehension, and new philosophy; damning them *ad infernos, ad gehennam*. The oration being ended, some honorary degrees were conferred, and the convocation dissolved.[7]

The inclusive reference to Cromwell, fanatics, the Royal Society and the new philosophy, as well as to "comprehension", seems to indicate that South saw all of them as different aspects of the same danger—a danger to the universities as well as to the public order in Church and State. Throughout his career, South often inveighed both against the new science—centering mostly on its materialistic, worldly, and atheistic implications—and against religious enthusiasm, prevalent among both radical sectarians and Catholics. In his printed sermons, no explicit argument links the new science and religious enthusiasm, although he may have made such a connection in his sermon at the opening of the Sheldonian.[8]

Attacks on the new science were published that same year and the following one by Meric Casaubon and Henry Stubbe. Casaubon did not deal with the new experimental science in his *Treatise Concerning Enthusiasme*, though he did include Descartes among the "philosophical enthusiasts" as we saw in the preceding chapter. His attack on experimental philosophy came over a decade later, in his Letter to Peter du Moulin, which was largely instigated by Glanvill's *Plus Ultra* but was also a response to Sprat's *History of the Royal Society*.[9]

At the same time as Meric Casaubon criticised the Royal Society,

---

[7] Letter to Robert Boyle, 11 July, 1669, in *The Works of the Honourable Robert Boyle*, ed. Thomas Birch, (London, 1772), vol. VI, p. 459; see also his letter to Oldenburg, secretary of the Royal Society, in A.R. Hall and M.S. Hall, eds., *The Correspondence of Henry Oldenburg* (Madison: University of Wisconsin Press, 1969), vol. VI, p. 129.

[8] For South's sermons see Robert South, *Sermons Preached Upon Several Occasions*, 7 vols. (Oxford: Clarendon Press, 1823).

[9] The "Letter to Peter du Moulin" is reproduced in Spiller, *"Concerning Natural Experimental Philosophie": Meric Casaubon and the Royal Society* (The Hague: Nijhoff, 1980), pp. 151–186. See also Spiller's introduction, pp. 145–147, and the discussion which sets Casaubon's critique of the Royal Society in the context of reactions to the new science. Peter du Moulin (1601–84), though not a scientist himself, was Casaubon's only contact with the new experimental philosophers. An expatriate from France, he was interested in educational reform during the Interregnum. Casaubon received a copy of Glanvill's *Plus Ultra* from him, probably before its publication in July 1669.

a more extended and virulent attack came from the pen of Henry Stubbe. Like Casaubon's Letter to Peter du Moulin, Stubbe's argumentation, in a series of pamphlets, was directed mostly at Glanvill's *Plus Ultra*, but it also referred to Sprat's *History of the Royal Society*.[10] Whereas Casaubon was a divine, Stubbe was a practising physician in the 1660's. His career—a republican and religious radical during the Interregnum, a protégé of the king and an avowed defender of Church, State and the College of Physicians after the Restoration— was enigmatic. According to James Jacob, Stubbe never in fact abandoned his radical religious views, and his post-Restoration conservatism was largely a facade.[11] His attack on the Royal Society, however, whatever its motives, was written, at least explicitly, from a perspective very similar to that of Casaubon's—that of conservative humanism and scholasticism.

The Social and Institutional Dimension

Both Casaubon and Stubbe wrote in defence of traditional institutions: the established church, the universities, and, in the case of Stubbe, the College of Physicians. They therefore criticised the new science primarily for its innovative character and for that reason associated it also with "enthusiasm" and "fanaticism". Casaubon was writing in 1669, still under the impact of the period of the Interregnum, when the universities were fiercely attacked by the radicals. The views of Sprat, Glanvill and the experimental scientists evoked in his memory the various plans of educational reform published in the 1640's and 1650's. For that reason, he sensed a real danger to the universities and to traditional learning in general in the kind of criticism coming from the new scientists. Their criticism was no different from the attacks on the universities made by the alchemists or by "Puritan" reformers like Hartlib and Dury before the Restoration. They were all in a sense "enthusiasts" because they all wished to discard scholastic and humanistic culture and, in one way or

---

[10] For a bibliographical reconstruction of Stubbe's controversy with Glanvill in 1670–71 see Spiller, *"Concerning Natural Experimental Philosophie"*, pp. 33–34.

[11] See J.R. Jacob, *Henry Stubbe, Radical Protestantism and the Early Enlightenment* (Cambridge: Cambridge University Press, 1983); and N.H. Steneck, "Greatrakes the Stroker: The Interpretations of Historians", *Isis* 73 (1982): 161–177.

another, find shortcuts to knowledge; in the case of the experimental philosophers—to useful knowledge.[12]

It was in this context that Casaubon compared Glanvill's *Plus Ultra* to *The Reformed Schoolmaster* by John Dury and to other projects for the improvement of knowledge, by Comenius, Lull and Ramus.[13] What Casaubon said about Dury's *Reformed Schoolmaster* is especially significant because he thought that it alleged something resembling direct commission from God:

> Indeed I never read any man that did not pretend to immediate com-
> mission from God, speak more magisterially, and as it were authenti-
> cally; but withal I must say, I never read any thing more whimsical
> and chimerical, then his *Reformation* doth appear unto me.[14]

Claims to novelty and their concomitant self-confidence could be founded, according to Casaubon, only on true or pretended direct divine inspiration, that is, on enthusiasm. For Casaubon, the experimental philosophers, like Descartes, were to be suspected of enthusiasm in consequence of their claim to be innovators, their rejection of traditional learning, and their disparagement of established institutions, especially the universities.

Henry Stubbe similarly attacked the new science's claim to innovation. Whereas, for Casaubon, the apologists of the Royal Society seemed dangerously close to the educational reformers of the Interregnum, Stubbe associated the experimental scientists with the opponents of the College of Physicians, opponents whom he regarded as empirics and "pseudochymists". He was referring particularly to the "Society of Chymical Physitians", or "A Noble Society for the Advancement of Hermetick Physick", as it was called in an earlier declaration. Established in 1665, as the plague was beginning to spread in London, this "anti-college", which never received a formal Royal patent, claimed to provide an alternative type of medicine to that of

---

[12] Casaubon, "Letter to Peter du Moulin", pp. 13–14, reproduced in Spiller, *"Concerning Natural Experimental Philosophie"*, pp. 163–164.

[13] On proposals for educational reform during the Interregnum with extracts of texts, including Dury's *The Reformed Schoolmaster*, see Charles Webster, ed., *Samuel Hartlib and the Advancement of Learning* (Cambridge: Cambridge University Press, 1970). It is worth mentioning here that in those same years, Samuel Maresius (Desmarets) in the Netherlands similarly debated with Comenius and suspected him, as well as Descartes, of enthusiastic leanings. See Chapters 1 and 4 above.

[14] Casaubon, "Letter to Peter du Moulin", p. 13, reproduced in Spiller, *"Concerning Natural Experimental Philosophie"*, p. 163.

the College of Physicians.[15] According to Stubbe, however, the moving spirits behind this project were members of the Royal Society:

> At first they would have incorporated the College of Physicians into their Society: but that the prudent and grave did decline: then they promoted the Anti-College of Pseud-Chymists, encouraging Odowde and his ignorant Adherents in opposition to the Physicians. And this is not more notorious to the world, than it is also that those objections with which M.N. and other Quacksalvers amuse the Age were suggested unto them by the Virtuosi and derived their repute from them.[16]

The physician and courtier Thomas O'Dowde was indeed a leading figure in the "Society of Chymical Physitians" and was influential in gaining support for that project among courtiers, noblemen and politicians, including Archbishop Sheldon himself.[17] Stubbe was not the only one to accuse him of ignorance. He was similarly portrayed by a rival within the society itself, George Thomson, who also alleged that it was O'Dowde who gave the society the reputation of being "a company of Fanaticks", that is, enthusiasts.[18] "M.N.", whom Stubbe mentions in the quotation above, is clearly Marchamont Nedham (or Needham), the prominent journalist and physician who was also involved in the "Society of Chymical Physitians."[19] The extent

---

[15] See Sir Henry Thomas, "The Society of Chymical Physitians, an Echo of the Great Plague of London, 1665", in E. Ashworth Underwood (ed.), *Science, Medicine and History: Essays on the Evolution of Scientific Thought and Medical Practice in Honour of Charles Singer* (Oxford: Oxford University Press, 1953), vol. II, pp. 55–71, and P.M. Rattansi, "The Helmontian-Galenist Controversy in Restoration England", *Ambix* 21 (1964): 1–23.

[16] Henry Stubbe, *Campanella Reviv'd or, an Enquiry into the History of the Royal Society, whether the Virtuosi there do not pursue the Projects of Campanella for the reducing of England into Popery* (London, 1670), "To the Reader". For a similar argument, aimed at the "Baconian Philosophers", see *The Lord Bacon's Relation of the Sweatening-Sickness Examined* (London 1671), "The Epistle Dedicatory", addressed to the College of Physicians.

[17] Thomas O'Dowde, a Groom of the King's Privy Chamber, was also a practising physician. His *The Poor Man's Physician* (1665) included a long list of chemical cures, the "Copy of the Engagement" subscribed by practitioners of Chemical Physick who wished to join the society, and a "Copy of the Paper" subscribed by the noblemen and "Persons of Honour" who registered their support of that society. See Thomas, "The Society of Chymical Physitians", pp. 65–71, and Rattansi, "The Helmontian-Galenist Controversy", pp. 13–18.

[18] See Thomas, "The Society of Chymical Physitians", p. 66. Thomson, an Helmontian physician, presented himself as a learned chemist in contradistinction from both Galenists and pseudo-chemists. He later engaged in a controversy with Stubbe, who wrote *Lord Bacon's Relation of the Sweatening-Sickness Examined* in reply. See also *D.N.B.* vol. XIX, pp. 720–721.

[19] On Marchamont Nedham, see *D.N.B.*, vol. XIV, pp. 159–164. In 1665 he published *Medela Medicinae, A Plea for the Free Profession and a Renovation of the Art of*

to which these chemical physicians indeed co-operated with the Royal Society is unclear, though they themselves regarded Boyle as one of their company.[20] The important point is that, in the eyes of Stubbe, the "chemical physicians" and the experimental scientists were joined in opposition to the traditional institution of the College of Physicians. Stubbe presented himself as defending the State, the Church and the Universities—the bulwarks of the social order—vis-à-vis the new scientists, who like the Paracelsians and empirics, were subverting public tranquillity.[21]

The scientists' criticism of established institutions was linked by their opponents with the rejection of traditional learning, which Stubbe took to be their ignorance of accepted knowledge. In that connection, he referred to them as "fanatics" and compared them to other enthusiasts such as the Spanish Alumbrados:

> Whatever Folly and Ignorance I charge upon them, they furnish me with new Arguments to prove it: I advise them hereafter to write against me in the Universal Character, that the Ignominy of our Nation may be more conceal'd: or to retire into some Deserts (fit receptacles for such Plagiaries, Cheats and Tories) least this second sort of worth-less Fannaticks, these Alumbrados in Religion and all Sciences (for 'tis now manifest, that they understand Chymistry as little as the Languages, Rhetorick, Logick and History) continue the Infamy of our Kingdom.[22]

Stubbe made the accusation in response to the arguments of Glanvill who treated with disdain Stubbe's adherence to Aristotle in matters of chemistry. According to Stubbe, however, "Neither the Grecians nor the disputing Ages were as ignorant of Chemistry as Mr. Glanvill asserts."[23] The apparent rupture between chemistry and traditional natural philosophy was the doing of Paracelsus and his disciples. Yet, although Stubbe was aware, unlike Casaubon, of the differences

---

Physick, a fierce attack on the College of Physicians which was answered by several champions of the College.

[20] See Rattansi, "The Helmontian-Galenist Controversy", p. 13.

[21] See, for example, Stubbe's "Letter of Dedication" in *A Censure upon certain Passages contained in the History of the Royal Society* (Oxford, 1670), the first pamphlet in his series of attacks on the new science. That dedication was addressed to Dr. John Fell, another critic of the Royal Society. For Stubbe's links with the universities, see Hunter, *Science and Society in Restoration England*, pp. 137, 152–153.

[22] Stubbe, *A Reply unto the Letter written to Mr. Henry Stubbe in Defence of the History of the Royal Society* (Oxford, 1671), p. 29. The anonymous letter (pp. 3–11) was in fact written by James Arderne, a London minister and a fellow of Brasenose College, Oxford. For the whole text, see Stubbe, *Censure*, Appendix to the second edition.

[23] Stubbe, *The Plus Ultra Reduced to a Non Plus* (London, 1670), p. 57.

between the Paracelsians and the experimental philosophers—the former looking back to antiquity and in particular to Hermes Trismegistos as their source of inspiration, the latter claiming to be innovators, or "novellists" as Stubbe called them—he nevertheless saw the similarity between them in their rejection of humanistic and Aristotelian culture:

> But when *Paracelsus* was seized with the same *Spirit* that seems to sway some of the *Virtuosi*: then did *he* begin to decry the study of *Languages*, as loss of time, our *Wits* call it *Pedantry*. He villified *Logick* as that which caused *endless disputes*, and darkened rather than discovered *Nature*.[24]

In their ignorance of traditional knowledge, in their rejection of scholastic and humanistic learning, and in their revolt against established institutions, the experimental scientists were no different from the Paracelsian alchemists. For Stubbe, as for Casaubon, they were "fanatics", enthusiasts, in both religion and the sciences.

It is in view of these types of argument that one should understand some of the points made by Sprat in defence of the new science. Sprat did not deny the novel character of the experimental philosophy, he tried to argue that this did not set it in conflict with traditional institutions. On the contrary, Sprat stressed that the experimental philosophers were the men who saved the universities from ruin during the Interregnum:

> . . . I may venture to affirm, that it was in good measure, by the influence, which these Gentlemen [John Wilkins and his colleagues gathering at Wadham College, Oxford] had over the rest, that the *University* it self, or at least, any part of its Discipline, and Order, was sav'd from ruine. And from hence we may conclude, that the same Men have now no intention, of sweeping away all the honor of Antiquity in this their new Design: seeing they imploy'd so much of their labor, and prudence, in preserving that *most venerable Seat* of antient Learning, when their shrinking from its defence, would have been the speediest way to have destroy'd it.[25]

This passage has an apologetic ring to it, but Sprat may have been making more than a polemical point in stressing the links between the university and the new science.[26]

---

[24] Ibid., p. 55.

[25] Sprat, *History of the Royal Society*, pp. 53–54. Sprat distanced himself from the "modern zealots" in philosophy and religion, who wished to destroy "root and branch" university education and "whatever has the face of Antiquity". (Ibid., pp. 323–329.)

[26] Michael Hunter, *Science and Society in Restoration England* (Cambridge: Cambridge

Beyond the educational realm, however, Sprat sought to legitimize the innovative character of the new science by an analogy with Protestantism. Pointing to the similarities between the Royal Society and the Church of England, he said:

> They both may lay equal claim to the word *Reformation*; the one having compass'd it in *Religion*, the other purposing it in *Philosophy*. They both have taken a like cours to bring this about; each of them passing by the *corrupt Copies*, and referring themselves to the *perfect Originals* for their instruction; the one to the *Scripture*, the other to the large Volume of the *Creatures*. They are both unjustly accus'd by their enemies of the same crimes, of having forsaken the *Ancient Traditions*, and ventur'd on *Novelties*. They both suppose alike, that their *Ancestors* might err; and yet retain a sufficient reverence for them.[27]

As this analogy also shows, Sprat insisted that the innovative character of science was not subversive of the social order. On the contrary, he presented the new science as providing a firm foundation for the social order, and, as such, an appropriate response to the challenge of enthusiasm.[28] For Sprat, enthusiasm was not as anti-traditional as Casaubon or Stubbe had held; he saw it primarily as a manifestation of a private, idiosyncratic, individualistic spirit, which claimed divine illumination and put forward a subjective interpretation of Scripture. Experimental philosophy, on the contrary, was a co-operative and, indeed, public and universally valid enterprise. The new science was public because the experimental method demanded the co-operation of several scientists and was a method that could be publicly seen, checked and verified.[29] It was universal, because the Royal Society

---

University Press, 1981), chapter 6; see also Mordechai Feingold, *The Mathematicians' Apprenticeship: Science, Universities and Society in England, 1564–1640* (Cambridge: Cambridge University Press, 1984); Edward G. Ruestow, *Physics at Seventeenth and Eighteenth Century Leiden: Philosophy and the New Science in the University* (The Hague: Nijhoff, 1973); L.W.B. Brockliss, *French Higher Education in the Seventeenth and Eighteenth Centuries: A Cultural History* (Oxford: Clarendon Press, 1987), chapter 7; and Michael Heyd, *Between Orthodoxy and the Enlightenment: Jean-Robert Chouet and the Introduction of Cartesian Science in the Academy of Geneva* (The Hague: Nijhoff; Jerusalem: Magnes Press, 1982).

[27] Sprat, *History of The Royal Society*, p. 371.

[28] See particularly Wood, "Methodology and Apologetics"; and Margaret C. Jacob, *The Newtonians and the English Revolution: 1689–1720* (Ithaca: Cornell University Press, 1976), pp. 36–39.

[29] On "enthusiasm" as a manifestation of a "private" spirit, see Sprat, *History of the Royal Society*, p. 363. On the experimental method as a "public" procedure, see ibid. pp. 91–92; Wood, "Methodology and Apologetics", pp. 19–20; and Steven Shapin and Simon Schaffer, *Leviathan and the Air Pump: Hobbes, Boyle and the Experimental Life* (Princeton: Princeton University Press, 1985).

". . . freely admitted Men of different Religions, Countries, and Professions of Life . . . For they openly profess, not to lay the Foundation of an *English, Scotch, Irish, Popish,* or *Protestant* Philosophy; but a
Philosophy of *Mankind.*"[30]

Sprat was suggesting a new intellectual basis for the social order,
a foundation which was well in line with the Latitudinarian views
obtaining within the Church of England in the 1660's.[31] The important point, however, is that Sprat suggested an alternative intellectual outlook to the conservative humanism of men like Casaubon, or
the professed Aristotelianism of Stubbe. For Sprat, Wilkins, Glanvill
and other experimental scientists—mostly young scholars whose formative years had been passed during the Interregnum—the traditional
intellectual basis of the social order, both humanistic and scholastic,
was hardly proof against enthusiasm.[32] This traditional outlook only
led to incessant disputes, which ultimately erupted in a civil war,
and it was by no means a bulwark against the surge of fanaticism. A
new intellectual foundation was needed for the social order and only
experimental philosophy could provide such an alternative, since it
avoided disputes and was an effective means of "abolishing or re-
straining the fury of *Enthusiasm*".[33] In performing these functions, the
new philosophy also reinforced the political order, inculcating civil
obedience to the ruler rather than disobedience and revolt, as the
"fanatics" had done.[34] The debate over the question whether the
new science was a manifestation of enthusiasm or an antidote to it
was primarily a debate concerning the intellectual foundation of the
social and political order.

---

[30] Sprat, *History of the Royal Society*, p. 63. This point was sharply criticised by
Stubbe; see Stubbe, *A Censure*, pp. 1–36.
   [31] Barbara Shapiro, "Latitudinarianism and Science", *Past and Present* 40 (1968):
16–41; James R. Jacob, and Margaret C. Jacob, "The Anglican Origins of Modern
Seience: The Metaphysical Foundations of the Whig Constitution", *Isis* 71 (1980):
251–267.
   [32] Joseph Glanvill, *Essays on Several Important Subjects in Philosophy and Religion* (London, 1676), Essay VII, p. 49; see also the earlier version, in manuscript in the
University of Chicago Library, "Bensalem, being A Description of A Catholick and
Free Spirit both in Religion and Learning", esp. p. 10; and Jackson I. Cope, "'The
Cupri-Cosmits': Glanvill on Latitudinarian Anti-Enthusiasm", *The Huntington Library
Quarterly* 17 (1954): 269–286.
   [33] Sprat, *History of the Royal Society*, p. 428.
   [34] Ibid., pp. 427–430.

The Epistemological and Moral Issues

The social and intellectual dimension of the new experimental philosophy was intimately linked with epistemological questions. In the
eyes of its critics, the experimental practice of the new science was
easily confused with the empirical tendencies of the alchemists or the
quack doctors. Thus, according to Casaubon, the experimental philosophers were no different from the "empiricks" in their exclusive
reliance on experience "and meer *Empiricks* have always been accounted
dangerous men".[35] For Casaubon, the empirical method was as use-
less, indeed as subversive, as its epistemological opposite, that is, the
excessive contemplation of the "contemplative enthusiasts"—mystics,
and philosophers like Descartes.[36] According to Casaubon, the proper
response to both dangers was Aristotelian philosophy. Aristotle presented the ideal balance between general theories and particular
observations. His epistemology was by no means over-theoretical and
contemplative, as Glanvill, for example, alleged.[37] Indeed, Casaubon
felt that in reacting against one type of enthusiasm, that of the contemplative philosophers, the experimental scientists ran the risk of
espousing the other, that of the empirics. In rejecting the Aristotelian
via media, they refused the only balanced epistemology on which an
intellectual and social order could be constructed.[38]

Henry Stubbe directed his attack against another aspect of the
epistemology of the new science, namely, its presumptuous claim to
unravel the secrets of nature. Though not using the term "enthusiasm", he clearly had it in mind when he characterised such presumption as "Rosicrucian":

---

[35] Casaubon, "Letter to Peter du Moulin", p. 10, reproduced in Spiller, *"Concerning Natural Experimental Philosophie"*, p. 160.

[36] Casaubon, *Treatise Concerning Enthusiasme*, chapter III. On his reference to
Descartes, see ibid. pp. 172–173; Spiller, *"Concerning Natural Experimental Philosophie"*,
chapter IV, and pp. 195–214, and Chapter 4 above.

[37] Casaubon, "Letter to Peter du Moulin", pp. 9–10 (in Spiller, *"Concerning Natural
Experimental Philosophie"*, pp. 159–160).

[38] The efforts of scientists like Boyle and apologists like Wilkins and Sprat to
dissociate the experimental method from the experience of the mystics on the one
hand, and the methods of the empirics on the other, should be seen against the
background of this type of criticism. See Wood, "Methodology and Apologetics" pp.
17–18. On Boyle, see James R. Jacob, *Robert Boyle and the English Revolution* (New
York: Burt Franklin, 1977), pp. 108–112, 127–128. For Sprat's criticisms of the
contemplative philosophers, see his *History of the Royal Society*, pp. 334–335.

All that is said about the erecting of *Mechanical* or *Sensible Philosophy of Nature* is but empty talk; *Human nature* is not capable of *such achievements*; 'tis evidently impossible to attain any *exact knowledge* of the surface of our whole *Terrestrial Globe*; and the *depths of the Earth and water*, are no less *unsearchable*: and as to the *component particles*, their *nature, figure, motions* and *combinations* are known only to the *Deity*; so that no prudent person is to be amused with their *Rosicrucian* promises.[39]

Against this background, it is worth looking at Stubbe's comments on Glanvill concerning this point. Glanvill, in *Plus Ultra*, attempted to dissociate the type of chemistry preached under the auspices of the Royal Society from the Paracelsian and Rosicrucian kind:

... [I]ts late *Cultivators*, and particularly the Royal Society, have refined it from its *dross*, and made it *honest, sober*, and *intelligible*, an excellent *Interpreter* to *Philosophy*, and *help* to *common Life*. For *they* have laid aside the *Chrysopoietick*, the *delusory Designs* and *vain Transmutations*, and *Rosicrucian vapours*, *Magical Charms* and *superstitious Suggestions*, and formed it into an *Instrument* to know the *depths* and *efficacies* of Nature.[40]

Stubbe quoted that passage in his *The Plus Ultra Reduced to a Non Plus*, but was not convinced by it. In the margin he made the following comment:

... I am sure the projects some go upon are delusory, have much of the Rosicrucian humour in them and the design of introducing sensible Philosophy is the pretence of Crollius and the Rosicrusive Order.[41]

The imputation of "presumption" raised by Stubbe against the new scientists leads from the epistemological aspect of the debate to the ethical and religious one. The reproach of "spiritual pride" was frequently levelled against enthusiasts in the Restoration period.[42] Yet, whereas critics like Stubbe charged the experimental scientists with undue pride, their defenders such as Sprat and Glanvill argued that the new science was an effective cure for intellectual arrogance. Sprat

[39] Stubbe, "To his ever honoured friend N.N.", in *Campanella Reviv'd*, appendix, p. 15. Stubbe had earlier compared Sprat to Alphonso King of Portugal, who professed "that if he had assisted God almighty at the Creation, he could have amended the fabric of the world" (*A Censure*, p. 44).
[40] Glanvill, *Plus Ultra*, p. 12.
[41] Stubbe, *Plus Ultra Reduced to a Non Plus*, p. 70. On the alchemist Oswald Croll, to whom Stubbe refers here, see Owen Hannaway, *The Chemists and the Word: The Didactic Origins of Chemistry* (Baltimore: Johns Hopkins University Press, 1975).
[42] James P. Murray, "Charity, Zeal and Spiritual Authority in Britain, 1660–1700", Ph.D. diss., Johns Hopkins University, Baltimore, 1986.

emphasized the careful and sceptical attitude of the experimental philosophers towards the enthusiasts' claims to have received new revelations or to perform new miracles. He was also referring here to the pretensions—not only of radical sectarians, but of many Puritans during the Interregnum—to interpret various calamities on earth as the expression of specific divine retribution for particular human transgressions. These interpretations, Sprat argued, were the figments of a private and proud imagination. In reaction to such pride, Sprat advocated intellectual "humility".[43] However, this was not the humility before the accumulated knowledge of past generations for which Casaubon and other humanist critics of enthusiasm contended, but a humility before the phenomena of nature. Experimental philosophy taught men to be very cautious in interpreting natural phenomena, and called for patient experimental gathering of data rather than projecting one's own fancies in ascribing meaning to these phenomena. Sprat used this Baconian theme to refute the enthusiasts' claims to detect direct and specific signs of divine judgement in natural occurrences. In fact, the experimental philosopher—far from being a proud enthusiast as some critics alleged—was the true embodiment of Christian humility, whereas the speculative philosopher was guilty, like the enthusiasts, not only of excessive contemplation, but of spiritual pride:

> The spiritual *Repentance* is a careful survey of our former Errors, and a resolution of amendment. The spiritual *Humility* is an observation of our Defects, and a lowly sense of our own weakness. And the *Experimenter* for his part must have some Qualities that [must] answer to these: He must judge aright of himself, he must misdoubt the best of his own thoughts; he must be sensible of his own ignorance, if ever he will attempt to purge and renew his Reason . . . it may well be concluded, that the doubtful, the scrupulous, the diligent *Observer of Nature*, is neerer to make a modest, a severe, a meek, an humble *Christian*, than the man of *Speculative Science*, who has better thoughts of himself and his own *Knowledge*.[44]

---

[43] Sprat, *History of The Royal Society*, pp. 356–365.

[44] Ibid., p. 367. See also Glanvill, *Philosophia Pia: or, a Discourse of the Religious Temper and Tendencies of the Experimental Philosophy which is profest by the Royal Society* (London, 1671), chapter V, esp. pp. 57–59. Glanvill puts the spiritual pride and reliance on fancy of the enthusiasts in the context of a medical account of the phenomenon. *Philosophia Pia* was written in response to Casaubon's *Letter to Peter du Moulin*. See Jackson I. Cope, *Joseph Glanvill, Anglican Apologist* (St. Louis: Washington University Studies, 1956), pp. 31–32.

The Religious Dimension: Science and Orthodox Christianity

The issue of spiritual pride is connected with the religious dimension of the question whether the new science was an antidote to enthusiasm or a manifestation of it. Here it is necessary to begin with Sprat himself, because critics like Casaubon and Stubbe referred to his arguments specifically.[45] When Sprat spoke of "enthusiasts", he meant not only "new prophets" who claimed direct divine inspiration, but also those millenarians who "translate the ancient *Prophecies* from those times, and Countries, which they did properly regard, to others, which they do not concern". Similarly, he denounced "false interpretations of *Providences* and *Wonders*". He criticised the tendency to interpret natural events as omens, wonders and miracles, or to misinterpret the significance of true miracles "when we make general events to have a private aspect, or particular accidents to have some universal signification".[46] Just as in the social sphere, so in the realm of nature, the enthusiasts were said to confuse the private with the universal. More generally, Sprat criticised the confusion of the natural and the supernatural in the thought of the enthusiasts, a confusion which by no means sustained the Christian religion but rather polluted it:

> ... [T]he *Enthusiast* goes neer to bring down the price of the True and Primitive *Miracles*, by such a vast, and such a negligent augmenting of their number.[47]

At this point Sprat presented the new experimental philosopher as a supporter of Christian orthodoxy rather than as one who was undoing it. It was the natural philosopher's scepticism towards alleged omens and miracles or towards pretended prophecies which demonstrated his Christian orthodoxy:

> Let it be allow'd, that he is alwayes alarm'd, and ready on his guard, at the noise of any *Miraculous Event*, lest his judgment should be surpriz'd by the disguises of *Faith*. But does he by this diminish the *Authority* of *Antient Miracles*? or does he not rather confirm them the more, by confining their number, and taking care that every falsehood should not mingle with them? Can he by this undermine *Christianity*, which does not now

---

[45] On Sprat's arguments against enthusiasm, see also Wood, "Methodology and Apologetics", pp. 16–21.
[46] Sprat, *History of the Royal Society*, p. 358.
[47] Ibid., p. 362.

stand in need of such extraordinary Testimonies from *Heaven*? or do not they rather indanger it, who still venture all its Truths on so hazardous a chance?[48]

The natural philosopher thus supported a growing tendency in Protestant and Anglican thought of the seventeenth century to confine miraculous events to the apostolic period, or at least to the first centuries of Christianity.[49] The systematic study of nature was the best corrective to the enthusiast's failure to distinguish the natural from the supernatural, the best guarantee against the exaggerated recourse to miracles and prophecies.

The theological function of the new philosophy was not merely negative. The experimental philosophers also offered a new avenue to knowledge of God. As Sprat himself said, in diminishing the supernatural intervention of God, the scientists were by no means denigrating divine providence:

> They make no comparison between his power, and the works of any others, but only between the several ways of his own manifesting himself. Thus if they lessen one heap yet they still increas the other: In the main they diminish nothing of his right. If they take from the *Prodigies*, they add to the ordinary *Works* of the same *Author*. And those ordinary *Works* themselves, they do almost rais [sic!] to the height of *Wonders*, by the exact Discovery, which they make of their excellencies.[50]

For Sprat, divine providence manifested itself in God's *Potentia Ordinata* more than in his *Potentia Absoluta*. The seventeenth-century natural philosophers' appreciation of *Potentia Ordinata* was at least partly sustained by them in order to dissociate themselves from the dangers of enthusiasm Yet regular providence, no less than extraordinary miracles, was a manifestation of God's will.[51] For Sprat, as for Wilkins, Boyle, Glanvill and other members of the Royal Society, the investigation of the "book of nature" was the best way to understand divine providence, indeed, to worship God by glorifying his works.[52]

---

[48] Ibid., p. 360.
[49] See Chapter 1 above.
[50] Sprat, *History of the Royal Society*, pp. 361–362.
[51] Wood, "Methodology and Apologetics", p. 16.
[52] See Barbara Shapiro, *John Wilkins, 1614–1672* (Berkeley: University of California Press, 1969), pp. 236–238; J.E. McGuire, "Boyle's Conception of Nature", *Journal of the History of Ideas* 33 (1972): 523–542; and Jacob, *Robert Boyle and the English Revolution*, pp. 98–118. Boyle's main text on this theme is Part I of "Some Considerations Touching the Usefulness of Experimental Natural Philosophy", in Thomas

This was precisely the point on which critics like Casaubon and Stubbe criticised Sprat. Excessive concentration on the investigation of nature seemed to them dangerously close to the naturalism and materialism of the "atheists". By exclusive preoccupation with secondary causes, the new philosophers ran the risk of ignoring the first cause. Such arguments were apparently common before Casaubon and Stubbe published their attacks on the Royal Society, indeed, before Sprat's own *History*, since Sprat tried to answer these accusations in his book. In response to the argument that the experimental philosophers abjured the Christian precept to despise "the world" and became excessively engrossed in *this* life instead of contemplating the next, Sprat made the distinction between carnal, lustful desires and a pious involvement in worldly affairs or in the investigation of nature.[53]

However, critics like Casaubon accused the new scientists not only of "atheism", but also of "enthusiasm". For Casaubon, the programme of the Royal Society—discovering the glory of God in the works of nature—was no different from the programme of the alchemists. Commenting on Glanvill's declaration, he said:

> ... I should have been very suspicious, if not confident, he had borrowed this goodly language from some profane Chymist, such as our *Robert Fludd* was, with whom such professions of zeal for the glory of God are very frequent and ordinary.[54]

Historically, there may indeed have been some traces of the influence of alchemical attitudes on the new scientific view of the world.[55] Casaubon however ignored the real differences between the alchemical programme and the experimental one. Though he relied on Mersenne's and Gassendi's opposition to Fludd, he did not see that the new experimental philosophers were likewise critical of alchemy; nor

---

Birch (ed.), *The Works of the Honourable Robert Boyle* (London, 1772), vol. II. For Glanvill's views see especially his *Philosophia Pia*, and Cope, *Joseph Glanvill*.

[53] Sprat, *History of the Royal Society*, pp. 365–369.

[54] Casaubon, *Letter to Peter du Moulin*, p. 21, reproduced in Spiller, *"Concerning Experimental Natural Philosophie"*, p. 171. Robert Fludd (1574–1637) was one of the most influential alchemical physicians in England of the early seventeenth century, and a chief supporter of the Rosicrucian fraternity.

[55] See Charles Webster, *From Paracelsus to Newton: Magic and the Making of Modern Science* (New York: Cambridge University Press, 1982); and P.M. Rattansi, "Paracelsus and the Puritan Revolution." *Ambix* 40 (1963): 24–32, and most recently, with respect to Newton, B.J.T. Dobbs, *The Janus Faces of Genius: The Role of Alchemy in Newton's Thought* (Cambridge: Cambridge University Press, 1991).

did he acquaint himself well with Fludd's work once he had decided
that it contained nothing "but what I judged ... impertinent and
blasphemous".[56] For him, the new corpuscular philosophers were as
presumptuous as Fludd had been in "applying all or most mysteries
of the Scripture to it [the Philosophers' stone], as that wherein onely,
or chiefly, the Goodness, Power and Wisdom of God is to be seen
and admired".[57] According to Casaubon, the programme of the Royal
Society—like the programme of the alchemists—purported to suggest a "short-cut" not only to secular knowledge but to the knowledge of God. Circumventing both Scripture and humanistic learning, the new experimental philosophers wished to discover God in
the works of nature, just as the alchemists pretended to do. Casaubon
came out against the language, not only of extravagant chemists "but
of all men generally, who professing Christianity, would raise admiration, by broaching unheard of mysteries".[58] He admitted "that there
is nothing in nature, in sight so inconsiderable, but may give an
intelligent man matter and occasion to admire and magnifie the Power
and Wisdom of God";[59] but that was so in the most regular and
daily occurrences, not in the extraordinary phenomena with which
the alchemists, astrologers and scientists dealt.

Once again, Casaubon failed to perceive the difference between
the alchemists and the new scientists. It was precisely in concentrating on the regular and common, that the new natural philosophers
sought to distinguish themselves from the alchemists and astrologers.
The distinction was incomplete, however. In the early years of the
Royal Society, investigations of regular phenomena and of "extraordinary curiosities" were often mixed.[60] For Casaubon, however, the
exclusive preoccupation with the investigation of nature, and the
investment of this activity with religious significance, threatened to
undermine the role of traditional learning and traditional theology as
an avenue to achieve a saving knowledge of God. Referring to the
Hebrew term in Proverbs for wisdom or salvation as signifying this
type of saving knowledge, he expressed the hope that Glanvill was
not making such extravagant claims for experimental philosophy:

---

[56] *Letter to Peter du Moulin*, p. 21, reproduced in Spiller, *"Concerning Natural Experimental Philosophie"*, p. 171.
[57] Ibid.
[58] Ibid.
[59] Ibid., p. 22, reproduced in Spiller, p. 172.
[60] See Hunter, *Science and Society in Restoration England*, pp. 66–67.

> After all this, we need less wonder, that your Author . . . should appro-
> priate *substantial wisdom* to this kind of Experimental Philosophy: though
> I hope he doth not intend thereby *Solomon's* תושיה in our English, *sound
> wisdom*: intended by *Solomon* of the true fear and sanctifying knowledge
> of God, to which the promises of eternal life are annexed: from whence
> it would follow, that according to him, none can be saved but by this
> way of Philosophy. But I will be more charitable then to think he
> could forget himself so much, though some may justly stumble at such
> superlative expressions, and his Philosophy (with sober men) more likely
> to lose than to gain by them.[61]

Thus the danger was nevertheless there. The advocates of experimental philosophy were setting up a new channel of direct access to
divine secrets, and as such, their theology was "somewhat mystical"
and their philosophy was nothing short of "enthusiasm".

Henry Stubbe, like Casaubon, was troubled by the religious significance with which Sprat invested the new experimental philosophy. He took umbrage at Sprat's statement that the natural and
experimental philosopher

> will be led to admire the wonderful contrivances of the *Creation*, and so
> to apply and direct his *praises* aright: which *no doubt*, when they are
> offer'd up to *Heaven*, from the mouth of one that hath well studied
> what he commends, will be more suitable to the *Divine Nature*, than the
> blind *Applauses of the Ignorant*.[62]

To this claim for the theological merit of scientific knowledge Stubbe
responded:

> The former part of this passage is contrary to the *Analogy of Faith* and
> *Scripture*, in that it makes the acceptableness of mens prayers to depend
> more or less on the study of Natural Philosophy. Whereas the *Apostle*
> suspends the *acceptableness of all Prayers unto God*, in being made unto
> him *in the name*, and *for the mediation of Christ Jesus*, applied by *faith*.[63]

Here, the issue was clearly that of the way to salvation. Stubbe took
Sprat to mean that the new natural philosophy provided such a way,
and he saw this as contradicting the articles of faith, particularly those
of the Protestants who regarded the mediation of Christ to the faithful

---

[61] Casaubon, *Letter to Peter du Moulin*, pp. 23–24, reproduced in Spiller, *"Concerning
Experimental Natural Philosophie"*, pp. 173–174.
[62] Stubbe, *A Censure*, p. 36. The quotation is from Sprat, *History of the Royal Society*,
p. 349.
[63] Stubbe, *A Censure*, p. 36.

as the exclusive bridge to salvation.[64] Stubbe argued in a manner almost identical with Casaubon, saying that natural knowledge performed no such "bridge":

> [A] *Psalm* of *David*, the *Te Deum*, or *Magnificat*, in a *blind* and *ignorant*, but *devout Christian*, will be better accepted than a *Cartesian Anthymne*.[65]

The reference to Descartes is significant, of course. Both Cartesianism and the new experimental science were regarded by Stubbe as claiming to be avenues to salvation—alternatives to the Protestant reliance on Scripture. Though he did not mention or even hint at alchemy or enthusiasm in this context, as Casaubon had done, their arguments were strikingly similar.

Stubbe reversed this argument in the same tract, a few pages later. Defending theological disputation as a necessary support of religious orthodoxy, he denounced Sprat's appeal for reliance on the "bare promulgation" of Scripture.[66] According to Jacob, Stubbe's defence of scholastic disputations and his critique of a reliance on the "bare promulgation" of Scripture was ironic and "left handed" and served to cover his own radical views. Otherwise, how is the sudden shift from a call to rely on the Psalms and *Te Deum* to a declaration of the need for scholastic terminology to be explained? However, the same shift occurs in Sprat's own text. When criticising the traditional "scaffolding" of Christianity, i.e. Aristotelian scholasticism, he had recourse to mere "Scripturalism". Yet Sprat was far less anti-intellectual when offering his own alternative underpinnings for orthodoxy, namely, the new natural philosophy. Stubbe might simply have been following, and responding to Sprat's own shift in his arguments. In addition, Stubbe was careful to present the Aristotelian and scholastic notions merely as useful, not as absolutely true or essential means towards the knowledge of God.[67] According to Stubbe—at least that

---

[64] Stubbe was also quoting article 13 of the 39 Articles—there is no value to works before Grace. James Arderne in his anonymous letter to Stubbe denied that Sprat claimed for the new philosophy the status of a soteriological bridge in place of Christ. Stubbe reiterated his own arguments in *A Reply unto the Letter*, pp. 6–7, 25–26.

[65] Stubbe, *A Censure*, p. 39; Cope, *Glanvill*, p. 33. Casaubon made a similar statement in *Letter to Peter du Moulin*, pp. 22–23, reproduced in Spiller, *"Concerning Experimental Natural Philosophie"*, pp. 172–173. God was indeed to be glorified by observing His works, yet what was needed for that was not scientific expertise but Grace.

[66] Stubbe, *A Censure*, pp. 40–52, referring to a passage in Sprat's *History of the Royal Society*, p. 355.

[67] Jacob, *Henry Stubbe*, pp. 92–93; and Stubbe, *A Reply unto a Letter*, pp. 25–26.

was his manifest view—"Peace in the Church" depended on the resort to "those transcendental notions, and Scholastic terms", even if they involved some disputations.[68] Removing them would only contribute to the growth of heresy; replacing them with the experimental investigation of nature, or with the mere reading of Scripture as expounded by Reason would only further subvert the social and ecclesiastical order.[69] Although Stubbe did not apply here the term "enthusiasm" to the new experimental philosophy, his explicit argument was very similar to that of Casaubon. True, for Stubbe, the main danger of the new science was its latent materialism, even atheism, but as in the case of Casaubon, and as many of the critics of enthusiasm pointed out, there was a paradoxical affinity between enthusiasm and atheism.[70] Both these tendencies rejected the traditional role of Christ, the Church, and the Christian intellectual heritage, as mediators between man and God. For Casaubon as well as Stubbe, the new experimental science was doing precisely that. Whether Stubbe refrained from associating the new science more explicitly and systematically with enthusiasm at this point because of his own covert, radical religious leanings must remain an open question.

For the apologists of the Royal Society, the new experimental philosophy was the best antidote to enthusiasm—the enthusiasm of the radical sects, the prophesiers and even the Puritans who claimed to interpret natural events as divine omens. For the critics of the Royal Society, on the other hand, the new science was dangerously close not only to materialism and atheism, but also to the "fanaticism" or enthusiasm of the Rosicrucians, the alchemists, and "empirics" who claimed to discover the secrets of nature and find shortcuts to secular and divine knowledge alike. The terms "enthusiasm" or "fanaticism" may have referred to somewhat different groups when used by Sprat and Glanvill or by South, Casaubon and Stubbe, but the outlook which both sides denounced was the same. The enthusiasts were those who rejected established institutions, threatened the social and political order and pretended to have direct access to certain knowledge, and, indeed, to divine knowledge as well. For the opponents of the Royal Society, the new experimental scientists clearly

---

[68] Stubbe, *A Censure*, p. 51.
[69] Ibid., pp. 53–55.
[70] See, e.g. More, *Enthusiasmus Triumphatus*, Section I, in *A Collection of Several Philosophical Writings of Henry More*, (London, 1662), vol. 1, and Chapter 3 above.

fell into this category. The experimental philosophers themselves, how-ever, regarded the new science as the best defence against the enthu-siasts in providing a firm intellectual basis for the social and political order, in inculcating a modest attitude towards knowledge, and in delimiting supernatural interventions in natural and human affairs.

The question whether the new science was a manifestation of enthusiasm or an antidote to it thus highlights the special social and cultural place science came to occupy in Restoration England. It also manifests the profound change which took place in that generation in the intellectual basis for the social order in general, and in the responses to enthusiasm in particular. The experimental philosophers admitted that they were innovators, but only in the sense of offering a new foundation for the existing social, political, cultural and reli-gious order. Their conservative critics, however, saw the new science as subversive of that order rather than as supportive of it. In this respect they detected an important point: the experimental scientists did not merely offer a new basis for the socio-cultural order, but implicitly suggested change in the nature of that order itself, weaken-ing the hold of traditional authorities, and putting greater emphasis on the individual and on co-operation between contemporary indi-viduals, as well as on the religious value of the investigation of na-ture, thus offering a new alternative to the social and cultural order.

The debate whether the new science was linked with enthusiasm or was an appropriate "antidote" to it thus highlights the change which was gradually taking place in the ideological basis of the so-cial and cultural order. In the post-1660 period, first in England, but later also on the Continent, the critique of enthusiasm was signifi-cantly transformed. From a critique based on tradition (whether theo-logical, medical or intellectual), it increasingly turned to new founda-tions, to new theological, medical and scientific arguments. In the present chapter, this change was examined through the discourse of natural philosophers on enthusiasm. The next two chapters will look at the parallel transformations in the theological and medical dis-course on enthusiasm in the late seventeenth century.

CHAPTER SIX

SCRIPTURE AND REASON: THE NEW THEOLOGICAL DISCOURSE ON THE EVE OF THE ENLIGHTENMENT

In the earlier parts of this book I discussed the theological critique of enthusiasm from the Reformation to the middle of the sixteenth century, going on to analyse the medical critique of enthusiasm and the relationship between the new science and enthusiasm. It is time now to return to the theological discourse and examine the extent to which it was influenced by the new intellectual currents surveyed in previous chapters. This investigation will lead us to the central question this study seeks to answer: How far was the critique of enthusiasm "secularized" on the eve of the Enlightenment, and in what ways was the challenge of enthusiasm itself one of the causes of the secularization of the ideological basis of the social and political order by the beginning of the eighteenth century?

As we have already seen, the challenge of "enthusiasm" reached a certain climax in the mid-seventeenth century, especially in England during the Interregnum period, but also in other countries, such as the Dutch Republic. It was to re-emerge from the late 1680's onwards, with the movement of the "petits prophètes" in the Cévennes following the Revocation of the Edict of Nantes, and later with the Camisard revolt of 1702–1704.[1] Movements such as the Quakers, the Dutch Collegiants, and later the Pietists, as well as the followers of Jean Labadie and Antoinette Bourignon, similarly fuelled the critique of enthusiasm in the late seventeenth and early eighteenth centuries.[2]

---

[1] On the "petits prophètes" and the Camisard revolt see the classic articles by Charles Bost, "Les Prophètes du Languedoc en 1701–1702", *Revue historique* 136 (January–April, 1921): 1–37; 137 (May–June, 1921): 1–31; idem., "Les 'Prophètes des Cévennes' au XVIIIe siècle", *Revue d'Histoire et de Philosophie Religieuses*, 5 (1925): 401–430. For recent studies see especially Philippe Joutard, *La légende des Camisards: Une sensibilité au passé* (Paris: Gallimard, 1977), as well as his shorter book, *Les Camisards* (Paris: coll. Archives, 1975), and finally, Daniel Vidal, *Le Malheur et son Prophète: Inspirés et Sectaires en Languedoc Calviniste (1685–1725)* (Paris: Payot, 1983).

[2] On the Quakers in the late seventeenth and early eighteenth centuries see the classic book by W.C. Braithwaite, *The Second Period of Quakerism* (London, 1921), and Arnold Lloyd, *Quaker Social History: 1669–1738* (London: Longmans, 1948). On the

Although some of these various enthusiasts preached doctrines which mainstream Protestants could consider heretical, the most striking feature of the theological critique of these movements is the paucity of doctrinal debate as such. Contrary to the controversies with the enthusiasts of the sixteenth and early seventeenth centuries, after 1660 the emphasis seems to have been on the legitimacy of enthusiasts' claims to have direct divine inspiration, rather than on the content of their preaching.[3] Indeed, in many cases, like that of the Cévennes prophets, the doctrine preached by the enthusiasts was orthodox Calvinist teaching, sometimes more traditionalist than that of the official churchmen of the time.[4] What distinguished them was usually the millenarian thrust of their preaching, and more important, their claim as laymen to prophesy and receive direct divine revelations.

In fact, after 1660, the central challenge of "enthusiasm" was conceived as an anti-clerical one, and in this respect, it was paradoxically often associated with atheism. The association between enthusiasm and atheism was made already by Henry More in his *Enthusiasmus Triumphatus*:

Collegiants see the recent study by Andrew C. Fix, *Prophecy and Reason: The Dutch Collegiants in the Early Enlightenment* (Princeton: Princeton University Press, 1991), especially chapter 2. For the history of Pietism in that period see Erich Beyreuther, *Geschichte des Pietismus* (Stuttgart: J.F. Steinkopf Verlag, 1978). It should be stressed, however, as Beyreuther does, that the Pietists themselves were ambivalent, and often opposed to enthusiasm. On Antoinette Bourignon and Jean Labadie, see Leszek Kolakowski, *Chrétiens sans Eglise* (Paris: Gallimard, 1969), chapters X, XI.

[3] Not all the tracts against "enthusiasm" in those years manifest this change. Some of the theological critique on the Continent, especially in academic milieus, aimed at Pietists, Quakers and mystical trends, continued to deal with doctrinal issues as well. Among the texts dealing with enthusiasm in the early eighteenth century which should be mentioned are: Friedrich Spanheim Jr., *Selectae Controversiae cum Enthusiastici*, in his *Opera Omnia*, tome 3. (Spanheim the younger was the son of Friedrich Spanheim, discussed in Chapter 1 above); Ch. Sonntag, *Animadversiones centum miscellae in Fanaticismum tam veterem quam recentiorem* (1701); S. Edzardi, *Impietas cohortis fanaticae, ex propriis Speneri, Rechenbergii, Petersenii, Thomasii, Arnoldi, Schützii, Böhmeri, aliorumque fanaticorum scriptis* (Hamburg, 1703); Johann Georg Neumann, *Synopsis errorum fanaticorum quos Tremuli moderni fovent, disputationibus aliquot academicis exposita* (Wittenberg, 1703); H.J. Gerdessen, *De Enthusiasmo schediasma inaugurale . . . contra fanaticos nov-antiquos* (Wittenberg, 1708; inaugural lecture delivered in 1694 but published fourteen years later). For a detailed contemporary bibliography see Ch. M. Pfaff, *Introductio in historiam theologiae literariam* (Tübingen, 1725), Part II, section XI, pp. 350–397. I am indebted to Prof. Pierre Fraenkel for directing my attention to this important bibliographic source. In the following pages, however, we shall deal mostly with polemical tracts aimed at a broader public, especially in England, but also with Continental reactions to the Huguenot prophets from the Cévennes.

[4] See Philippe Joutard, *La légende des Camisards*, pp. 39–40, 47–48.

Atheism and *Enthusiasm*, though they seem so extremely opposite one to another, yet in many things they do very nearly agree. For, to say nothing of their joynt conspiracy against the true knowledge of God and Religion, they are commonly entertain'd, though successively, in the same Complexion ... those that have only a fiery *Enthusiastick* acknowledgement of God ... will as confidently represent to their *Phansy* that there is no God, as ever it was represented that there is one....

More went on to stress the mutual support which the atheist and enthusiast bestowed on each other:

For the *Atheist*'s pretence to Wit and natural Reason ... makes the *Enthusiast* secure that *Reason* is no guide to God: And the *Enthusiast*'s boldly dictating the careless ravings of his own tumultuous *Phansy* for undeniable Principles of Divine knowledge, confirms the *Atheist* that the whole business of Religion and Notion of a God is nothing but a troublesome fit of over-curious *Melancholy*.[5]

The common substratum of both atheism and enthusiasm was melancholy, as we have seen in previous chapters. But they also had a common enemy—"the true knowledge of God and Religion"—and their arguments reinforced each other. Similar arguments were repeated in the next two generations, as the challenge of atheism became increasingly menacing. In 1680, Bishop Burnet, discussing the disastrous consequences of the execution of Charles the First, included among them "the advantage that many weak and prejudicial persons took against the appearance of Religion, Prayers, and the Motions of God's Spirit: all these having been so much pretended at that time".[6] A few years later Charles Leslie declared that the devil had "arm'd the atheists and deists to joyn with the more plausible enthusiasts, and Latitudinarians" to form an alliance to destroy the church.[7] And following the affair of the French Prophets the Low Churchman Josiah Woodward considered the unfounded pretensions of the enthusiasts as one of the causes of the languishing state of true religion:

For when People have sounded these Pretensions, and found them nothing more than the *Fancies* of Men's *distempered Brains*, or the *suggestions*

---

[5] *Enthusiasmus Triumphatus*, Section I, pp. 1–2.
[6] G. Burnet, *A Fast Sermon on the 30th of January 1680 before the Aldermen of the City of London* (London, 1681), p. 9.
[7] Charles Leslie, *The Snake in the Grass* (third edition, 1698), preface, p. xii. I am indebted for this quotation to James P. Murray, "Charity, Zeal and Spiritual Authority in Britain, 1660–1700", unpublished Ph.D. diss., Johns Hopkins University, 1986, chapter 6.

of evil *Spirits*; they are apt to think so, even of Things truly *Sacred* and *Divine*, without taking just care to discern the vast *difference* betwixt the one and the other.[8]

The French Prophets, critics said, gave the libertines a pretext to claim that the biblical prophets "were such of men as the *Camisards* now are".[9] Sir Richard Bulkeley, one of the chief patrons of the Prophets, was accused of setting "the whole Tribe of Atheists, Deists etc. upon the giggle."[10] On the other hand, the Low Churchman Benjamin Hoadly held that the spread of atheism and profaneness encouraged the manifestation of enthusiasm.[11]

The link between enthusiasts and atheists is not that odd, however. Both were deeply anticlerical and wished to undermine the ecclesiastical order. At least, this is how the ministers perceived them. Josiah Woodward quoted the Preface of Lacy's *Cry from the Desert* to the effect that "when God shall pour out his Spirit on all Flesh, there will manifestly be little need of the Clergy, they will stand upon a Level with the rest."[12] Another Anglican minister, Edmund Chishull, was quick to note that the obliteration of any distinctions between clergy and laymen was not only the theme of French Prophets like Cavalier, but also of deists such as Matthew Tindal in his *Rights of the Christian Church Asserted* (1706).[13] Beyond their common anti-

---

[8] J. Woodward, *Remarks on the Modern Prophets, and on Some Arguments Lately published in their Defence* (London, 1708), pp. 5–6.

[9] *Clavis Prophetica: or, a Key to the Prophecies of Mons. Marion, and the other Camisars, With some Reflections on the Characters of these New Envoys, and Mons. F.—their Chief Secretary* (London, 1707), pp. 5–6. The same argument was voiced in 1698, before the French Prophets arrived in England, by W. Whitfeld in *A Discourse of Enthusiasm*, p. 19. Other critics of the French Prophets made the same point: George Hickes in his "Epistle Dedicatory to Sir George Wheeler" in the fourth ed. of *The Spirit of Enthusiasm Exorcised* (London: 1709), B2; Edmund Calamy, *A Historical Account of My Own Life*, vol. II (ed. by John T. Rutt, London, 1829), p. 103; Marc Vernous, *A Preservative Against the False Prophets of the Times* (London, 1708), p. 19. Several years later Samuel Turrettin in Geneva used the same argument in his *Préservatif contre le fanatisme* (Geneva, 1723), pp. 430–431.

[10] *Reflections on Sir Richard Bulkeley's Answer to Several Treatises* (London, 1708), Preface, p. vi.

[11] Benjamin Hoadly, *A Brief Vindication of the Antient Prophets* (London, 1709), Preface.

[12] J. Woodward, *Remarks on the Modern Prophets*, p. 55.

[13] E. Chishull, *The Great Danger and Mistake of all New Uninspired Prophecies, Relating to the End of the World, Being a Sermon Preached on Nov. 23rd, 1707* (London, 1708), pp. 41–42. Chishull regarded Cavalier's assemblies in the Cévennes where sacraments were distributed by laymen as the first church to practise the principles advocated by deists like Tindal. He did not mention Tindal by name, however, alluding only to Tindal's book.

clericalism, enthusiasts and deists were united, according to their critics, in rejecting Scripture as the exclusive authority in religious matters. Both groups also set up private judgment as a substitute for tradition, making "every private Christian a Pope" in the words of George Hickes, the famous non-juror.[14] This is a crucial point to which I shall return below. For all these reasons, it is not surprising that behind the enthusiasts' pretensions to prophecy and inspiration, critics saw an atheistic design.[15]

Yet, no less important than the anti-clerical challenge was the threat enthusiasm posed to political authority and the social order. In England of the Interregnum period, this threat was especially lively, but it remained in force after the Restoration as well. Thus in 1674 the following poem with its somewhat awkward rhyming scheme appeared at the end of an Anglican Almanac:

See you not here blind ignorant heady zealots
How first the church was governed by Prelates;
Christ's holy Apostles, and the seventy were
Most of them bishops, placed here and there
In sundry Churches, for the Propagation
O'the Christian faith within each several Nation;
And were those lights put out by bold intrusions,
What would be in the church but mad confusions?
Each Cobbler then would say he had the spirit
and Preach such Doctrine as would Bedlam merit.[16]

The reference to "Bedlam" merits attention, given our discussion of the medical interpretation of enthusiasm in previous chapters. Here however it is important to note that the threat to the ecclesiastical order was conceived as a threat against the social order in general.[17] Several years later, Robert South similarly alluded to the Interregnum

---

[14] George Hickes, *The Spirit of Enthusiasm Exorcised*, pp. 37–38 in the first ed. of 1680, p. 62 in the 4th ed. of 1708.

[15] This was indeed the main argument of the anonymous tract *Clavis Prophetica* quoted above, which was principally directed against the scientist Nicolas Fatio de Duillier. Several historians have recently pointed out the possible social and intellectual links between deists and enthusiasts. Deism in the early eighteenth century may in fact be regarded as a kind of religious reform movement in search of a pristine form of Christianity. See for example, Hillel Schwartz, *The French Prophets* (Berkeley: University of California Press, 1980), pp. 62–64.

[16] *An Episcopal Almanac for the year 1674*, C 8v.

[17] The reference to the cobbler, the standard symbol of the lower orders, is significant. Indeed, the poem concluded with the classical proverb: "let the cobbler stick to his last"—"ne sutor ultra crepidam".

experience and to the political and social threat of enthusiasm. He reminded his listeners that the Spirit taught the enthusiasts "to bind kings with chains, and their nobles with fetters of iron". Indeed, he analysed the political and anti-clerical threat of enthusiasm in clear economic terms, writing ironically:

> ... [W]hen the yoke of government begins to sit uneasy upon their unruly necks, or when they have run themselves out of their estates, and so come to cast a longing eye upon the revenues of the church, or of their rich neighbors about them; why then the word, that commands obedience, and forbids all violence and injustice, presently becomes not only a dead, but a killing letter, and a beggarly rudiment, and in comes the Spirit with a mighty controlling force to relieve and set them at liberty....[18]

Oblique references to the Interregnum experience were common also among critics of the French Prophets after 1706, and once again they insisted on the link between the anti-clerical challenge and the danger to the social order as a whole. Said one opponent of the new "pretended prophets":

> When they have railed against us Ministers, till they have the Rabble about them, then the levelling Principle is always taken up, and from preaching against Priests, they turn their Doctrines against the Rich.[19]

The terms "levelling" and "levellers" were of course loaded with memories of the English Civil War. Not by chance did they appear in quite a few of the tracts written against the French Prophets in England.[20] Most important, however, the ministers were never tired of insisting that the enthusiasts' claim to direct divine inspiration did not threaten merely the authority of the Church. It also endangered the social order as a whole, economic, political, even familial.[21]

Faced with this challenge, how did theologians and preachers react to it in the late seventeenth and early eighteenth centuries? To

---

[18] Robert South, Sermon LV, "Enthusiasts, not led by the Spirit of God", in *Sermons* (New York, 1870), vol. III, p. 165. On Robert South see above, Chapter 5, note 6.

[19] Francis Hutchinson, *A Short View of the Pretended Spirit of Prophecy* (London, 1708), p. 39.

[20] See for example [Anon.], *Observations upon Elias Marion and his Book of Warnings Lately Published* (London, 1708), pp. 9–10; Francis Atterbury, *The Voice of the People No Voice of God* (London, 1710), p. 24.

[21] See for example, Henry Nicholson, *The Falsehood of the New Prophets Manifested with their Corrupt Doctrines and Conversations* (London, 1708), p. 24.

what extent did their response to the enthusiasts differ from that of their predecessors? As I noted above, post-1660 ministers focused less on doctrine and more on the question of authorization. I shall now go on to examine the changes in theological discourse concerning enthusiasm in that period, focusing on references to a key text already referred to in Chapter 1—I John 4:1:

> Beloved, believe not every spirit, but try the spirits whether they are of God: because many false prophets are gone out into the world.

The traditional commentaries on this verse, as we have seen, tended to associate "spirit" with doctrine, and identified false prophets as false teachers.[22] Even those who referred to the pretended inspiration of the false prophets paid more attention to the doctrinal content of their teaching than to the credibility of their claims to inspiration. I have discussed Luther's use of I John 4:1 in Chapter I above.[23] Calvin referred to the same verse in his biblical commentaries, taking the term "spirit" indeed "as meaning a man who claims the gift of the spirit, so that he may assume the office of a prophet."[24] Still, the trial of spirits was primarily the testing of the doctrine taught by these "spirits". Believers should be watchful, Calvin said, "not to accept any doctrine lightly and without judgment."[25] Seventeenth century Reformed theologians similarly stressed the doctrinal criterion in the

---

[22] This interpretation may be found already in the medieval glosses, for example, that of Nicholas of Lyra. See *Biblia cum glossa ordinaria* (1586 ed.) fol. 232v. I am indebted to Irena Backus from the Institute for Reformation History in Geneva for this reference, as well as for other bibliographical help on this topic. In the sixteenth century we find this interpretation in the Commentaries of Zwingli, Tyndale and Gualtherus, to take but a few examples: Huldreich Zwingli, *Exegetica Novi Testamenti Residua*, in M. Schuler and J. Schulthess, eds., *Huldreich Zwinglis Werke*, vol. VI, t. 2 (1838), p. 333; William Tyndale, *The Exposition of the fyrste Epistle of Seynt John* (1531), pp. 42v–43r; Rudolphus Gualtherus, *In Joannis Apostoli et Evangelistae Epistolam Canonicam Homiliae XXXVII* (Zürich, 1553), Homilia XXII, pp. 149–157, esp. p. 150r. In the seventeenth century, see for example Jean Mestrezat, *Exposition de la première epistre de l'Apostre S. Jean*, t. II (1651), p. 11.

[23] See also his "Vorlesung über den 1. Brief des Johannes. 1527", in *WA*, I, 20, pp. 724–728, and Christoph Windhorst, "Luther and the 'Enthusiasts', Theological Judgements in his Lecture on the First Epistle of St. John (1527)", *Journal of Religious History* 9 (1977): 339–348.

[24] Jean Calvin, *Commentaries*, tr. and ed. by J. Haroutunian, "The Library of Christian Classics", vol. XXIII (Philadelphia: The Westminster Press, 1958), pp. 86–88. The quotation is on p. 86. The original Latin text reads as follows: ". . . [E]o, qui spiritus dono se praeditum esse iactat ad abeundum prophetae munus." J. Calvin, *Opera quae supersunt omnia*, vol. LV, in *Corpus Reformatorum*, vol. 83, cols. 345–349, quotation from col. 347.

[25] Calvin, *Commentaries*, ibid.

trial of spirits.[26] As late as 1680, George Hickes, the future non-juror, posed Christological doctrine as the first rule by which to try the spirits.[27]

In this respect, the use of that same verse in at least some of the critique of enthusiasm at the end of the seventeenth and early eighteenth centuries marks a very significant change: here the focus was clearly not on doctrine, but on the enthusiasts' claims to divine inspiration. As far as doctrine was concerned, the teaching of the "petits prophètes" in the Cévennes was typically Calvinist. Indeed, their stress on sin and repentance represented a tradition of popular Calvinism which had become increasingly alien to many official Huguenot ministers. True, it was a millenarian type of Calvinism, strongly influenced by the Old Testament. However, by the time the French Prophets had come to England in the early eighteenth century, their millenarian and apocalyptic message had been somewhat watered down, and their preaching was vague enough to be found acceptable by a variety of theological ears, including Anglican ones.[28] One of the chief spokesmen of the prophets themselves, John Lacy, dwelt on this point in the Preface to his *Warnings*: "This Mission brings no new Doctrine with it".[29] Similarly, Henry Nicholson, a follower turned critic of the French Prophets confessed that he had always remained a good Anglican

> But as these Men did not, at first, seem to assault any of my *Tenets* in that point; so they insensibly gained on my Judgment to believe several things, which now, upon more serious Consideration, I look upon as Delusion.[30]

With the French Prophets, the established Churches thus confronted not so much a heretical challenge, but one of enthusiasts who threatened to circumvent the clerical channels for transmitting the Christian message by arrogating to themselves direct divine inspiration. Opponents therefore focused their attention on these claims, rather

---

[26] See for example, Johan Piscator, *Commentarii in Omnes Libros Novi Testamenti* (Herborn, 1613), pp. 1469, 1472; Franciscus Gomarus, *Analysis Primae Epistolae Johannis*, in *Opera Theologica Omnia* (Amsterdam, 1664 ed.), p. 731.

[27] George Hickes, *The Spirit of Enthusiasm Exorcised* (1680 ed.), pp. 18–19. In the 1709 edition of that same text, p. 38.

[28] See Hillel Schwartz, *The French Prophet*, pp. 37–71, 85–98.

[29] Quoted by Schwartz, *The French Prophets*, p. 90.

[30] Henry Nicholson, *The Falsehood of the New Prophets Manifested*, p. 7. Italics in the original.

than on the content of the enthusiasts' preaching. The elderly John Humfrey admitted that the French Prophets' call to repentance was in itself positive, but he disliked their tendency to pronounce particular prophecies and warnings, adding:

> This is the point then at the bottom, whether that which they call Inspiration be not really their own Fancy only, Imagination, or Delusion?[31]

He then proceeded to quote I John 4:1. The Huguenot minister Marc Vernous was even clearer on this point:

> But tho' these Prophets teach nothing contrary to the Holy Scriptures, that does not hinder but that we may deny the Truth of their Commission, at least reserve to ourselves the Liberty of examining it, according to the Rules delivered to us in the Holy Scriptures.[32]

The trial of spirits therefore had to rely on other criteria by which to examine the prophets' claims to be in possession of direct divine inspiration. As we have seen above, the principal traditional sign of divine inspiration was the ability to perform miracles. Precisely on the eve of the Enlightenment, miracles assumed particular importance because doctrine was less of a shibboleth by which to judge the pretensions of the prophets. Moreover, as we have seen in Chapter 5, miracles became specifically crucial as unambiguous proofs of divine mission in a generation which was influenced by the new scientific conceptions of evidence. Such evidence had to be not only public, but verifiable by controllable methods. Hence the claims of the prophets to predict the future were carefully scrutinized and even mocked at. This was notably so after the failed resurrection of Dr. Emes, foretold to take place on May 25, 1708.[33] Indeed, the background to this careful scrutiny was the Protestant principle that miracles ceased to occur after the Apostolic period. As we have seen in Chapter 1, this was a basic Protestant supposition since at least the middle of the sixteenth century. Faced with the challenge of the

---

[31] John Humfrey, *An Account of the French Prophets, And their Pretended Inspirations, in Three Letters sent to John Lacy* (London, 1708), pp. 29–30.

[32] Marc Vernous, *A Preservative against the False Prophets of the Times* (London, 1708), p. 45.

[33] [Anon.], *Reflections on Sir Richard Bulkeley* (London, 1708), Preface, pp. 12–13; Nathaniel Spinckes, *The New Pretenders to Prophecy Examined* (London: 1709), Postscript; See also Edmund Calamy's report on his discussion before May 25 with Francis Moult, a supporter of the Prophets, in Calamy's *Historical Account of My own Life*, p. 105. On the failed resurrection of Dr. Emes and its repercussions, see also Schwartz, *The French Prophets*, p. 120.

French Prophets, it was a principle repeated by Protestants of all persuasions. Nonjurors like Hickes and Spinckes, High Church bishops such as Blackall, Broad Churchman like Benjamin Hoadly, the non-conformist Edmund Calamy, as well as Continental Calvinists like Bénédict Pictet in Geneva—all relied on this idea of the cessation of miracles in their controversy with the Huguenot prophets of the early eighteenth century.[34]

On the basis of this principle, and under the growing influence of the new experimental science, scepticism increased concerning the reliance on alleged miracles in that generation. Protestant theologians tended to give naturalist accounts for any such miracles, or at least to claim the existence of natural causes, even if unknown. We find this already in a sermon originally delivered by John Tillotson in 1679.[35] The most sceptical attitude towards miracles as public signs of inspiration was expressed by Benjamin Bayly in his *Essay upon Inspiration* of 1707.[36] This position, significantly enough, drew criticism from High Church quarters. Thus Henry Leavery, in a manuscript letter to Nathaniel Spinckes of February 20, 1711, criticised this aspect of Bayly's *Essay*. Leavery basically approved of Bayly's *Essay* (a noteworthy reaction from a High Churchman and friend of Hickes and Spinckes!), but he was very uneasy with Bayly's scepticism towards miracles:

---

[34] George Hickes, *The Spirit of Enthusiasm Exorcised* (1709 ed.), pp. 51–52, 62; Nathaniel Spinckes, *The New Pretenders to Prophecy Examined*, p. 362, also quoting Hickes; Offspring Blackall, *The Way of Trying Prophets: A Sermon preached before the Queen at St. James's November 9, 1707* (London, 1707), pp. 18–20; Benjamin Hoadly, *A Brief Vindication of the Ancient Prophets*, pp. 241–242. Edmund Calamy, *A Caveat against New Prophets*, pp. 10–11. Bénédict Pictet, *Lettre sur ceux qui se croyent inspirez*, pp. 29–36. Pictet was a relatively conservative theologian in Geneva who struggled to defend Calvinist orthodoxy in that period. See on Pictet, Eugène de Budé, *Vie de Bénédict Pictet, théologien genevois, (1655–1724)* (Lausanne: Bridel, 1874). See also the anonymous *A Dissuasive against Enthusiasm*, p. 49, ff., and Marc Vernous, *A Preservative Against the False Prophets of the Times*, p. 45.

[35] See Sermon XII in *The Works of Dr. John Tillotson . . . containing four sermons and discourses* (London, 1696), pp. 211–212.

[36] [Benjamin Bayly], *Essay upon Inspiration* (London, 1707), pp. 97–134. Bayly (1671–1720) was educated at St. Edmund's Hall and Wadham College, Oxford, and served for most of his career as rector of St. James's at Bristol. See *D.N.B.* vol. I, p. 1368. The first edition of *An Essay upon Inspiration* was published anonymously in 1707 and was directed mostly against the Quakers with whom Bayly had to deal in Bristol. The section on the French Prophets was added in the second edition of 1708, pp. 383–415.

I am afraid Mr. B. ascribing so much to the powers of Nature may give encouragement to the Doctrine of that half witty Philosopher Spinoza who reckons God only Nature . . . and his allowance of such almost unlimited power in the Divel [sic!] to delude any man by wonders may countenance Mani's mad haeresy of an Independent Supreme Being, and by both weaken the evidence for the truth of Christianity by miracles.[37]

Once again we see the delicate position in which churchmen found themselves in that generation, between the enthusiasts and their claims to contemporary miracles on the one hand, and the sceptical critics, who were too close to Spinoza in denying the possibility of divine miracles, on the other.

Alongside miracles, the other traditional criterion for the trial of spirits was Scripture itself. The sufficiency of Scripture as a guide to Christian life and doctrine was the standard Protestant argument against the enthusiasts, as we have seen in Chapter 1. It remained so in the late seventeenth and early eighteenth centuries as well, and it was presented as the surest rule by which to "try the spirits".[38] Scripture was thus brought forward not only as containing orthodox doctrine, but as the basis for examining the nature and legitimacy of inspiration itself. Said one anonymous minister in a sermon in 1707:

Prophesie itself, though a Gift immediate from God, and one would think had no need of any further Tryal than present Miraculous Operation, yet is subjected by command from God to be tryed by the authority of Holy Scriptures.[39]

The lack of any new message was a strong argument for the redundancy of new inspirations.[40] But a new doctrine could also not be reconciled with Scripture. The enthusiasts who claimed to have direct divine revelation were thus caught in a 'no win' dilemma in which their message either fitted Scripture, and was therefore redundant,

---

[37] Bodleian Library Mss., Rawl. C. 105, p. 588r.

[38] This was the theme of Blackall's Boyle Lectures in 1700, *The Sufficiency of a Standing Revelation* (London, 1717 ed.), as well as his later tract against the French Prophets, *The Way of Trying Prophets*, pp. 7–8. See also George Hickes, *The Spirit of Enthusiasm Exorcised* (1709 ed.), pp. 43–54; William Whitfeld, *A Discourse of Enthusiasm* (London, 1698), p. 6; James Hog, *Notes about the Spirit's Operations* (Edinburgh, 1709), pp. 21–22, 98–103.

[39] G. Philadelphus [pseudo.], *An Answer to the Right Way of Trying Prophets by F.M. [Francis Moult]* . . . *as delivered in a Sermon, November 9, 1707* (London, 1708), p. 20. For similar views see W. Stephens' Sermon on I John 4:1 in his *Sermons on Several Subjects* (Oxford: 1737 ed.), vol. II, p. 369, and *A Dissuasive against Enthusiasm*, pp. 2–3.

[40] See for example, Calamy, *A Caveat against New prophets*, pp. 10–11.

or contradicted it, and was hence false.[41] Scripture also provided the
critics of enthusiasm with a model of true prophecy, in comparison
with which contemporary prophets seemed hardly credible, a point
to which I shall return below. The conclusion was clear, and expressed most succinctly by the Scottish Presbyterian James Hog:

> Hence Visions, voices and Dreams, are no bottom on which we may
> build, and we ought to cease from regard to them.[42]

Side by side with the traditional standards of miracles and Scripture,
however, another, new criterion appeared by which to "judge the
spirits", namely reason. Indeed "Reason and Scripture" were the twin
rules to which almost all critics had recourse in that generation. For
Protestant ministers of all persuasions towards the end of the seventeenth century, and the beginning of the eighteenth, Scripture and
Reason, so far from clashing with each other, were considered to be
the two grand bulwarks against the threat of enthusiasm, indeed, the
double foundation of the social and religious order.

The growing role of reason as a critical factor in Protestant thought
in the late seventeenth century, especially in England, but not only
in England, is well known, of course.[43] My point, however, is that
this new role of reason emerged specifically in the confrontation with
enthusiasm. Indeed, the debate with the enthusiasts may well have
been a leading cause for the increased emphasis on reason in the
theological discourse of that generation. Already in the 1660's and
70's Anglican theologians like Robert South presented reason, together with Scripture and miracles, as the means by which to judge
the spirits and the reliability of faith.[44] Similarly, John Tillotson in a
sermon on I John 4, preached at Whitehall in 1679, declared that

---

[41] This dilemma was clearly posed by Thomas Morer in his Preface to *Sermons on
Several Occasions* (London, 1708), p. ix. See also Blackall, *The Way of Trying Prophets*,
p. 18; Pictet, *Lettre sur ceux qui se croyent inspirez*, pp. 29, 33, 35, 66.

[42] James Hog, *Notes about the Spirit's Operations*, pp. 23–24.

[43] Among the extensive literature on that subject, see especially, G.R. Cragg, *From
Puritanism to the Age of Reason* (Cambridge: Cambridge University Press, 1950); H.R.
McAdoo, *The Spirit of Anglicanism: A Survey of Anglican Theological Method in the Seven-
teenth Century* (London: Adams and Charles Black, 1965); and Phillip Harth, *Swift and
Anglican Rationalism: The Religious Background of A Tale of A Tub* (Chicago: Chicago
University Press, 1961). I shall return to some of the literature on parallel Continen-
tal developments below.

[44] See his sermon "Enthusiasm not led by the Spirit of God", in Robert South,
Sermons, pp. 169–174. South also argued in connection with the doctrine of the
Trinity, that reason ought to be the criterion by which we judge the reliability of
faith. See Robert South, "The Doctrine of the Blessed Trinity Asserted, and Proved

Reason is the faculty whereby Revelations are to be discerned; or to use the phrase in the *text*, it is that whereby we are to judge what *Spirits are of God, and what not.* For all Revelation from God supposeth us to be men, and to be endued with Reason; and therefore it does not create new Faculties in us, but propounds new Objects to that Faculty which was in us before. Whatever Doctrines God reveals to men are propounded to their Understandings, and by this Faculty we are to examine all Doctrines which pretend to be from God, and upon examination to judge whether there be reason to receive them as Divine, or to reject them as Impostures.[45]

Tillotson contended that in revealing Himself to men, God did not transform our faculties, but rather presented new objects before them, for their rational judgment. I shall presently return to this important point. The role of reason in the "examination of spirits" was also stressed by more conservative theologians. A year after Tillotson's sermon, George Hickes, soon to become a non-juror, in his sermon *The Spirit of Enthusiasm Exorcised*, refuted the Quaker George Keith. Keith had denied both the principle of the cessation of inspiration and the role of Scripture and reason in the "trial of spirits". Hickes retorted:

> . . . [L]et me shew you what a dangerous, damnable, and precarious principle that is, which asserts, that immediate Revelation, or Inspiration is not ceased, but is a standing, and perpetual gift in the Church of Christ . . . And that this Spirit of immediate Revelation or Spiritual light, is not, like the *Spirits* in Primitive times, to be tryed by the Scriptures, and reason, but that both of them are to be tryed by it.[46]

Seen against this background, the better known views of John Locke on this subject cannot be seen as exceptional, though they were surely influential in the next generation. Already in the early 1680's, in his *Journals*, Locke introduced reason as the judge of faith, determining

---

not Contrary to Reason", in I. Simon, *Three Restoration Divines: Barrow, South, Tillotson. Selected Sermons* (Paris: Société Les Belles Lettres, 1967), vol. II, pp. 261–262, and Simon's Introduction, vol. I, pp. 96–98.

[45] John Tillotson, Sermon XXI, in *The Works of the Most Reverend Dr. John Tillotson* (London, 1696), pp. 209–221. The quotation is from p. 210.

[46] George Hickes, *The Spirit of Enthusiasm Exorcised* (1680 ed.), pp. 37–38. A few years later, Elie Merlat, the French Huguenot theologian who took refuge in Lausanne, also gave reason a role in the "trial of spirits" in a sermon preached against the "petits prophètes" of the Cévennes. The sermon was again based on I John 4:1. E. Merlat, *Le moyen de discerner les esprits* (Lausanne, 1689), pp. 20, 25–27, 63–64. On Merlat, see Eug. et Em. Haag, *La France Protestante* (Paris, 1846–1859; Geneva: Slatkine reprints, 1966), vol. VII, pp. 374–378.

whether a revelation was truly divine or not.[47] He discussed this systematically in the *Essay concerning Human Understanding* published in 1690:

> Whatever God hath revealed is certainly true; no Doubt can be made of it. This is the proper object of *Faith*: but whether it be a divine Revelation or no, *Reason* must judge.[48]

Locke distinguished between the certainty of knowledge and the trust generated by faith. Yet faith was possible only if its authenticity was confirmed by reason.[49] In the case of enthusiasm reason indeed denied the authentic character of pretended inspiration. Locke discussed the topic of enthusiasm already in his *Journals*, in an entry on February 19, 1682, where he defined it in the following way:

> A strong and firme perswasion of any proposition relateing to religion for which a man hath either noe or not sufficient proofs from reason but receives them as truths wrought in the minde extraordinarily by god himself and influences comeing immediately from him seemes to me to be Enthusiasme, which can be noe evidence or ground of assureance at all nor can by any meanes be taken for knowledg [sic!].[50]

Enthusiasm was thus carefully defined in contradistinction from reason. It was a persuasion lacking sufficient proofs from reason. Locke returned to the subject in the mid 1690's when he added a chapter on enthusiasm as the penultimate chapter to the fourth edition of the *Essay Concerning Human Understanding*, which was published in 1700.[51] In that chapter Locke stated very clearly:

> He therefore that will not give himself up to all the Extravagancies of Delusion and Error must bring this Guide of his *Light within* to the Tryal. God when he makes the Prophet does not unmake the Man.

---

[47] See R.I. Aaron and J. Gibb, eds., *An Early Draft of Locke's Essay together with Excerpts from his Journals* (Oxford: The Clarendon Press, 1936), pp. 114–116, 124.

[48] John Locke, *An Essay Concerning Human Understanding*, chapter XVIII, section 10, see edition by Peter H. Nidditch (Oxford: Clarendon Press, 1975), p. 695.

[49] See also Maria Cristina Pitassi, *Le Philosophe et l'Ecriture: John Locke exégète de Saint Paul. Cahiers de la Revue de Théologie et de Philosophie*, 14 (Geneva, Lausanne, Neuchâtel, 1990), pp. 37–39, 58–61. For a somewhat different view of the relationship between faith and reason in the thought of Locke see David C. Snyder, "Faith and Reason in Locke's *Essay*", *Journal of the History of Ideas* 47 (1986): 197–213.

[50] Aaron and Gibb, *An Early Draft of Locke's Essay*, pp. 119–121, the quotation is from p. 119. See also Pitassi, *Le Philosophe et l'Ecriture*, pp. 57–58, note 17.

[51] See Locke's letter to Molyneux on April 26, 1695 in *The Correspondence of John Locke*, ed. by E.S. De Beer, vol. V (Oxford: Oxford University Press, 1979), letter 1887, p. 352. Locke made the first reference to the possibility of adding a chapter on enthusiasm in his letter to Molyneux on March 8 of that year. See ibid., letter 1857, p. 287.

He leaves all his Faculties in their natural State, to enable him to judge of his Inspirations, whether they be of *divine* Original or no.... Every Conceit that throughly warms our Fancies must pass for an Inspiration, if there be nothing but the Strength of our Perswasions, whereby to judge of our Perswasions; If *Reason* must not examine their Truth by something extrinsical to the Perswasions themselves; Inspirations and Delusions, Truth and Falshood, will have the same Measure, and will not be possible to be distinguished.[52]

It was by reason then, that one could distinguish true inspiration from false enthusiasm. Yet Locke did not rule out the two traditional criteria for the judgment of true inspiration—Scripture and miracles:

If this internal Light, or any Proposition which under that Title we take for inspired, be conformable to the Principles of Reason, or to the Word of GOD, which is attested Revelation, *Reason* warrants it, and we may safely receive it for true ... If it receive no Testimony nor Evidence from either of these Rules, we cannot take it for a *Revelation*, or so much as for true, till we have some other Mark that it is a *Revelation*, besides our believing that it is so. Thus we see the holy Men of old, who had *Revelations* from GOD, had something else besides that internal Light of assurance in their own Minds, to testify to them, that it was from GOD. They ... had outward Signs to convince them of the Author of those Revelations.[53]

Nevertheless, reason was "our last judge and guide in everything", including the judging of those very signs. Locke, like contemporary theologians, thus offered another criterion, along with those of Scripture, by which to compare contemporary claims to inspiration.

In the following years, especially after the spread of the Camisard prophets in Europe, the emphasis on reason and Scripture as the twin rules by which to judge claims of inspiration became standard argument.[54] The Broad Churchman Benjamin Bayly put the point most succinctly:

Whether a Man be inspired or not, Reason is the judge; the only faculty that can distinguish between Enthusiasm and true and Divine Inspiration.[55]

---

[52] Locke, *An Essay Concerning Human Understanding*, chapter XIX, section 14, p. 704 in the Nidditch ed.

[53] Ibid., section 15, pp. 704–705 in the Nidditch ed.

[54] In addition to Hickes whom we have mentioned already and who published a new edition of *The Spirit of Enthusiasm Exorcised* in 1709, see also the words of the Huguenot minister in London, Philippe Mesnard, *Les faux prophètes convaincus*, pp. 77–78.

[55] Bayly, *Essay on Inspiration* (1707 ed.), p. 17. See also the second ed. of the *Essay*, published in 1708, pp. 173–179, and on p. 414, as the concluding remarks of his

Bayly's formulation specifically echoed that of Locke or possibly Tillotson.[56] Not all the commentators expressed themselves in the same distinct manner, but the differences were essentially those of emphasis.[57] Samuel Turrettin in Geneva made a very similar statement a few years later: "Nous ne pouvons d'ailleurs nous assurer de la verité de la Révélation sans les secours de la Raison."[58] Just as reason judged the reliability of sense-data, said Turrettin, so it was the judge of the data of revelation, and of the claims of the enthusiasts to direct divine inspiration. In confronting the enthusiasts, Protestant theologians on the eve of the Enlightenment thus reversed the traditional relationship between faith and reason, and turned the latter into a judge of the former.

It is important to note, however, that the concept of reason itself was undergoing significant changes in that period. The historian should be sensitive to the various transformations in the meaning of the concept of reason in different cultures and periods.[59] In the late sixteenth and early seventeenth century, "reason" was understood by Protestant theologians in the traditional scholastic sense of syllogistic reason. It had an instrumental function, the drawing of logical conclusions from presuppositions expounded in Scripture, or the faithful

---

text "Let us try therefore all Pretences to immediate Revelation by sound Reason and Scripture, and if Men soar beyond these, out of sight of the Reveal'd Word and Human Reason, let them go—". Indeed, in his Sermon "Of Enthusiasm", given as the Lent Lectures founded by the High Churchman Edward Colston, Bayly laid greater stress on Scripture, *Fourteen Sermons on Various Subjects* (London, 1721), pp. 274–302. W. Stephens relied on reason as the exclusive judge: "It was by Reason that Christians had to judge the credibility of the claims to inspiration made by the enthusiasts, and whether they were indeed of divine origin." *Sermons on Several Subjects*, vol. II, pp. 336–337.

[56] Note, however, that Bayly took the position of Stillingfleet, rather than that of Locke, in distinguishing between apprehension and comprehension, and in arguing that certain revealed matters like the Trinity could be apprehended by human reason, though not fully comprehended. See ibid., pp. 203–213.

[57] See also Edmund Calamy, *A Caveat against New Prophets*, pp. 32–40, who also relied on Elie Merlat to whom I referred above, for arguments that the inspirations were not from God; Benjamin Hoadly, *A Brief Vindication of the Antient Prophets* (London, 1709), in Hoadly, *Several Tracts* (London, 1715), p. 266, and Thomas Morer, "A Sermon Concerning Agitations", in *Sermons on Several Occasions* (London, 1708), p. 222.

[58] Samuel Turrettin, *Préservatif contre le fanatisme, ou réfutation des pretendus inspirez des derniers siècles* (Geneva, 1723), p. 160, see also pp. 8–9, 162, 440.

[59] See for example the pertinent remarks to this effect in François Laplanche, *L'Evidence de Dieu chrétien. Religion, culture et société dans l'apologétique protestante de la France classique (1576–1670)* (Paris: Association de publication de la faculté de théologie protestante de Strasbourg, 1983), p. 137.

interpretation of these tenets. In the course of the seventeenth century, as the result of continual inter-confessional debate, some theologians, both Anglican and Huguenot (especially in the Academy of Saumur in France), increasingly emphasized the ability of human reason to understand and prove the basic tenets of Christianity—the existence of God the creator, Providence, the immortality of the soul, the principles of natural law and those of reward and punishment, both in this world and the next. Nevertheless, the close link between human reason and divine grace on these issues was strongly maintained. Protestant theologians distinguished between "Carnal Reason" and "Right Reason". The latter was dependent on "Prevenient Grace", on the pre-disposal of reason by grace. On the other hand, the reason which recognized the natural and moral order merely prepared the believer to accept the articles of faith. Theologians like Amyraut in France or Tillotson in England, while modifying the extreme Calvinist distrust of reason, were nevertheless loyal to the Thomistic tradition which insisted upon the dependence of human reason on divine grace.[60]

In the course of the second half of the seventeenth century the concept of human reason underwent a far-reaching, if not always explicit, transformation among Protestant ministers and preachers. The scholastic terminology was gradually losing ground, or at least modifying its character and function. The dimension of divine grace was pushed backwards, sharply separated from the realm of human reason, or conversely, conceived in almost naturalist terms, as we shall see below. Whereas for an Anglican theologian like Tillotson, human reason was dependent on divine grace and closely linked with it, in the next generation, especially among Low Churchmen in England, but also among Protestant theologians on the Continent, human reason was increasingly viewed as autonomous, precisely because it was seen as a divine gift.[61] Benjamin Hoadly, the Bishop of Bangor, put it clearly:

---

[60] For the concept of reason among Latitudinarians, especially Tillotson, see Roger L. Emerson, "Latitudinarianism and the English Deists" in J.A. Leo Lemey, ed., *Deism, Masonry and the Enlightenment. Essays honoring Alfred Owen Aldridge* (Newark: University of Delaware Press, 1987), pp. 19–48. For the concept of reason in the Saumur school, see F. Laplanche, *L'Evidence de Dieu chrétien*, pp. 97–133, and more extensively, in *L'Ecriture, Le sacré et l'histoire* (Amsterdam and Maarssen: APA—Holland University Press, 1986).
[61] See Bayly, *An Essay on Inspiration*, p. 159; Samuel Turrettin, *Préservatif contre le fanatisme*, p. 420.

> This indeed is certainly true, that his Ways in many things are far out
> of our Sight, nor can we possibly Judge of all the *Reasons* and *Ends* he
> hath in view: But what then? Doth it follow therefore that we must
> swallow everything as his Prescription? Doth it follow that we are *Judges*
> of nothing relating to him? Why then doth he himself subject his
> Revelations to our tryal and Judgement?[62]

These theologians were clearly influenced by the new conception of
reason as expounded by Cartesian philosophy on the one hand, and
the philosophy of Locke on the other. This conception emphasized
the role of reason as an independent criterion of truth, and as the
basis for certain knowledge. It also stressed the need to rely on univocal
language, in contrast to Thomistic philosophy which relied on
multivocal and equivocal terminology.[63]

Most important, however, reason as conceived by the late seventeenth and early eighteenth centuries had a social role to play in the
critique of enthusiasm. As we have seen above, enthusiasm was viewed
as dangerous to the social order because of its subjective and idiosyncratic character. The criteria for judging claims to divine inspiration had therefore above all to be public. Such indeed were miracles
in the biblical period, and such was Scripture itself. Reason had to
be public too in order to serve as a criterion by which to "try the
spirits". Yet it was individual reason which played such a public role.
Once again, Locke provides the clearest and most influential expression of this notion:

> But it is not the strength of our private perswation within ourselves,
> that can warrant it [divine inspiration] to be a Light or Motion from
> Heaven: Nothing can do that but the written Word of God without us,
> or that Standard of Reason which is common to us with all Men.[64]

The reason of the individual was thus a public criterion, side by side
with Scripture, to set against the subjectivist pretensions of the enthusiasts. It offered a firm foundation to the social order. This was
also the view adopted by many Low Churchmen in their controversies with the Quakers and the Huguenot prophets in the following
years. We find it even before Locke published the fourth edition of

---

[62] Benjamin Hoadly, *A Brief Vindication of the Antient Prophets*, in *Several Tracts*,
p. 266.

[63] On this subject, see Amos Funkenstein, *Theology and the Scientific Imagination from
the Middle Ages to the Seventeenth Century* (Princeton: Princeton University Press, 1986),
pp. 28–31.

[64] Locke, *Essay Concerning Human Understanding*, Book IV, Ch. XIX, section 16.

the *Treatise*, in the sermon by W. Stephens, commenting on I John 4:1 and the rules by which the spirits should be judged:

> Amongst these Rules, the First is, the having Recourse to our private Judgments, and a rational Weighing, in our own Minds, the merits of the Pretension.[65]

The individual judgment of reason was thus a public criterion, alongside Scripture, though by no means instead of it, in the eyes of Anglican Whigs. Moreover, it was posed as an antidote to "private persuasion".

Besides the problem of the criteria by which the spirits were to be judged, there was another, no less important question: Who was entitled to "try" them? In the early years of the Reformation, Luther—as against the Roman Catholics—emphasized each individual Christian's responsibility to judge the spirits.[66] The Calvinist answer was twofold, distinguishing between private and public trial. Such a distinction enabled Protestants to assign responsibility to individual Christians without creating spiritual anarchy and confusion. Calvin's own position in commenting on I John 4:1 laid down the principle for his followers:

> By private testing, each one establishes his own faith, and accepts only the teaching which he knows to be from God ... Public testing of doctrine has to do with the common consent and polity of the church. Since there is a danger that fanatical men may rise up and boast rashly that they have the Spirit of God, believers should seek remedy by coming together and reasoning their way to an honest and godly agreement.[67]

The public trial of spirits was thus specifically aimed at the pretensions of enthusiasts *fanatici homines*—who set up their own private

---

[65] W. Stephens, *Sermons on Several Subjects*, vol. II, Sermon XV, p. 366.

[66] "Non curet Christianus, quid totus mundus iudicet, si eciam totus mundus, omnes angeli contra sentirent, quia Christianus est iudex super omnes creaturas et angelos, quia habet spiritum sanctum, qui est iudex, dominus super omnia in celis et terris." "Predigt am Tage Kreuzes Erhöhung", 14/9/1524, *WA*, vol. 15, p. 684. On this sermon, see also Chapter 1 above. For Martin Bucer's view on this issue, similarly stressing the responsibility of every Christian to judge the spirits, see: "Martin Butzers ein christlichen Rath und Gemeyn der statt Weissenburg Summary seiner Predig daselbst gethon 1523", in *Martin Bucers Deutsche Schriften*, vol. I (Gütersloh: Gütersloher Verlagshaus Gerd Mohn; Paris: P.U.F., 1960), p. 84, and his "Ein kurtzer wahrhafftiger bericht von Disputationen und gantzem handel, so zwischen Kuonrat Treger ... und den predigern des Evangelii zuo Strassburg sich begeben hat", in *Martin Bucers Deutsche Schriften*, vol. 2, p. 97.

[67] John Calvin, *Commentaries*, pp. 87–88. For the Latin text see "Commentarius in epistolae catholicas" in *Opera Calvini*, *CR*, vol. 83, p. 348.

claims to inspiration. Whereas for Calvin, such public testing consisted of believers "coming together and reasoning their way to an
honest and godly agreement", subsequent Reformed commentators
interpreted public examination more clearly as resting with the ecclesiastical authorities.[68]

Towards the end of the seventeenth century, however, the balance
clearly shifted in favor of individual examination, and John's exhor-
tation was taken to be addressed to every believer. This is manifest
already in Tillotson's 1679 sermon on I John 4:1, where a great part
of his polemics is directed against the Catholic restriction of such
examination exclusively to the ecclesiastical authorities.[69] By the early
eighteenth century, critics of the French Prophets similarly laid stress
on the individual responsibility of every Christian to try the spirits
for himself, though some Huguenot and Presbyterian ministers adhered to the Calvinist dual examination—public and private.[70] The
individualistic requirement was emphasized especially by Broad
Churchmen, and was put succinctly by Stephens:

> In matters of so great an Importance as Religion is, Men have a na-
> tive, inherent, and unalienable Right of Judging for themselves.[71]

These words have a strikingly modern ring. Indeed, Protestant ministers were led to stress the same individualistic, even non-clerical
orientations which they criticised in their opponents. Lay critics of
enthusiasm supported this individualistic approach even more warmly.[72]
By the beginning of the eighteenth century, the delicate balance

---

[68] See for example, Gomarus, *Opera Theologica Omnia*, p. 731a; J. Piscator, *Commentarii
in Omnes Libros Novi Testamenti*, p. 1472b; J. Mestrezat, *Exposition de la première epistre
de l'Apostre S. Jean*, vol. II, p. 25.

[69] Tillotson, Sermon XXI, *Works*, pp. 213–215.

[70] Merlat, *Lettre sur ceux qui se croyent inspirés*, pp. 11–18; Mesnard, *Les faux prophètes
convaincus*, p. 86; Hog, *Notes about the Spirits' Operations*, p. 98, though he did not
elaborate on public examination; S. Turrettin, *Préservatif contre le fanatisme*, pp. 440, 446.

[71] W. Stephens, *Sermons on Several Subjects*, vol. II, p. 366. For similar views see
Calamy, *A Caveat against New Prophets*, p. 31; G. Philadelphus, *An Answer to the Right
Way of Trying Prophets*, p. 5; and G.L. Le Sage the elder referred to in the following note.

[72] Thus in Geneva, George-Louis Le Sage the elder voiced the principle of individual examination in the following words: "L'on ne sauroit douter que châque
particulier ne puisse examiner lui-même la nature des esprits, savoir si la Vocation
Divine que quelques particuliers se pourroient attribuer pour faire recevoir quelque
nouvelle opinion, est véritablement Divine; Douter que châcun ne puisse faire cet
examen, c'est rendre inutiles les exhortations si précises et si souvent rëiterées, que
les Ecrivains Sacrez nous adressent, d'éxaminer la Doctrine que l'on nous propose."
G.L. Le Sage, *Essai sur les caractères d'une vocation divine* (Amsterdam, 1721; 1st ed.,
1708), pp. 18–19.

between ecclesiastical authority and private judgment was tipping in the direction of the latter.

Finally, let us look at the interpretation Protestant ministers in that generation gave to true prophecy and to the genuine operation of the Holy Spirit, as distinct from the false pretenses of the enthusiasts. This is, of course, a vast topic which cannot be dealt with exhaustively within the limits of this study, but it is worth pointing out at least some important aspects of this account, both of biblical prophecy and the operation of the Holy Spirit.

The Cambridge Platonist John Smith (1618–1652) devoted a chapter in his discourse *Of Prophesie* to "The Difference of the True Propheticall Spirit from Enthusiastical Imposture".[73] He relied largely on Jewish medieval sources, principally Maimonides, in addition to scriptural verses, classical sources, and Patristic authorities. Indeed, he understood true prophecy primarily in rationalist terms, as distinguished from false prophecy:

> ... [T]he *Prophetical* spirit doth never alienate the Mind, (seeing it seats it self as well in the *Rational* powers as in the *Sensitive*,) but alwaies maintains a consistency and clearness of Reason, strength and soliditie of Judgment, where it comes; it doth not *ravish* the Mind, but *inform* and *enlighten* it: But the *Pseudo prophetical* spirit, if indeed without any kind of dissimulation it enters into any one, because it can rise no higher then the Middle region of Man, which is his *Fancy*, it there dwells as in storms and tempests, and being ἄλογόντι in it self, is also conjoyned with alienations and abreptions of mind.[74]

Whereas false prophecy appeals only to the senses and imagination (fancy), true prophecy also addresses the mind. The former was often caused by melancholy, fortified by a strong power of divination.[75] Nevertheless, Smith did not deny the similarities between true prophecy and false enthusiasm as far as the external manifestations are concerned, since "both of them make strong impressions upon the *Imaginative* powers", and both involve visions upon the stage of fancy.[76] Indeed,

---

[73] The Discourse *Of Prophesie* appeared in John Smith, *Select Discourses* published posthumously by John Worthington in 1660. I have used the 1672 edition where that discourse is on pp. 161–274. Chapter IV, pp. 183–202, is devoted to "The Difference of the true Prophetical Spirit from all Enthusiastical imposture".

[74] Ibid., p. 190.

[75] Ibid., pp. 183, 188, where Smith refers to Plato's *Phaedrus*, but interprets Plato's reference to mania as a negative one, and p. 190.

[76] Ibid., pp. 183–184.

... [W]e must not mistake the business, as if there were nothing but
the most absolute *Clearness* and *Serenitie* of thoughts lodging in the Soul
of the *Prophet* amidst all his *Visions.*[77]

Panic fears, consternations, affrightments and tremblings were emotions frequently accompanying prophecy as Jeremiah, Ezekiel, Daniel
and many other biblical prophets testified, and as medieval Jewish
philosophers like Maimonides, Albo and Abarbanel emphasized.
Neither were physical phenomena such as voices foreign to them, or
dramatic signs like the trumpets and seals in the book of Revelation.[78] The distinction between true prophecy and false enthusiasm,
therefore, was not altogether easy and clear-cut. Smith inclined to
distinguish between the two not only in terms of the "matter", the
message—the false prophets "tending to nourish immorality and
prophaneness", but also in terms of the "Energy" and "the manner
of inspiration" which was *"more dilute* and *languid.* Whereas *true Prophesie*
entred upon the Mind *as a fire,* and *like a hammer that breaketh the rock
in pieces."*[79] Though stressing the rational element in true prophecy,
Smith, like the medieval Jewish philosophers on whom he relied, did
not ignore the emotional and physical side-effects of divine inspiration. Enthusiasm, in contrast, was based exclusively on ecstasies and
on the imagination, and even there, the passions and perceptions it
aroused were less vigorous and lively than in true prophecy.[80]

Edward Stillingfleet, later Bishop of Worcester, was more tradi-
tional than Smith. In his *Origines Sacrae,* written a few years after
Smith, Stillingfleet relied on Thomas Aquinas rather than on
Maimonides when he said

... [I]n *Prophetical illumination* the mind of the *Prophets* was so *moved*
by the *Spirit of God,* as an *instrument* in the *hand* of an *Artificer,* which
bears no proportion with the *skill* of the workman.[81]

In case the prophet was endowed with a *lumen propheticum,* he knew

---

[77] Ibid., p. 192.

[78] Ibid., pp. 192–199.

[79] Ibid., p. 200. Smith is quoting here Jeremiah 23:29.

[80] Ibid., pp. 200–202. In the following chapter, Smith presented the *Intellectus agens*
or "Immediate Efficient" of true prophecy as an angel, working upon the prophet
by dream or vision. Ibid., pp. 202–212.

[81] Edward Stillingfleet, *Origines sacrae: or a Rational Account of the Grounds of Christian
Faith, as to the Truth and Divine authority of the Scriptures, and the matters therin contain'd* (1st
ed. 1662; 3rd ed. corrected and amended, London, 1666), p. 182. See Thomas
Aquinas, *Summa Theologica,* 2, 2, 9. 1, 173, art. 3.

indeed with certainty that the revelation he received came from God. Stillingfleet, however, entertained the possibility that something might be represented to the fancy of a visionary who lacked the ability to understand the meaning of those "imaginary species". Such were the dreams of Pharaoh, or Nebuchadnezzar, which required the interpretations of Joseph or Daniel respectively.[82] Nevertheless, Stillingfleet held that neither prediction nor miracles were essential features of true prophecy. Miracles were needed only when the prophets were sent to bear testimony to the truth of their way of religion to people not convinced of it. Indeed, the prophets had to be judged primarily by the doctrine which they preached, not by the miracles which they truly or allegedly performed.[83]

In the second half of the seventeenth century the rational element in true prophecy was further stressed, as against mere enthusiasm. Critics of enthusiasm made a sharp distinction between biblical prophecy and contemporary "prophets". The latter, such as the "petits prophètes", were ecstatic prophets who hardly understood what they were saying. The prophets of the Bible, on the other hand, operated by means of reason and understood very well the message they were transmitting. Thus, Elie Merlat in Lausanne, one of the first critics of the "petits prophètes", stressed that true divine inspiration worked on man's mind, not on his senses or imagination.[84] English ministers said the same thing a few years later as the Huguenot prophets crossed the Channel. Relying, among other sources, on Stillingfleet, ministers stressed that God addressed the mind of the prophets and their understanding, not their physical ear, and surely did not talk directly through their mouths.[85]

A similar intellectualist interpretation is noticeable among Protestant theologians in this generation with respect to the regular and contemporary operations of the Holy Spirit. In his *Essay on Inspiration*, Benjamin Bayly remarked that

> the Assistance of the Spirit not a little consisting in giving the Objects of Faith this agreeable and rational Appearance.[86]

---

[82] Ibid.

[83] Ibid., pp. 170, 174, 199–204.

[84] Elie Merlat, *Le moyen de discerner les esprits*, pp. 32, 73.

[85] Benjamin Hoadly, *A Brief Vindication of the Antient Prophets*, p. 265; Thomas Morer, *A Sermon Concerning Agitations* (London, 1708), pp. 221–222.

[86] B. Bayly, *An Essay on Inspiration*, p. 175.

A similar view was held by Reformed theologians like the Dutch Frans Burman, the Frenchmen Jean Claude and even more so Claude Pajon, and the Genevan Bénédict Pictet.[87] All of them presented the operation of the Holy Spirit and of divine grace largely in cognitive, almost "psychological" terms, and they did so especially while confronting the threat of enthusiasm.

Indeed, Reformed theologians at the end of the seventeenth century and the early eighteenth were unwilling to give up the indispensability of the operation of the Holy Spirit in the process of conversion, but vis-à-vis the enthusiasts, they tended to give it an increasingly intellectualist and naturalist interpretation. Thus, one of Pictet's students in Geneva, Samuel Turrettin, devoted a whole chapter in his tract against fanaticism to the difference between the fanatical interpretation of the operation of the Holy Spirit, and the Orthodox one. On the face of it, Turrettin emphasized the traditional Protestant link between Scripture and the operation of the Holy Spirit, and he quoted his predecessors, such as Bénédict Pictet, to that effect. Yet he tended to give a concrete and specific account of the operation of the Holy Spirit, and he did so in cognitive, medical and psychological terms. The Holy Spirit gave us first of all the instruction we needed concerning the way of sanctity by the communication of Scripture, since "La première chose dont on a besoin pour suivre une certaine route, c'est de la bien connoitre".[88] It then operates on our bodies:

> Le Saint Esprit peut agir sur nôtre corps pour rectifier jusqu'à un certain point nôtre temperament, et par là diminuer l'empire qu'il a sur nôtre ame, et la violence des tentations qu'il nous livre.[89]

We have here an analysis parallel to the medical account of enthusiasm which has been discussed in Chapters 3 and 4 above, and to which I shall return in the following chapter. The Holy Spirit works on our temperament in such a way as to diminish its hold over our soul, and the strength of the temptations it poses. Here, the "medical" analysis refers to the positive process of sanctification, but in

---

[87] See Laplanche, *L'écriture, le Sacré et l'histoire*, pp. 584–586, 618–619, 652–653.
[88] Samuel Turrettin, *Préservatif contre le fanatisme*, p. 400.
[89] *Ibid.*, p. 401. Turrettin went on to give the example of the choleric person: God can affect the constitution of his blood in such a way that he would not give way to anger so easily. For Pictet's view, see Laplanche, *L'Écriture, le sacré et l'histoire*, pp. 618–619.

both cases men's religious motives are understood in physiological or at least psychological terms. This is how Turrettin presented the operation of the Holy Spirit on our soul:

> Le S. Esprit peut agir sur nôtre ame même, pour perfectionner les facultez dont elle doit faire usage, afin de surmonter les tentations auxquelles elle se trouve exposée. . . . Dieu peut aussi agir immédiatement sur nôtre ame pour perfectionner et pour fortifier ces facultez, il peut disposer nôtre ame d'une telle manière, qu'elle pourra dans la suite résister avec plus de facilité à l'impression que font sur elle les objets extérieurs, jusqu'à ce qu'elle ait examiné ce qu'elle doit faire pour s'acquitter de ses devoirs.[90]

Turrettin thus wished to give as naturalist an account as possible for the operation of the Holy Spirit. The Holy Spirit did not need to provide any new revelations, as the enthusiasts claimed, it only mitigated the force of the bodily temptations, and directed man's attention away from ideas which could inflame his passions, and towards the Christian virtues.[91] Turrettin thus translated the classical Protestant view of the operation of the Holy Spirit into empirical and concrete terms.[92] The challenge of enthusiasm required Turrettin, as it required other Protestant ministers in his generation, to give a naturalist, psychological, even medical account of the regular operation of the Holy Spirit, which in itself they were careful not to deny.

Faced with the challenge of enthusiasm on the one hand, and the danger of deism and atheism on the other, both of which endangered the clerical monopoly on the religious message—Protestant ministers on the eve of the Enlightenment, in England and on the

---

[90] Ibid., pp. 401, 402.

[91] "[P]our produire ces divers effets il n'employe aucune Nouvelle Révélation, il peut agir sur nôtre corps pour en rectifier les mouvemens et sur nôtre ame pour perfectionner ses faultez, sans lui donner pour cela aucune nouvelle idée, et par conséquent aucune Nouvelle Révélation." Ibid., p. 403, and see also pp. 403–404.

[92] The orthodox Protestant view regarded the Holy Spirit as operating both on the Intellect and, more important, on the Will. (In this respect, the Saumur school from John Cameron to Claude Pajon had already shifted the emphasis in an intellectualistic direction). Yet, the manner of operation of the Holy Ghost usually remained somewhat abstract and described in metaphorical terms, relying on scriptural verses. See for example, the Articles of the Synod of Dort on this matter, chapters 3 and 4 (concerning the doctrine of the Fall and Conversion) article 11, *Acta Synodi Nationalis. . . . Dordrechti Habitae* (Leiden, Dordrecht, 1620), p. 258. For an English translation see Thomas Scott, *The Articles of the Synod of Dort* (Philadelphia: Presbyterian Board of Publication, 1856), p. 210. This specific article is also quoted and translated into English in Brian G. Armstrong, *Calvinism and the Amyraut Heresy*, pp. 63–64.

Continent, had to renew the theological basis of their own status
and of the ecclesiastical order. They did so by adding individual human
reason to the traditional reliance on Scripture, by recourse to the
new experimental science, and by the incorporation of medical and
psychological terminology even in explaining the operation of the
Holy Spirit. They primarily employed this medical terminology,
however, in their account of enthusiasm itself. Indeed, some of the
ministers were remarkably abreast of the changes in the medical
theories of that period. We should therefore turn now to the diffusion
of a new medical critique of enthusiasm in the late seventeenth century.

CHAPTER SEVEN

THE NEW MEDICAL DISCOURSE AND THE THEOLOGICAL CRITIQUE OF ENTHUSIASM

The churchmen's critique of enthusiasm was largely transformed in the second half of the seventeenth century, not only due to the impact of the new conception of reason and its role in theological matters, or the influence of the new experimental science, but also through the increasing penetration of the medical discourse concerning enthusiasm. Such "medicalization" of the critique of enthusiasm, whose origins have been discussed in Chapters 2 and 3, had far-reaching implications.[1] It may also be seen as another manifestation of the growing "secularization" of the problem of enthusiasm, since by the early eighteenth century, some ministers, at least, tended to relegate that problem to the care of the physicians.

That medical discourse itself changed significantly in the post-1660 period, and these changes had important effects on the critique of enthusiasm. Until the second half of the seventeenth century, the Galenic conception of melancholy was predominant among critics of enthusiasm who wished to rely on a medical tradition in their discussion. As we have seen in previous chapters, Burton, Casaubon and even Henry More were deeply influenced by the humoral doctrine. Nevertheless, the humoral paradigm, reigning supreme for over two thousand years, was under growing attack in the sixteenth and seventeenth centuries, first by Paracelsus and his disciples, the "iatrochemists", who employed chemical concepts and methods of treatment, and later, from within, by members of the medical establishment itself. The crisis within Galenic medicine paved the way for a mechanistic alternative. The new mechanistic philosophers rejected the doctrine of humours just as they rejected the classical conception of qualities with which it was closely associated. This is especially

---

[1] Both historians and literary scholars have focused mostly on the influence of Burton, Casaubon and More on Swift's *Tale of a Tub* and the *Mechanical Operation of the Spirit*. (See note 1 in Chapter 3 above). Less attention has been given to the penetration of the medical discourse into regular Anglican and Protestant sermons in the post 1660 period.

clear in the case of René Descartes who essentially rejected the humoral theory by simply ignoring it almost entirely.[2] By the second half of the seventeenth century, the mechanist account in physiology had increasingly spread among physicans both in England and on the Continent.[3]

What were the effects of the decline of the humoral theory and the rise of mechanistic philosophy on specific medical views concerning melancholy? This is, of course, a vast and complicated question which cannot be dealt with exhaustively in this chapter.[4] According to one historian of melancholy, Esther Fischer-Homberger, the decline in the credibility of the theory of humours led to a transition from aetiological definitions of melancholy to symptomatic ones. When the existence of black bile was no longer taken for granted, melancholy lost its unified aetiological explanation. One turned, therefore, to the symptoms of melancholy for a definition of that condition.[5] By the end of the seventeenth century melancholy was usually defined as a feverless delirium with symptoms of sadness (associated traditionally with the heart), and dotage (idée fixe, or head-melancholy, linked with disturbances of the mind). Other symptoms of melancholy were more and more relegated to other diseases, primarily hysteria and hypochondria, usually referred to as the "spleen".[6] As we shall see below, critics of enthusiasm in the late seventeenth and early eighteenth centuries would also refer to the spleen, or to vapours rising from hypochondria, as causes for some of the delusions of the enthusiasts.

---

[2] On Descartes' physiological thought see Thomas S. Hall, "Descartes' Physiological Method: Position, Principles, Examples", *Journal of the History of Biology* 3 (1970): 53–79. See also G.A. Lindeboom, *Descartes and Medicine* (Amsterdam: Rodolpi, 1979), chapters V–VII. For older studies, see the classical article by Auguste Georges-Berthier, "Le mécanisme Cartésien et la physiologie au XVIIe siècle", *Isis* 2 (1914): 37–89, and the more philosophically oriented study by Pierre Mesnard, "L'esprit de la physiologie Cartésienne", *Archives de Philosophie* 13 (1937): 181–220.

[3] See on this topic, Theodore Brown, *The Mechanical Philosophy and the "Animal Oeconomy"* (New York: Arno Press, 1981).

[4] For a detailed recent discussion of this topic see Stanley W. Jackson, *Melancholia and Depression: From Hippocratic Times to Modern Times* (New Haven, London: Yale University Press, 1986), chapters 6, 7.

[5] Esther Fischer-Homberger, *Hypochondrie. Melancholie bis Neurose: Krankheiten und Zustandsbilder* (Bern, Stuttgart, Wien: Huber, 1970), pp. 17–19; idem., *Das Zirkuläre Irresein* (Zürich, 1968), pp. 25–32. Nevertheless, as Fischer-Homberger herself points out, the transition from an aetiological to a symptomatic definition of melancholy constituted a gradual shift of emphasis, rather than a drastic turn-about.

[6] In addition to the studies by Fischer-Homberger mentioned above see also Jackson, *Melancholia and Depression*, pp. 274–310.

Although discussions of the symptoms (and even cure) of melancholy remained strikingly traditional in the late seventeenth and early
eighteenth centuries, and although there was no one, clear, substitute for black bile as a unified explanation of melancholy, a crucial
change may nevertheless be detected in the account of both melancholy and hypochondria given by medical writers in this period. Two
aspects of this change are especially relevant to our topic: the increased emphasis on the role of the so-called "animal spirits" and
their malfunctions in causing the symptoms of melancholy (or hypochondria), and the marked tendency of many of these writers to
understand such malfunctions in corpuscular and mechanical terms.

In accounting for the causes of melancholic symptoms, greater stress
was laid by the medical writers on the role of the animal spirits and
their malfunctions. The animal spirits (*pneuma psychikon, spiritus animalis*)
were seen in the Galenic tradition as instruments of the soul, transmitting to it sensations from the external senses and transmitting from
it voluntary motion to the various members of the body. They originated in the external air which the body breathed. In the lungs this
air was digested, and, reaching the heart, it was assimilated into the
blood, thus forming the vital spirits (*pneuma zotikon*) which were trans-
ported to the whole body. In the arteries of the *rete mirabile* these
spirits were further refined and, by a process of exhalation (*anathymiasis*),
became animal spirits in the brain. From the brain they entered the
(hollow) nerves as the substratum for motive and sensitive soul-
faculties.[7] Yet, whereas according to the Galenic tradition, the "animal spirits" were the affected part in the melancholic condition, not
the immediate cause of melancholy,[8] in the seventeenth century, with

---

[7] See O. Temkin, "On Galen's Pneumatology" *Gesnerus* 8 (1950): 180–189. Rudolph
E. Seigel, *Galen's System of Physiology and Medicine* (Basel, New York: S. Karger, 1968),
pp. 182–195. For the Galenic texts see *De Usu Partium*, Liber IV, Cap. 17 (in C.G.
Kühn's ed. of Galen's *Opera Omnia*, vol. 3, Leipzig, 1822, pp. 492–500); there is an
English translation of this text by M.T. May, *Galen on the Usefulness of the Parts of the
Body* (Ithaca, N.Y.: Cornell University Press, 1968), vol. I, p. 324. Also *De Usu
Respirationum*, Cap. 5 in Kühn, vol. 4 (1822), pp. 501–502.
[8] See Galen, *On the Affected Parts*, tr. from the Greek text with explanatory notes
by Rudolph E. Seigel (Basel: S. Karger, 1976), p. 88. For the Greek text and Latin
translation see Galen, *De Lociis Affectis*, Liber III, Cap. 9 in C.G. Kühn, *Galeni Opera
Omnia*, vol. 8 (1824), p. 174. The same approach was taken in the seventeenth
century by Robert Burton who summarized the long medical tradition on melancholy.
The animal spirits were affected by black humor (whether cold or hot and dry) but
did not play an important role in his account of melancholy. See for example, *The
Anatomy of Melancholy*, Part I, Section 1, Memb. 3, Subsect. 3 (pp. 173–174 in the

the decline of humoral medicine, they, or more precisely, their mal-
function, assumed a more active role in the aetiology of melancholy.[9]

No less important was the increasingly mechanistic and corpuscular interpretation of "animal spirits" in the medical literature of
that period.[10] It was first developed systematically by Descartes, although, as we have seen above, he did not deal with the issue of
melancholy at all. Unlike Galen, Descartes regarded the animal spirits
as originating and pre-existing in the blood, as its most subtle and
agitated element. Moreover, he gave the animal spirits a strict corpuscular and mechanistic re-interpretation. The "esprits animaux" were
small corpuscles and as such belonged to the human (or animal) body
which was essentially a machine.[11] In this corpuscular orientation,
Descartes was also heir to sixteenth century psychological thought
which tended to give a physiological account for the activities of the
soul. Yet, whereas the naturalist thought of the Renaissance tended
to identify the animal spirits with the soul, and to blur the distinction
between matter and spirit, body and soul, Descartes developed his
mechanistic account in order to emphasize the distinction between
body and soul; he may have done so partly in reaction to thinkers
such as Melanchton, Servetus, Telesio and Campanella.[12]

Everyman ed.). In fact, "animal spirits" do not appear at all in the Index of the *Anatomy*.

[9] This is already clear in Daniel Sennert's *Institutiones* of 1611, where he saw the
"dark and black animal spirits" as the proximate cause of melancholy which was
"offending the imagination". See Daniel Sennert, *Institutionum medicinae libri V*
(Wittenberg, 1611), Book 2, Part 3, Sect. 2, Ch. IV. For an English translation see
Nine Books of Physick and Chirurgy Written by that Great and Learned Physitian, Dr. Sennertus
(London, 1658), p. 106; D. Sennert, *Medicinae Practicae Lib. I* (1628), Part II, Ch.
VIII, in *Opera Omnia* (Paris, 1641), pp. 125–127.

[10] The changing views concerning "animal spirits" in the second half of the seventeenth and early eighteenth centuries represent a complex topic which needs a
separate discussion. In this chapter I can only provide a very brief summary of
these developments.

[11] See letter to Buitendijck, *AT*, vol. 4, pp. 64–65. On Descartes' indebtedness to
previous sources concerning the subject of "animal spirits" see also Franz Rüsche,
"Zur Lehre Descartes' von den 'Lebensgeistern'", in *Philosophisches Jahrbuch* 60 (1950):
450–456.

[12] Michael Servetus identified the soul (indeed, the divine spirit itself!) with vivi-
fied blood. See Michael Servetus, *Christianismi Restitutio*, 1553 (rpt. ed. Nuremberg,
1790), p. 170. For an English translation, see Charles D. O'Malley, *Michael Servetus*
(Philadelphia: American Philosophical Society, 1953), pp. 202–208, esp. 204. Unlike
Servetus, however, Descartes clearly distinguished the animal spirits from the rational
soul, see *Traité de l'homme*, AT, vol. 11, 129–38, (pp. 20–30 in Hall's English translation,
Treatise of Man). *Les Passions de l'Ame*, part I, article X, (AT, vol. 11, pp. 334–342).
See also Descartes' letter to the Marquise of Newcastle (April 1645?), AT, vol. 4,
p. 191. See also the article "Descartes: Physiology" by Theodore M. Brown in the

The influence of Descartes over many of the medical writers in the next generation is clear, although its precise nature is still an open question, and the topic cannot be dealt with in detail in the present chapter.[13] One prominent example which is relevant to us is that of the English physician Thomas Willis. Sedlian Professor of Natural Philosophy in Oxford from 1660 till 1668, Willis combined a chemical interpretation with a mechanical one which was more clearly divorced from traditional Galenic notions.[14] The animal spirits were seen as chemical liquors distilled from the blood which, in melancholic distempers, became highly salty, acetous and corrosive like vinegar, and its particles, very moveable and unquiet.[15] Willis

---

D.S.B, vol. IV, pp. 61–65. On other sixteenth century tendencies to identify the animal spirits with the soul see Daniel P. Walker, "Medical *Spirits* and God and the Soul" in *Spiritus, IV Colloquio Internazionale del Lessico Intellettuale Europeo*, eds. M. Fattori and M. Bianchi (Rome: Edizioni dell'Ateneo, 1984), pp. 223–244. I am grateful to Professor Owsei Temkin for directing my attention to this interesting collection of articles. Whereas Walker stresses the thrust to give a corporeal interpretation to the soul in this identification, I would emphasize the tendency to "spiritualize" the medical spirits themselves by linking them (as Servetus and even Melanchton had done and the Cambridge Platonists were to do later in the seventeenth century) with the rational soul and even the Holy Spirit itself. A similar tendency to link melancholy with divine inspiration in the positive sense is manifest in the sixteenth century.

[13] See Hall, "Descartes' Physiological Method", p. 61, Brown, *The Mechanical Philosophy and the "Animal Oeconomy"* pp. 81–104. See also J.S. Spink, *French Free Thought from Gassendi to Voltaire* (New York: Greenwood, 1960), pp. 215–225. On the impact of Descartes on the Leiden School of Medicine see Antonie M. Luyendijk-Elshout, "Oeconomia Animalis, Pores and Particles", in Th. H. Lunsingh Scheurleer and G.H.M. Posthumus Meyjes, eds., *Leiden University in the Seventeenth Century: An Exchange of Learning* (Leiden: Brill, 1975), pp. 295–307.

[14] On Thomas Willis see the article "Willis, Thomas" by Robert G. Frank in the D.S.B, vol. XIV, pp. 404–409; Hansruedi Isler, *Thomas Willis 1621–1675, Doctor and Scientist* (New York, London: Haefner, 1968); Kenneth Dewhurst, *Thomas Willis as a Physician* (William Andrews Clark Memorial Library, Los Angeles: University of California Press, 1964). Willis responded to the challenge of the Paracelsian chemists and "chemical physicians" by adopting some of their principles and integrating them into a mechanical framework. See Brown, *The Mechanical Philosophy and the "Animal Oeconomy"*, pp. 152–160. Whereas Brown stresses Willis's mechanical approach, T.H. Jobe and Stanley Jackson emphasize his chemical understanding of melancholy: J.H. Jobe, "Medical Theories of Melancholia in the 17th and early 18th Centuries", *Clio Medica* 11 (1976): 217–231, esp. pp. 221–224; Jackson, *Melancholia and Depression*, pp. 110–115. For a caution against any strict and artificial distinction between Iatrochemical and Iatromechanistic approaches in the late seventeenth century see Lester S. King, *The Philosophy of Medicine: The Early Eighteenth Century* (Cambridge Mass.: Harvard University Press, 1978), chapter V.

[15] T. Willis, *Two Discourses Concerning the Soul of Brutes*, Part I, Ch. IV, pp. 23–24. Part II, Ch. XI, pp. 188–192, in Dr. Willis's *Practice of physick, being the Whole Works*, tr. by S. Pordage (London, 1684). The work was first published in Latin under the title *De Anima Brutorum* in 1672. For his lectures on this subject, see Kenneth Dewhurst,

explained the "disturbed phantasies" of melancholic persons as the result of the irregular and diffuse motion of these particles within the brain, instead of their regular motion into the nerves as in the case of healthy persons. In such irregular motion, these saline particles could also carve out new pores and passages in the brain causing "unwonted and incongruous notions".[16] Emotions and passions, in turn, could cause disturbances of the animal spirits. Strong passions such as love, hate, fear, envy, and shame, but also inordinate study— distracted the animal spirits from their regular motion. Consequently, the heart grew weaker, the blood became more fixed and saline, and hence, the animal spirits degenerated further, leading in turn to melancholic disturbances.[17] We shall return to this circular mechanism between "animal spirits" on the one hand, and passions and imagination on the other. At all events, Willis's chemico-mechanical account of melancholy was highly influential in the late seventeenth and early eighteenth centuries, though not undisputed, and it is to him that some of the preachers against the enthusiasts referred.

Clerical Use of Medical Arguments Against the Enthusiasts

In examining the penetration of the medical theories concerning melancholy into the clerical critique of enthusiasm, we should pay attention therefore to the changing character of that medical critique. How up-to-date were the Protestant ministers in their use of medical arguments against the enthusiasts in the late seventeenth and early eighteenth centuries? The answer to such a question can reveal much about the extent to which clerics were committed to the corpuscular philosophy. It may also disclose some of their views concerning the mind-body relationship.

Thomas Willis's Oxford Lectures (Oxford: Sanford Publications, 1980), pp. 122–130. See also Jobe, "Medical Theories of Melancholia", p. 222, and Jackson, "Melancholia and the Waning of the Humoral Theory", *Journal of the History of Medicine and Allied Sciences* 33 (1978): 370–371.

[16] *Concerning the Soul of Brutes*, pp. 190–191.

[17] Willis, *Concerning the Soul of Brutes*, p. 192. The passions of the soul were themselves one of the six "non-naturals" traditionally regarded as the causes of health or disease. (The others were air, food and drink, sleep and vigilance, motion and rest, evacuation and repletion). See on this topic, L.J. Rather, "The 'Six Things Non-Natural': A Note on the Origins and Fate of a Doctrine and a Phrase", *Clio Medica* 3 (1968): 337–347, and Peter H. Niebyl, "The Non Naturals", *Bulletin of the History of Medicine* 45 (1971): 486–492.

The traditional concept of melancholy by no means disappeared in the second half of the seventeenth century, though it was often invested with new meanings and new interpretations. For Henry Wharton in England, who aimed his critique at the Catholic Church, the enthusiasts were not just superstition-ridden, but also melancholic. His analysis of the physiological mechanism which gave rise to such delusions was, however, clearly influenced by the medical notions of the day:

> Such Persons are commonly endued with weak Brains and diseased bodies; often suffer irregular motions of the Blood, which creates gross and turbulent Spirits, and fills the Brain with strong and active Vapours. These continuing a violent motion in the Brain, will reproduce so strong and lively Images of those things, which have been the most frequent Objects of their Meditations, and made deepest Impression in them, that they will really believe themselves to act those things which they only imagine; and to see, hear, and feel all those Objects, which are so lively represented to them. This is manifest even in Melancholly and Hypochondriack Persons, who are so far deluded by the Action of the undigested Vapours of their Bodies upon their Brain, that they frequently believe the reality of those things, which their disturbed Imagination representeth to them.[18]

Irregular motions of the blood, turbulent animal spirits and vapours arising from the stomach, not the traditional humours, were now the cause of deluded imagination.

In the tracts written against the French Prophets traditional themes and concepts such as "melancholy" nevertheless still appeared. The Low-Church minister, Benjamin Bayly, who tended to give a strict naturalist account of the behaviour of the Prophets, still relied on traditional themes in explaining why they were mad even though only when engaged in prophecy. Did his opponent never hear, he asked, "of a Man's being mad *quoad hoc*, in one particular thing, altho' in other Matters he may speak and act with common Discretion and Sobriety"?[19] In 1721, the Genevan theologian Bénédict Pictet

---

[18] Henry Wharton, *The Enthusiasm of the Church of Rome* (London, 1688), p. 11.
[19] Benjamin Bayly, *An Essay upon Inspiration*, in two parts, 2nd ed. (London, 1708), p. 409. A similar point, also in traditional terms, was made by Bayly in a sermon "Of Enthusiasm" which was published in 1721:

> *Enthusiasm* is a Sort of religious *Madness*. For as, in Madness, Men frequently fancy themselves Kings, or Emperors, so, under the Power of Enthusiasm, Men very seriously fancy themselves Prophets, divine, and heavenly Ambassadors.

Benjamin Bayly, *Fourteen Sermons on Various Subjects* (London, 1721), Sermon IX, "Of Enthusiasm", pp. 269–302, quotation from p. 272.

counted melancholics among the chief groups of enthusiasts. As late
as the third decade of the eighteenth century, the term was not yet
obsolete.[20]

On the whole, however, melancholy was no longer that prominent in the medical critique against the French Prophets, and other
diseases and medical concepts appeared instead, as they did indeed
in the medical thought of the time. Thus, the anonymous author of
Observations upon Elias Marion compared the forced or preternatural
(i.e., pathological) affections of the body of a "prophet" like Marion
to "what happens many times to Women in Hysterick Fitts, arising
from the strength of their Fancies and Passions".[21] George Philadelphus made the same point: the agitations of the prophets were *Praeternatural* rather than *Super-natural* motions. Addressing Francis Moult, an
apothecary who acted as missionary, scribe and host of the Prophets,
he made the following significant comment:

> Had you read more of Physic and less of *Jacob Bekmen* (sic!), you might
> find several Instances of *Men*, *Women*, and *Children*, acted by *Involuntary
> Motions in Hysteric Fitts*, nay, Sing to perfection, tho' in their natural
> State of Health, never could Sing the least Note, Climb up Walls like
> Cats, and do abundance of such Prodigious wonderful Actions (*vid. Dr.
> Willis De Passione Hysterica*) All which no sober Men, can, or will At-
> tribute to a *Supernatural Agency*, but all must own to be *Praeter-natural*. So
> that your first Evidence, I presume, of their Divine Mission drawn
> from a Supernatural Power falls to the Ground.[22]

The confrontation between Jacob Boehme and books of "Physick"
exemplifies the extent to which Anglican ministers, in trying to account for the convulsions and involuntary motions of the enthusiasts,
preferred the medical corpus of knowledge to the interpretation found
in the writings of the mystics. Furthermore, the reference to Willis's
work indicates that the clerical critics of the French Prophets were
pretty up-to-date as far as the medical thought of the time was concerned. More common than hysteria, however, was the concept of
"vapours" which was linked with hypochondria, a malady which, as
mentioned above, tended to replace melancholy in the medical thought

---

[20] Bénédict Pictet, *Lettre sur ceux qui se croyent inspirez* (Geneva, 1721), pp. 22–23.
[21] [Anon.], *Observations upon Elias Marion and his Book of Warnings, Lately Published,
Proving this Elias to be a false Prophet, and a dangerous Person* (London, 1707), pp. 7–8.
[22] George Philadelphus [pseud.], An Answer to F.M. [Francis Moult] in *The Right
Way of Trying Prophets ... by F.M. ... To which is added, An Answer thereunto, Paragraph
by Paragraph ... by G. Philadelphus* (London, 1708), p. 13.

of that period. Thus, one of the anonymous answers to the prophet John Lacy explained the visions of the prophets as "the Effect of an *over-heated* Brain and of *Vapors*."[23] Yet, in assigning the causes of such vapours, the critics often fell back upon causes traditionally ascribed to melancholy too, such as fasting and troubles of mind.[24]

Since, however, according to their critics, the visions of the prophets were imaginary, the principal question to be elucidated was the nature of their imagination. Here, indeed, discussion relied on the concept of "animal spirits". We see such use of the animal spirits in explaining visions and imagination already in the 1688 sermon by Henry Wharton against the Roman Catholics, whom he regarded as enthusiasts. The tendency of Roman Catholic enthusiasts to fix their attentions and meditate upon certain objects "and employ all their Spirits in continuing their Ideas of them . . .", Wharton said, "create a mighty Fermentation in the Blood, whence new Clouds and Vapours are transmitted into the Brain, and render the Imagination more intense and strong."[25] For Wharton, as for future critics of enthusiasm, there was thus a mutual or circular relationship between the imagination and the physiological functions. The imagination could excite the passions and disturb the spirits which in turn rendered the imagination more confused and intense.[26] The irregular motion of the spirits

---

[23] [Anon.], *An Answer to a Letter of John Lacy Esq. dated July 6 1708 and directed to Josiah Woodward* (London, 1708), p. 28. The letter referred at this point to Edward Stillingfleet's *Fanaticism of the Church of Rome*, or as the full title read, *A Discourse Concerning the Idolatry Practised in the Church of Rome, and the Hazard of Salvation in the Communion of it: In Answer to some Papers of a Revolted Protestant. Wherein A Particular Account is given of the Fanaticisms and Divisions of that Church* (London, 1671). This text was answered already at that time by Hugh Cressy, *Fanaticism fanatically imputed to the Catholick Church by Doctor Stillingfleet: and the imputation refuted and retorted* (Paris, 1672).

[24] Elie Merlat in Lausanne compared the convulsions of the "petits prophètes" to epilepsy and suggested the possibility that some of their pronouncements were due to hysteria or hot vapours, but he did not pursue this line of argument any further. See Merlat, *Le Moyen de discerner les esprits* (Lausanne, 1689), pp. 34, 62. In England some years later, the anonymous author of *A Dissuasive against Enthusiasm* (London, 1708), attributed the prophetic effusions of the French Prophets to vapours and whimsies which filled their brain. These in turn were caused by fastings and troubles of mind which were unavoidable during the revolt in southern France. *A Dissuasive against Enthusiasm: Wherein the Pretensions of the modern Prophets to Divine Inspiration, and the Power of Working Miracles, are examined and confuted by Scripture and Matter of Fact* (London, 1708), pp. 45–46.

[25] Wharton, *The Enthusiasm of the Church of Rome*, p. 12.

[26] As I indicated above, this circular relationship was also a common theme in traditional medicine. Yet there, the humours alongside the spirits performed a crucial role, being affected by the imagination directly or indirectly, via the passions. See

could also produce various effects upon the body—extraordinary motions, suspension of life activities and ecstasy. In short, while adhering to a model in which psychological factors interacted with physiological ones, Wharton stressed the corporeal nature of enthusiasm, in contradistinction to the divine character of real inspiration:

> ... [T]he Enthusiast himself believes all this to proceed from a Divine influence, and mistakes the phrensies of his Brain for the dictates of the Holy Ghost; and the credulous Multitude, which ever refers those things to a Divine original, whose causes it cannot comprehend, proclaimeth his Dreams to be Inspirations, ascribeth the extatick motions of his Body to the operation of the Spirit acting in him, and admireth his high-flown Nonsense as Divine Sublimity.[27]

Critics of the French Prophets were similarly aware of the influence of the imagination on the animal spirits, and hence of the circular nature of the mechanism they were describing. Thus, Henry Nicholson, an ex-Prophet, but also a physician himself, analysed this psychological/physiological mechanism:

> And perhaps this might have been my Case, had I suffered my Imagination to be led, as theirs apparently are, by an intoxicated Fancy, which, as we may perceive in several other Cases, inflames the animal Spirits to an unnatural Pitch: and the Violent Motions of the Body, serve to heat the agitated Blood, and afford a constant supply of overheated Spirits to the Nerves, to strengthen and carry on the violent Agitations, and delusive Impressions.[28]

The imagination heated the animal spirits and they in turn caused further delusions.

The role of the animal spirits in accounting for deluded imagination was emphasized by other critics of the French Prophets as well. The words of the anonymous author of *A Dissuasive against Enthusiasm* were typical:

> For, First, A Delirium, or natural Enthusiasm, arising from a disorder'd Brain, occasion'd by great Fervency of Temper, or violent Agitations of the animal Spirits, will necessarily impregnate the Fancy, cause the

---

Stanley W. Jackson, "Burton and Psychological Healing", *Journal of the History of Medicine and Allied Sciences* 44 (1989): 160–178.

[27] Wharton, *The Enthusiasm of the Church of Rome*, p. 13.

[28] Henry Nicholson, *The Falsehood of the New Prophets Manifested* (London, 1708), p. 13. Nicholson was born in Ireland and was educated at Trinity College, Dublin, and University College, Oxford. He later went to Cambridge and to Middle Temple, London. See Schwartz, *The French Prophets*, pp. 303, 328.

Images of Things to come into it very fast, and produce a very ready Invention of Matter, and copious Fluency of Words.[29]

The phenomenon of the French Prophets, however, was not merely an individual affair. It was a social movement in which claims to inspiration spread rapidly. Such contagion needed explanation too, and once again, the imagination, together with the "animal spirits", served as an explanation. For certain critics with a Platonic orientation like the ex-Quaker George Keith, the animal spirits were associated with some "subtile effluvium" by which the inspiration of one person could induce the inspirations of others who heard him.[30] At the same time, Keith tended to give a corpuscular interpretation to these "effluvia":

> But that called the Corpuscular Philosophy, seems best to resolve the Phenomena of many natural effects, by the efflux or effluviums of subtle little particles of Bodies of different figures and shapes, with various differing Motions that go from Bodies to Bodies both of Minerals and Vegetables, as well as of brute and rational Animals.[31]

Keith thus combined the Renaissance naturalist account of enthusiasm and the way it spread with the contemporary corpuscular one, turning the animal spirits into an interpersonal medium in addition to being a medium between soul and body.

The Low-Church minister Benjamin Bayly analysed in similar terms the way in which John Lacy became inspired:

> I rather believe it [Lacy's inspirations] first arose from the Impressions that the Acting and Discourses of these French Prophets made upon his Imagination or Fancy. And this is no such Wonder; for the Spirits of some Men are very susceptible of Impressions, and what Power the Fancy has to make Men diseased, all acute Physicians know . . . The sight of what other Men do, doth strangely dispose us to do the same; and if some Men were every day to see mad Men, and believe them Divinely Inspir'd, and consequently look upon Madness as the highest

---

[29] *A Dissuasive against Enthusiasm*, p. 45.

[30] On the emission of spirits from men to men Keith quoted Pico della Mirandola, Marsilio Ficino, Paracelsus, Cornellius Agrippa, Johannes Baptista Porta, as well as Francis Bacon. See *The Magick of Quakerism or, the Chief Mysteries of Quakerism Laid Open* (London, 1707), pp. 75–80.

[31] *The Magick of Quakerism*, p. 60. On the animal spirits as the substratum of the effluxes and effluvia see also pp. 41–42, 50–52, 55. See also on this subject, Schwartz, *Knaves, Fools, Madmen*, pp. 48–54. Schwartz does not, however, emphasize Keith's peculiar combination of the Renaissance magical view with the contemporary corpuscular one.

and greatest Gift they were capable of, we should see what Effect it would have.[32]

The imagination was the medium which was influenced by the sights and sounds of other inspired persons, and which in turn caused similar agitations and motions in the bodies of those present.[33] The same point was made by the anonymous author of the *Observations upon Elias Marion*; by the Presbyterian minister Edmund Calamy; and by the Huguenot ministers Claude Grosteste de la Mothe and Philippe Mesnard.[34] Mesnard admitted, however, that the role of the imagination in this process was one of the hardest issues in medicine:

> ... [L]'imagination s'y laisse surprendre, et communique les mêmes mouvemens. Ne demandez pas comment cela se peut faire. Rien n'est plus difficile dans la Physique que d'expliquer la force ou la faiblesse de l'imagination. Ce n'est pas icy le liëu d'entrer dans cette discussion. Je ne say même si les plus habiles Philosophes sont en état de nous dire sur cela quelque chose de satisfaisant. Ils sont réduits comme le vulgaire à s'en tenir à l'expérience, et à reconnoître que la chose est, sans expliquer comment elle est ...[35]

We have here an interesting case of a clerical reliance on medicine together with an awareness that medical knowledge does not have yet a clear answer to the question.

Nevertheless, most ministers and critics of enthusiasm in that generation adhered to a corpuscular account of individual and collective imagination. They made use of the Cartesian distinction between mind and body in order to re-define the difference between true inspiration, which was a matter of the mind, and mere agitations, convulsions and alleged visions, which were purely physiological phenomena. This was already stated quite clearly by the Cambridge Platonist, John Smith, in the middle of the seventeenth century:

---

[32] Benjamin Bayly, *An Essay on Inspiration*, pp. 409–410.

[33] It should be stressed, however, that this was also one of the functions of the imagination according to George Keith. See *The Magick of Quakerism*, p. 70.

[34] *Observations upon Elias Marion and his Book of Warnings*, pp. 7–8. Edmund Calamy, *A Caveat against New Prophets, in Two Sermons* (London, 1708), p. 30. Quoted also by Schwartz, *Knaves, Fools, Madmen*, p. 50, note 55. Calamy (1661–1732), a well-known historian of non-conformity, was apparently of Huguenot ancestry, though several generations in England. See Schwartz, p. 83, and *D.N.B.* vol. 3 pp. 683–687. Claude Grosteste de la Mothe, *Caractère des Nouvelles Prophécies en quatre Sermons, Prononcez dans l'Eglise Française de la Savoye* (London, 1708), p. 91.

[35] Philippe Mesnard, *Les faux prophètes convaincus* (London, 1708), fourth sermon, pp. 79–80.

Whereas the *prophetical Spirit* acting *principally* upon the *Reason* and *Understanding* of the Prophets, guided them consistently and intelligibly into the understanding of things ... this *Pseudo-prophetical* Spirit being not able to rise up above this low and dark Region of Sense or Matter, or to soar afloat into a clear Heaven of vision, endeavoured always as much as might be to strengthen it self in the *Imaginative* part.[36]

Similar views were expressed by Edward Stillingfleet a few years later.[37] In the next generation, the Broad Churchman Benjamin Hoadly stressed that the bodily agitations, which accompanied the prophecies of contemporary pretenders to inspiration, were never characteristic of the ancient biblical prophets, who were always in a clear state of mind while prophesying.[38]

Social and Political Implications

The distinction between mind and body, true inspiration and false enthusiasm, had a social correlate as well, since it implied a clear demarcation line between the two professions: the physicians, dealing with the body, and the ministers, caring for the salvation of the soul. More important, by giving a medical interpretation to the phenomenon of enthusiasm, the ministers not only relied on a body of knowledge alien to their theological training, they also relegated the treatment of the so-called enthusiasts to the medical profession. Claimers to direct divine inspiration were hence not regarded as heretics needing ecclesiastical, or even secular, punishment, but rather as sick people who needed medical care.

Thus, already Robert South, in a sermon preached at Oxford in the late 1670's or early 80's, stressed that the best cure for enthusiasm, being essentially an expression of melancholy, was by the efforts of a physician, not a divine; by purging, not by promise or prophecy;

---

[36] John Smith, "Of Prophecy", in Smith, *Select Discourses* (Cambridge, 1673), p. 186. The text was edited posthumously by John Worthington and first published in 1660. There is also a reprint of that edition in Scholars' Facsimiles and Reprints, Delmar, N.Y., 1979.

[37] Edward Stillingfleet, *Origines Sacrae or a Rational Account of the Grounds of Christian Faith, as to the Truth and Divine Authority of the Scriptures and the matters therein contain'd*, Book II, Chapter 5, pp. 165–204 in the third edition of 1666; the first edition appeared in London in 1662.

[38] Benjamin Hoadly, *A Brief Vindication of the Antient Prophets, from the Imputation and Misrepresentation of such as adhere to our Present Pretenders to Inspiration. In a Letter To Sir Richard Bulkeley* (published anonymously in London, 1709), pp. 13–31.

by blood-letting, not by the sacrificial blood of Christ.[39] In the early eighteenth century, the moral implications of the medical critique were explicitly formulated by the anonymous author of *A Dissuasive against Enthusiasm*:

> And if this be the real Case of the Modern Enthusiasts; they are become Objects of Pity and Charity, and deserve to be pray'd for, as Lunaticks, and the Unfortunate, rather, than condemn'd of Hypocrisy, or of worse Design.[40]

Daniel Defoe similarly recommended an indulgent attitude towards the Prophets, since they were essentially deluded.[41]

The practical implications were also clear. George Philadelphus formulated them hypothetically in lines addressed to Francis Moult:

> Had it been a Composition of your own single Pen, and not the result of a Club of your pretended Inspir'd Society, as it seems evident enough to me so to be; I should have thought you had wanted more the advice of a Physician to rectifie your Constitution, than such an one as me to confute you by Reason, and Argumentation.[42]

Some, indeed, drew these practical conclusions. John Tutchin, the editor of *The Observator*, argued that there was no point in prosecuting the prophets by law "For what law can control or rectify Nature?" He recommended instead to construct a religious Bedlam for them.[43] The ex-prophet and physician Henry Nicholson reported the case of one Robert Wise, a sawyer near London Wall, who was one of the agitated:

> His Friends perceiving him to forsake his Trade, and to neglect to provide for his Wife and Family, put him some time into a Mad-House,

---

[39] Robert South, *Sermons Preached upon Several Occasions*, vol. III (New York, 1870), pp. 61–62, 81–82.

[40] *A Dissuasive against Enthusiasm*, p. 46. The same point was made by the Scottish Episcopalian Robert Calder in his letter to Cunninghame: "If a Delusion, as you say well in your Warnings to the City of *Edinburgh* . . . we should pity and pray for you, which I still do . . .". Calder, *A True Copy of Letters Past betwixt Mr. Robert Calder . . . and Mr. James Cunninghame* (Edinburgh, 1710), p. 8. See also the quotation from *Observations upon Elias Marion and his Book of Warnings*, p. 14, cited above.

[41] Daniel Defoe, *A Review of the State of the British Nation*, vol. V, no. 12 (April 12, 1708), in facsimile reproduction entitled *Defoe's Review*, ed. by Arthur W. Secord (New York: Columbia University Press, 1938).

[42] George Philadelphus [Pseud.], Postscript to *The Right Way of Trying Prophets* (London, 1708), p. 25. On Francis Moult, see Schwartz, *The French Prophets*, esp. p. 302.

[43] *The Observator*, July 23–26, 1707. Quoted by Schwartz, *Knaves, Fools, Madmen*, pp. 51–52.

and there by bleeding, and the usual Methods of those Places, he was freed from his Agitations: But they return'd upon him, after he came out of that Confinement.[44]

Benjamin Bayly referred to the theme of Bedlam from the opposite direction. Had it been given out that the madmen presently at Bedlam were in fact inspired, he said,

> [T]is not impossible but some upon frequent hearing and seeing them, in time, might, to their great Joy, find the Symptoms of the same Spirit coming on them apace, as it happens it seems to such as attend the present Prophets.[45]

George Philadelphus tended to see conspiracy behind the claims of the prophets, but, as has been shown above, he did not rule out the possibility of individual madness and hence, the need for medical treatment. Finally, some years later, Samuel Turrettin, who was Pictet's disciple and younger colleague in Geneva, similarly recommended confinement in serious cases of enthusiasm.[46]

Whether explicitly advocating confinement to Bedlam or not, the analogy between the enthusiasts and the mad was significant enough in the writings of many of the critics. Confinement was by no means a light infliction in that period. Indeed, the present study can serve as another illustration of Michel Foucault's thesis, according to which seclusion for alleged or real mental disturbances became a major means of excluding deviants in the "classical period".[47] Nevertheless, for our purposes, the important point to stress is that the ministers were thus relegating some of their authority to the carriers of medical knowledge. Indeed, both physicians and ministers underwent similar intellectual influences in that generation, primarily that of Cartesianism which stressed the sharp distinction between mind and body. For the ministers, that distinction served to underpin their own professional identity as ministers of the soul. It also helped to distinguish between present-day enthusiasts, false claimers to divine inspiration on the one hand, and biblical, true prophecy, on the other. Yet, this distinction between body and soul also defined the boundaries between the two

---

[44] Nicholson, *The Falsehood of the New Prophets Manifested*, pp. 28–29.

[45] Bayly, *An Essay on Inspiration*, p. 411.

[46] Samuel Turrettin, *Préservatif contre le fanatisme, ou réfutation des prétendus inspirés des derniers siècles* (Geneva, 1723), pp. 57–58, 65–66, and also pp. 231–32, 442. It is also worth noting that in his medical interpetation, Turrettin relied explicitly on Henry More. Ibid., p. 368.

[47] Michel Foucault, *Folie et déraison: Histoire de la folie à l'âge classique* (Plon: Paris, 1961).

professions, and clearly circumscribed their respective spheres of activity. The new common intellectual ground shared by physicians
and ministers thus contributed to a sharper division of labour between the two professions and at the same time, to close co-operation.
Moreover, this new type of collaboration between physicians and
ministers, based on a corpuscular and mechanistic natural philosophy, indicates a measure of "secularization" of public consciousness
in Protestant communities at the turn of the eighteenth century.
Ministers relied on a secular discipline, that of medicine, in analysing
the phenomenon of enthusiasm, and sometimes even delegated to
the physicians the treatment of that problem. In this respect, the
medical critique of enthusiasm as adopted by clerical circles, contributed to the secularization of religious sensibilities on the eve of the
Enlightenment.

Nevertheless, the combination of a medical account with a clerical
critique was by no means the only approach to the issue of enthusiasm
at the end of the seventeenth century and the early eighteenth. To
begin with, not all ministers shared that medical discourse, and some
clerical voices were raised against the new medical explanation of
enthusiasm. The most famous objection against the new medical and
mechanical account was that of Jonathan Swift in his *Mechanical
Operation of the Spirit*, first published anonymously in 1704. Swift did
not ignore the medical interpretation. On the contrary, he gave it some
prominence, especially in *A Tale of a Tub*, published in that same
volume.[48] Yet, in the *Mechanical Operation of the Spirit*, Swift ridiculed,
in words which have become classic, some of the contemporary versions of the medical critique, especially the concept of "animal spirits":

> For, it is the Opinion of Choice *Virtuosi*, that the Brain is only a Crowd
> of little Animals, but with Teeth and Claws extremely sharp, and there-
> fore, cling together in the Contexture we behold, like the Picture of
> *Hobbes's Leviathan*, or like Bees in perpendicular swarm upon a Tree, or
> like a Carrion corrupted into Vermin, still preserving the Shape and

---

[48] See *A Tale of a Tub. Written for the Universal Improvement of Mankind*, fifth edition
(London, 1720), Sections VIII–XI, in A.C. Guthkelch and D. Nichol Smith, eds.,
*A Tale of a Tub to which is added The Battle of the Books and the Mechanical Operation of
the Spirit by Jonathan Swift* (Oxford: At the Clarendon Press, 1920), pp. 150–205.
Swift was directly influenced by Burton, Casaubon and More in their medical analysis
of enthusiasm. See C.M. Webster, "Swift and Some Earlier Satirists of Puritan Enthusiasm" *PMLA* 48 (1933): 1141–53; *idem.*, "The Satiric Background of the Attack
on the Puritans in Swift's *A Tale of a Tub*", *PMLA* 50 (1935): 210–23; Phillip Harth,
Swift and Anglican Rationalism (Chicago: Chicago University Press, 1961), pp. 105–116.

Figure of the Mother Animal. That all Invention is formed by the Morsure of two or more of these Animals, upon certain capillary Nerves, which proceed from thence, whereof three Branches spread into the Tongue, and two into the right Hand ... That if the Morsure be Hexagonal, it produces Poetry; the Circular gives Eloquence; If the Bite hath been Conical, the Person, whose Nerve is so affected, shall be disposed to write upon the Politicks; and so of the rest.[49]

This brilliant satire was obviously aimed principally at the new corpuscular philosophy and the way it was incorporated into medical theory. Yet Swift's more immediate purpose here was to stress that "natural enthusiasm" was primarily artificial enthusiasm, namely, intentionally induced. True, that artifice could make use of the temper and complexion of individuals, but it was nevertheless essentially contrived.[50]

Some critics of the French Prophets came out explicitly against the medical interpretation and the indulgent attitude that it implied toward the Camisard leaders who came from France:

> There are say, those who are inclin'd to favour them Enthusiasticks or distemper'd Persons, who should not be molested, if we had but the least compassion of the Infirmities of Human Nature. This Pity increases when one is perswaded that their Distemper has been occasion'd by their great Suffering in Prison, where the Terror of the Cruelties they were threatened with, disorder'd their Imagination. If this were true, who would not show some Indulgence to Persons whose Distemper proceeds from such a cause? But the case will be very much altered, when we are convinc'd, that those are Impostors whom we took for Persons distemper'd; we shall then have a just Abhorrence of those Blasphemies which we could hardly bear with before.[51]

Thus, quite a few critics could not give up a religious, moral or political censure of enthusiasm. They suspected the prophets either of disguised Catholicism, disguised atheism, or political conspiracy, and condemned their personal moral behaviour.[52] Such censure had

---

[49] [Jonathan Swift], *A Discourse Concerning the Mechanical Operation of the Spirit. In a Letter to a Friend. A Fragment* (London, 1710), in Guthkelch and Smith, eds., *A Tale of a Tub*, pp. 261–291; the quotation is from p. 279.

[50] Ibid., pp. 279–285.

[51] [N.N.] *An Account of the Lives and Behaviour of the Three French Prophets, Lately come out of the Cevennes and Languedoc; And of the Proceedings of the Consistory of the Savoy in Relation to them* (London, 1708), p. 2. In the following pages the anonymous writer argued, on the basis of a French attestation, that Jean Cavalier, one of the prophets who came from France, was in fact a rogue, a hypocrite and a traitor.

[52] George Philadelphus [pseud.], in *The Right Way of Trying Prophets*, p. 18; [Anon.],

practical implications as well. Whereas the medical account meant
that the enthusiasts should be sent to Bedlam, the accusations of
heresy, subversion and immorality, necessarily led to calls for legal
action. The Huguenot minister Philippe Mesnard declared clearly:

> Il s'agit d'imposteurs, qui savent très bien qu'ils ne sont rien moins
> que Prophètes, et qui ne font ce personnage que par un intérest sordide,
> ou par quelque autre principe encore plus criminel . . . Ne parlons donc
> point des égards que l'on doit à ceux qui errent de bonne foy; nous
> avons affaire à des Imposteurs.[53]

He therefore justified legal proceedings against the "prophets".

Another group which rejected the medical critique of the ministers was of course that of the enthusiasts themselves. Interestingly
enough, however, the defenders of the prophets did not necessarily
deny the physiological component of prophecy. They admitted that
there was a certain resemblance between "inspired" agitations and
natural, corporeal phenomena. Yet, they kept saying that their critics' exclusive reliance on a medical explanation necessarily led to
Deism, as it undermined all revelation. This is especially manifest in
the debate between Sir Richard Bulkeley, the most important patron
of the prophets, and the Anglican Low Churchman, Benjamin
Hoadly.[54] Bulkeley wished to show, in adducing the example of the

---

Clavis Prophetica; or a Key to the Prophecies of Mons. Marion, and the other Camisars (London, 1707), Part 2, pp. 7, 21–22. See also Schwartz, *Knaves, Fools, Madmen*, pp. 56–
57. According to Schwartz, older critics tended to suspect Catholic plots whereas
younger critics feared religious scepticism and freethinking. Ibid., p. 57, note 83.
The anonymous N.N., whom I have just quoted above, compared Fatio to John
Dee, the Elizabethan hermetic mathematician who associated himself with Edward
Kelley, and who claimed to have discoursed with the angels. *An Account of the Lives
and Behaviour of the Three French Prophets*, pp. 33–34. See also Schwartz, *Knaves, Fools,
Madmen*, pp. 60–65.
[53] Philippe Mesnard, *Les faux prophètes convaincus* (London, 1708), third sermon,
p. 71. See also pp. 29, 34, 58, 104. As we shall see below, Shaftesbury criticized
primarily the *French* ministers who wished to take harsh measures against the Prophets, thus playing largely into their hands, longing, as they did, for martyrdom.
[54] Richard Bulkeley, *An Answer to Several Treatises Lately publish'd on the Subject of the
Prophets, The First Part* (London, 1708). Hoadly, *A Brief Vindication of the Antient Prophets*. Sir Richard Bulkeley (c. 1661–1710) was an Irish Baronet, Member of Parliament at Dublin and an active fellow of the Dublin Philosophical Society. On Bulkeley
see *D.N.B.*, vol. 3, p. 233 (which gives a wrong birth date), and K. Theodore Hoppen,
The Common Scientist in the Seventeenth Century: A Study of the Dublin Philosophical Society
(London: Routledge and Kegan Paul, 1970), pp. 39–40. Benjamin Hoadly (1676–
1761), Bishop successively of Bangor, Hereford, Salisbury, and Winchester was one
of the leaders of the Low Church party, a strong defender of the 1688 revolution,
and a fierce polemicist with the nonjurors. See *D.N.B.*, vol. 9, pp. 910–915.

evil spirit of Saul (Samuel 18:10), that the Bible used the term "prophesying" even in a case of melancholy like that of Saul, because that melancholy involved agitation—regularly the sign of divine inspiration.[55] In making that point, however, Bulkeley unwittingly blurred the distinctions between true prophesying and mere melancholy, even in the Bible itself.[56] For Bulkeley and other enthusiasts, the divine spirit employed natural, and indeed, what seemed as "clinical" means in order to achieve its purpose.

This fusion of the spiritual and physiological dimension is most strikingly manifest in a statement ascribed to Fatio de Duillier, the scientist who became a spokesman of the French Prophets. The anonymous N.N. in his *Account of the Lives and Behaviour of the Three French Prophets* claimed the following concerning Fatio:

> Our Mathematician is known to be skilfull in Gardening ... Besides his being a Gardener, he professes to be a Philosopher; They say, that in his system he explains Prophecy by the Exaltation of Matter to a certain Degree, in which it has the Virtue, even of foretelling things to come.[57]

The reference is used by an opponent, in an ironic tone, but the substance of the view ascribed to Fatio may well be authentic. Fatio apparently did not see any contradiction between a physiological, even "materialistic" account of prophecy, and a commitment to its inspirational character. Unlike their critics, the prophets and their spokesmen stressed the close interconnection of physiological phenomena and mental or even supernatural ones.

This was a point which a third group—the deists, were also inclined to pick up. Influenced, like many of the enthusiasts themselves, by Renaissance notions of harmony, sympathy and antipathy,

---

[55] Bulkeley, *An Answer to Several Treatises*, pp. 33–34. Bulkeley also relied on the French translation of the biblical phrase which says concerning Saul—"Il faisoit du Prophète".

[56] The same point is still clearer in his commentary on the story of the child prophet whom Elisha sent to Jehu (II Kings, 9). According to Bulkeley, the agitations of that boy led one of the servants to ask Jehu "Wherefore came this mad fellow to thee". Moreover, he prefers the Septuagint version which translates "epileptic" instead of "mad", "for so, or like to that, it did appear to them." Ibid., p. 35. Bulkeley thus emphasized even more the similarity between prophetic and pathological behaviour.

[57] [N.N.], *An Account of the Lives and Behaviour of the Three French Prophets*, pp. 33–34. Quoted also in Schwartz, *The French Prophets*, p. 236, note 45. Unfortunately, I have not been able to find any reference in Fatio's own writings to this physiological account of inspiration.

the deists similarly tended to blur the distinctions between mind and body, body and soul.[58] Such a position also led them to question the distinction between contemporary claims to inspiration and biblical prophecy. Indeed, both enthusiasts and deists wished to obliterate the distinction between body and soul, and both sought to undermine the distinction between classical prophecy in Scripture and contemporary claims of divine inspiration. Yet, whereas the enthusiasts wished to obliterate that distinction in order to give legitimacy to their own "prophecies", the deists wished to do the same in order to de-legitimize, at least implicitly, both types of prophecy. Indeed, as will be shown in the following chapter, deists such as the third Earl of Shaftesbury were to draw far-reaching conclusions from the medical approach which the ecclesiastical establishment adopted in that generation. The clerical recourse to a medical account could open the way to a far more radical view of enthusiasm, a view which in fact would give it a new rehabilitation.

---

[58] See for example, [John Trenchard], *The Natural History of Superstition* (London, 1709), pp. 11–15, 37–48. On the one hand, Trenchard relied on Burton and traditional medicine in accounting for the phenomena of alleged inspiration; on the other, he referred to Renaissance naturalist views which blurred the distinction between body and soul.

CHAPTER EIGHT

SHAFTESBURY AND THE LIMITS OF TOLERATION
CONCERNING ENTHUSIASM

The most famous text of the early eighteenth century dealing with enthusiasm is undoubtedly Shaftesbury's *Letter Concerning Enthusiasm*. Written in the late summer of 1707, at the height of the controversy surrounding the French Prophets, it circulated in manuscript form for a few months before being published anonymously in the early summer of 1708.[1] By that time, the agitation around the Prophets had abated somewhat, especially after their predictions concerning the "resurrection" of Dr. Emes failed to materialize.[2] Nevertheless, Shaftesbury's letter created a storm of its own, mainly because of its thinly disguised deistic implications.

Indeed, historians have seen Shaftesbury's *Letter* mostly in the context of the deistic controversies in England of the early eighteenth century.[3] For my part I shall focus on his attitude towards enthusiasm, and on the reactions to his call for a more indulgent attitude towards the enthusiasts. I shall analyse this debate against the background of the earlier critiques of enthusiasm discussed in the present book, also examining the limits set to the toleration of enthusiasm in a society where a certain toleration had been, since 1689, a constitutive part of the social and political order.

The Toleration Act of 1689 established limited tolerance of

---

[1] For a new scholarly edition of this text, including a detailed introduction reconstructing the history of its writing and publication see Richard B. Wolf, *An Old-Spelling, Critical Edition of Shaftesbury's "Letter Concerning Enthusiasm" and "Sensum Communis: An Essay on the Freedom of Wit and Humour"* (New York and London: Garland, 1988). I have used, and shall henceforth refer, however, to the original edition, *A Letter Concerning Enthusiasm, to My Lord ****** (London, 1708). The *Letter* was addressed to Lord Somers, Lord Chancellor and one of the leaders of the Whig party, but his name was not mentioned explicitly on the title page until the 1732 edition. See Wolf, pp. 17–18, 110–111, and *D.N.B.*, vol. XVIII, pp. 629–637.

[2] On the expected resurrection of Dr. Emes on May 25, 1708, its failure, and the effect of this on the movement of the French Prophets, see Schwartz, *The French Prophets* (Berkeley: University of California Press, 1980), pp. 113–125.

[3] See especially, Alfred Owen Aldridge, "Shaftesbury and the Deist Manifesto", *Transactions of the American Philosophical Society* 41 (1951): 297–385.

Nonconformists, but excluded, as is well known, Roman Catholics and Anti-Trinitarians. Deists, Jews, and other non-Christians were not mentioned at all by the Act. Strictly speaking, the Act did not even grant explicit toleration to Nonconformists, but only suspended the penalties imposed on them by previous laws. The Corporation and Test Acts, which barred Nonconformists and Roman Catholics from holding royal and municipal offices, were not repealed.[4] In practice, however, over 2,500 "meeting-houses" for Nonconformist public worship were approved during the next twenty years. The expiration of the Licensing Act in 1695 opened the gates to a flood of pamphlets and books, including deistic ones, whose heretical content would previously have barred their publication. The extent of toleration and its precise meaning were to become a constant topic of public and Parliamentary debate in the next decades. After the accession of Queen Anne in 1702, the Tory opponents of toleration tried repeatedly to curtail its implications, especially the wide-spread practice of "occasional conformity" whereby Nonconformists could be appointed to public office by a one-time partaking of High Communion according to the Anglican rite. These attempts, however, were unsuccessful up to 1711. Yet, the constant cries of High Church ministers that the "Church was in danger", required the Low Church establishment to be doubly cautious concerning heretics, radical Nonconformists and enthusiasts.[5] Shaftesbury's *Letter*, and the reactions to it, should be seen against this background.

Shaftesbury's Letter *and his Attitude towards* "*Enthusiasm*"

Anthony Ashley Cooper, third Earl of Shaftesbury (1671–1713), was an avowed spokesman for toleration in the generation after the

---

[4] The Toleration Act, its import and significance, have been the subject of some lively debate. Whereas some scholars of the previous generation tended to emphasize its limitations, in recent years historians have shown the impact of the Act in practice, in spite of the narrow and circumscribed formulation of the Act itself. Among the numerous studies, see especially the oft-quoted article by G.V. Bennett, "Conflict in the Church", in Geoffrey Holmes, ed., *Britain after the Glorious Revolution* (1969; repr. paperback, London, Macmillan, 1982), pp. 155–175, and O.G. Grell, J.I. Israel and N. Tyacke, *From Persecution to Toleration: The Glorious Revolution and Religion in England* (Oxford: The Clarendon Press, 1991), especially the articles by Jonathan I. Israel and Hugh Trevor-Roper. This collection also contains a facsimile of the printed text of the Toleration Act (Appendix ii).

[5] On mounting Tory and High Anglican pressures during the reign of Queen

"Glorious Revolution". A "Roman Commonwealthman", as he regarded himself, he belonged to that circle of Country Whigs who,
while strongly supporting both King William and later the Hanoverian
succession, were nevertheless critical of the ascendancy of the "Court
Whigs".[6] The grandson of the first Earl of Shaftesbury, Anthony
Ashley's education was mostly entrusted to John Locke, protégé of
the first Earl. His circle of friends later in life was also largely Locke's
circle. Two visits to Holland, in 1687, as part of his "Grand Tour",
and a more extended stay in 1698–99, established his many Dutch
connections, with Remonstrants like Philip van Limborch, with the
English Quaker Benjamin Furly, and with Huguenot refugees like
Pierre Bayle and Jean Le Clerc. He thus became acquainted with
the continental Republic of Letters, and with the special atmosphere
of tolerance in Dutch society, which served as a model for the English Whigs.[7] Yet, Shaftesbury's own intellectual orientation was increasingly influenced in the 1690's by the Cambridge Platonists. His
first published undertaking was an edition in 1698 of twelve sermons
by Benjamin Whichcote to which he added an Introduction.[8] To
what extent he managed to combine Lockean psychology and epistemology with Platonism, is a matter of some debate among scholars.[9] The tensions may be seen most specifically, however, in his
views on enthusiasm.

Shaftesbury's attitude towards enthusiasm has engaged the attention

---

Anne see, in addition to the references mentioned in the previous note, Geoffrey
Holmes, *The Trial of Doctor Sacheverell* (London: Methuen, 1973), pp. 29–41.

[6] This paragraph is largely based on the recent biography of Shaftesbury by Robert
Voitle, *The Third Earl of Shaftesbury. 1671–1713* (Baton Rouge and London: Louisiana State University Press, 1984). On his political allegiances and self designation as
a "Roman Commonwealthman" see ibid., pp. 206–209. On his political activities as
a member of Parliament in 1695–1698 see ibid., pp. 70–78. On the "Commonwealthmen", see the classical study by Caroline Robbins, *The Eighteenth Century Commonwealthmen* (Cambridge, Mass: Harvard University Press, 1958). Shaftesbury never held
public office, however, except for the largely honorific title of "Vice-Admiral of
Dorset" which he inherited after his father's death in 1699, and from which he was
dislodged with the accession of Queen Anne. In 1702, a few months before his
death, William III offered Shaftesbury the post of Secretary of State, but the offer
was declined. See Voitle, pp. 201–202, 212–213.

[7] On Shaftesbury's education, and Locke's role in it, see Voitle, chapter 1. On
his later links with Locke, and Locke's circle, see ibid., pp. 60–70, and *passim*. On
his visits to the Dutch Republic, see pp. 18, 84–93.

[8] *Select Sermons of Dr. Whichcote* (London, 1698). See also Voitle, *Shaftesbury*, pp. 111–118.

[9] On Shaftesbury's critical attitude towards Locke see Voitle, *Shaftesbury*, pp. 64–
67, 118–122.

of several scholars.[10] His views have been compared mostly to those of his mentor, John Locke, as he expressed them at the end of his *Essay concerning Human Understanding*. Shaftesbury's debt to Henry More's *Enthusiasmus Triumphatus* has also been noted. However, the significance of Shaftesbury's new view of enthusiasm, and especially, his "rehabilitation" of that concept, can be fully appreciated only against the background of the Platonic and medical tradition on enthusiasm which has been delineated in previous chapters of the present study.

Indeed, in order to understand Shaftesbury's attitude towards enthusiasm we should see him first of all as a critical disciple of the seventeenth century Cambridge Platonists. On this issue, Shaftesbury went beyond the ambivalent attitude we have detected in Henry More.[11] Not only was he much more tolerant towards enthusiasm than More had been, but he was ready to entertain a positive conception of enthusiasm, though the rehabilitation he proposed was very different from that of the Renaissance. Only by seeing both the continuities and differences between the traditional discourse on enthusiasm and that of Shaftesbury can his radical re-interpretation of the debate with the enthusiasts be fully appreciated. We shall start, therefore, with Shaftesbury's medical critique of enthusiasm in the *Letter*.

Shaftesbury accepted the seventeenth century medical critique of enthusiasm, but drew far-reaching conclusions from it. His first reference to the medical perspective clearly goes back to Burton:

> There is *a Melancholy* which accompanys all Enthusiasm. Be it *Love* or *Religion* (for there are Enthusiasms in both) nothing can put a stop to the growing mischief of either, till the Melancholy be remov'd, and the Mind at liberty to hear what can be said against the Ridiculousness of an Extreme in either way.[12]

---

[10] See especially: Aldridge, "Shaftesbury and the Deist Manifesto", esp. pp. 314–322. Voitle, *Shaftesbury*, pp. 313–333. F. Paknadel, *"Lettre Concernant L'Enthousiasme* de Shaftesbury", in D. Bulckaen, *L'Enthousiasme dans le Monde Anglo-Americain aux XVIIe et XVIIIe Siècles"* (Actes du Colloque tenu à Paris les 20 et 21 octobre 1989), pp. 109–119. And finally, Wolf, *Shaftesbury's "Letter"*, Introduction.

[11] It should be noted, however, that Shaftesbury pointed out More's ambivalence towards enthusiasm. Recommending to a young friend some books of "our Divines and *Moralists*", including Henry More's *Enchiridion Ethicum*, Shaftesbury wrote:

> Dr. More's *Enchiridion Ethicum*, is a right good Piece of sound Morals; tho' the Doctor himself, in other *English* Pieces, could not abide by it; but made different Excursions into other Regions, and was perhaps as great an Enthusiast as any of those, whom he wrote against. However, he was a learned and a good Man.

[Anon.], *Several Letters Written by a Noble Lord to a Young Man at the University* (London, 1716), Letter IX, December 30, 1709, p. 43.

[12] *Letter Concerning Enthusiasm*, p. 13.

The liberty of judgment alluded to in the quotation above reflects Shaftesbury's own particular position, to which I shall return below. Yet in regarding the melancholic temper as the source of mischief in religion, he was saying nothing new.

Neither did Shaftesbury ignore the collective aspect of enthusiasm. He stressed the psychological dynamic as well, analysing the phenomenon of "pannick" by going back to the Classical origins of that term in the story of Pan and Bacchus who struck terror among the enemy by clamours echoing from rocks and caverns. He continues:

> ONE may with good reason call every Passion *Pannick* which is rais'd in a Multitude, and convey'd by Aspect, or as it were by Contact, or Sympathy. Thus popular Fury may be call'd *Pannick*, when the Rage of the People, as we have sometimes known, has put them beyond themselves; especially where Religion has to do. And in this stage their very Looks are infectious. The Fury flies from Face to Face: and the Disease is no sooner seen than caught ... Such force has Society in ill, as well as in good Passions: and so much stronger any affection is for being *social* and *communicative*.[13]

The radicalization of this medical or psychological account came in the next sentence, when Shaftesbury proceeded to apply this analysis to religion in general:

> THUS, my Lord, there are many *Pannicks* in Mankind, besides merely that of fear. And thus is Religion also *Pannick*; when Enthusiasm of any kind gets up; as oft, on melancholy occasions, it will do.[14]

It is here that Shaftesbury has crossed the Rubicon, characterizing religion itself, at least in certain conditions, as a "pannick". Indeed, he went on to stipulate those conditions which were conducive to such "pannicks":

> For Vapors naturally rise; and in bad times especially, when the Spirits of men are low, as either in publick Calamitys, or during the Unwholesomeness of Air or Diet, or when Convulsions happen in Nature, Storms, Earthquakes, or other amazing Prodigys.[15]

Later in the *Letter* he referred to "a sort of Enthusiasm of second hand":

---

[13] Ibid., pp. 15–16.
[14] Ibid., p. 16.
[15] Ibid., p. 16.

> [W]hen Men find no original Commotions in themselves, no prepossessing *Pannick* which bewitches 'em, they are apt still, by the Testimony of others, to be impos'd on, and led credulously into the Belief of many false Miracles.[16]

It is within this context of "Enthusiasm of second hand" that Shaftesbury discussed the commotion caused by the "new Prophesying Sect", the French Prophets in London that year, and the "signal miracle" they allegedly performed.[17] He posed the critical question whether among the hundreds of witnesses to that miracle there had been anyone "wholly free of *Melancholy*". Surely there were some, Shaftesbury implied ironically

> For otherwise the *Pannick* may have been caught; the Evidence of the Senses lost, as in a Dream; and the Imagination so inflam'd, as in a moment to have burnt up every Particle of Judgment and Reason. The combustible Matters lie prepar'd within, and ready to take fire at a spark; but chiefly in a Multitude seiz'd with the same Spirit.[18]

In his psychological analysis of the collective type of enthusiasm, as it characterized many of the French Prophets' assemblies, Shaftesbury did not differ from other critics. But, he took the further dangerous step of seeing such mechanisms of "pannick" as typical to religion in general, thus implicitly broadening the seventeenth century medical discourse on enthusiasm to include various types of religious inspiration.

He did so primarily by blurring the distinctions, not only between the biblical prophets and the contemporary French Prophets, but also between Christian prophecy and the "Heathenish" one. As far as the external symptoms were concerned, Shaftesbury found no difference between the prophets of the Old or New Testament, and the prophets of his own time. Referring to the working of the Spirit, whether good or bad, he said:

> I find by present Experience, as well as by all Historys Sacred and Profane, that the Operation of this *Spirit* is every where the same, as

---

[16] Ibid., p. 43.
[17] Scholars have long debated as to which "signal miracle" Shaftesbury was referring. Most probably the reference is to a miracle performed in the Cévennes in France by a bricklayer named Clary who endured a fire and emerged, as he had predicted, unscathed from it, a miracle attested by hundreds of people. The story was reported in Lacy's *Cry from the Desert* published earlier in 1707, and was subsequently widely discussed in the English pamphlets dealing with the Prophets. See Wolf, *Shaftesbury's "Letter"*, pp. 118–121, for a detailed discussion of this question.
[18] *Letter Concerning Enthusiasm*, pp. 44–45.

to the bodily Organs. . . . whether the Matter of Apparition be true or false, the Symptoms are the same, and the Passion of equal force in the Person who is Vision-struck.[19]

Significantly, he relied on John Lacy's Preface to *A Cry from the Desert* in comparing the ecstasies of the biblical prophets to the agitations of the contemporary ones. In this respect, the deist critic Shaftesbury outwardly shared the assumptions of the enthusiasts themselves. However, he added the pagan prophets too to that comparison:

> I only know that the Symptoms he describes, and which himself (poor Gentleman!) labors under, are as *Heathenish* as he can possibly pretend them to be *Christian*.[20]

Shaftesbury proceeded to cite the medical labels given by the classical authors to vision-struck people with such symptoms, whether "Nympholepti" by the Greeks, or "Lymphatici" by the Romans.[21] Were such labels appropriate only to the pagan prophets? Shaftesbury was careful not to push the similarities between Christian and pagan prophecies beyond the level of the bodily manifestations, but as we shall see below, he refrained from offering any other criterion for distinguishing between the two.

Shaftesbury, then, clearly extended the medical account of enthusiasm to include at least the bodily symptoms of all prophets, whether heathen or Christian, ancient or contemporary. Yet, unlike his seventeenth century predecessors, including Burton, Casaubon and Henry More, who associated the medical critique with a moral one, Shaftesbury adopted a far more indulgent attitude toward those "humours". He was also much more sceptical of the physicians' methods of curing such distempers:

> There are certain Humours in Mankind, which of necessity must have vent. The Human Mind and Body are both of 'em naturally subject to Commotions: and as there are strange Ferments in the Blood, which in many Bodys occasion an extraordinary discharge; so in Reason too, there are heterogeneous Particles which must be thrown off by Fermentation. Shou'd Physicians endeavour absolutely to allay those Ferments of the Body, and strike in the Humours which discover themselves in such Eruptions, they might, instead of making a Cure, bid fair perhaps

---

[19] Ibid., pp. 45, 50.
[20] Ibid., p. 46.
[21] Ibid., p. 50.

to raise a Plague, and turn a Spring-Ague or an Autumn-Surfeit into an epidemical malignant Fever.[22]

The attempt to cure these ferments with harsh methods ran the risk of making them much more acute. Shaftesbury therefore discarded, not only the punitive measures against enthusiasm, but also the strictly medical solution to melancholy and enthusiasm. Since the "distemper" which arises on such occasions was a natural one, the role of the Magistrate was not to suppress that distemper, but rather to soothe it:

> [A]t this season the *Pannick* must needs run high, and the Magistrate of necessity give way to it. For to apply a serious Remedy, and bring the Sword, or *Fasces*, as a Cure, must make the Case more melancholy, and increase the very Cause of the Distemper. To forbid Mens natural Fears, and to endeavour the overpowering them by other Fears, must needs be a most unnatural Method. The Magistrate, if he be any Artist, shou'd have a gentler hand; and instead of Causticks, Incisions, and Amputations, shou'd be using the softest Balms; and with a kind Sympathy entering into the Concern of the People, and taking, as it were, their Passion upon him, shou'd when he has sooth'd and satisfy'd it, endeavour, by chearful ways, to divert and heal it.[23]

We have here in a nutshell, Shaftesbury's plea for toleration with regard to enthusiasm. He has taken the seventeenth century medical discourse, and turned it into a basis for a tolerant attitude towards the various manifestations of enthusiasm. Seeing that distemper as a natural one, he relied on Epicurus in calling for a tolerant attitude towards enthusiasm:

> SO necessary it is to give way to this Distemper of *Enthusiasm*, that even that Philosopher who bent the whole Force of his Philosophy against Superstition, appears to have left room for visionary Fancy, and to have indirectly tolerated Enthusiasm . . . 'TWAS a sign that this Philosopher believ'd there was a good stock of *Visionary Spirit* originally in Human Nature. He was so satisfy'd that Men were inclin'd to see Visions, that rather than they shou'd go without, he chose to make 'em to their hand.[24]

Shaftesbury based his plea for a tolerant attitude, however, not only on the naturalist and medical accounts of enthusiasm. He also relied

---

[22] Ibid., p. 14.
[23] Ibid., pp. 16–17.
[24] Ibid., pp. 48–49. The last sentence hints at Shaftesbury's own view as to the appropriate attitude towards enthusiasm to which I shall return below.

on another seventeenth century tradition, that of English Erastianism. Indeed, he combined the plea for toleration with the insistence on a national church, and on the leading role of the Magistrate in public religious matters.

> For to deny the Magistrate a Worship, or take away a National Church, is as mere Enthusiasm as the Notion which sets up Persecution.[25]

His distinction between "public" and "private" here is also highly important. (At this point he adduced the analogous distinction between private gardens and "publick Walks", or between public libraries and private domestic tutors.)

Shaftesbury also argued, however, that persecution was counterproductive. By that time, this had become a "classical" argument for toleration and against persecution. Persecution, he claimed, only enhanced and gave greater popularity to the views and beliefs which were censored. Significantly, he started with the literary case:

> I CAN hardly forbear fancying, that if we had a sort of Inquisition, or formal Court of Judicature, with grave Officers, and Judges, erected to restrain Poetical Licence, and in general to suppress that Fancy and Humour of Versification ... if the Poets, as Ringleaders and Teachers of this Heresy, were under grievous Penaltys forbid to enchant the People by their vein of Rhyming; and if the People, on the other side, were under proportionable Penaltys forbid to hearken to any such Charm ... we might perhaps see a new *Arcadia* arising out of this heavy Persecution: Old People and Young wou'd be seiz'd with a versifying Spirit; we shou'd have Field-Conventicles of Lovers and Poets ...[26]

He then went on to the more relevant and "burning" example, that of the Camisard prophets:

> THERE are some, it seems, of our good Brethren, the *French* Protestants, lately come amongst us, who are mightily taken with this Primitive way. They have set a-foot the Spirit of Martyrdom to a wonder in their own Country; and they long to be trying it here, if we will give 'em leave, and afford 'em the Occasion; that is to say, if we will only do 'em the favor to hang or imprison 'em; if we will only be so obliging as to break their Bones for 'em, after their Country fashion, blow up their Zeal, and stir a-fresh the Coals of Persecution. But no such Grace can they hitherto obtain of us ... tho' the Priests of their own Nation wou'd gladly give 'em their desir'd Discipline, and are earnest

---

[25] Ibid., p. 17.
[26] Ibid., p. 21.

> to light their probationary Fires for 'em; We *English* Men, who are
> Masters in our own Country, will not suffer the Enthusiasts to be thus
> treated.[27]

In this well-known, brilliant, and ironic passage, Shaftesbury hardly
said very much that was new, and as we shall see below, nor did
most of his critics dispute his opposition to persecution.

However, Shaftesbury went one step further, and argued that a
more tolerant attitude on the part of the Jews and the Romans towards the early Christians might have dealt a mortal blow to Christianity right from the start.

> 'Twas more the Misfortune indeed of Mankind in general, than of
> Christians in particular, that some of the earlier *Roman* Emperors were
> such Monsters of Tyranny, and began a Persecution, not on religious
> Men merely, but on all who were suspected of Worth or Virtue. What
> cou'd have been a higher Honour or Advantage to Christianity, than
> to be persecuted by a NERO?[28]

Once again, Shaftesbury placed the Christians of the Apostolic period
on the same level as the contemporary "prophets". Moreover, he
obliquely counter-posed the fortunes of Christians to those of humanity in general in a spirit which harbingered Enlightenment attitudes.

If neither persecution nor medical treatment was the right response
to enthusiasm, and if, nevertheless, it was a melancholic "distemper", how then should it be dealt with? The cure which Shaftesbury
advocated was raillery and laughter, rather than "Causticks, Inci-
sions, and Amputations":

> IT was heretofore the Wisdom of some wise Nations, to let People be
> Fools as much as they pleas'd, and never to punish seriously what
> deserv'd only to be laugh'd at, and was, after all, best cur'd by that
> innocent Remedy.[29]

Raillery, not physick, was the best antidote to enthusiasm. In a way,
Shaftesbury took an Erasmian atttitude towards Folly, but without
the Christian and metaphysical dimensions that concept had for
Erasmus.[30] Fools had to be taken lightly, and "Good Humour" was
the best response to the "melancholic humour"; it was indeed, the

---

[27] Ibid., pp. 26–27.
[28] Ibid., pp. 24–25.
[29] Ibid., pp. 13–14.
[30] For Erasmus's conception of Folly see M.A. Screach, *Ecstasy and the Praise of Folly* (London: Duckworth, 1980).

right way of dealing with any issue, including religion.[31] The specific example Shaftesbury had in mind, an example which was to resonate angrily in many of the responses to the *Letter*, was that of the Puppet-Show at Bart'lemy-Fair, where the French Prophets and their agitations were mocked at in the summer of 1707.[32] That type of satire, Shaftesbury argued, was the best and most effective remedy for enthusiasm.

Towards a "Rehabilitation" of Enthusiasm

Only towards the end of the *Letter*, does Shaftesbury hint at the positive connotations of the term "enthusiasm". There, he clearly adhered to the Platonic tradition, going back to the Pseudo-Aristotelian *Problemata* when he said:

> NO *Poet* . . . can do any thing great in his own way, without the Imagination or Supposition of *a Divine Presence*, which may raise him to some degree of this Passion we are speaking of.[33]

His conclusion was clear, even though he kept his own evaluation shrouded in irony:

> THE only thing, my Lord, I wou'd infer from all this is, that ENTHUSIASM is wonderfully powerful and extensive; that it is a matter of nice Judgment, and the hardest thing in the world to know fully and distinctly; since even *Atheism* is not exempt from it.[34]

Outwardly, Shaftesbury subscribed to the conventional distinction between enthusiasm and true divine inspiration:

---

[31] *Letter Concerning Enthusiasm*, pp. 21–23. On the role of humour and raillery in Shaftesbury's thought see also Stanley Grean, *Shaftesbury's Philosophy of Religion and Ethics: A Study in Enthusiasm* (Athens, Ohio: Ohio University Press, 1967), pp. 120–128.

[32] *Letter Concerning Enthusiasm*, pp. 27–29. Clearly, a satire on the French Protestants in a puppet show linked with St. Bartholomew had a sharp bite, considering the memory of the St. Bartholomew massacre of 1572.

[33] *Letter Concerning Enthusiasm*, p. 51. He added that "Even the cold LUCRETIUS makes use of Inspiration, when he writes against it; and is forc'd to raise an Apparition of *Nature*, in a Divine Form, to animate and conduct him in his very Work of degrading Nature, and despoiling her of all her seeeming Wisdom and Divinity." (Ibid., pp. 51–52) In this positive view of enthusiasm, or inspiration, Shaftesbury of course diverged from the critical view of Locke, as he did in adopting the Platonic philosophy in general. Locke, it should be remembered, had not left any room for a positive evaluation of enthusiasm in the chapter he added on that subject in the 4th edition of the *Treatise Concerning Human Understanding*.

[34] *Letter Concerning Enthusiasm*, p. 52.

> For Inspiration is *a real* feeling of the Divine Presence, and Enthusiasm
> *a false one.*[35]

Yet he was quick to add a caveat of far-reaching consequence:

> But the Passion they raise is much alike. For when the Mind is taken
> up in Vision, and fixes its view either on any real Object, or mere
> Spectre of Divinity; when it sees, or thinks it sees any thing prodigious,
> and more than human; its Horror, Delight, Confusion, Fear, Admira-
> tion, or whatever Passion belongs to it, or is uppermost on this occa-
> sion, will have something vast, *immane*, and (as Painters say) *beyond Life.*[36]

Having made the distinction between real inspiration and false,
Shaftesbury was quick to put it into question. From the subjective
point of view, it was extremely hard to distinguish between the two
because the passion they raised "is much alike". Indeed, Shaftesbury
gave a subjectivist twist to the Platonic interpretation of enthusiasm,
seeing it primarily as a human passion:

> . . . *Inspiration* may be justly call'd *Divine* ENTHUSIASM: for the Word
> it-self signifies *Divine Presence*, and was made use of by the Philosopher
> whom the earliest Christian Fathers call'd *Divine*, to express whatever
> was sublime in human Passions.[37]

This subjectivist interpretation of both the term "enthusiasm", and
the Platonic understanding of it, was a crucial step with portentous
ramifications for Shaftesbury's own views on the topic, as well as for
the later history of the term.[38] Whereas Henry More saw genuine
enthusiasm as the work of the divine spirit, Shaftesbury emphasized
the psychological and epistemological perspective.[39] Enthusiasm was

---

[35] Ibid., p. 53.

[36] Ibid., p. 53.

[37] Loc. cit. Shaftesbury was referring to Plato's *Phaedrus*, as well as to the *Apologia*,
and to Plutarch. In fact, as his recent editor, Richard Wolf, remarks, Shaftesbury
misquoted the passages from Plato and Plutarch to suit his own purpose. See Wolf,
Shaftesbury's "Letter", p. 126. On the increasing, though still guarded, subjectivist
perspective of Shaftesbury's ethics see Charles Taylor, *Sources of the Self* (Cambridge
Mass.: Harvard University Press, 1989), pp. 248–259. Whereas in the concept of the
"Good", Shaftesbury still adhered to the classical—Platonic and Stoic—objectivist
view, his idea of inspiration and "enthusiasm" seems to me more clearly subjectivist.

[38] See Susie I. Tucker, *Enthusiasm: A Study in Semantic Change* (Cambridge: Cambridge University Press, 1972), p. 138. For an interpretation which stresses the objective
features of enthusiasm according to Shaftesbury, see Stanley Grean, *Shaftesbury's
Philosophy of Religion and Ethics*, especially chapter 2, and pp. 256–259.

[39] On More's views concerning genuine enthusiasm, see Chapter 3 above. It should
be noted, however, that already in the 1662 edition of *Enthusiasmus Triumphatus*, More

an apprehension of the divine, rather than an action of the divine spirit itself.

Was there, then, a distinction between "positive" enthusiasm, and the melancholic distemper which should be cured, or at least restrained by "good humour"? And who was to judge? Once again, Shaftesbury relied on traditional answers, but carried them to a more radical conclusion. What may seem surprising, but is highly interesting—he referred to the same verse from I John 4:1, which, as we have seen in Chapter 6 above, was a scriptural commonplace among clerical critics of enthusiasm. Yet he added to this verse a second part which gave it a radically new interpretation

> For *to judg* [sic] *the Spirits whether they are of God*, we must antecedently *judg our own Spirit*; whether it be of *Reason*, and *sound Sense*; whether it be fit to *judg* at all, by being sedate, cool, and impartial; free of every bypassing Passion, every giddy Vapor, or melancholy Fume.[40]

As we have seen already, the principle of individual judgment and the criteria of reason and good sense were by no means foreign to the critics of enthusiasm in the early eighteenth century, even the ecclesiastical ones. Shaftesbury, however, took this criterion one step further by focusing on introspection and self-examination. Moreover, whereas Christian critics of enthusiasm had recourse to individual reason alongside with Scripture, Shaftesbury did not refer to Scripture as a measuring-rod by which to judge enthusiasm.[41] Indeed, he implied that some of the negative characteristics of enthusiasm might be found among Old Testament Prophets as well. Serious introspection was a necessary antecedent to any "trial of spirits", and only good humour could serve as an effective antidote to enthusiasm.

The positive connotations of enthusiasm were broadly explicated in other texts by Shaftesbury which he published after the *Letter*. Indeed, he had developed his positive view of enthusiasm already in *The Social Enthusiast*, a philosophical dialogue written in 1703 or 1704

---

added a more subjective interpretation of enthusiasm, closer to that of Shaftesbury— "the triumph of the Soul of man inebriated, as it were with the delicious sense of the divine life"—with which he declared himself "as much a friend, as I am to the vulgar fanatical Enthusiasm a professed enemy". (*Enthusiasmus Triumphatus*, section 63, in *A Collection of Several Philosophical Writings*, 1662, vol. I, p. 45).

[40] *Letter Concerning Enthusiasm*, p. 54.
[41] Even Henry More, as we have seen in Chapter 3 above, required the reliance on Scripture alongside with Reason, in judging whether enthusiasm was genuine or not.

which circulated only in manuscript form among some of his friends.[42] In 1709 he published a revised version of that text under the title *The Moralists; a Philosophical Rhapsody*.[43] There he made a significant distinction between "serene enthusiasm" and the vulgar sort of enthusiasm of "modern *Zealots*". The sceptic Philocles characterizes his "enthusiast" Platonist friend Theocles in the following words:

> I MUST confess ... he had nothing of that savage air of the vulgar enthusiastick Kind. All was serene, soft, and harmonious. The manner of it was more after the pleasing Transports of those antient *Poets* you are often charm'd with, than after the fierce unsociable way of modern *Zealots*; those starch'd gruff Gentlemen, who guard Religion as Bullys do a Mistress, and give us the while a very indifferent Opinion of their Lady's Merit, and their own Wit, by adoring what they neither allow to be inspected by others, nor care themselves to examine in a fair light. But here I'll answer for it; there was nothing of Disguise or Paint. All was fair, open, and genuine, as Nature herself.[44]

The distinction between the two types of enthusiasm here was social as well as psychological ("vulgar", "savage" versus "serene, soft and harmonious"). Still more important, the one type was secretive, the other open to public examination. It was a distinction between zealous enthusiasm which does not allow any inspection of its objects by others (or by oneself, for that matter), and a critical enthusiasm which withstands examination. As he says in the following lines:

> And tho the Object here was very fine, and the Passion it created very noble; yet *Liberty*, I thought, was finer than all.[45]

At this point, Shaftesbury returned implicitly to the concept of toleration. As far as genuine, critical and "serene" enthusiasm was concerned, there was no contradiction between it and a tolerant attitude:

> That tho he had all of the *Enthusiast*, he had nothing of the *Bigot*. He heard every thing with Mildness and Delight; and bore with me when I treated all his Thoughts as visionary; and when, Sceptick-like, I unravel'd all his Systems.[46]

---

[42] See on that text, Voitle, *Shaftesbury*, pp. 313–323, and Grean, *Shaftesbury's Philosophy of Religion and Ethics*, Chapter 2.

[43] On some of these revisions, partly written in response to the criticisms of his *Letter*, see Voitle, *Shaftesbury*, pp. 347–349.

[44] *The Moralists*, Part I, Sect. 3, in *Characteristicks of Men, Manners, Opinions, Times*, vol. II, pp. 218–219. The book first appeared in 1711. I have used the 1732 edition of this work.

[45] Ibid., p. 219.

[46] Loc. cit.

The subjective attitude of the enthusiast, not just the object of his enthusiasm, was the critical criterion in Shaftesbury's rehabilitation of the term.[47]

This becomes even clearer in the next text Shaftesbury wrote concerning enthusiasm, partly in response to criticism levelled against the *Letter*. I refer here to Part II of the "Miscellaneous Reflections" written in 1709–1711, and first published in the third volume of his *Characteristicks* in 1711.[48] In that text, Shaftesbury once again posed the question of the difference between the positive and the danger-ous type of enthusiasm. Here, he started with the criterion of degree. In and of itself, enthusiasm was a natural passion, but it needed constant restraint and the exercise of moderation:

> Now as all Affections have their Excess, and require Judgment and Discretion to moderate and govern them; so this high and noble Affec-tion, which raises Man to Action, and is his Guide in Business as well as Pleasure, requires a steddy [sic!] Rein and strict Hand over it. All *Moralists*, worthy of any Name, have recogniz'd the Passion; tho' among these the wisest have prescrib'd Restraint, press'd *Moderation*, and to all TYRO'S in Philosophy forbid the forward Use of Admiration, Rap-ture, or Extasy, even in the Subjects they esteem'd the highest, and most *divine*.[49]

Once again, the object of rapture and enthusiasm was less relevant. While as a young man Shaftesbury had been willing to declare him-self an "enthusiast" in admiring the Artificer of nature,[50] in his later years, and following the affair of the French Prophets, he stressed

---

[47] In this respect, it should be stressed, Shaftesbury's rehabilitation of the term "enthusiasm" was not only in an aesthetic sense, as some of his Romantic followers interpreted him. See Voitle, *Shaftesbury*, pp. 322–323, and Grean, *Shaftesbury's Philosophy of Religion and Ethics*, who both stress the broader meaning of enthusiasm for Shaftesbury.

[48] See Voitle, *Shaftesbury*, pp. 305, 338–339.

[49] "Miscellaneous Reflections", Part II, Chapter 1, in *Characteristicks*, vol. III, p. 36–37.

[50] See "Exercises", Public Record Office, 30/24/27/10, Ex. 153, written in 1700, quoted by Voitle, *Shaftesbury*, p. 329. See also the passages in the "Excercises" pub-lished by Benjamin Rand:

> Why fear enthusiasm? Why shun the name? Where should I be ecstasied but here? Where enamoured but here? Is my subject true, or is it fiction? If true, how can I forsake it?. . . . Is the beatific vision enthusiasm? Or suppose it enthusiasm, is it not justifiable and of a right kind? What can be more highly reasonable? What greater folly, poorness, and mis-ery than be without it? Is there a rational and admired enthusiasm that belongs to archi-tecture, painting, music, and not to this?

(Benjamin Rand, *The Life, Unpublished Letters, and Philosophical Regimen of Anthony, Earl of Shaftesbury* (London: Macmillan, 1900), pp. 32–33.

that enthusiasm could be excessive even if its object was divine. The reins which ought to restrain such enthusiasm were the reins of Reason. Without them, the natural passion of enthusiasm degenerated into frenzy and zeal:

> This Passion is experienc'd, in common, by every worshiper of the *Zealot*-kind. The Motion, when un-guided, and left wholly to it-self, is in its nature turbulent and incentive. It disjoints the natural Frame, and relaxes the ordinary Tone or Tenor of the Mind. In this Disposition the Reins are let loose to all Passion which arises; And *the Mind*, as far as it is able to act or think in such a State, approves the Riot, and justifies the wild *Effects*, by the suppos'd Sacredness of *the Cause*. Every Dream and Frenzy is made INSPIRATION; every Affection, ZEAL.[51]

At first sight, Shaftesbury seems to be using the traditional language in distinguishing between false enthusiasm and true inspiration. Yet, as we have seen already, for him, the subjective, "psychological" perspective was the principal (though not the exclusive) one from which to view the issue. Without having recourse to Scripture, Reason and moderation remained the antidotes to exaggerated enthusiasm, which, when well-tempered, and critical, as Shaftesbury had noted earlier, was a natural and positive passion.[52]

Moreover, Christianity in general, or at least, clerical Christianity, in contra-distinction to Pauline Christianity, has now been relegated to the realm of exaggerated and intolerant enthusiasm. Shaftesbury devoted the second half of the second chapter in Part II of the *Miscellaneous Reflections* to an historical analysis of the growth of intolerance in early Christianity. He saw the roots of Christian intolerance in the combination of the roles of philosopher and priest, where priestly claims to divine inspiration merged with philosophical claims to possess rational certainty concerning that revelation.[53] The result was that

---

[51] "Miscellaneous Reflections", Part II, Chapter 1, *Characteristicks*, vol. III, p. 40.

[52] One should be careful, of course, not to give an overly "subjectivist" interpretation to Shaftesbury's concept of "enthusiasm". Though without a personal God as its object, genuine enthusiasm nevertheless was directed at the True, the Good and the Beautiful which had an objective existence in the order of nature. Indeed, Stanley Grean rightly stresses that Shaftesbury saw the experience of beauty as the means to transcend the separation of subject and object. (*Shaftesbury's Philosopohy of Religion and Ethics*, p. 257.) Nevertheless, it is important to note that Shaftesbury's distinctions between true and false enthusiasm were essentially subjective or psychological ones.

[53] *Miscellaneous Reflections*, Part II, Chapter 2, in *Characteristicks*, vol. III, pp. 74–82. Shaftesbury also referred to the historical circumstances of growing Roman oppression

Liberty of Judgment and Exposition taken away: No Ground left for Inquiry, Search, or Meditation: No Refuge from the *dogmatical* Spirit let loose. Every Quarter was taken up; every Portion prepossess'd. All was reduc'd to *Article* and *Proposition*. Thus, a sort of *Philosophical* ENTHUSIASM overspread the World.[54]

Appropriately enough, Shaftesbury presented the Emperor Julian "the Apostate" as a prime example of a tolerant and moderate attitude in religious matters.[55]

Shaftesbury, like his predecessors, the Cambridge Platonists, linked enthusiasm with the natural temperament of melancholy. Indeed, quoting More, Shaftesbury explicitly stated that melancholy was the natural cause behind "devotional enthusiasm" too.[56] Like More, within that temperament he distinguished between a genuine, positive enthusiasm, and a reprehensible one. Yet he drew the line separating the two in a radically different place, and based it on radically different foundations. Much less convinced of his ability to identify direct divine inspiration with certainty, Shaftesbury relied on subjective, primarily psychological criteria. For the same reason, he did not see any contradiction between genuine enthusiasm and toleration towards other people's views. And, of course, he carried the seventeenth century critique of enthusiasm to the threshold, indeed, beyond the threshold, of Christianity itself.

In spite of important continuities, then, Shaftesbury's critique of enthusiasm radically re-interpreted the meaning of the term, and the distinctions between positive and negative enthusiasm. Yet, the important point for us is to emphasize the continuities as well as the break that Shaftesbury represents in the history of the critique of enthusiasm. What he did in the *Letter* was to draw far-reaching conclusions from traditional lines of argument against the enthusiasts, such as the medical interpretation, and the need of a "trial of spirits". This is precisely why the *Letter*, anonymous at the time, attracted such heated responses, which would in turn influence the discourse on enthusiasm in the early eighteenth century. I shall now turn to some of these responses.

---

which fostered seeing the expectation of the Second Coming as the coming of the Messiah in a temporal sense. Ibid., p. 78.

[54] Ibid., p. 81.
[55] Ibid., pp. 86–89.
[56] Ibid., pp. 65–68.

Reactions to Shaftesbury's Letter

The anonymous publication of Shaftesbury's *Letter Concerning Enthusiasm* in the early summer of 1708 attracted several heated replies in the next few months, some of which were likewise unsigned. Critics were quick to detect the barely disguised deistic thrust of the *Letter*, and the debate it aroused constituted indeed an important part of the deistic controversy in England in the early eighteenth century. Nevertheless, the *Letter*, and the reactions it elicited, were also part of the debate concerning enthusiasm, and it is important to examine the extent to which they changed the nature of that debate. Especially significant for us is the fact that the call for a tolerant attitude towards the enthusiasts was perceived, on the eve of the Enlightenment, as a threat to the foundations of Christianity itself.

Not all of those who responded to Shaftesbury's *Letter* can be definitely identified.[57] The first reaction, apparently from the nonjuror Samuel Parker, appeared in two consecutive issues of *Censura Temporum*, in August and September 1708.[58] The next was *Remarks upon the Letter to a Lord concerning Enthusiasm*, written in all probability by the Bishop of Gloucester, Edward Fowler, who in fact had been one of the staunch opponents of the non-jurors since the Glorious Revolution.[59] Fowler was the target of Shaftesbury's ironic reference

---

[57] For the most recent discussion of these responses see Wolf, *Shaftesbury's "Letter"*, pp. 6–16. See also Aldridge, "Shaftesbury and the Deist Manifesto", especially the bibliography on pp. 371–382. There were also several Continental responses to Shaftesbury's *Letter*, most interesting, perhaps, that by Leibniz, in reaction to the *Letter* sent to him by Coste: C.I. Gerhardt, ed., *G.W. Leibniz, Philosophischen Schriften* (reprint edition, Hildesheim: Olms Verlag, 1978), vol. III, pp. 423–424, pp. 405–431 for the whole exchange between Coste and Leibniz concerning this issue. Leibniz's ambivalent attitude towards enthusiasm is currently being studied by Daniel J. Cook. Like Shaftesbury, Leibniz could find some positive aspects in enthusiasm, yet he was upset by Shaftesbury's tone of raillery concerning such a serious matter. I am grateful to Professor Cook for letting me read a draft of his paper "Leibniz on Enthusiasm" prior to publication.

[58] [Samuel Parker] in *Censura Temporum: The Good or Ill Tendencies of Books, Sermons, Pamphlets, etc. Impartially consider'd, In a dialogue between Eubulus and Sophronius* (London, printed for H. Clements: For the Month of August 1708, pp. 244–254; For the Month of September, pp. 263–265). See also A.O. Aldridge, "Shaftesbury and the Deist Manifesto", pp. 320–322. Samuel Parker was the son of Samuel Parker Sr., the Restoration Bishop of Oxford who in 1670 published the famous *Ecclesiastical Polity*. Samuel Parker Jr. published the periodical *Censura Temporum* between 1708 and 1710, defending the principles of the High Church party. See *D.N.B.*, vol. XV, pp. 275–276.

[59] [Anon.], *Remarks upon the Letter to a Lord Concerning Enthusiasm. In a Letter to a Gentleman. Not written in Raillery, Yet in Good Humour.* (London: Printed by W.D., for

in the *Letter* to "an Eminent, Learned, and truly Christian Prelate you once knew, who cou'd have given you a full account of his Belief in *Fairys*".[60] That might have well been the reason for Fowler's quick response to the *Letter*. The *Remarks*, nevertheless, were written in a moderate tone, and tried to examine Shaftesbury's text in a fair manner. The same cannot be said of another response to Shaftesbury published anonymously in 1709, entitled *Reflections upon "A Letter Concerning Enthusiasm"*, which according to some authorities, may also have been written by Fowler.[61] This text elaborated some of the points raised in Fowler's *Remarks*, but was written in a much harsher tone. The last extended response to Shaftesbury, also published in 1709, was probably written by Mary Astell, and was entitled *Bart'lemy Fair: or, an Enquiry after Wit*.[62] Mary Astell (1668–1731), was well-known as a polemicist and a "Daughter of the Church of England", who defended traditional Anglican doctrine against the Roman Catholics, against Locke's *Reasonableness of Christianity*, as well as against Tillotson's views on eternal punishment in Hell.[63]

English responses to Shaftesbury's *Letter Concerning Enthusiasm* thus came from Broad Churchmen like Fowler as well as High Anglicans like Samuel Parker, from ecclesiastics as well as lay people who, as

---

John Wyat, 1708). 91 pp. On Fowler (1632–1714) see *D.N.B.*, vol. VII pp. 524–526. On Fowler as the probable author of that tract see Aldridge, "Shaftesbury and the Deist Manifesto", p. 371, and Wolf, *Shaftesbury's "Letter"*, pp. 7–8.

[60] *Letter Concerning Enthusiasm*, p. 6. The allusion here was to Fowler providing Henry More with several accounts of ghosts and spirits, which were incorporated in Glanvill's *Sadducismus Triumphatus*. See Wolf, *Shaftesbury's "Letter"*, pp. 3–5. Indeed, the sentence quoted above was one of the reasons why Shaftesbury at first did not want the *Letter* to be published, given the position Bishop Fowler held, and the services he had rendered the Whig cause after the Glorious Revolution. The sentence quoted is already more careful with respect to Fowler than the reference in the original manuscript had been, since it mentions him in the past tense, as a "Prelate you once knew". As we know, the original manuscript had circulated quite widely for a few months before the official publication of the *Letter*.

[61] [Anon.] *Reflections upon a Letter concerning Enthusiasm, to my Lord *****. In another Letter to a Lord*. (London: Printed for H. Clements, 1709). Voitle, as well as the British Library Catalogue, ascribe this text, rather than the *Remarks*, to Bishop Fowler.

[62] [Anon.] *Bart'lemy Fair: Or, an Enquiry after Wit: In which due respect is had to a Letter Concerning Enthusiasm, to my Lord ****, by Mr. Wotton* (London: Printed for R.W. Wilkin, 1709). A second edition which included an "Advertisement to the Reader", appeared in 1722 under a slightly different title, [Anon.], *An Enquiry after Wit: Wherein the Trifling Arguing and Impious Raillery of the Late Earl of Shaftesbury, in his Letter concerning Enthusiasm, and other Profane Writers, Are fully Answered, and justly Exposed*. (Second Edition: London: Printed for John Bateman, 1722).

[63] On Mary Astell see Ruth Perry, *The Celebrated Mary Astell: An Early English Feminist* (Chicago: Chicago University Press, 1986). See also "Astell, Mary", *D.N.B.*, vol. I, pp. 201–202.

in the case of Astell, sympathized with the High Church party. The critique of the *Letter*, like the critique of enthusiasm we surveyed in Chapter 6 above, brought together the various trends of ecclesiastical and theological thinking in England of the early eighteenth century. In discussing Shaftesbury, we began with his medical critique, proceeded to the implications he drew from that critique as to the tolerant attitude towards enthusiasm, then moved to "raillery" as the best antidote to enthusiasm, and finally examined his distinction between positive and negative enthusiasm. In the case of his opponents, however, one should go the other way round since they observed first of all the ambivalence in Shaftesbury's own concept of enthusiasm. They were struck by the "good humour" which he advocated, not only with respect to enthusiasm, but with regard to religion in general, a humour which they took as unqualified cynicism. They then had to come to terms with Shaftesbury's plea for toleration concerning enthusiasm, in the context of the problem of toleration in general in England at that time. Finally, the radical conclusions which Shaftesbury had drawn from the medical critique led his opponents to re-examine that critique and to seriously qualify it.

Shaftesbury's critics were quick to seize upon the deep ambivalence and hardly disguised irony in his treatment of enthusiasm. Was it indeed a distemper, so universal as to underlie all religions, or was it a normal, natural, indeed, positive temper? Was it his aim to ridicule all religious beliefs, or perhaps, to rehabilitate enthusiasm itself? On the one hand, Fowler remarked, Shaftesbury called inspiration— "Divine Enthusiasm", following Plato on this matter. On the other, "he ... calls Enthusiasm in *general* a *Distemper* ...".[64] How then, to reconcile these two views? Was there still any distinction between true inspiration and false enthusiasm in Shaftesbury's view? Critics like Fowler realized that Shaftesbury was re-defining the term itself, especially when he was talking about "atheistic enthusiasm":

> But besides his *Heroine, States-Mans, Poetical, Oratorical, Musical*, and *Philosophical* Enthusiasms, to which he adds elsewhere the *Furious* one too, he tells us ... of an *atheistical enthusiasm*, which, I suppose, is no *Divine* Inspiration, nor taken so to be by the *Atheist*.[65]

It was indeed Shaftesbury's irony in using that label which principally angered Fowler.

---

[64] *Remarks*, p. 50.
[65] *Remarks*, pp. 51–52.

The suggestion that religious matters should be approached with "good humour" of course incensed all of Shaftesbury's critics. Religion should be taken seriously, they argued. But the deep cause of the contention, which is not always sufficiently noticed, was the issue of salvation. Shaftesbury, like other deists, pushed to the extreme the growing indifference in his generation towards the soteriological dimension of Christianity.[66] In reaction, his critics reiterated the importance of that dimension. Religion could not be taken "in good humour" because it involved too serious an issue—the salvation of our souls. That issue, Shaftesbury's critics noted, hardly bothered him at all. Mary Astell referred to his passion for the "Anti-saving of Souls":

> Unless that Anti-*saving of Souls* which *is now the Heroic Passion of* your *exalted Spirits, and is become in a manner your chief Care, and the very end of* all your Consultations, has inspir'd you with that *hopeful Project* of instructing the Valiant Youth of the Nation, to reconcile the Luxuries of their Winter Quarters to the Rigors of a Camp.[67]

Whereas Natural Theology was indeed the first foundation of Christianity, it was by no means a sufficient basis, Fowler and the author of the *Reflections* argued, and had to be supplemented by Revealed Theology. Natural Theology assured us of the existence of God, and even of his Goodness, "But is Goodness *all* perfections? Is not *Wisdom* a Perfection, and *Righteousness*, and *Purity*, or Holiness, to name no more?"[68] Addressing himself to the crucial point in the debate with deism, Fowler stressed that God was not just absolutely Good, but also the supreme Governor of the world, enacting laws, rewarding the just and punishing the wicked, in this life and the next.[69] Furthermore

> ... God would not study *universal* Good, nor promote the *whole* Interest of the whole World, if he had not as great a regard, at least, to the Spiritual and Eternal Interest of Men, as to their Bodily and Temporal ...[70]

---

[66] See C.J. Betts, *Early Deism in France* (The Hague: Martinus Nijhoff, 1984), pp. 164–166, for a similar indifferene towards the issue of salvation in the French deistic text *Examen de la Religion*, published around the same time as Shaftesbury's *Letter*.

[67] *Bart'lemy Fair*, p. 10. The thrust of her argument here was Shaftesbury's negligence of the real issues at hand, the war with Louis XIV, as well as the social needs of the poor or the state of the Church.

[68] *Remarks*, p. 32.

[69] Ibid., pp. 33–35.

[70] Ibid., pp. 36–37.

God was thus not just supremely Good, he was the Judge, as well as the Redeemer of mankind. These functions could not be grasped by Natural Theology. Furthermore, the central mysteries of God, such as the Trinity and the Resurrection, could only be dealt with by Revelation.[71]

Religion, then, was too serious a matter to be treated simply by "good humour", and could not be reduced merely to the discourse of Natural Theology. Significantly, in the view of Shaftesbury's critics, the issue of salvation and the question of enthusiasm also set limits to the practice of toleration. Shaftesbury's Whig opponents, Bishop Fowler and the author of the *Reflections*, were indeed in a delicate position. They shared his opposition to persecution, yet they could not accept his practice of ridicule towards religion, nor his indulgent attitude towards enthusiasm. Fowler posed the question succinctly, in terms which seem pretty modern:

> ... Whether Liberty may be denied to the Ridiculing of every thing ... Whether there be any such things as *Sacred* ... If there be, Whether it be a decent or *innocent* thing to Ridicule them.[72]

Fowler agreed with Shaftesbury in his harangue against persecution, but he couched that agreement in heavy irony:

> For a good many Pages after the 21st, we meet with very notable high Flights against *Persecution* upon the score of Religion. And I wish I had *his* Pen to tell you my Thoughts of them. Yet take from my *own*, such a one as it is, what follows, *viz*. That I feel myself in so *Good a Humour*, as not onely disables me to give them one angry Cast, but makes me not a little pleased with the Eloquence and Wit he has shewed *here*.[73]

Fowler went on veiling his own view with irony:

> If ever I could be so Bigotted to my own Religious Sentiments, as to hate other Folks that differ from mine, while I am ignorant of what is to be said for them, I should be in danger of hating the Religion of all Persecutors, (however dignifi'd or distinguish'd) without any other Reason, but because 'tis *theirs*: And of concluding all those *Modes* of Religion arrant *Priestcraft*, in which the Doctrine of *Persecution* is a *fundamental* Article; and that cannot be propagated nor defended but by *Club-Law*. And thus, Sir, you see how far I am from having any Dispute with our Gentleman upon *this* Argument.[74]

---

[71] See *Reflections*, pp. 6–9, 83–93,
[72] *Remarks*, pp. 15–16.
[73] Ibid., pp. 25–26.
[74] Ibid., p. 26–27.

While agreeing with Shaftesbury on the principle, he warned, in a round-about-way, against condemning as "arrogant Priestcraft" any defence of persecution, and urged taking into account the doctrine in question, which indeed may be "dignifi'd". In other words, not every persecution was reprehensible, and not every type of toleration commendable. Fowler hinted here that there were indeed limits to toleration, as well as to the effectiveness of "good humour".[75]

The author of the *Reflections* took a similar view. He was incensed by Shaftesbury's sarcastic attitude to the claims of the secular authority to take care of matters regarding the salvation of souls in the after-life:

> It would move a little Choler, to see a Person, in a Publish'd, and sort of Triumphing, Letter to some Great Lord (and that is Design'd for all he can Infect), so scornfully speaking of a certain *New sort of Policy which extends it self to another World, etc.* and of *the Magistrate's so concerning himself in it.* As if, on Supposition of its Truth, it was not their Indispensable Duty; and they could Concern Themselves in any thing better or higher.[76]

Any doctrine related to salvation, if true, should indeed be the concern of the Magistrate. In this respect, neither the *Remarks* nor the *Reflections* adopted the position of Locke who sharply distinguished between matters of state and the question of salvation.[77] Both texts rejected the dividing line between the public realm of religion, that of external worship, and the private sphere of belief and opinions. According to Shaftesbury's opponents, belief had public significance too, since it involved matters of salvation. Nevertheless, the writer of the *Reflections* explicitly agreed with Fowler's guarded and qualified view on the issue of persecution:

> By the way, *my Lord,* I cannot but take notice, what Advocates these Gentlemen are of late grown, for *Liberty of Conscience:* and against the

---

[75] A detailed analysis of Fowler's arguments on the necessary limits of toleration and "ridicule" is beyond the limits of my present concern. But see *Remarks*, pp. 15–24.

[76] *Reflections*, pp. 16–17.

[77] On the similarities as well as differences between Locke's views concerning toleration and those of the Whigs after 1689 see J. Waldron, "Locke: Toleration and the Rationality of Persecution", in S. Mendus, ed., *Justifying Toleration: Conceptual and Historical Perspectives* (Cambridge: Cambridge University Press, 1988), pp. 61–86; John Dunn "The Claim to Freedom of Conscience: Freedom of Speech, Freedom of Thought, Freedom of Worship?" and Mark Goldie, "The Theory of Religious Intolerance in Restoration England", both in O.P. Grell, J.I. Israel and N. Tyacke, eds., *From Persecution to Toleration*, pp. 171–193, 331–368, esp. 362–363.

Violence of *Persecution*. I am, with that worthy Person that made the *Remarks*, entirely against the Ways of Persecution; and subscribe to all that Wise Persons have ever said against it; though at the same time a Man may lament the Divisions, and unhappy Separations, there are amongst us. But it is worthy of Observation, with what excellent Charity, and true Christian Zeal, these enthusiasts for *Deism*, or at least *Scepticism* (if I may thus speak) press a general Liberty for all Persuasions, or Enthusiasms, of Men. And what is the true Original of this? *Divide et Impera*. I desire to be pardon'd, if I think it to be from somewhat the same Grounds, that the *Romanists*, in a late reign, were so much for an Universal Liberty of Conscience; *i.e.*, to shelter themselves well, at first, under it; and when that was done, to engross, if possible, by degrees the Chief Rule to themselves. And as at this Day, nothing delights the *Papists* more than our Varieties of Division, which they also further to the utmost of their Power; so these *Libertines* of ours, *Theists*, or no *Theists*, seem to please themselves not a little with our Varieties of religion (or, as they love rather it should be term'd, of Superstition, or Enthusiasm) and to spread in triumph their Tokens and Banners upon them.[78]

While adhering to the principle of Toleration, and opposed to persecution, Whigs such as Fowler and the author of the *Reflections* shied from interpreting the opposition to persecution as an acceptance of liberty of conscience for *all* views, including those of the deists, atheists, and enthusiasts. They reminded themselves and their readers that such a universal liberty of conscience had not long ago been declared by James II in his 1687 "Declaration of Indulgence" in order to further the cause of Roman Catholicism. And they suspected Shaftesbury of a similar design, in favour not just of the enthusiasts, but of the deists and atheists as well. Indeed, and especially significant for our present topic, they regarded "enthusiasm" as parallel to "deism" and "atheism". The phenomenon of enthusiasm, and the spread of deistic tracts in those years, presented the Whig ministers with a difficult dilemma. Subscribing to the Act of Toleration of 1689, they were nevertheless reluctant to extend it to the French Prophets, or to those deists like Shaftesbury who were tolerant towards enthusiasm.[79]

The non-juror Samuel Parker had fewer problems with the issue of toleration. He poured derision on Shaftesbury's suggestion, quoted

---

[78] *Reflections*, pp. 54–55.
[79] On the complex attitude of the "Established Whigs" to toleration and its limits after 1689 see above, as well as G.V. Bennett, "Conflict in the Church", in Holmes, *Britain after the Glorious Revolution*, pp. 155–175, and the articles by J. Israel, M. Goldie and H.R. Trevor-Roper, in *From Persecution to Toleration*.

above, to establish an Inquisition in Britain to restrain Poetical License. Parker chose not to understand Shaftesbury's irony, retorting:

> ... [M]ethinks 'tis somewhat surprizing, that there should be need of
> an Inquisition to compel Men to gratifie their Lusts and Follies. I thought
> the Business of Authority and correction had been to restrain them
> from it. But, it seems, the State of Things is chang'd. We must be
> dragg'd to Pleasure![80]

Mary Astell too had no qualms concerning toleration. Indeed, her
ironic response to Shaftesbury was directed principally at Whig critics such as Fowler, who tended to take—what seemed to her—an
indulgent attitude towards the *Letter*:

> For there are among those whose Business is Religion, Men so far
> from Bigotry, such avow'd Enemies to Superstition, and to any thing
> called by these Names, that tho' they do not think it Decent to chant
> Encomium upon all your Actions, yet are such excellent Distinguishers,
> as not to confound the *Less* with the *More* Praise-worthy.... They don't
> justify you as *Atheists*, but they tolerate you as *Deists* and *Socinians*, by a
> peculiar Act of Indulgence over and above the *Act of Toleration*; and
> they Adore you as Patriots. They expect not that you shou'd be with
> out Fault, alas! we live not in *Plato's* Commonwealth, but in the Dregs
> of *Gothic* Monarchy! Your public Spirit, your honest and unwearied
> Industry, *perfas & nefas*, to serve your Country, are Virtues that atone
> for every thing!.[81]

Her words were thus an oblique critique of the Toleration Act itself
and its far-reaching, if unintended consequences.[82] Astell carried her
critique further and ironically pointed out its social implications later
in her treatise:

> For the best way in our Great Men's Opinion, is to remove the Ter
> rors of Religion, the "Melancholy and Formal" manner of treating it,
> and to render it so gentle, that it may not disturb us in any Jollity.
> This wou'd, doubtless, recommend it to Men of Wealth and Quality,
> who love their Ease and Pleasures, and can't endure the thought of
> being call'd to account for following their own Humour. And he who
> prepares the way to such noble Proselytes, must needs be thought to
> have done a considerable Service to Religion![83]

---

[80] *Censura Temporum*, September, 1708, p. 264.

[81] *Bart'lemy Fair*, pp. 14–15.

[82] See on these unintended consequences the articles by Jonathan Israel and H.R.
Trevor-Roper in the collection *From Persecution to Toleration*.

[83] *Bart'lemy Fair*, pp. 44–45.

Indeed, the reaction to Shaftesbury's *Letter* dwelt on the threat it posed
to the social order no less than to religious Orthodoxy. Mary Astell
put it sharply:

> For until this Blessed Age of *Liberty*! . . . it was never thought a Service
> to the Public to expose the Establish'd Religion, no not when it was
> ever so false and ridiculous in it self, to the contempt of the People.
> The strongest Prejudice and most plausible Argument, that the Wise
> and Good, among *the mighty Princes and Emperors of the World*, had against
> that subduing force of Reason and Miracle by which Christianity made
> its way thro' all Opposition, was the Danger of Innovating upon the
> Receiv'd Religion and Faith of their Ancestors, the Maintenance of
> which was so necessary to the Public Peace, as they suppos'd.[84]

Astell took a dangerous step when arguing for *any* established religion, since Christianity itself was, as she herself noted, an innovative
religion, threatening the established one. This was precisely the enthusiasts' point: Christianity, and even more specifically, Protestantism, showed that "innovation" was not necessarily a bad thing. For
Christians, the problem had always been how to reconcile this real-
ization with the maintenance of the social order. On the eve of the
Enlightenment that problem had become especially acute.

Why did a tolerant attitude towards contemporary enthusiasm seem
so dangerous, not only in the eyes of High Church sympathisers like
Astell, but also Broad Churchmen like Fowler? First of all, because,
as we have seen above, it involved blurring the lines between biblical
prophecy and the contemporary prophets. Shaftesbury's *Letter* only
showed that if contemporary enthusiasts were taken lightly, the constitutive prophecies of Christianity, whether of the Old or New Testament, could be taken lightly too. A sharp line had to be drawn
between the two types of prophecy in order to safeguard the special
status and authenticity of the biblical message. The deistic challenge
thus called for a renewed emphasis on Scripture as an antidote to
enthusiasm.

Edward Fowler reiterated the criteria we have noted already in
Chapter 6 above:

> But I am perswaded, that without all this *ado*, we may know real Divine
> Inspirations from mere Pretensions, if we please, and would but sin-
> cerely set about it. Whosoever will so do, may quickly be satisfied, that
> the onely course to be taken is considering what *rational* Evidence ap-
> pears of their not being deluded, nor Impostors, who profess to come

---

[84] Ibid., p. 23.

upon God's Errand, and to be Inspir'd by His Spirit. And a very little Thinking will put it out of doubt, that our Minds can be rationally satisfi'd about this Matter, onely by enquiring what *Credentials* these pretended Ambassadors bring with them. Now nothing is more evident, than that 'tis necessary these should demonstrate their being divinely Inspir'd, by *first* delivering nothing in GOD'S Name, but what is *God-like*, and *worthy of God*; and *next*, that what they deliver should be confirm'd by *Miracles*, or Works surpassing the Power of mere Natural Causes.[85]

The criteria which Fowler considered as rational evidence were the content of the message, namely, it had to be "worthy of God", and a confirmation by miracles which surpassed the power of natural causes. Yet, these signs, and indeed, special inspiration itself, were only necessary when a new doctrine—not an old and known one—was put forward. To incite sinners to repentance, Fowler declared (in direct response to the arguments of some of the "prophets") no extraordinary inspiration or divine message was required. Only when new doctrine was proposed, on the basis of direct divine inspiration, both criteria had to be met—the content of that doctrine had to be worthy of God, and the claim to inspiration had to be confirmed by miracles, including successful predictions not foreknowable in their causes.[86]

The author of the *Reflections* preferred an argument on the ground of probability in distinguishing the ancient prophets from the modern ones:

> ... [H]ow much more likely is it, (a Thousand times more likely) that these Few comparatively, and Giddy, Prejudic'd, or Debauch'd Infidels, should be under the Delusions of their Looseness or Pride; and that this Sort of Madness and Enthusiasm of theirs should be very *Catching*, and pass, as a kind of Natural Contagion, from One to Another; than that all things should be turn'd Topsy-turvy, and the Wise and Sober become Fools and Madmen, to make way for these Libertines, and Irreligious Ranters, to Ride, as it were, in Triumph over their Heads![87]

Finally, the use Shaftesbury and other Deists made of the medical account of enthusiasm laid bare the inherent dangers of such a naturalist account of religious phenomena. Could not the same account be applied to biblical prophecy and to religious experiences deemed

---

[85] *Remarks*, pp. 59–60.
[86] Ibid., pp. 60–62.
[87] *Reflections*, p. 47.

truly divine? Some of those who responded to Shaftesbury continued nonetheless to adhere to the medical account of enthusiasm. Edward Fowler declared himself satisfied with what he called a "mechanical" account of enthusiasm, according to which

> It may be, in short, wholly resolved into Brains well heated with Thoughts; which, according to Mens very different *Make*, and the *Things* thought on, must needs be more or less intense and fixed, and the Brains subject to be *over-heated*, more or less; and especially in those in whom the *Melancholick* Humour is predominant in a higher or a lower degree. The onely Fault I can spy in *this* Account is, that 'tis too simple for Men of Wit and Fancy. This gives a *Mechanical* Account of those strange Commotions he has describ'd.[88]

Fowler added that "those *nervous* Maladies which commonly accompany this disorder of the Brain . . . naturally proceed from thence as does Heat from Fire".[89] No less significant, he relied on Henry More's *Enthusiasmus Triumphatus* in giving such an interpretation.[90] Cambridge Platonism could thus serve as a source both for Shaftesbury and Fowler, each arriving at contrary conclusions from that tradition. Fowler therefore did not dispute the medical or "mechanical" account. Indeed, he criticised Shaftesbury precisely from that perspective, claiming that such an account was too simple for "men of wit". At the same time he pointed out that characterizing enthusiasm as "a very Catching disease" ran the risk of a regression *ad infinitum*, unless one explained how it started.[91] The problem was not with the medical account per se, but with the lack of understanding of that account, with the tendency to rely exclusively on it, as we shall presently see, and of course, with the facile generalization of such an explanation to cover *all* types of divine inspiration.[92]

Faced with this challenge of the broadening of the medical account, Fowler himself, and Shaftesbury's other critics, resorted once again to the traditional diabolical account of enthusiasm. It is highly interesting to see that such a demonological explanation of the agitations and alleged inspirations of the French Prophets resurfaced mainly *after* the publication of Shaftesbury's *Letter*.[93] Thus, Fowler argued,

---

[88] *Remarks*, pp. 48–49.
[89] Ibid., p. 49.
[90] Ibid., p. 50.
[91] Ibid., pp. 53–54.
[92] Ibid., pp. 46–48.
[93] On reservations concerning the medical critique following Shaftesbury's *Letter*

phenomena such as Speaking in Tongues, as well as the contagious nature of enthusiasm, indicated that it could not be interpreted in medical terms alone:

> As to these People being possessed with what is called a *Quoad hoc Madness*, as many would have them to be, how so great a Number should, all of a sudden, be seiz'd with this Disease . . .? Sure *Madness* has not hitherto been reputed a *Catching* Disease, whatever *Enthusiasm* may be. And could *Madness* give that Gentleman *in his Agitations, a Pompous Latin Style of which out of his Exstasies it seems he is wholly uncapable*? as we now saw our Gentleman's Words are.[94]

If enthusiasm seemed like inspiration, this was only because God permitted the evil spirit to act in this way so as to harden the hearts of the unbelievers and the infidels.[95] Fowler emphasized the demonological account also in order to point out that miracles alone were not a sufficient criterion to verify claims to direct divine inspiration. Evil spirits too could perform miracles and therefore, as we have seen above, the content of the alleged inspiration had to be carefully examined. Fowler thus claimed the existence of "Daemoniacal Enthusiasm", although "it is grown very Modish (however it comes to pass) to *seem* at least to disbeliev [sic!] it."[96] This is a significant comment which indicates that Fowler realized that in such demonological interpretation of enthusiasm he was "old-fashioned". He determined to be so not only because of the limitations of the medical account, nor even to explain away the French Prophets' claims to perform miracles. Like seventeenth century theologians before him, Fowler feared that the denial of demons was but a first step towards the denial of God, and in an age of growing infidelity, it was paramount to insist on the permission which God had given for the intervention of the devil:

> If I may make any Conjecture concerning the Design of Providence, in permitting such a Spirit of Delusion thus to prevail here at *this* time, I cannot but greatly fear it is intended in just Judgment, for the more hardening of Infidels (who so lamentably now Abound, beyond the

---

see also Schwartz, *Knaves, Fools, Madmen and that Subtile Effluvium* (Gainsville: University Presses of Florida, 1978), pp. 53–54. Schwartz, however, tends to ascribe the recourse to demonological arguments mostly to the older opponents of the French Prophets, rather than to the challenge posed by Shaftesbury. Ibid., pp. 52, 55.

[94] *Remarks*, p. 70. The author of the *Reflections* agreed with Fowler that the agitations and appearances of the Prophets were *Daemoniacal* in origin. *Reflections*, p. 2.

[95] *Remarks*, pp. 69–70.

[96] Ibid., p. 68.

Example of former Ages) by a *Mock-effusion of the Holy Spirit,* and an *Aping* (tho' most wofully) *of the Great Day of Pentecost.* Yet were a *Possession* more generally acknowledg'd in the Case, this Permission, may be as *gracious* a Providence for the raising Mens Minds to a greater sense of the *reality* of Invisible Beings; and the Conviction of those whose Unbelief is not incurable.[97]

An exclusive medical account thus had serious drawbacks, especially once it had been used in an extended way by a Deist like Shaftesbury. Even the physician Richard Blackmore, in the next decade, was aware of the dangers of the medical interpretation of enthusiasm. Though ascribing enthusiasm to Melancholy and the Spleen, he was nevertheless quick to add:

> From this Observation, some Men of Wit have reproach'd all Devotion as the Effect of a distemper'd Brain, and an Imagination overagitated by the Spleen.[98]

Both ministers and some laymen were therefore reluctant to view the enthusiasts merely as sick people, entitled to pity rather than condemnation. Therefore, traditional demonological accusations against the enthusiasts still persisted in the early eighteenth century and indeed, resurfaced, in response to the deist broadening of the medical critique to include religion as a whole. As has been shown in a previous chapter, the opponents of enthusiasm also resorted to a "political" account, seeing the symptoms of the enthusiasts as mere imposture aimed at subverting the social, political or clerical order.[99] The challenge of enthusiasm thus set clear limits to toleration in England on the eve of the Enlightenment. In the next generation, the question would be re-opened following the emergence of Methodism, but that is already a new story, which requires another study. For my part, I would like finally to return to the issue of the links between enthusiasm and the new mechanical philosophy, since on that level too, one can find a transition from sharp antagonism in the seventeenth century to some cases of a more tolerant attitude in the eighteenth.

---

[97] Ibid., pp. 69–70.

[98] Richard Blackmore, "An Essay Upon the Spleen", in *Essays upon Several Subjects,* vol. II (London, 1717), p. 216. The whole essay is on pp. 167–237. Blackmore indeed ascribed enthusiasm to the spleen and melancholy.

[99] See Chapter 7 above.

CHAPTER NINE

MECHANISM AND ENTHUSIASM: FROM EXPLICIT
ANTAGONISM TO IMPLICIT ALLIANCE

Tendencies towards the rehabilitation of enthusiasm in the eighteenth
century may be seen not only on the religious but also on the philosophical and scientific level. From the early eighteenth century onwards, certain scientists could view enthusiasm with more tolerant
eyes, sometimes even actively supporting the enthusiasts. It is time,
therefore, to return finally to a theme which has preoccupied us in
previous chapters of this book—the relationship between enthusiasm
and the new mechanical philosophy.

In the second half of the seventeenth century, notwithstanding the
criticism of conservative opponents, the new natural philosophy, both
Cartesian and experimental, was increasingly regarded as an effective antidote to enthusiasm. The mechanistic philosophy which saw
nature strictly in terms of matter and motion was especially appropriate for that purpose. The mechanical investigation of nature could
no longer be understood as a means to discover hidden divine truth
or to acquire direct divine inspiration. Indeed, Continental natural
philosophers were drawn to a mechanistic view precisely because it
avoided mixing the spiritual with the natural, and since it carefully
distinguished between theology and philosophy. This was true not
only for Catholic thinkers like Mersenne and Descartes, but also for
Protestant professors of philosophy like the Genevan Jean-Robert
Chouet, or his former student, Pierre Bayle.[1]

In England, too, the mechanical philosophy first seemed attractive
as a healthy antidote to the various trends of enthusiasm and the

---

[1] For Mersenne, see the classic study by Robert Lenoble, *Mersenne ou la naissance
du mécanisme* (Paris: Vrin, 1943). Descartes' attitude towards tendencies which conflate
the theological and the philosophical, spirit and matter, is expressed most clearly in
his 1638(?) letter concerning the views of Comenius. See AT, vol. 2, Letter CLX,
pp. 345–48. On Chouet see my book *Between Orthodoxy and the Enlightenment: Jean-
Robert Chouet and the Introduction of Cartesian Science in the Academy of Geneva* (The Hague,
Jerusalem: Martinus Nijhoff, The Magnes Press, 1982). On Pierre Bayle see Elisabeth
Labrousse, *Pierre Bayle*, 2 vols. (The Hague: Martinus Nijfhoff, 1963, 1964), esp. vol. I,
chapter 5, pp. 94–112, vol. II, chapters 8, 10.

interest in alchemy and other occult sciences which became manifest
during the Interregnum period. In Chapter 5 above we saw how
propagandists like Sprat and Glanvill presented the new experimental
science as the best response to the challenge of enthusiasm. The same
was true for the practising scientists themselves, though their reaction
to enthusiasm was often implicit rather than explicit. English mechanical philosophy should be distinguished, however, from that of
the Continent on several accounts: First of all, unlike Cartesians
across the Channel, English natural philosophers did not completely
dissociate experimental philosophy from religious concerns. Indeed,
even corpuscular philosophers like Boyle tended to see their role as
equivalent to that of ministers, presenting themselves as "priests of
nature."[2] Consequently, and this is the second point, they were weary
of the "materialistic" and "atheistic" implications of Cartesianism.
They had to distance themselves, after all, from Hobbes as well as
from the enthusiasts. "Spiritual" elements were, therefore, never completely banished from the thought of most English natural philosophers. Writers like Sprat, Glanvill, Boyle and above all, Henry More,
tried to give a "naturalist" account of spirits and spiritual phenomena in order to combat the claims of both atheists and enthusiasts.[3]
Very soon, however, in the course of the 1660's, important differences emerged. Whereas More believed that the mechanical philosophy could not account for natural phenomena, and that experiments
had proved the existence of a "hylarchic spirit", Boyle and Hooke
defined the limits of experimental philosophy in a way which excluded the discussion of an "hylarchic principle". Such a "Spirit of
Nature" was not a physical principle but rather a metaphysical one,
and was thus outside the realm of experimental philosophy which
should be kept autonomous and immune to external metaphysical

---

[2] See Steven Shapin and Simon Schaffer, *Leviathan and the Air-Pump* (Princeton:
Princeton University Press, 1989), pp. 310–319, and note 52 in Chapter 5 above.
See also James R. Jacob, *Robert Boyle and the English Revolution* (New York: Burt Franklin,
1977). The establishment of the "Boyle Lectures" for the purpose of confuting the
dangers of atheism by an appeal to Natural Philosophy is well known. See especially
Margaret C. Jacob, *The Newtonians and the English Revolution* (Hassocks, Sussex: The
Harvester Press, 1976), chapter 4.
[3] Shapin and Schaffer, *Leviathan and the Air-Pump*, pp. 207–212. On Henry More's
"Spirit of Nature" see Michael Boylan, "Henry More and the Spirit of Nature",
Journal of the History of Philosophy 18 (1980): 395–405; John Henry, "Henry More
versus Robert Boyle: The Spirit of Nature and the Nature of Providence", in Sarah
Hutton, ed., *Of Mysticism and Mechanism: Tercentenary Studies of Henry More (1614–1687)*
(Dordrecht: Kluwer, 1989). See also Chapter 3 above.

considerations.[4] Robert Boyle, after all, adopted a corpuscular view of nature as a clear reaction to the alchemical and mystical tendencies current during the Interregnum. Yet even Boyle was not as strict a mechanical philosopher as his Continental colleagues were, and was ready at times to entertain the possibility of active or vital forces in nature.[5] As has recently been shown, the experimental method was a response to the authoritarian materialism of Thomas Hobbes on the one hand, and the pretensions of the enthusiasts on the other.[6] The emphasis on experiments and on the audience as visual witnesses of a public performance was clearly a means to counter the claims of various enthusiasts to private and un-mediated visions of their own.[7]

English mechanical philosophers thus differed from their Continental colleagues both in the ways they responded to the challenge of enthusiasm, and in the modifications they introduced within mechanical philosophy itself. Indeed, the main challenge to the mechanistic and corpuscular view of nature was posed by the problem of gravitation and attraction. Could such an action-at-a-distance be explained in mechanistic terms, and without having recourse to some type of occult qualities or "spirits", a recourse which would run the

---

[4] Shapin and Schaffer, *Leviathan and the Air-Pump*, pp. 212–219. In their stress on the autonomy of experimental philosophy, Boyle and Hooke were not so different from Cartesian natural philosophers on the Continent such as Chouet. Yet, as Shapin and Schaffer stress (ibid., p. 209), Boyle did not deny the reliability of "spirit testimonies", and in this respect he diverged from the Cartesians. (See also following note.)

[5] For studies which stress Boyle's mechanical and corpuscular orientation see Marie Boas, *Robert Boyle and Seventeenth-Century Chemistry* (Cambridge: Cambridge University Press, 1958), chapter V; and to some extent, though from a different historiographical and methodological perspective, also Jacob, *Robert Boyle and the English Revolution*. For a discussion emphasizing Boyle's divergences from strict Continental mechanistic philosophy see Shapin and Schaffer, *Leviathan and the Air-Pump*, and John Henry, "Occult Qualities and the Experimental Philosophy: Active Principles in Pre-Newtonian Matter Theory", *History of Science* 24 (1986): 333–381, an article to which I shall return below.

[6] Shapin and Schaffer, *Leviathan and the Air-Pump*. Shapin and Schaffer focus their attention, however, on the challenge of atheism, rather than on that of enthusiasm.

[7] The *Micrographia* of Robert Hooke was also an implicit response to the challenge of enthusiasm in its stress on the mediate knowledge of nature through experiments which ought to be constantly reviewed by the public. I am indebted for this point to a paper by Michael Dennis, "Graphic Understanding: Instruments and Interpretation in Robert Hooke's *Micrographia*". Hooke similarly criticized the "hylarchic spirit" of Henry More, and like his mentor Boyle, stressed the autonomy of experimental work. See Shapin and Schaffer, *Leviathan and the Air-Pump*, p. 223, and Robert W.T. Gunther, *Early Science in Oxford*, vol. 8: *The Cutler Lectures of Robert Hooke* (Oxford: Dawson of Pall Mall, 1931), pp. 187–88.

risk of once again introducing enthusiasm into natural philosophy? Recent scholarship has pointed out that "hidden" or "occult" qualities were by no means expelled from English experimental philosophy; neither were "spirits", if their existence could be deduced from phenomena and proven experimentally.[8] Indeed, experimental proof, as I have remarked above, was the guarantee which English natural philosophers relied upon to counter the danger of enthusiasm. With respect to the problem of attraction and gravitation, the recurring response of English mechanical philosophers was the use of the concept of *aether*. This was the course already taken by Hooke, who tried to explain gravity and attraction on the basis of vibration in the aether which was the medium among the stars. How mechanistic his solution was is a matter of debate among historians.[9] At all events, even Hooke could not avoid some reference to the spirit of God as the ultimate cause of motion in general and gravitation in particular.[10]

The central figure in this connection is of course Newton himself. Whereas his major scientific achievement was the mathematical formulation of the law of universal gravitation, he continued to search throughout his life for some explanation of the cause of gravity. There is some disagreement among scholars as to how seriously to take his various speculations on this subject.[11] These "hypotheses" are nevertheless highly important for the ensuing scientific discussion of this

---

[8] John Henry, "Occult Qualities and the Experimental Philosophy", esp. pp. 361–363, and Keith Hutchinson, "What Happened to Occult Qualities in the Scientific Revolution?" *Isis* 73 (1982): 233–253, who deals with the broader changes in the meaning of the term "occult" in seventeenth century natural philosophy.

[9] On Hooke's account of gravitation and attraction see F.F. Centore, *Robert Hooke's Contribution to Mechanics: A Study in Seventeenth Century Natural Philosophy* (The Hague: Martinus Nijhoff, 1970), pp. 97–105; R.S. Westfall, *Force in Newton's Physics* (London: Macdonald; New York: American Elsevier, 1971), pp. 269–271; and finally, John Henry, "Occult Qualities and the Experimental Philosophy", pp. 346–348, who stresses the points where Hooke preceded Newton in introducing the notion of "active principles" in nature.

[10] See especially *A Discourse of the Nature of Comets* in Robert Hooke, *Posthumous Works* (London, 1705), pp. 174–175.

[11] A. Rupert Hall and Marie Boas Hall, for example, tend to play down the importance of Newton's evolving "speculations" on this matter. See their article "Newton's Theory of Matter", *Isis* 51 (1960): 131–144, esp. pp. 136, 142. They rely among other things on a sentence in Newton's famous 1678/9 letter to Boyle (to which I shall presently return) where he says: "For my own part I have so little fansy to things of this nature that had not your encouragement moved me to it, I should never I think have thus far set pen to paper about them." H.W. Turnbull, ed., *The Correspondence of Isaac Newton*, vol. II (Cambridge: Cambridge University Press,

topic in the eighteenth century, and particularly relevant to the question of the relationship between mechanism and enthusiasm.

In his earlier years, Newton tended to subscribe to what may seem a "mechanistic" view of nature. Since his student notebooks in the 1660's he had tended to assign the cause of gravitation to the mechanical operation of subtle particles of matter, or aether. The tensions within that view became increasingly clear in the course of the 1670's, however, as Newton tried to fuse this mechanical account with his speculations on the role of an active spirit in vital and alchemical processes.[12] The two famous texts in which he put forward the aether hypothesis in the 1670's were "An Hypothesis explaining the Properties of Light" which was sent to Oldenburg on December 7, 1675, and his letter to Boyle of February 28, 1678/9.[13] It is important to note, however, that neither text reached a wider public till the middle of the eighteenth century, when Birch published *The Life and Works of the Honourable Robert Boyle* in 1744, and later his *History of the Royal Society*, in 1756–57.[14] In the "Hypothesis explaining the Properties of Light" Newton developed a theory of aether which, on the face of it, was not very different from that of Hooke. On the basis of that aether he explained not only attraction and

---

1960), p. 295. Westfall, on the other hand, does not take such deprecations seriously, in view of the fact that Newton then and there went on to compose some four thousand words on these "fancies". R.S. Westfall, *Never at Rest: A Biography of Isaac Newton*, (Cambridge: Cambridge University Press, 1980), p. 372. Most recently, the late Professor Dobbs has forcefully argued for the seriousness of Newton's lifelong search for a causal account of gravitation, B.J.T. Dobbs, *The Janus Faces of Genius: The Role of Alchemy in Newton's Thought* (Cambridge: Cambridge University Press, 1991).

[12] See on this subject, Westfall, *Force in Newton's Physics*, pp. 329–331, 335–336, 363–370, idem, *Never at Rest*, and most extensively now, Dobbs, *The Janus Faces of Genius*, chap. 4. Dobbs discovered, analysed and published (ibid., Appendix A) the crucial text which attempted to combine the mechanical and alchemical account— "Of natures obvious laws and processes in vegetation" (Dibner MSS 1031 B, now at the Smithsonian library in Washington), which was apparently written around 1672.

[13] The "Hypothesis explaining the Properties of Light" is now published in H.W. Turnbull, ed., *The Correspondence of Isaac Newton*, vol. I (Cambridge: Cambridge University Press, 1959), pp. 362–388. It may also be found in I.B. Cohen, ed., *Isaac Newton's Papers and Letters on Natural Philosophy and Related Documents* (Cambridge Mass.: Harvard University Press, 1978), pp. 178–190. The letter to Boyle is in *The Correspondence of Isaac Newton*, vol. II, pp. 288–296.

[14] The "Hypothesis explaining the Properties of Light" was published by T. Birch, *The History of the Royal Society* (London, 1756–57), vol. III, pp. 247–269; the letter to Boyle was published by Birch in *The Life and Works of the Honourable Robert Boyle* (London, 1744), vol. I, pp. 73–74.

gravity, but also the reflections and refractions of light as well as the muscle motions in the body, equating the "animal spirits" with the aether.[15] "Thus—he said—perhaps may all things be originated from aether."[16] Gravity was explained specifically on the basis of the circulation of aether. While air, exhalations and vapours continually rise up to space and become aether, the spirit of aether tends to condense and descend from above with great celerity "In wch descent it may beare downe with it the bodyes it pervades with force proportionall to the superficies of all their parts it acts upon."[17] Nevertheless, as has recently been shown, the "Hypothesis" is suffused with alchemical and theological assumptions, which render it far from "mechanical" in the strict sense of the word.[18]

Some three years later, at the end of his famous letter to Boyle, Newton returned to aether as the cause of gravity. Now his hypothesis was somewhat different. In the center of the earth only finer aether can enter its pores, whereas in open spaces the aether is grosser. The further one is from the center of earth, the grosser the aether becomes. Hence, in the upper parts of a given body, the aether is grosser, but being less apt to be lodged in these pores than the finer aether below, "it will endeavour to get out and give way to ye finer aether below, wch cannot be wthout ye bodies descending to make room above for it to go out into."[19] Here, then, gravitation is the consequence of grosser particles of aether getting out of the body, and thus pushing it downwards. This letter, then, presented a more mechanical account. Indeed, on the face of it, both these texts of the 1670's seem to present a mechanistic account of gravity. This is how they were read in the middle of the eighteenth century, and this is also how they have been viewed by historiography in the three centuries following. Yet, as recent scholarship has pointed out, these texts,

---

[15] Newton himself hinted at the similarity of his views to those of Hooke on the aether issue (in contradistinction to their disagreements concerning the nature of light). See *The Correspondence of Isaac Newton*, vol. I, p. 363. I shall return to this analogy or even identification of aether with the "animal spirits" since it has direct bearing on the issue of enthusiasm.

[16] Ibid., p. 364.

[17] Ibid., p. 366. As the editors note, this last sentence served Newton to argue ten years later (in a letter to Halley) that he had then already turned his thoughts to universal gravitation. See also on this subject Dobbs, *The Janus Faces of Genius*, pp. 105–106. Dobbs tends to accept Newton's argument that the "Hypothesis" already contained a suggested cause for universal gravitation.

[18] See Dobbs, *The Janus Faces of Genius*, pp. 102–117.

[19] *The Correspondence of Isaac Newton*, vol. II, p. 295.

especially the "Hypothesis", cannot be understood without due attention to the alchemical terms with which they are imbued, and without the theological (indeed, Arian) context of the views they present. Even at this stage, Newton was not an outright mechanical philosopher.[20]

In fact, soon after his letter to Boyle, Newton seems to have undergone a profound conversion. Under the combined influence of alchemy and the problem of orbital mechanics, he abandoned the subtle aether as the cause of attraction and repulsion, and adopted the notion of action at a distance. In the early 1680's, he began to view force acting between particles as the ultimate agent of nature, rather than moving particles themselves. Newton thus moved from a kinetic mechanical philosophy to a dynamic one.[21] This new view was of course crystallized in the *Principia* and the various drafts written around it. During the middle period of his career, from the early 1680's till at least 1713, Newton did not refer to aether, and explained gravitation as the direct result of God's will.[22]

This point is highly significant for our purpose. Newton re-introduced direct divine intervention into the core of physics, closely linked with his new conception of force. He regarded this account of force as somewhat speculative, hinting at it in his published writing but elaborating it more explicitly only in his private papers. Nevertheless, one cannot ignore such an account's being part of his natural philosophy, and as is well known, this description of force as the direct manifestation of God's will was highly influential among contemporary theologians.[23]

---

[20] This is true especially with regard to terms such as "sociability" by which Newton attempts to explain some of the functions of the aether in his "Hypothesis of Light" and in the letter to Boyle. See on this subject, B.J.T. Dobbs, *The Foundations of Newton's Alchemy: or "The Hunting of the Greene Lyon"* (Cambridge: Cambridge University Press, 1975, paperback ed., 1983), pp. 204–213, idem., *The Janus Faces of Genius*, pp. 96–121, and Westfall, *Force in Newton's Physics*, pp. 367–369, as well as his biography of Newton, *Never at Rest*, pp. 307–309, 371–377.

[21] Westfall, *Never at Rest*, p. 390. Dobbs dates this "conversion" to 1684, *The Janus Faces of Genius*, pp. 130–146.

[22] See Dobbs, *The Janus Faces of Genius*, chapter 6.

[23] Westfall, *Force in Newton's Physics*, pp. 395–400. The hints in the published work may be found in the General Scholium in the 1713 edition of the *Principia* which stresses the dominion of God over nature, largely in response to Leibniz; and in the queries of the *Opticks*, first added to the 1706 Latin edition of the *Optice*, and later published as queries 28 and 31 in the 1717/18 edition of the *Opticks*. See E. Cajori, ed., *Sir Isaac Newton's Mathematical Principles*, vol. II (Berkeley and Los Angeles: University of California Press, 1966), pp. 543–547; and Isaac Newton, *Opticks; or a Treatise*

Recent scholarship has shown that Newton never gave up this dynamic concept of force once he adopted it around 1680, and that in the period between 1687 and 1713, he indeed saw divine will as the direct cause of gravitation.[24] Nevertheless, he also continually searched for mediating causes which could explain forces such as gravity. Indeed, from 1706 onwards, active principles were increasingly seen as the immediate causes of various forces.[25] The concept of "aether" re-appeared a few years later, first in the General Scholium of the 1713 edition of the *Principia*, then in the 1717/18 edition of the *Opticks*, yet now it was no longer a mechanistic principle. In fact, in the General Scholium Newton used aether to explain only electrical phenomena, not gravity, clearly distinguishing the one from the other, especially in the original versions of the text. Although in the 1717/18 edition of the *Opticks* he implied that such a subtle elastic aether could explain gravity as well, the extreme rarity of the aether, whose particles repelled each other in inverse proportion to their size, embodied the principle of action at a distance rather than providing a mechanistic account to supplant it. Such an aether was clearly a dynamic medium, not by any means a mechanical fluid.[26]

We must return, however, to the notion of force as a manifestation of divine power, the conception which Newton entertained especially in the period 1687–1713, and which even in his later period did not disappear completely. That view owed much to the influence on Newton of Henry More, Ralph Cudworth and Renaissance Naturalism in general, and indeed, to Platonic and Stoical sources.[27] In

---

of the Reflections, Refractions, Inflections and Colours of Light (New York: Dover, 1952; based on the 4th edition, London, 1730), pp. 362–370, 375–406, especially pp. 401–404. On the Newtonian natural theologians who relied on this view see below.

[24] See especially now, Dobbs, *The Janus Faces of Genius*, chapter 6.

[25] See J.E. McGuire, "Force, Active Principles, and Newton's Invisible Realm" *Ambix* 15 (1968): 154–208, esp. pp. 164–174; Westfall, *Force in Newton's Physics*, pp. 391–395.

[26] J.E. McGuire, "Force, Active Principles, and Newton's Invisible Realm", pp. 194–197, 206–207. See also P.M. Heimann and J.E. McGuire, "Newtonian Forces and Lockean Powers: Concepts of Matter in Eighteenth-Century Thought", *Historical Studies in the Physical Sciences* 3 (1971): 237–246; P.M. Heimann, "'Nature is a perpetual Worker': Newton's Aether and Eighteenth-Century Natural Philosophy", *Ambix* 20 (1973): 1–8. See also Ernan McMullin, *Newton on Matter and Activity* (Notre Dame, Indiana: University of Notre Dame Press, 1978), especially pp. 96–101, and Dobbs, *The Janus Faces of Genius*, chapter 7.

[27] See Westfall, *Force in Newton's Physics*, pp. 395–399. See also J.E. McGuire, "Force, Active Principles and Newton's Invisible Realm", pp. 184–185, 204–207; and his "Neoplatonism and Active Principles: Newton and the *Corpus Hermeticum*" in *Hermeti-*

fact, the foremost of Newton scholars has argued that Newton gave up a mechanical explanation of gravity for the possible quantification of it, even if that involved a certain 'flirtation' with mystical and Pythagorean conceptions.[28]

Did this mean, however, a 'flirtation' with enthusiasm as well? Quite the contrary. Like More, Newton maintained a distance from enthusiasm. On the basis of both his public writings and those private papers which historians have examined so far, it is quite clear that Newton's attitude towards enthusiasm was a cool one, although Margaret Jacob has argued that he manifested some interest regarding the French Prophets, for example.[29] While Newton clearly paid much attention to millenarian speculations, his interest (at least his recorded one) seems to have been mostly based on Scripture, not on visions or contemporary claims to divine inspiration. In discussing the principles of scriptural interpretation in a Ms. *Treatise on Revelation* for instance, he warned that "Too much liberty in this kind savours of a luxuriant ungovernable fansy and borders on enthusiasm."[30] Yet, like More and other English natural philosophers, the mature Newton responded to the challenge of enthusiasm not by adhering to strict mechanism, but rather by incorporating non-mechanical factors in his natural philosophy. Claims to direct divine inspiration could be countered not by a mechanistic view which removed God from nature almost entirely (this to Newton and his followers would amount

---

cism and the Scientific Revolution (Los Angeles: William Andrews Clark Memorial Library, 1977), pp. 95–142. In the latter article McGuire argues that a clear distinction has to be made between the Neoplatonic tradition to which Newton was exposed in Cambridge and which deeply influenced him, and the Hermetic tradition which at most served him only as a legitimizing ideology in the early 1690's. This difference may be accounted for on the basis of Newton's commitment to a transcendental conception of God. Loyal as he was to that conception, he replaced the hermetic notion of *anima mundi* with that of the will of an omnipresent God. Recently, Professor Dobbs has also stressed the ancient, classical sources, especially Platonic and Stoic, for Newton's conception of God's direct role in nature, rather than the biblical, or even alchemical ones. *The Janus Faces of Genius*, chapter 6.

[28] Westfall, *Force in Newton's Physics*, pp. 395–400. See also J.E. McGuire and P.M. Rattansi, "Newton and the 'Pipes of Pan'", *Notes and Records of the Royal Society* 21 (1966): 108–143.

[29] See Margaret C. Jacob, "Newton and the French Prophets: New Evidence", *History of Science* 16 (1978): 134–142. For a view which stresses Newton's reserve concerning predictions and visions, see Frank E. Manuel, *Isaac Newton Historian* (Cambridge: Cambridge University Press, 1963), p. 156.

[30] Yahuda Ms. 1, 12v, National Library, Jerusalem. See also Frank E. Manuel, *The Religion of Isaac Newton* (Oxford: The Clarendon Press, 1974), Appendix A, p. 117. See also Westfall, *Never at Rest*, pp. 654–655.

to materialistic atheism), but by transferring the emphasis from the supernatural to the natural means by which God manifested Himself to man. As is well known, this view was used by Newton, as well as by contemporary theologians, to develop a natural theology which would answer the challenge of atheism.[31] It also lay at the heart of the Leibniz-Clarke Correspondence. Leibniz equated natural with mechanical and therefore saw the Newtonian force as a "perpetual miracle". Newton and Clarke, in contrast, believed that a regular activity, subject to clearly formulated laws, could be natural even if it was not mechanical and was the direct result of divine activity.[32]

Herein lies a fundamental difference between the English and the Continental conceptions of natural philosophy, a difference which influenced their respective endeavours to counter the enthusiasts' over-emphasis on the supernatural dimension. Although Newton and Clarke were accused by Leibniz of introducing "supernatural" elements into Nature, their tendency to see all God's interventions in the world as natural, and to blur the distinctions between God's *Potentia Ordinata* and God's *Potentia Absoluta* could mean that no room was left for a supernatural dimension at all.[33] I shall return to this important point

---

[31] The pioneering study on this topic is Hélène Metzger, *Attraction universelle et religion naturelle chez quelques commentateurs anglais de Newton*, "Philosophie et histoire de la pensée scientifique", IV–VI (Paris: Hermann, 1938). For the use of the above argument in the Boyle lectures, see especially Jacob, *The Newtonians and the English Revolution*, chapters 4–7. The lectures most relevant to this theme were those of Bentley in 1692 and Clarke in 1705. See also William Whiston, *Astronomical Principles of Religion, Natural and Reveal'd* (London, 1717). For Newton's own use of this argument to counter the claims of atheism see Query 28 of the *Optice*, and the Ms. draft *Quaestio* 23 quoted by Westfall, *Force in Newton's Physics*, note 181 on pp. 419–420. See also the earlier article by McGuire, "Force, Active Principles and Newton's Invisible Realm", 187–194.

[32] The Leibniz-Clarke Correspondence was published in Leroy E. Loemker, ed., *Gottfried Wilhelm Leibniz: Philosophical Papers and Letters* (Chicago: Chicago University Press, 1956), vol. II, pp. 1081–1210. Another edition was published separately by H.G. Alexander, *The Leibniz-Clarke Correspondence* (New York: Manchester University Press, 1956), see especially, pp. 12, 20. The literature on that controversy is of course enormous, but on the particular point stressed here see J.E. McGuire, "Force, Active Principles, and Newton's Invisible Realm", pp. 181–182, 197. As McGuire suggests, Newton's stress in Query 31 of the 1717/18 edition of the *Opticks* that active principles were part of the natural order, might have been an oblique response to Leibniz. See now also Dobbs, *The Janus Faces of Genius*, pp. 218–230.

[33] Clarke expressed himself in a highly significant manner on this point in the correspondence with Leibniz: "*natural* and *supernatural* are nothing at all different with regard to God, but distinctions merely in our conceptions of things." H.G. Alexander, *The Leibniz-Clarke Correspondence*, p. 24. See also McGuire, "Force, Active Principles, and Newton's Invisible Realm", pp. 202–204, and Dobbs, *The Janus Faces of Genius*, pp. 230–243.

below. In England, in any case, the explanation of gravity as the manifestation of the direct intervention of God in nature fulfilled several functions. It was not only a solution to a problem in natural philosophy, a solution which opened the way for mathematical dynamics. It was also a decisive argument against atheists and enthusiasts alike.

The Scientist as Enthusiast: Nicolas Fatio de Duillier

It is against this background that one may see the various attempts to provide a mechanistic account of gravitation in the eighteenth century. For our purpose, the crucial and fascinating point is that such attempts were sometimes linked with a favourable, or at least indulgent, attitude towards enthusiasm. Whereas in the seventeenth century mechanistic natural philosophy was seen as an effective antidote to enthusiasm, in the eighteenth it could be coupled with an active interest in prophecy and "enthusiastic" movements.

This is most clearly manifest in the career and intellectual development of one of Newton's closest and most brilliant disciples, the Genevan Nicolas Fatio de Duillier (1664–1753).[34] Nicolas Fatio was born in Basel to a noble family of Italian origin. His father bought the Duillier estate near Geneva and moved there when Nicolas was a boy. In 1678 Fatio became a student at the Genevan Academy of Jean-Robert Chouet, from whom he received a Cartesian conception of physics as well as a Cartesian view of the relationship between philosophy and theology.[35] Contrary to the wishes of his father who wanted him to be a minister, Nicolas did not continue to study theology but rather devoted himself to scientific pursuits. With the help of Chouet, he established contact with the Abbé Nicaise and with Jean Dominique Cassini, the foremost astronomer in Paris at that

---

[34] Fatio de Duillier has been the subject of several studies in recent years, but no one has yet attempted to write a systematic biography of him. Three studies which contain important biographical information are: Charles A. Domson, *Nicolas Fatio de Duillier and the Prophets of London* (New York: Arno Press, 1981); Hillel Schwartz, *The French Prophets: The History of A Millenarian Group in Eighteenth-Century England* (Berkeley, Los Angeles, London: University of California Press, 1980); Horst Zehe, *Die Gravitationstheorie des Nicolas Fatio de Duillier* (Hildesheim: Gerstenberg Verlag, 1980), chapter 1.

[35] On Chouet see my book *Between Orthodoxy and the Enlightenment*. On the relationship between theology and philosophy see especially ibid., chapter 2.

time. Coming to Paris, he participated with Cassini in observations of the Zodiacal light and of what was later to be known as Halley's Comet. As anti-Protestant pressure mounted in France, he returned to Geneva in 1683 and there continued with his astronomical observations. He came to England for the first time in 1687, and was soon captivated by the new natural philosophy of Isaac Newton, and by the *Principia*, then just published. By 1689 he had rejected Descartes and adopted the Newtonian view, as is clear from a letter he wrote to his former teacher, Chouet.[36] After a brief stay in Holland, Fatio returned to England in 1691 and a few years was one of Newton's most intimate friends.[37] Yet his Cartesian tendencies were not completely dissipated as is evidenced by his principal scientific research programme which had already crystallized in those years—the attempt to give a mechanistic account of gravitation.

Fatio rejected the Cartesian notion of a plenum and adhered to the Newtonian concept of an infinite vacant space. Yet in that space, he argued, there existed in addition to solid matter, elastic particles of aether of varying shape, size and speed. The difference between the speed with which they hit a body and the speed with which they rebound from it is what causes the body to be pushed. Were there only one body in the world, such a push would be balanced by the similar push of particles all around that body. Once there are two bodies, they "screen" the effects of the particles between them, and are thus pushed towards each other with a force which is greater the closer they are to each other, that is, in inverse proportion to the distance between them. And since all bodies are extremely porous in their structure, that subtle matter can penetrate into them and its effects are greater in direct proportion to the mass of those bodies.

---

[36] The letter is extant among the extensive Fatio papers in the Bibliothèque publique et universitaire in Geneva (henceforward BPU), Ms. Fr. vol. 602, fol. 58r (December 1, 1689).

[37] On the relationship between Newton and Fatio in the early 1690's see Frank E. Manuel, *A Portrait of Isaac Newton* (Cambridge, Mass.: Harvard University Press, 1968; London: Frederick Muller, 1980), pp. 191–212. Manuel believes that the relationship between them in those years may have been more than purely intellectual, and that Fatio may have been somehow connected with Newton's psychological collapse in 1693. See also Westfall, *Never at Rest*, pp. 493–97, 531–33, 538–39. The correspondence between Fatio and Newton has been published in *The Correspondence of Isaac Newton*, vol. III (Cambridge: Cambridge University Press, 1961). For the collaboration between Newton and Fatio in alchemical studies in those years see Dobbs, *The Janus Faces of Genius*, pp. 170–175, 181–185. The late Professor Dobbs was kind enough to send me those sections prior to the publication of her book.

Fatio thus combined a Newtonian world view with some mechanistic hypotheses congruent with the way of thinking of Continental scientists.[38] He never published his theory systematically and completely, reworking and correcting it throughout his life, but it was relatively well-known, especially in Geneva, his native town, as we shall see below.[39] Although Fatio claimed that Newton was seriously interested in his hypothesis, we have a testimony from the astronomer and mathematician David Gregory, according to whom Newton was sceptical already in 1691 concerning Fatio's theory. In his memorandum of December 12, 1691, Gregory wrote—"Mr. Newton and Mr. Halley laugh at Mr. Fatio's manner of explaining gravity".[40]

The important point for us, however, is that the mixture of a Newtonian and mechanistic outlook was ultimately connected, in the

---

[38] On Fatio's theories of gravitation, see Zehe, *Die Gravitationstheorie des Nicolas Fatio de Duillier*, chapters 2 and 8, and the references to Fatio's texts in the following note. For Fatio's conception of space and his critique of Descartes see Zehe, pp. 216–226, and Domson, *Nicolas Fatio de Duillier*, pp. 116–128. Though rejecting the Cartesian theory of plenum and vortices, Fatio followed Descartes in searching for a mechanistic account of gravitation in terms of matter and motion. As Zehe puts it: ". . . Fatios Schweretheorie ist ebenso wie die Huygensche eine Theorie im Sinne der cartesischen Prinzipien." (*Die Gravitationstheorie*, p. 53, see also p. 181). What distinguished it, however, from both the Cartesian explanation and that of Huygens was its ability to account for the Newtonian law of universal gravitation. Huygens, Leibniz and Jacob Bernoulli in fact expressed great interest in Fatio's hypotheses.

[39] The only public expression of his views was the lecture Fatio gave before the Royal Society in February 1689/90 entitled "De la cause de la pesanteur". Bernard Gagnebin has attempted to reconstruct that original text with its later additions on the basis of manuscripts found in the BPU in Geneva. See Bernard Gagnebin, *"De la cause de la pesanteur*: Mémoire de Nicolas Fatio de Duillier. Présenté à la Royal Society le 26 février 1690", in *Notes and Records of the Royal Society* 6 (1949): 105–160. There are other manuscripts of that text, however, which Gagnebin ignored. More complete and reliable is the version published earlier in this century by K. Bopp, using a copy of the 1701 text under the same title, sent by Fatio to Jacob Bernoulli in Basel (now at the Gotha Library). See K. Bopp, "Die wiederaufgefundene Abhandlung von Fatio de Duillier: *De la cause de la pesanteur*", in *Drei Untersuchungen zur Geschichte der Mathematik* (*Schriften der Strassburger Wissenschaftlichen Gesellschaft in Heidelberg*, Neue Folge, 10 heft), (Berlin, Leipzig, 1929), pp. 19–66. However, Bopp did not include later additions written by Fatio in 1706 and 1742. For the various versions of Fatio's text, and a critique of Gagnebin's edition, see Zehe, *Die Gravitationstheorie*, pp. 56–63, 286–309.

[40] H.W. Turnbull, ed., *The Correspondence of Isaac Newton*, vol. III, p. 191. Indeed, it is clear that Newton did not wish that Fatio's comments on gravitation should be included in the next edition of the *Principia*. See Zehe, *Die Gravitationstheorie*, p. 181. For Fatio's claim that Newton took him seriously see Gagnebin, "De la cause de la pesanteur", p. 117 and Dobbs, *The Janus Faces of Genius*, pp. 188–189. Dobbs argues that for Newton, "Fatio's hypothesis probably foundered on the problem of the lack of retardation of celestial bodies moving in the subtle fluid". Ibid., p. 189.

case of Fatio, with manifest enthusiasm, and with a deep involvement with the French Prophets who came to London in 1706, and
to whom I have already referred in previous chapters. Fatio was
caught up in this group and soon became their spokesman.[41] With
him, enthusiasm seems to have penetrated once again into the realm
of science and scientific activity. Fatio's involvement with the Prophets, we now know, did not mean the cessation of his scientific work.
Socially, he indeed retreated from the scientific community, apparently long before the French Prophets appeared in England.[42] His
active sympathy with these "fanatics" undoubtedly sealed his fate and
caused him social and scholarly ruin from which he would never
recover.[43] Yet he did not give up his scientific activities and his work
on a mechanistic account of gravitation. The numerous versions and
additions to "De la cause de la pesanteur", his 1729 poem "De Causa
Gravitatis" written in the style of Lucretius, as well as his correspondence after 1707, all testify to his continuing scientific interests, indeed, even to some surviving links with Newton.[44] True, he retreated
from the public arena, and between 1713 and Newton's death in
1727 he did not publish any scientific papers. However, his involvement with the French Prophets, and his interest in Cabbalah and
mystical theology did not preclude his scientific interests and his
persevering wish to provide a mechanistic explanation of Newton's
law of universal gravitation. The relationship between the two orien-

---

[41] On this group, and Fatio's role in their movement see Hillel Schwarz, *The French Prophets*, esp. chapters III, IV, VII. See also Chapters 6, 7 and 8 above.

[42] In December 1707, after he was placed in a pillory as a punishment for his involvement with the subversive activities of the Camisard prophets, Nicolas Fatio wrote to his brother, Jean-Christophe, à-propos the meetings of the Royal Society: "Il y a très longtemps que je n'ai été dans leurs Assemblées: et je ne crois pas qu'il faille que je me presse d'y retourner." BPU, Ms. Fr. 602, fol. 24r.

[43] Zehe, *Die Gravitationstheorie*, pp. 43–50.

[44] For the different versions of "De la cause de la pesanteur" see note 39 above. See also Domson, *Nicolas Fatio de Duillier*, chapter IV. On his hexameter composition in imitation of Lucretius see below. Fatio's correspondence often refers to scientific matters, but see especially his letter to his nephew François Calandrini of August 27, 1745. There, as an old man, Fatio summarized his life, referring principally to his work on the cause of weight. BPU, Ms. Fr. 602, fols. 182r–183v. This letter is also published in Domson, *Nicolas Fatio de Duillier*, Appendix C, pp. 157–162. François Calandrini (1677–1750) was the son of Fatio's sister, Sybille-Catherine. He was first syndic in Geneva a couple of times during the 1740's. The possibility of some continuation in Fatio's relationship with Newton after 1707 has been raised in a recent paper by Karin Figala and Ulrich Petzold, "Physics and Poetry: Fatio de Duiller's *Ecloga* on Newton's *Principia*", *Archives Internationales d'Histoire des Sciences* 37 (1987): 316–349.

tations thus poses an intriguing problem for the historian.

According to one recent student of Fatio, the late Charles Domson, the crucial turning point in Fatio's religious beliefs had occurred already in 1692–93, and the chief source of inspiration for his "enthusiastic" inclinations was none other than Newton himself, in his method of scriptural interpretation, in his conception of divine Providence, and in his reliance on the so-called "hermetic tradition" in general. Yet, unlike Newton, or even Henry More, Fatio did not see prophecy merely as a past, historical phenomenon. His involvement with the French Prophets indicates that he regarded direct divine inspiration as a present possibility.[45] While Newton followed Burton, Casaubon and More in equating enthusiasm with lunacy and melancholy, Fatio can be clearly designated as an enthusiast himself.[46]

Fatio thus diverged from Newton both in his scientific theories and in his religious orientation. Can these two divergencies be connected? Most scholars have not dealt explicitly with this problem, concentrating either on Fatio's scientific theories on gravitation, or on his millennial and "enthusiastic" tendencies.[47] To the extent that they deal with the relationship between Fatio's scientific theories and his religious millenarian commitments, historians rightly stress that there was no necessary contradiction between the two orientations at that period. They place Fatio within Newton's circle and explain the links between his scientific and prophetic tendencies by referring to the conceptions of Providence and millenarianism prevalent in that circle.[48] Yet, as we have just seen, Fatio differed from Newton in his

---

[45] Domson, *Nicolas Fatio de Duillier*, chapter II. Domson recognizes the difference between Newton and Fatio, seeing it as a difference in their attitude towards mysticism (ibid., pp. 64–66). Yet on the whole he tends to play down the significance of that difference.

[46] On Newton's attitude towards enthusiasm see above. On his tendency to equate enthusiasm with lunacy and melancholy see also Manuel, *The Religion of Isaac Newton*, pp. 65–66, 87.

[47] Among historians concentrating on Fatio's scientific theories see especially Zehe, *Die Gravitationstheorie*, and Gagnebin, "De la cause de la pesanteur". For studies focusing on Fatio's involvement with the French Prophets, see Hillel Schwartz, *The French Prophets*, and Charles Domson, *Nicolas Fatio de Duillier*.

[48] This is indeed the central thesis of Domson's book, see especially chapter IV. See also Schwartz, *The French Prophets*, pp. 233–242. Similarly, the article by Figala and Petzold, "Physics and Poetry" (see note 44 above), analyses Fatio's *Ecloga* of Newton in 1728 and deals with the way Fatio's enthusiasm coloured his view of Newton and the *Principia*. The article includes the Latin text and an English translation of that poem. Yet like Domson and Schwartz, Figala and Petzold stress the affinities between Fatio and Newton, rather than the differences. I am grateful to Professor Figala for giving me a full manuscript version of the paper prior to publication.

prophetic and millenarian tendencies as well. True, on the question of gravitation, Fatio diverged from Newton as early as 1689–90, while on the issue of enthusiasm, such a turning point took place later, perhaps when the "prophets" came to England in 1706, or much earlier, indeed, as early as 1693, when the close relationship between Fatio and Newton seems to have ended abruptly.[49] Fatio's mystical and millenarian interests can be clearly dated to the period before 1706, but it is not known whether he espoused the possibility of contemporary prophecy prior to the arrival of the Camisard prophets in the summer of 1706.[50]

Be this as it may, Fatio evidently became an enthusiast only years after he began working on a mechanistic account of gravitation. His original motivation for developing such an account was surely influenced by his former Cartesian background, as well as by his links with Continental natural philosophers, and probably had little to do with any religious views.[51] His mechanistic orientation, however, might

------

[49] According to Domson, 1692–93 was in fact the year when Fatio got from Newton his millenarian interests and his method for interpreting Scripture. This was also the year when they collaborated very closely in alchemical studies, as has been noted above. How then is one to explain the rupture between them following Newton's breakdown in late 1693? Did Fatio then already go one step beyond Newton and adopt an "enthusiastic" way of thought? Or did he begin to take such a course following the end of the relationship with Newton, as Westfall argues? According to Westfall, Fatio then underwent a personal crisis of his own, never to regain his place within the scientific community. See *Never at Rest*, pp. 538–539.

[50] Even before the French Prophets affair, Fatio was evidently interested in the hermetic and mystical literature, for example in Raymond Lull. See the letter of August 21, 1704 from one Ritter to Fatio de Duillier, concerning an edition of Lull (BPU, Ms. Fr. 601, fols. 264r–265r). Among the Fatio papers are six notebooks entitled "Elucidation du Testament de Raimond Lull" (Ms. Fr. 605, No. 6). By 1706 Fatio was known as a "Cabaliste" and indeed asked his brother to get him a copy of Rosenroth's *Kabbala Denudata*. See copy of a letter by Jean-Christophe to Nicolas Fatio of January 22, 1706, in Ms. Fr. 601, fol. 139, and copies of a letter by Nicolas Fatio to Jean-Christophe 19/12/1707, Ms. Fr. 602, fol. 24v, and fol. 115v. These letters make it clear that Nicolas Fatio knew the book quite well, and might have seen it in Newton's library. See J. Harrison, *The Library of Isaac Newton* (Cambridge: Cambridge University Press, 1978), no. 873. I am indebted to Professor Figala for this last reference. See also Ms. Fr. 603, fols. 37–61 for Fatio's Cabbalistic interests, and Domson, *Fatio de Duillier*, pp. 133–135.

[51] It should be mentioned, however, that there are contemporary hints of some type of deistic or sceptical leanings of the young Fatio. One of these contemporary allusions was that of Edward Calamy in his *Historical Account of my own Life*, ed. by John T. Rutt (London, 1829), where he called the young Fatio a "Spinozist". See also Domson, *Nicolas Fatio de Duillier*, pp. 43–44, and pp. 43–51 in general for Domson's view of Fatio's scepticism till 1693. Thomas Hearne characterized Fatio as "a sceptic in religion" as late as 1709, *Reliquiae Hearnianae* (Oxford, 1857), vol. I, 147–150, quoted by Domson, p. 79. As we have seen throughout this study, however, there

have affected the way he interpreted Newton's interests in divine providence and millenarian prophecies. Caught up from 1693 onwards in such interests as alchemy, Scriptural exegesis and later, the Cabbalah, Fatio may have given a new interpretation to his mechanistic theories as well. In contrast to Descartes and his Protestant followers, Fatio's mechanistic theory of gravitation after the mid 1690's was not meant to "push" God out of nature as much as possible, but on the contrary, to provide a clear medium by which to account for, and prove, the constant intervention of God in the world. In this respect Fatio was not so far from Newton's approach. Indeed, in the 1706 additions to his treatise "De la cause de la pesanteur", he also entertained the possibility that the will of God was the direct cause of gravitation, and it may not be a coincidence that this was the year in which Newton hinted at this view publicly, in the Latin edition of the *Optice*.[52] Later, however, in the Latin poem *De Causa Gravitatis*, and in the 1742 version of "De la cause de la pesanteur" Fatio adopted a more reserved attitude toward that alternative.[53] Nevertheless, Fatio thought—and here his earlier Cartesian origins may still be noticeable—that such divine intervention in nature should preferably be formulated in mechanistic terms, and he felt that his aether provided such a medium of God's general providence.[54] Indeed, Fatio regarded his mechanistic theory of gravitation as the most effective "antidote" to atheism. The treatise in verse, *De Causa Gravitatis*, that he composed in 1729 for a competition announced by the Académie des Sciences expounded his theory as an explicit response to Lucretius' *De Rerum Natura*. While Lucretius banished divine presence from the regular course of nature, Fatio—like Newton (and up

---

was a dialectic affinity between "scepticism" and "enthusiasm" in the seventeenth century.

[52] "De la cause de la pesanteur", section 44, in Gagnebin, p. 149. See also Domson, *Nicolas Fatio de Duillier*, chapter IV, pp. 104–116. The *Optice* put clear emphasis not only on God as the first cause, but on his role in the constant renewal of motion. See also note 23 above.

[53] Gagnebin, "De la cause de la pesanteur". Whereas in 1706 he wrote "Mais j'avoue que je ne me tiens point trop assuré que la pesanteur ne soit un effet immédiat de la volonté de Dieu...", in 1742 he wrote—"chacun est en liberté de croire que la pesanteur ne soit un effet immédiat de la volonté de Dieu...". On his Latin poem *De Causa Gravitatis* see below. It is significant to note, however, that in 1741 he added a line to that poem which emphasized, à propos the cause of gravity, that it was not equivalent to the will of God ("Quae non synonyma est Vox ipsi Velle Jehovae"). BPU, Ms. Fr. 603, fol. 241v.

[54] See on this point, Schwartz, *The French Prophets*, pp. 235–236.

to a point, one may say, Descartes too)—wanted to show that without God's constant intervention, everything would fall into nothingness.[55] As he wrote two years later to a friend à propos that poem: "... my Theory proves the Intervention of an Almighty Power governing in the whole extent of Infinite Space."[56] Yet Fatio provided the proof by resorting systematically to a mechanistic medium—the aether, by which God operates in nature, particularly with respect to gravitation. The recourse to direct divine intervention seemed to him too simplistic an answer, which did not even satisfactorily explain natural phenomena such as the decrease and increase of motion in the world.[57] Fatio claimed that his aether supplied a mechanistic explanation not just for gravitation, or for the means by which lost motion was supplemented, but also for fermentation and other phenomena which Newton ascribed to "active principles".[58] Such a

---

[55] The text submitted to the Académie has not been found so far, nor did Fatio ever receive a response, but copies of this treatise are in the BPU, Ms. Fr. 603, fols. 114–127, 231–275, 276–307. See also Domson, *Nicolas Fatio de Duillier*, p. 123, note 42, and Figala and Petzold, "Physics and Poetry", note 80. This philosophical poem still awaits systematic study, and in what follows, I can only touch in a tentative manner on a few points relevant to our present concerns.

[56] Letter to John Conduitt, August 26, 1730, Keynes Ms. 96 in Kings College, Cambridge. A copy of the letter is in Cambridge University Library, Add. 3996, fol. 717–720. It has been published by Domson, *Nicolas Fatio de Duillier*, Appendix B, pp. 152–156, the quotation is on p. 154. Fatio made a similar comment at the dedicatory opening of a 1731 ms. version of his poem *De Causa Gravitatis* where he said that gravitation was a proof of the "divine wisdom and omnipotent activity, ceasing neither in time nor place". ("... imo Divinam illud in Orbe regendo Sapientiam, et omnipotentem Operationem, nullo Tempore nulloque Loco cessantem locupletissime demonstrat.") BPU, Ms. Fr. 603, fol. 235r. I am indebted to Professor Figala for calling my attention to this citation. See also Fatio's letter to François Calandrini of August 27, 1745, referred to in note 44; see also Domson, *Nicolas Fatio de Duillier*, pp. 122–125, for a discussion of some of these issues.

[57] Were God's will the direct cause of motion, Fatio argued, the amount of motion would have been constant, rather than decreasing and increasing. BPU, Ms. Fr. 603, fol. 241. See also fol. 270 for another copy.

[58] "Ex gravitate ergo incassum, <u>Newtone</u>, petatur\ Ipsa mera—imperitans si sit Divina Voluntas,\ Subsidium amisso pro Motu restituendo:\ Quam Vim rite tamen tribuis *CAUSAE Gravitatis*.\ Hanc igitur Causam statuis quoque Mechanicam esse;\ Et caecos Motus propria Vi posse creare.\ ... Unica quod queat illa Theoria verior esse;\ Si modo mechanica est Gravitatis Causa creandae:\ Hic, Veri clara perfusus Luce, fateris\ Servari Rerum Motus, et in Orbe novari,\ Ab CAUSA per quam Gravitas generatur et ipsa;\ Vel CAUSA unde potest quoque Fermentatio nasci;\ Activis uti Principiis tibi nomine dictis;\ (Cui generi adscribi videantur Luxque Calorque.)\ Hanc, merito, Motus amissos restituendi\ Vim sibimet descripta Theoria vindicat ultra." BPU, Ms. Fr. 603, fol. 241v. See also fols. 270–271. Fatio indeed referred explicitly to Newton's 31st query in the 1721 edition of the *Opticks*, see fols. 241r, 269.

mechanistic account, however, did not mean that God was not both the first and ultimate cause of nature. Indeed, Fatio went so far as to exclaim that Nature was nothing but God, Mind. Yet, in a manner typical to Continental thinkers, he argued that God was the metaphysical source of gravity, but that the philosopher should search for the inferior and intermediate causes of natural phenomena.[59]

The older Fatio thus combined in a curious way a Platonic philosophy with a mechanistic conception of nature. This use of mechanistic philosophy as a means to express and reinforce God's involvement in nature rather than to "push" Him away from nature, meant a certain blurring of distinctions between the natural and the supernatural. As I noted above, such blurring of distinctions was potentially already present in Newton's thought. Whereas many of his disciples might interpret this tendency in a deistic direction, others, like Fatio, would give an "enthusiastic" interpretation to that same tendency, positing a certain infusion of the divine into the material and mechanical operations of nature.

Do we have here some clue to Fatio's attitude towards contemporary prophecy and enthusiasm, the second issue on which he diverged from Newton? Fatio clearly did not see his mechanistic approach as in any way contradicting his acquired faith in the divine inspiration of contemporary prophets, and he apparently upheld both these attitudes from 1706 till the end of his life. Yet, there might even have been a positive link between the two orientations. As we saw in Chapter 7 above, one of Fatio's opponents in the affair of the French Prophets ascribed to him a materialistic explanation of prophecy itself. "They say, that in his System he explains Prophecy by the Exaltation of Matter to a certain Degree, in which it has the virtue of even foretelling things to come."[60] The critics of enthusiasm, as we know, themselves tended to give a naturalist account of claims to alleged divine inspiration, ascribing them to clinical disturbances such as melancholy, the influence of animal spirits or to some subtle

---

[59] "Hic etenim Natura nihil; sed cuncta DEUS, MENS.\ Prima et si Deus est, Idemque est Ultima Causa;\ Quaerere Philosophum Causas decet Inferiores,\ Perque Gradus medios Coelestem ascendere Scalam;\ Sed Regis meminisse sedentis Vertice summo.\ Qui, licet et proprio Mundum pro Velle gubernet,\ Possit et Ipse tamen Motuque et Legibus uti:\ Quem videor Casum satis hactenus esse secutus.\ Ipsi, quomodo vult, remanent sua Jura, regendi." BPU, Ms. Fr. 603, fols. 271–272.

[60] N.N., *An Account of the Lives and Behaviour of the Three French Prophets* (London, 1708), p. 34. Quoted also in Schwartz, *The French Prophets*, p. 236, note 45.

effluvium.[61] Yet Fatio seems to call on his mechanistic account in order to strengthen, rather than to refute such claims. In this respect, he shared the hermetic attitudes of early seventeenth-century science which did not clearly distinguish between the natural and the supernatural, yet he combined such a conception with Continental and Cartesian tendencies to give a mechanistic explanation for natural phenomena.[62]

Conversely, during the period of his involvement with the French Prophets, Fatio presented his theory of aethereal fluid itself as the result of divine inspiration.[63] This seems to have been his conviction ever since.[64] Towards the end of his life he wrote to his nephew, François Calandrini:

---

[61] See Chapter 7 above.

[62] On the relationship between "hermetic" and alchemical attitudes and the French Prophets see Schwartz, *The French Prophets*, pp. 233–251. It may be worth directing attention at this point to Fatio's links with another former Newtonian of millenarian and mystical tendencies—the physician George Cheyne. According to one of Cheyne's recent historians, the relationship between Fatio and Cheyne started indeed around 1706, when the French Prophets reached England. See G.S. Rousseau, "Mysticism and Millenarianism: 'Immortal Dr. Cheyne'", in R.H. Popkin, ed., *Millenarianism and Messianism in English Literature and Thought 1650–1800*, Clark Library Lectures 1981–1982 (Leiden: Brill, 1988), pp. 81–126. Almost thirty years later, Cheyne put his signature on Fatio's manuscript "De la cause de la pesanteur". BPU, "Dossiers ouverts d'autographes: Newton", fol. 11. The signature reads "seen at Bath May 20 1735". This fragment was clearly part of the original manuscript "De la cause de la pesanteur". See on this point Zehe, *Die Gravitationstheorie des Nicolas Fatio de Duillier*, pp. 59, 290–293, Gagnebin, p. 123; and *The Correspondence of Isaac Newton*, vol. III, p. 69, Note 1. I am grateful to Professor Karin Figala for directing my attention to this significant document. Cheyne's signature should by no means be taken as an approval of Fatio's theories, however, since the same document bears also the earlier signatures of Newton, Halley and Huygens. Nevertheless, Cheyne himself was very much preoccupied by the problem of gravitation throughout his life, and perhaps like Fatio, he tended to give a Platonic, spiritualist, almost "enthusiastic" interpretation to Newtonian natural philosophy. See on that issue Rousseau, "Mysticism and Millenarianism", p. 117. On Cheyne's evolving theories concerning gravitation see G. Bowles, "Physical, Human and Divine Attraction in the Life and Thought of George Cheyne", *Annals of Science* 31 (1974): 473–488.

[63] See the testimony of Chevalier Ramsey in April 1730, in Joseph Spence, *Observations, Anecdotes and Characters of Books and Men*, vol. 1 (Oxford: At the Clarendon Press, 1966), p. 469, No. 1260. See also p. 283 for a similar testimony by Dr. Lockier, Dean of Peterborough. See also Domson, *Nicolas Fatio de Duillier*, p. 101.

[64] It should be observed, however, that Fatio also ascribed such inspiration to Newton. Indeed, in his 'Ecloga' on the *Principia* Fatio presented Newton as mediator between Creator and Creation, replacing Christ in this function, his birth coinciding with that of Christ and with the Creation itself. As Professor Figala points out, "one may well see in the parallels between the birth of Christ and the birth of Newton a final manifestation of Fatio's earlier millenaristic enthusiasm". Figala and Petzold, "Physics and Poetry", note 54. At the same time, it may not be a coincidence that

It seems to me that Providence has had particular reasons to wish that it would be I who would be the first to perceive them [the mechanical causes of gravity]. While it [Providence] works in the Spiritual [realm] to make a New World, it expresses most of the foundations [of this world] in the astronomical systems of the learned; and we discover [both] a new Earth, much more glorious, and a new Heaven, of which we are given the exact measures.[65]

For Fatio de Duillier, his mechanistic explanation of gravity was itself a divine announcement of "a new earth" and "a new heaven", paralleling and complementing the prophecies of the enthusiasts. For that reason too, a mechanistic view of nature was the other side of an "enthusiastic" religious consciousness.

George-Louis Le Sage

The ideas of Fatio de Duillier, both his mechanistic account of gravitation and his curious combination of mechanism and enthusiasm, were to have an interesting impact in his town of origin, Geneva. In spite of the strong Newtonian influence on Genevan scientists in the second quarter of the eighteenth century, the mechanistic tradition in Geneva could not be easily uprooted, and Fatio de Duillier's specific attempt to give a mechanistic interpretation of gravitation clearly had some influence among his compatriots. In 1731, a straightforward mechanistic account of gravitation was offered by Jean Jallabert, in theses which he sustained under the presidency of Gabriel Cramer.[66] Although Cramer and Jallabert did not mention the earlier attempt

---

Fatio saw Newton's discoveries as prophesied since the beginning of the world, while viewing his own theories as the result of contemporary particular providence, that is, the consequence of enthusiasm or immediate inspiration. In this respect he seems to have diverged not only from Halley, as Figala points out, but from other Newtonian natural theologians.

[65] "... [I]l me semble que la Providence a eu des Raisons particulières, pour vouloir que ce fût moi qui les apperçusie le premier. Pendant qu'elle travaille dans le Spirituel à faire un Monde Nouveau; elle rendesse dans le système Astronomique des Savans, la plupart de ses Fondemens; et nous découvre une Terre nouvelle et beaucoup plus glorieuse; et un Ciel nouveau, duquel elle nous donne en Toises et en Pies une très exacte mésure." BPU, Ms. Fr. 602, fols. 183r–183v. See also in Domson, *Nicolas Fatio de Duillier*, p. 161, and Schwartz, *The French Prophets*, p. 236.

[66] Gabriel Cramer had been a professor of mathematics in the Genevan Academy since 1724; he was later to become a professor of natural philosophy. See the article on him in *D.S.B.*, vol. III, pp. 459–469. Jean Jallabert was the son of Etienne Jallabert, the first professor of mathematics in Geneva. On Gabriel Cramer and Jean Jallabert see also Charles Borgeaud, *Histoire de l'Université de Genève*, vol. I: *L'Académie*

by a Genevan to give such an account, that of Fatio de Duillier, it
is quite clear that they were directly influenced by him. In fact, among
Nicolas Fatio de Duillier's papers I have found a note in which he
himself described how his ideas reached Cramer: one of the manuscript versions of "La cause de la pesanteur" was copied by Nicolas'
brother, Jean-Christophe, around 1700, and upon the latter's death
in 1720 was transferred to his son, Nicolas' nephew:

> Par où elle a été communiqué à Mr. *Cramer* Professeur en Philosophie
> à Genève, qui a réduit ma Théorie en des Thèses publiques; la publiant
> sans mon Nom, sans l'entendre à fond.[67]

Whether they understood Fatio's theory correctly or not, Cramer
and Jallabert evidently adopted it in 1731.[68] Like Newton, they rejected the idea of gravity as an essential and inherent quality of bodies
(for then, would a single body in the universe also possess that quality?), as well as the Newtonian explanation of gravity as caused immediately by God. One needed to refer to secondary causes, not just
to God as a universal primary cause, otherwise, universal gravitation
would turn out to be a perpetual miracle, a view which could not be
admitted in physics (this was also Leibniz's argument against Newton, as I recalled above). Cramer and Jallabert added that the
Newtonian account of gravitation was fraught with the same difficul-
ties as the system of the Occasionalists, a significant comparison between Newton and Malebranche![69]

---

de Calvin 1559–1798 (Geneva: Georg et Co., 1900), pp. 502–504, 564–572. The
theses he defended under Cramer were published in 1731 under the title *Theses
Physico-Mathematice de Gravitate* (Geneva, 1731). Jallabert was later to become professor of experimental philosophy (1739–1750), of mathematics (1750–1752) and of
philosophy (1752–1757). He became especially known in the scientific community
owing to his experiments in electricity. Indeed, his account of electricity was also
mechanistic, presupposing a rarefied and vast elastic fluid, filling all the universe as
well as the pores of physical bodies in which electricity was propagated like waves.
See Isaac Benguigui, *Théories électriques du XVIIIe siècle: Correspondance entre l'Abbé Nollet
(1700–1770) et le physicien genevois Jean Jallabert (1712–1768)* (Geneva: Georg, 1984),
pp. 20–23 for biographical information on Jallabert, and pp. 82–84 for an outline
of his theory of electricity. I am grateful to Simon Schaffer for directing my attention to this book.

[67] BPU, Ms. Fr. 603, fol. 64r.

[68] The similarity of their views is also attested by the French natural philosopher
Dortous de Mairan who, upon receiving Cramer's and Jallabert's *Thèses sur la pesanteur*
was struck by their similarity to Fatio's philosophical poem, submitted anonymously
for the 1728 prize of the Académie des Sciences. Indeed he concluded that the
poem had probably been written by Cramer himself. See copy of a letter from de
Mairan to Cramer, June 15, 1733, BPU, MS. Fr. 2065, fol. 103v.

[69] The same comparison was to be made by David Hume a few years later in his

The 1731 theses did not develop in detail the type of mechanistic account of gravitation they called for, beyond positing a "very rare fluid" as the medium which "pushed" bodies towards each other. In spite of some favourable reactions from French natural philosophers like de Mairan, Cramer seems to have later withdrawn from the attempt to provide such a mechanical account of gravitation.[70] Seventeen years after the Jallabert theses of 1731, when another student presented him with a mechanistic explanation of gravitation, Cramer reacted quite negatively, dismissing his own earlier speculations along these lines as "une Débauche passagère d'imagination."[71] This time, however, Cramer did mention to the student in question, that a similar attempt to explain gravitation mechanically had been made earlier by another Genevan, Fatio de Duillier.

The name of that student was George-Louis Le Sage, born in 1724. His father was a Huguenot refugee by the same name who spent many years in England, was himself interested in philosophy, and towards the end of his life was involved in the radical movement in Geneva.[72] Le Sage Junior (1724–1803) finished his studies in philosophy at the Academy of Geneva, and went first to Basel and afterwards to Paris for a few years to study medicine, at his father's

---

Enquiry into Human Understanding. See Heimann, "Voluntarism and Immanence: Conceptions of Nature in Eighteenth-Century Thought" *Journal of the History of Ideas* 39 (1978): 271–283, reference to Hume on pp. 277–279.

[70] For de Mairan's reactions see the copies of his letters to Cramer from June 15, 1733, and August 31, 1738, BPU, Ms. Fr. 2065 fols. 103r–104v. These letters were copied by George-Louis Le Sage to whom I shall presently return. On Dortous de Mairan and his loyalty to Cartesian and mechanistic principles, in spite of his readiness to accept many of Newton's experimental and mathematical discoveries, see Pierre Brunet, *L'introduction des théories de Newton en France au XVIIIe siècle* (Paris, 1931; reprint edition, Geneva: Slatkine Reprints, 1970), pp. 118–121. Towards the end of his life, however, Cramer seems to have returned to a mechanistic explanation of aether; see the extract of the Physics course he gave in 1751 "Sur la nature de la Pesanteur", BPU, Ms. Le Sage 17, 2, 19pp.

[71] The quotation is in the papers of George-Louis Le Sage, to whom we shall presently turn, BPU, Ms. Fr. 17a, sachet 7, 1st card.

[72] On Le Sage Senior (1676–1759) see *La France Protestante*, eds., Eugène and Emile Haag, first ed., tome VI (1856), pp. 568–570, A. de Montet, *Dictionnaire biographique de genevois et de vaudois* (1878), tome II, pp. 60–61, and the article by Gür referred to below. Ironically enough, in view of what would follow, Le Sage the father wrote a tract against the French Prophets when he was in England, republished in 1721. *Essai sur les Caractères d'une Vocation Divine* (London, 1708, Amsterdam, 1721). On his political activities in the 1750's see André Gür, "Un Précédent à la Condamnation du 'Contrat Social': L'Affaire Georges-Louis Le Sage (1752)", *Bulletin de la Société d'histoire et d'archéologie de Genève* 14 (1968): 77–94. He also corresponded with Rousseau during the 1750's.

wishes. There he began to develop his mechanistic theories of gravitation which he suggested to his former teacher Cramer upon returning to Geneva in 1748. Being only a *natif* of Geneva without citizenship *(Bourgeoisie)*, the younger Le Sage was unable to practice medicine, nor did he ever receive a post in the Academy. He made his living by private teaching and devoted most of his life to his scientific research, though like Fatio, he hardly published anything during his lifetime.[73]

It was Cramer's reference to Fatio which aroused Le Sage's interest in Fatio's thought and career, as well as in the relationship between science and enthusiasm.[74] Soon, Le Sage also discovered the 1731 theses sustained by Jallabert under Cramer's presidency, which made it harder for him to understand Cramer's coolness in 1748–49. He devoted many handwritten notes to an effort to explain Cramer's change of mind. Though he mentioned some scientific arguments which Cramer used against his own 1731 hypothesis, Le Sage tended to think that the main reasons for Cramer's change of mind were personal. He was influenced, Le Sage felt, on the one hand by the Cartesians in Paris who still adhered to Descartes's theory of vortices (rather than to that of the aether which posited some vacant space), and on the other, by Newton's own negative attitude towards Fatio de Duillier. The opposition of Cramer's colleague J.L. Calandrini to mechanistic explanations may also have contributed to his change of mind.[75] Le Sage did not impute to Cramer any anti-mechanistic views

---

[73] For a biography of Le Sage Jr. see the study of his former associate, and the executor of his papers—Pierre Prevost, *Notice de la vie et des écrits de George-Louis Le Sage de Genève* (Geneva, 1805), which includes also some of Le Sage's writings. Le Sage in fact received the *Bourgeoisie*, but only in 1768, after his father's death, when he was no longer interested in a medical career. Le Sage has not yet received the systematic attention of historians of science, which he clearly deserves, probably because of the daunting amount of manuscript material he left behind him, including some thirty thousand (!) playing cards on the backs of which he scribbled his notes. See Bernard Gagnebin, "Un Maniaque de l'introspection révélé par 35.000 cartes à jouer: Georges-Louis Le Sage" in *Mélanges d'histoire du livre et des bibliothèques offerts à M. Frantz Calot* (Paris, 1960), pp. 145–157. Among historians of science, Larry Laudan has treated briefly his use of hypothesis, see *Science and Hypothesis* (Dordrecht: Reidel, 1981), pp. 118–124.

[74] In fact, most of the Fatio papers now in the BPU in Geneva were acquired by Le Sage in 1765 from Ed. Ingram, the brother of John Ingram who was the creditor of Fatio's last landlord, Mr. Clare. See Gagnebin, "De la cause de la pesanteur", pp. 118–120. See also BPU, Ms. Fr. 602, fols. 245–265, and Ms. Fr. 2064, fols. 104–117.

[75] For Le Sage's notes on the possible reasons for Cramer's changed attitude see BPU, Ms. Le Sage, 17a, sachets 4, 7, 22.

in principle, however. Cramer continued apparently to search for a mechanistic explanation of gravity, though he suspended judgement with regard to Fatio's account.[76]

Le Sage, on the contrary, came to see his own scientific enterprise as a sort of continuation of that of Fatio, although he postulated inelastic particles rather than elastic ones as the medium accounting for the phenomenon of gravity. Indeed, like Fatio, he thought he was developing a line of thought latent in Newton himself. I shall not enter into an analysis of Le Sage's intellectual and scientific enterprise, a task far beyond the limits of this work, especially given the enormous amount of manuscript material available. My purpose here is only to examine how his lifetime project—to provide such a mechanistic account of gravity—was linked to his views concerning the relationship between science and religion, science and enthusiasm, particularly given the combination of the two in the life of his predecessor, Nicolas Fatio de Duillier.

George-Louis Le Sage, like many of his contemporaries in Geneva and in the Reformed camp in general, was concerned not only with scientific problems such as the explanation of gravity, but with theological questions too, and primarily, with the challenge of atheism which seemed to have become increasingly serious by the middle of the eighteenth century.[77] He was well aware of the insufficiencies of Newtonian natural theology, not only since it "secularized" religion itself, but also since it was open to the relentless criticism of Cartesian methodical doubt.[78] Le Sage thus keenly felt the need to find a better foundation for religion than the natural theology of the Newtonians, based, as it was, not only on the argument from design, but on the assumption of God's direct intervention in nature. He did

---

[76] In fact, as I mentioned above, Cramer returned to a mechanistic explanation in his 1751 Physics course, given the year before he died. An extract of the part of the course dealing with the account of gravity is in the BPU, Ms. Le Sage, 17, 2.

[77] In one of his notes concerning the question of miracles and the challenge of deism, Le Sage remarked that he was in agreement with "tous les philosophes laïques mes compatriotes, tels que Gabriel Cramer, Jean-André de Luc, Jacques Necker etc. y compris même J.J. Rousseau à certains égards." BPU, Ms. Le Sage, 17a, Sachet 8, 4th card. It should be noted that Le Sage included in his list both "established" intellectuals like Cramer and Necker who held academic posts as well as outsiders like de Luc and even radicals such as Rousseau "in some respects"! On Jean-André de Luc, the future geologist, and his links with Rousseau and the radicals in Geneva in the 1760's see R.A. Leigh, ed., *Correspondance complète de Jean Jacques Rousseau*, vol. 31 (Oxford, 1978), Letter 5479 and the notes to that letter, pp. 35–36.

[78] See his notes "Sur l'Athée vertueux", in BPU, Ms. Fr. 2056, section entitled "Personalités sur la Religion".

not object to natural theology per se; on the contrary, he sought to develop such theology, but he believed, like most Protestants on the Continent, that it should be based on a mechanistic view of nature in which God did not intervene time and again in the "machine" which he once set in motion.[79]

Le Sage's theories on the mechanistic explanation of gravity to which he devoted the best part of his long life can be seen as part of this broader project. He explained attraction by reference to "ultramundane particles," extremely small atoms supposedly moving at a very high speed (faster than light!) which impelled bodies towards each other, without themselves being subject to the law of gravity. Although material objects were porous enough to let most of these aethereal particles penetrate them without any interaction, some of the particles would impact with the constituent corpuscles of the object and thus cause it to move. An isolated mass of matter was kept in equilibrium by these particles pressing it from all sides, but any other mass at a given distance would block some of the particles between the two bodies, casting a "gravitational shadow" and thus they would be pushed towards one another. Le Sage tried to develop his theory in a way which would account specifically for the Newtonian law of universal attraction, namely, that the force of attraction between two bodies was proportional to the product of the masses of the two bodies and inversely proportional to the square distance between them.[80] However, in assuming the existence of such an "immaterial substance" and calling it "particules ultramondaines," Le Sage was consciously introducing a certain "transcendental" element into nature itself, while "pushing" God's direct intervention further away.[81] Indeed, whereas the Newtonian type of natural theology

---

[79] "Essai d'un nouveau système de Religion Naturelle fondé sur le Principe de l'Imitation de Dieu", BPU, Ms. Fr. 2056. Le Sage took exception, however, to the Leibnizian position that God necessarily created the best possible world. Rather, according to Le Sage, He created the best one among those which could be perpetuated by a small number of general laws. Ibid. Section 1.

[80] See Le Sage, "Lucrèce Newtonien" first published in *Mémoires de l'Académie Royale des Sciences et Belles-lettres de Berlin* (1784) and later reprinted in Prevost, *Notice de la vie et des écrites de George-Louis Le Sage*, pp. 561–604. See also on this subject Samuel Aronson, "The Gravitational Theory of George-Louis Le Sage", *The Natural Philosopher* 3 (1964): 51–74, esp. pp. 53–58, and Larry Laudan, "The Medium and its Message: a Study of some Philosophical Controversies about Ether", in G.N. Cantor and M.J.S. Hodge, eds., *Conceptions of Ether. Studies in the History of Ether Theories 1740–1900* (Cambridge: Cambridge University Press, 1981), pp. 164–165.

[81] On this point, it might be interesting to compare Le Sage's views to those of

practically abolished the realm of metaphysics (since physics was the sphere of divine power and presence, in so far as it was accessible to human reason), Le Sage reintroduced this discipline which dealt with God as the primary cause and with His mediated relationship with the created world.

Within the sphere of metaphysics, Le Sage could also explicate the principles of teleology which he felt Newtonian natural philosophy did not develop systematically enough. The investigation of natural phenomena, Le Sage believed, could point both to the intelligent cause which created them and to the ultimate end for which they were created, and the same held true for the particular ends of specific phenomena. Hence, the investigation of particular phenomena could also reveal the specific views which God had in mind in creating those objects. It also ensured the existence of particular providence, rather than just general providence.[82] Indeed, Le Sage argued, particular providence meant that there was a reason and an end for every object in nature, as minuscule as it might be, in contributing to universal happiness, and that only his own scientific theory provided for such particular providence.[83] Le Sage admitted that one

---

the Hutchinsonians in England at that period, like William Jones for example. Jones also combined a mechanistic interpretation of nature with a stress on God's transcendence. William Jones, *An Essay on the First Principles of Natural Philosophy* (Oxford, 1762), Book II, pp. 55–116, for his mechanistic account of gravitation, and Book IV, chapters V–VI, on the relationship between God and nature. On the Hutchinsonians as a group, see A.J. Kuhn, "Glory or Gravity: Hutchinson vs. Newton", *Journal of the History of Ideas* 22 (1961): 303–322. For the Hutchinsonians' links with the High Church party and with an Augustinian type of Christianity see the important article by C.B. Wilde, "Hutchinsonianism, Natural Philosophy and Religious Controversy in Eighteenth-Century Britain", *History of Science* 18 (1980): 1–24.

[82] See "Quelques fragmens de l'ouvrage projeté par Le Sage sur les Causes finales" published by E.S.F. Reverdil, in Prevost, *Notice de la vie et des écrits de George-Louis Le Sage*, pp. 495–560. Reverdil (1732–1808) was one of Le Sage's students and close associates when he stayed in Geneva in the late 1750's. He later became a professor of mathematics in Copenhagen, and adviser of Christian VII, before returning to his native Vaud towards the end of his life. The original manuscript notes, more extensive than those published by Reverdil, are in BPU, Mss. Suppl. 765/1, fols. 1–96. They were written by Le Sage around 1756. He was apparently influenced at this point by Christian Wolff's call (made in the introductory note to his Logic course of 1740) to develop a theory of *Téléologie* within Natural Philosophy. (See Reverdil's introduction to that text in Prevost, p. 496.)

[83] "On ne peut donc admettre la Providence particulière qu'en ce sens qu'il n'y a dans la nature aucun être si petit qu'il soit en lui même et si peu important pour les autres, aucun changement si léger dans aucune des choses qui existent qui n'ait été prévu, et qui ni soit entré dans le plan de la création à proportion de ce qu'il pouvait contribuer au bonheur total. Le dogme de la Providence particulière ainsi expliqué est une suite naturelle de la Théorie que je viens d'exposer, ou plutôt c'est

could find these ends only by presenting them as hypotheses which
were then checked, verified or falsified. Even the proof for the existence of a purposeful Creator (rather than sheer chance) as the cause
of the natural order, was founded merely on arguments of probability. The hypothetical method was the appropriate one not only in
physics, in the mechanistic explanations given for gravitation, but in
metaphysics as well. In this respect, Le Sage carried the Cartesian
hypothetical approach to its logical conclusion.[84]

Unlike many Cartesians, however, but similarly to Fatio, Le Sage
used his mechanistic theories not to distance God from nature, but
rather to ensure God's particular providence and specific involvement in nature, even if it was an indirect involvement. Moreover, as
in the case of Fatio, Le Sage's mechanistic approach made possible
a certain rehabilitation of enthusiasm. Yet, whereas Fatio seemed to
have done this by providing a mechanistic account for the phenomenon of inspiration itself, for Le Sage, the mechanistic view of nature
enabled the drawing of a clearer line of demarcation between physics and religion. Indeed, while Fatio had rejected the materialist view
of Lucretius, as we noted above, Le Sage in his "Lucrèce Newtonien"
tried to offer a synthesis of the Newtonian and Lucretian world view,
though of course he did not accept the atheistic implications of classical atomism and Epicureanism. The investigation of nature did not
rule out the existence of God and his involvement in creation, but
the spiritual truths of the Church had to be judged according to
criteria completely different from those applicable in physics.[85]

This principle of the segregation of religion from natural philosophy, which was traditionally linked with a mechanistic account of
nature, could now serve Le Sage for a new purpose. His scientific
debt to Fatio de Duillier as a precursor of his own mechanistic explanation of gravity presented Le Sage with a dilemma. Fatio's reputation was tainted, after all, by his involvement with the Camisard
prophets. How could a man be taken seriously on matters of natural
philosophy if he was an "enthusiast" and a "fanatic"? Le Sage thus
set out to try and "rehabilitate" Fatio and to explain, if not to justify,

---

cette Théorie même." BPU, Mss. Suppl. 765, fol. 70. This particular section was
omitted by Reverdil in his published version. See previous note.

[84] On Le Sage's hypothetical method see Laudan, *Science and Hypotheses*, pp. 118–
124.

[85] BPU, Ms. Le Sage 43a, sachet 29, card no. 25.

his "enthusiasm". He states that purpose clearly at the beginning of his collection of notes on that subject:

> Since it is important for the propagation of the true mechanism of gravity that one of the formulators of that doctrine should not be taken too much as a visionary, I thought it worthwhile to examine what exactly was involved in this misjudgement which Fatio had had, deluding himself he could perform miracles.[86]

Paradoxically enough, as we shall presently see, it was precisely Le Sage's mechanistic philosophy which helped him achieve that aim to partially legitimize "enthusiastic" tendencies, claims to direct divine inspiration and even arguments based on the possibility of new miracles.

Le Sage regarded with scepticism—though not with mockery— the claims of Fatio and the French Prophets to perform miracles, have visions and establish contacts with spirits. Yet, in order to show that Fatio was not that exceptional in the combination of enthusiasm and serious scientific activities, Le Sage compiled a list of prominent natural philosophers who had religious visions or claimed to have direct divine inspiration. Chronologically speaking, his list began with Michael Stifel, the German Lutheran mathematician of the first half of the sixteenth century who engaged in prophesying and in calculations concerning the end of the world, went on to the French Cabbalist Guillaume Postel and the Elizabethan scientist John Dee and his assistant Edward Kelley who allegedly held numerous conversations with Spirits.[87] Le Sage next proceeded to the visions of Descartes, as recorded in his *Olympiques*, to the visions of Pascal, and to Henry More—"a profound Theologian, well versed in all branches of Philosophy who pretended to have many conversations with superior

---

[86] "Come il importe à la propagation du vrai méchanisme de la gravité que l'un de ses inventeurs ne passe pas trop pour un visionnaire, j'ai crû l'avoir examiner en quoi précisement consistoit cet Ecart de jugement qui avoit Fatio, à se flater de pouvoir opérer des miracles." BPU, Ms. Le Sage 43a, boite, sachet 29, first card. This collection of cards is entitled "Citations et Reflexions étrangères à Fatio propres à justifier sa crédulité aux Inspirations modernes."
[87] On Michael Stifel (1487–1567) see the article by Kurt Vogel in *D.S.B.*, vol. XIII, pp. 58–62. On Guillaume Postel see W.J. Bouwsma, *Concordia Mundi, the career and thought of G. Postel* (Cambridge Mass.: Harvard University Press, 1957), and the numerous studies by François Secret, especially "G. Postel et les courants prophétiques de la Renaissance", *Studi Francesi*, 3 (1957). On Dee and Kelley see Peter J. French, *John Dee: The World of an Elizabethan Magus* (London: Routledge and Kegan Paul, 1972, paperback ed., 1984), esp. pp. 9–13, 113–125. As we mentioned in Chapter 3 above, it was Meric Casaubon who published in 1659 *A True and Faithful Relation of what passed for many Years Between Dr. John Dee ... and some Spirits.*

Intelligences and even with the Divinity itself."[88] Le Sage passed on
to Newton, mentioning his commentaries on the books of Daniel
and Revelation as a similar example of the "mystical" tendencies of
serious scientists.[89] He finally made reference to his own contemporary, the Swedish mystic Emmanuel Swedenborg, another case of a
serious mathematician, holding a mechanistic view of nature, who
claimed to have "sublime visions" and to have held thousands of
sessions with celestial spirits during the last thirty or forty years of
his life.[90] His survey thus purported to show that such claims were
quite common among scientists and mathematicians, and need not
cast any shadow on their scientific achievements proper. Le Sage's
justification ran partly along "psychological" lines. Indeed, he quoted
Seneca who referred to Pseudo-Aristotle's famous dictum in the *Problemata* 30 that "No great genius has ever existed without some touch
of madness", a notion which as we know was also highly influential
among "Proto-Romantics" of Le Sage's generation.[91] More specifically,
Le Sage argued that "Physico-Mathematicians" who were used to
clear distinctions and boundary lines, passed easily from faith to credulity, since in that sphere no such clear boundary line existed.

This last point indicates that Le Sage's argument went beyond the
psychological level, on to the epistemological one. For Le Sage, matters
of faith were not subject to the clear and distinct criteria of reason,

---

[88] ". . . [C]e Théologien si profondément instruit dans toutes les branches de la
Philosophie prétendait avoir eu plusieurs Entretiens avec des Intelligences supérieurs
et même avec la Divinité." BPU, Ms. Le Sage, 43a, sachet 29, card no. 3. See also
card 15, and sachet 31, card 5. On More see Chapter 3 above. On Descartes and
the role that the *Olympiques* played in his image as an "enthusiast" see Chapter 4
above. Le Sage relied on the *Eloge* of Descartes by Gaillard (Paris, 1765), pp. 27–28.

[89] BPU, Ms. Le Sage, 43a, sachet 29, card no. 7, sachet 31 card no. 5. In this
connection Le Sage quoted the Italian Abbé Farisi in his *Elogio del Cavaliere Isacco
Newton* (Milan, 1778), which ascribed Newton's commentaries on the books of Daniel
and Revelation to his weakening intellect in old age.

[90] BPU, Ms. Le Sage 43a, sachet 29, cards 10, 18. Le Sage relied on the *Gazette
littéraire de deux-ponts*, année 1773, Nos. 11, 12. On Swedenborg see the article by
Sten Lindroth in *D.S.B.*, vol. XIII, pp. 178–181.

[91] "Nullam magnam ingeniam, sine mixtura Dementia fuit." BPU, Ms. Le Sage,
43a, sachet 29, card 4. He quotes from Seneca, *De Tranquillitate Animi*, in *Dialogorum*,
Lib. IX, Cap. 17, 10. For a Latin text with English translation see Seneca, *Moral
Essays*, trans. J.W. Basore, vol. II (London: Heinemann, 1932). On the *Problemata* 30
see above, Chapter 2. On the conceptions of "Genius" among the Pre-Romantics
there is an extensive bibliography but for a convenient summary see the articles
"Genius from the Renaissance to 1770" by Giorgio Tonelli, and "Genius: Individualism in Art and Artists" by Rudolf Wittkower in the *Dictionary of the History of Ideas*,
vol. II, pp. 293–312.

and therefore one could understand, if not agree with, the "enthusiastic" ravings of serious scientists, without doubting the reliability of their scientific findings. It is not accidental that he noted down the following quotation from the French Cartesian Montmort:

> The clarity of mathematics and the holy obscurity of faith are two things completely opposed. I do not believe anyone would ever succeed in linking them together.[92]

No less significant is the fact that this citation comes from the end of Montmort's argument with John Craig's *Theologiae Christianae Principia Mathematica*. Craig, a friend and disciple of Newton, attempted in that book to prove the truth of the Christian religion—as against Jews and unbelievers—by computing the exact time of the Second Coming. Identifying a gradual diminution of faith, a diminution which could be precisely formulated in mathematical terms, Craig assumed that the Second Coming would occur when that faith had all but disappeared, around 3144 A.D. at the latest.[93] The Cartesian Montmort found such mathematical computations dubious and based on arbitrary presuppositions. This was also the opinion of Le Sage himself. In another note in the same batch of cards he referred explicitly to Craig as an example of a mathematician who falsely tried to apply the rules of mathematics to the question of the diminishing credibility of miracles, and hence the probability of new ones. Such probability or lack thereof, Le Sage argued, could not be judged by mathematical calculations.[94]

---

[92] "La Clarté des Mathématiques, et la sainte obscurité de la Foi sont des choses trop opposées. Je ne crois pas que personne réussisse à en faire jamais l'alliance." BPU, Ms. Le Sage 13a, sachet 29, card 5. The quotation is from the "Avertissement" of the second edition of Montmort's *Essai d'analyse sur les jeux de hazard* (published anonymously, Paris, 1713), p. xxxix. On Montmort (born Pierre Rémond) 1678–1719, see *D.S.B.*, vol. IX, pp. 449–501. See also the "Eloge de M. De Montmort" in *Histoire de l'Académie Royale des Sciences*, année 1719 (Paris, 1721), pp. 83–93.

[93] John Craig, *Theologiae Christianae Principia Mathematica* (London, 1699). See especially the Preface to the reader. On Craig see *D.N.B.*, vol. 4, pp. 1372–73.

[94] BPU, Ms. Le Sage, 43a, Sachet 29, card no. 21. Another important theme in Le Sage's attempts to rehabilitate Fatio was the question of the possibility of new miracles. On the question of the cessation of miracles see Chapter 1 above. Le Sage admitted that the majority of Protestant theologians believed that miracles had ceased since the Apostolic period or shortly thereafter, but he insisted that the question nevertheless remained open, and that according to quite a few theologians, the possibility of miracles had not disappeared. Fatio's error, Le Sage felt, was in the way he estimated the relative advantages and drawbacks which might accrue to the Church from the occurrence of miracles at the present time. Yet, Le Sage could well understand Fatio's misjudgement, not only because of the lack of clear and

The Genevan Le Sage thus clearly sided with some of the French Cartesians as against most of the Newtonians in England, not only in his attempt to provide a mechanistic account of gravity but also in the clear distinction which he drew between natural philosophy and matters of faith. Such a distinction, however, was as much Calvinist, well anchored in the Reformed tradition, as it was Cartesian. Protestantism gave rise not only to a type of natural theology which regarded scientific research as a way to glorify God and prove His Wisdom and Providence. The original message of Calvinism was in fact the separation of the realm of philosophy from that of theology and the stress on God's transcendence. This attitude could fit very well the attempts to provide a mechanistic account of nature. Yet, whereas in the seventeenth century such a programme served to combat the claims of enthusiasts who allegedly mixed religion and science, in the eighteenth century—as the case of Le Sage indicates— this "segregationist" streak in Protestantism could be employed to partially rehabilitate the enthusiasts by relegating their claims of visions and inspiration to the realm of "obscure" faith. This transformation was largely a response to the growing challenge of atheism, a response different from that given by Newtonian natural theology. While the latter ran the risk of "secularizing" religion itself by bringing it literally down to earth, Le Sage, like many other Christians of the later eighteenth century, sought to salvage the Christian religion by stressing its supernatural and fideistic nature. Indeed, this combination of mechanism and an indulgent attitude towards enthusiasm is also a clear harbinger of Romantic attitudes, and Le Sage, who died in 1803, can definitely be characterized as a "pre-Romantic" in Geneva.

The relationship between enthusiasm and science in the early modern period was thus neither simple nor static. It depended largely

---

authentic criteria by which to weigh the advantages and disadvantages of such renewed miracles, but also given the sorry state of the Church and particularly the spread of atheism in his generation. The important point for us, however, is that for Le Sage the possibility of miracles did not contradict his mechanistic conception of nature. In fact, in a different place he mentioned his indebtedness to Gabriel Cramer for the idea of the preordination of miracles, a conception which accounted for the possibility of miracles without the renewed intervention of God in the physical universe. Le Sage regarded that idea as a most satisfactory response to the deists who denied the possibility of miracles altogether. It also enabled him to view with indulgence Fatio's faith in the alleged miracles performed by the so-called French Prophets. See BPU, Ms. Le Sage, 43a sachet 29, card 28, and Ms. Le Sage 17a, sachet 8.

on the intellectual and ideological vantage point from which one saw and conceived both enthusiasm and the right methodology of natural philosophy. Nevertheless, the thrust of the new philosophy of nature, both Cartesian and Newtonian, was "anti-enthusiastic". Indeed, the reaction to enthusiasm, as we have seen in this book, was one of the important motivating forces in the emergence of corpuscular natural philosophy as well as the Newtonian one. When a century later some natural philosophers like Le Sage were ready to leave room for mystical speculations and religious enthusiasm, they did so by strictly limiting such speculations to the individual and private realm.

THE CRITIQUE OF ENTHUSIASM AND THE PROBLEM OF SECULARIZATION

Our story, which started with the Reformation critique of enthusiasm, has brought us to the pre-Romantic rehabilitation of enthusiasm, or at least to the eve of the emergence of Pietism, Methodism and other revivalist movements. The challenge of enthusiasm, I have tried to argue, and the reactions it aroused, point to some of the motivations leading the established Protestant élite to adopt more secular attitudes on the eve of the Enlightenment. The reaction to enthusiasm may indeed have been one of the factors contributing to the process of secularization in the early modern period.

At the same time, however, we have seen in the course of our study that enthusiasm was often associated with atheism. The so-called enthusiasts in their individualistic approach, in their rejection of traditional authorities, and of course, in their anti-clericalism, seem to be more modern than their clerical opponents. Was not the spread of enthusiastic movements a factor in undermining the authority and prestige of the clerical establishment, and thus indeed a factor contributing to the growing secularization of European society? Did not some of these movements in that period themselves undergo a significant process of secularization?[1] Furthermore, should not those who adopted a tolerant attitude towards enthusiasm, like the third Earl of Shaftesbury, be regarded as the true "secularists", much more than either the Protestant establishment or the enthusiasts themselves?

The problem of the relationship between enthusiasm and secularization thus reveals some of the basic ambiguities in the concept of secularization itself on the eve of the Enlightenment. If by secularization one means the gradual decline of the Church and of the authority of the ecclesiastical establishment, then the enthusiasts themselves indeed contributed to that process. If, however, we take secularization to

---

[1] For a case in point see, Andrew C. Fix, *Prophecy and Reason: The Dutch Collegiants in the Early Enlightenment* (Princeton: Princeton University Press, 1991).

mean the "disenchantment of the world", the retreat of the supernatural dimension from human and natural affairs, then it is the
reaction to enthusiasm of the clerical establishment which may be
taken as an indication of this process. Indeed, Christian intellectuals,
especially Protestant ones, in the early modern period rejected not
only magical and demonological beliefs, but also the claims of enthusiasts to have direct access to the supernatural realm.

How can these two contradicting meanings of secularization be
reconciled, and what is the exact relationship between enthusiasm
and secularization in the seventeenth and early eighteenth centuries?
The term "secularization", I would like to suggest, should denote,
with reference to that period, primarily a crisis in the symbolic and
institutional means which link the public sphere here on earth with
a transcendental source of meaning and legitimacy. The difficulty of
formulating and institutionalizing a "bridge" which would link the
transcendent God with the mundane sphere was of course common
to all monotheistic religions since the so-called "axial age" in the
first millennium B.C.[2] It was an acute problem in Christianity especially after the Reformation, when the role of the Church as a
mediating institution was thrown into doubt. Mainstream Protestants
continued to adhere to orthodox Christology which viewed the Incarnation, Crucifixion and Resurrection of the historic Christ as the
central mediating symbol for salvation. Yet, in contrast to the Roman Catholics, they saw Scripture as the sole epistemological road
to transcendent truth, and denied the sacral role of the priest as a
mediator between divine grace and the individual believer. The enthusiasts, in contrast, were viewed as challenging precisely the mediating

---

[2] The idea of an "axial age" with its crucial significance for world history was
first formulated by Karl Jaspers, *Vom Ursprung und Ziel der Geschichte* (Munich: Piper
and Co., 1949), English translation by Michael Bullock, *The Origin and Goal of History*
(New Haven and London: Yale University Press, 1953). This conception was further
elaborated, with particular stress on the notion of transcendence, in a special issue
of *Daedalus*, under the title "Wisdom, Revelation and Doubt: Perspectives on the
First Millennium B.C.", edited by Benjamin Schwartz (Spring, 1975). For a recent
systematic development of this theme which has very much influenced my own
thinking on the subject, see Shmuel N. Eisenstadt, "The Axial Age: the Emergence
of Transcendental Visions and the Rise of Clerics", *Archives Européennes de Sociologie*
29 (1982): 294–314; and idem., "Explorations in the Sociology of Knowledge: The
Soteriological Axis in the Construction of Domains of Knowledge", in S.N. Eisenstadt
and I. Friedrich Silber, eds., *Knowledge and Society: Studies in the Sociology of Culture Past
and Present*, vol. 7 (1988): *Cultural Traditions and Worlds of Knowledge: Explorations in the
Sociology of Knowledge*, pp. 1–71.

symbols which the Magisterial Reformation maintained, namely the central soteriological role of Christ, and the exclusive position of Scripture as an avenue to religious truth. As we saw in Chapter 1, the theological critique of enthusiasm focused precisely on these issues. In terms of doctrine, theologians like Bullinger focused on the enthusiasts' heretical views concerning the Incarnation. In terms of authorization, the standard theological critique relied on Scripture, and attacked the enthusiasts' wish to circumvent it. In social terms, critics insisted on the role of the ministers in spreading the Word of God, and saw with apprehension the anti-clerical thrust of the enthusiasts. In all these respects, enthusiasts were regarded as no less dangerous than atheists, and indeed, having some affinities with them. The historian may partly adopt this perspective in noting that the various groups and individuals who claimed to have direct divine inspiration in the early modern period undermined the orthodox mediating symbols and institutions, whether Church, Scripture, or the role of the historic Christ, and in this respect, contributed to a crisis in their credibility. Such a crisis in the symbols and institutions linking man to God, more than an outright rejection of the transcendental realm and its relevance altogether, seems to me to be the hallmark of secularization in the late seventeenth century, and in this sense, the enthusiasts may indeed have contributed to that process.

On the other hand, the clerical establishment in responding to that challenge, had increasingly to modify its own ideological arsenal, in ways which similarly weakened the traditional mediating symbols between God and man. This can already be seen in the medical account, first Galenic, later chemical or mechanical, which was given even by ministers for the phenomenon of enthusiasm in the seventeenth and early eighteenth centuries, and which I have outlined in Chapters 2, 3 and 7. By defining enthusiasm in medical, even physiological terms, clearly distinguished from religious inspiration proper, the clerical critics, from Burton onwards, attenuated the links between empirical reality and the transcendental dimension, between the natural realm and the supernatural one. The parallel distinction between body and mind, increasingly insisted upon in the second half of the seventeenth century, largely under Descartes' influence, had a similar effect. This distinction, as we have seen in Chapter 7, also had a social correlate, in stressing the division of labour between ministers and physicians. Most important, perhaps, the increasing emphasis on medical knowledge laid the foundations for a new, more secular, basis of the social and cultural order.[3]

True, Protestant ministers still regarded the supernatural realm, the content of which was incorporated in Scripture for all to read, as within the public domain. The message of Scripture also remained the principal criterion according to which claims for prophecy and direct divine inspiration were to be judged. Nevertheless, as was shown in Chapter 6, resort to Scripture was supplemented by a resort to human reason. By the end of the seventeenth century, Scripture—although still indispensable—was no longer sufficient on its own to serve as a "bridge" between the transcendental realm and human knowledge. The introduction of individual human reason as a mediating faculty between God and man, the emphasis laid on reason as a divine gift, as a source of genuine prophecy, in contradistinction to false claims to direct inspiration, all point to a significant secularization of the epistemological bridge linking the transcendental realm with the human one. Such secularization was taking place largely in response to the challenge of enthusiasm.

Yet, it may be argued, the rationalizing tendencies in Protestant theology of the late seventeenth and early eighteenth centuries, and the reliance on natural theology, were not so very different from those of medieval Scholasticism. Indeed, it is not a coincidence that in precisely that period the impact of Maimonides, the foremost rationalist Jewish philosopher of the Middle Ages, is so noticeable.[4] Nevertheless, the concept of reason as an antidote to enthusiasm in the late seventeenth century is significantly different from scholastic conceptions of reason. It is individual critical reason, not just logical and instrumental, but an autonomous source of religious, as well as

---

[3] In the next generation, the critics of the Cartesian approach, whether the enthusiasts themselves, the deists, or later, even some Newtonian ministers, with whom I have not dealt in this book—all challenged the clear distinction between mind and body, the supernatural and the natural. They thus contributed on their part to a more radical secularization of culture, typical to the Enlightenment, in which the distinction between the natural and the supernatural was obliterated altogether, and likewise, the separation between body and soul.

[4] On the impact of Maimonides in that period see Richard H. Popkin, "Newton and Maimonides" in *A Straight Path. Studies in Medieval Philosophy and Culture. Essays in Honor of Arthur Hyman*, ed. Ruth Link-Salinger, et al. (Washington D.C.: Catholic University of America Press, 1988), pp. 216–229; idem., "Some Further Comments on Newton and Maimonides", in James E. Force and Richard H. Popkin, *Essays on the Context, Nature and Influence of Isaac Newton's Theology* (Dordrecht, Boston, London: Kluwer Academic Publishers), pp. 1–7, as well as passing references in other articles in that volume. See also Frank E. Manuel, *The Broken Staff: Judaism through Christian Eyes* (Cambridge Mass.: Harvard University Press, 1992).

secular, truth. In this respect, especially in their openness to innovation and individual judgment, Protestant ministers clearly adopted some of the features of enthusiasm which they debated.

These changes can be seen most clearly in the intellectual armory to which ministers had recourse in their controversy with the enthusiasts. Up to the middle of the seventeenth century, theologians, as well as lay intellectuals, relied on the scholastic and humanistic tradition in defending the established order vis-à-vis the challenge of the enthusiasts. Indeed, as I have shown in Chapters 4 and 5, the critics of these traditions—alchemists, empirics, experimental philosophers, even Descartes—were themselves regarded as enthusiasts. From the 1660's onwards, however, the new natural philosophy offered itself as a more reliable antidote to the danger of enthusiasm than scholasticism or humanism had been. By the end of the seventeenth century, the natural physical world, side by side with Scripture, was presented as a bridge to the knowledge of God. This of course is a well-known phenomenon, but the argument of this book has been that the controversy with the enthusiasts was one of the important incentives to the increasing reliance of the theologians on both reason and nature, and that herein we may see another manifestation of the secularization of the symbolic bridge linking man to God.

Such secularization of the religious consciousness of the Protestant establishment itself could not fail to lead, however, to more radical secularization on the part of the opponents of that establishment, particularly the deists. As we saw in Chapter 8, deists like Shaftesbury drew far-reaching conclusions from the medical and rationalist critique directed against the enthusiasts. If enthusiasm was a medical phenomenon rather than a religious one, Shaftesbury argued, it was no longer that dangerous or subversive, and should be treated with ridicule, rather than by the harsh means of persecution. Indeed, should not biblical prophecy itself be seen in similar terms? If human reason is the judge with respect to the enthusiasts, should it not be the judge in matters pertaining to religious phenomena in general? The secularization of the symbolic and institutional links between God and man could thus be pushed one step further, doing away altogether with the traditional links of Scripture, faith and divine grace.

Yet, Shaftesbury's famous *Letter* also points to another far-reaching transformation with respect to enthusiasm. Whereas up to the end of the seventeenth century "enthusiasm" was a label ascribed to pretensions to direct divine inspiration, or claims to absolute truth, by the early eighteenth century, the term increasingly refers to subjective sentiment. Once again, the medical account may have contributed to this transformation; with Shaftesbury, however, enthusiasm does not necessarily have a negative connotation. He returns indeed to the Platonic and Renaissance rehabilitation of enthusiasm but now as a personal sentiment, rather than as a temperament with astrological and metaphysical implications. Here too, the links between empirical human experience and the transcendental realm are weakened, although Shaftesbury did not by any means renounce the Platonic ideal of contemplation, mostly, in his later years, in an aesthetic sense.

The increasingly subjective interpretation of enthusiasm in the eighteenth century, and the tendencies to rehabilitate it, are a topic beyond the confines of the present study. Yet, in Chapter 9 we saw one further manifestation of this trend in the realm of natural philosophy, particularly in the manuscript notes of the Genevan George-Louis Le Sage. Whereas in the second half of the seventeenth century the new experimental science was mostly viewed as a firm response to the challenge of enthusiasm, by the eighteenth century there appeared a scientist like Nicolas Fatio de Duillier, who could be at the same time a spokesman of the French Prophets, or George-Louis Le Sage, who could defend that combination of scientist and enthusiast, and who could place Fatio himself in a long line of such intellectuals.

Nevertheless, it is not by chance that both Fatio and Le Sage were considered outsiders, even eccentrics in the Enlightenment culture of the eighteenth century. The Enlightenment could accept the phenomenon of enthusiasm only in its restricted subjective and largely aesthetic sense. It is these connotations of the term which have remained in linguistic use up to the present. In rejecting any claims to direct divine inspiration, however, the Enlightenment on its part was largely heir to the Christian, mostly Protestant critique of enthusiasm in the sixteenth and seventeenth centuries, a critique which has been the subject of the present book. Was this critique an enlightened and rational attitude or was it a suppression of an important human urge? Should we at the end of the twentieth century be more indulgent to enthusiasm, not only in the aesthetic and psychological sense, but also in its original religious sense? Can the social order be defended without designating those who claim direct divine inspiration as madmen? The answer to these questions remains outside the realm of the historian's craft. His task however, is to pose the questions and to explore the historical circumstances which have led to our present condition, and thus, to open up certain avenues which may otherwise seem closed.

BIBLIOGRAPHY

MANUSCRIPT SOURCES

Geneva—Bibliothèque publique et universitaire:

Ms. Fr. 601–603, 605 (The papers of Nicolas Fatio de Duillier); 2056 (Papers of George Louis Le Sage); 2064; 2065, fols. 103r–104v (letters from Dortous de Mairan to Gabriel Cramer).
Ms. Le Sage, 17a; 17, 2; 43a; (Papers and card notes of George-Louis Le Sage).
Mss. Suppl. 765/1 (Papers of George-Louis Le Sage).

Cambridge—University Library

Add. 3996, fols. 717–720 (Letter of Nicolas Fatio de Duillier to John Conduitt, 26.8.1730).

Oxford—Bodleian Library

Mss., Rawl. C. 105, p. 588r. (Henry Leavery, letter to Nathaniel Spinckes of February 20, 1711).

Jerusalem—The National and University Library
Yahuda Ms. 1 (Newton's Ms. *Treatise on Revelation*).

PRINTED PRIMARY SOURCES

Acosta, Joseph. *De temporibus novissimis libri quatuor.* Rome, 1590.
Adams, Thomas. "The Sinners Passing-Bell or Phisicke from Heaven." A sermon published in *The Divells Banket.* London, 1614.
Alexander, H.G., ed. *The Leibniz-Clarke Correspondence.* New York: Manchester University Press, 1956.
An Answer to a Letter of John Lacy Esq. dated July 6, 1708 and directed to Josiah Woodward. London, 1708.
Aretaeus of Cappadocia. *Aretaeus, Opera Omnia.* Edited by C.G. Kühn. Leipzig, 1828. This edition includes the Greek text and a Latin translation.
——. *The Extant Works of Aretaeus, the Cappadocian.* Translated by F. Adams. London, 1856.
——. *Aetiologica, Simeiotica et Therapeutica Morborum acutorum et diuturnorum Aretaei Cappadocis.* Edited by G. Henisch. Augsburg, 1603.
——. *Libri Septem.* Venice, 1763. This edition is an amended version of the Latin translation by J.P. Crassus, first published 1552.
Aristotle. *Aristoteles Werke.* Edited by E. Grumach. Vol. 19, *Problemata Physica.* Edited by H. Flashar. Berlin: Akademie-Verlag, 1962.
Aristotle. *The Works of Aristotle.* Edited by W.D. Ross. Vol. VII. Oxford: Clarendon Press, 1927.
[Astell, Mary?] *Bart'lemy Fair: Or, an Enquiry after Wit: In which due respect is had to a Letter Concerning Enthusiasm, to my Lord***,* by Mr. Wotton. London: Printed for R.W. Wilkin, 1709. A second edition which included an "Advertisement to the Reader", appeared under the title, *An Enquiry after Wit: Wherein the Trifling Arguing*

and Impious Raillery of the Late Earl of Shaftesbury, in his Letter concerning Enthusiasm, and other Profane Writers, Are fully Answered, and justly Exposed. London: Printed for John Bateman, 1722).

Atterbury, Francis. *The Voice of the People No Voice of God.* London, 1710.

Avicenna. *Liber Canonis, De medicinis cordialibus, et cantica.* Venice, 1555.

Baillet, Adrien. *La vie de Monsieur Des-Cartes.* Paris, 1691. Reprint. The Philosophy of Descartes series edited by Willis Doney. New York and London: Garland, 1987.

———. *La Vie de Mons. Descartes . . . réduite et abrégé.* 1692. 2nd ed. 1693. This abridged version was translated into English by S.R. under the title *The Life of Monsieur Des Cartes containing the History of his Philosophy and Works. As also The Most Remarkable Things that Befell him during the Whole Course of his Life.* London, 1693.

Bayle, Pierre. *Dictionnaire historique et critique.* Geneva: Slatkine, 1969. Reprint of the 1820–1824 edition.

Bayly, Benjamin. *An Essay upon Inspiration.* In two parts. 1st edition, London, 1707. 2nd edition, London, 1708.

———. *Fourteen Sermons on Various Subjects.* London, 1721.

Birch, Thomas. *The Life and Works of the Honourable Robert Boyle.* London, 1744.

Birch, Thomas. *The History of the Royal Society.* London, 1756–1757.

Blackall, Offspring. *The Way of Trying Prophets: A Sermon preached before the Queen at St. James's November 9, 1707.* London, 1707.

———. *The Sufficiency of a Standing Revelation.* 1700. London, 1717.

Blackmore, Richard. "An Essay Upon the Spleen." In *Essays upon Several Subjects,* vol. II. London, 1717.

Boyle, Robert. *The Works of the Honourable Robert Boyle.* Edited by Thomas Birch. London, 1772.

Bruele, W. *Praxis Medicinae Theorica et Empirica Familiarissima.* Leiden, 1589.

———. *Praxis Medicinae, or The Physicians Practise: Wherein are Contained all Inward Diseases from the Head to the Foot.* 3rd edition. London, 1648.

Bucer, Martin. *Martin Bucers Deutsche Schriften.* Vol. I. Edited by Robert Stupperich. Gütersloh: Gütersloher Verlagshaus Gerd Mohn; Paris: P.U.F., 1960.

Budé, Guillaume. *Annotationes in XXIIII Pandectarum Libros.* Lyon, 1551.

Bulkeley, Richard. *An Answer to Several Treatises Lately publish'd on the Subject of the Prophets, The First Part.* London, 1708.

Bullinger, Heinrich. *Der Widertoeufferen vrsprung/ fürgang/ Secten/ waesen/ fürnemme vnd gemeine jrer leer Artickel/ . . . abgeteilt in VI. Buecher/ vnd beschriben durch Heinrychen Bullingern/ dienern der kirchen zuo Zürych.* Zurich, 1560. Reproduction of 1561 edition. Leipzig: Zentralantiquariat der DDR, 1975. Translated into Latin by J. Simler under the title *Adversus Anabaptistas libri VI nunc primum e Germanico sermone in Latine conversi, per Iosiam Simlerum.* Zurich, 1560.

Burnet, G. *A Fast Sermon on the 30th of January 1680 before the Aldermen of the City of London.* London, 1681.

Burton, Robert. *The Anatomy of Melancholy.* Edited by Thomas C. Faulkner, Nicolas K. Kiessling, Rhonda L. Blair. Introduction by J.B. Bamborough. Oxford: the Clarendon Press, vol. I, 1989; vol. II, 1990; vol. III, 1994.

———. *The Anatomy of Melancholy.* Edited by Holbrook Jackson. London: Everyman's University Library, 1932; republished in one volume, Totowa, New Jersey: Rowman and Littlefield University Library; London: Dent, 1975.

Calamy, Edmund. *A Caveat against New Prophets, in Two Sermons.* London, 1708.

———. *A Historical Account of My Own Life.* Edited by John T. Rutt. Vol. II. London, 1829.

Calder, Robert. *A True Copy of Letters Past betwixt Mr. Robert Calder . . . and Mr. James Cunninghame.* Edinburgh, 1710.

Calvin, Jean. *Opera quae supersunt omnia.* Edited by G. Baum, E. Cunitz, and E. Reus. In *Corpus Reformatorum.* Vols. 29–87. Brunswick, 1863–1900.

———. *Commentaries.* Translated and edited by J. Haroutunian. "The Library of Christian Classics", vol. XXIII. Philadelphia: The Westminster Press, 1958.

Cardano, Girolamo. *De Rerum Varietate Libri XVII.* Basel, 1557.

——. *De Subtilitate Libri XXX.* Nuremberg, 1550. Translated into French by Richard le Blanc, *Les Livres de Hiérome Cardanus . . . intitulés de la subtilité.* Paris, 1556.

Casaubon, Meric. *A Treatise Concerning Enthusiasme As it is an Effect of Nature: but is mistaken by many for either Divine Inspiration, or Diabolicall Possession.* First edition, London, 1655; second edition, 1656. A facsimile reproduction of the second edition with an Introduction by Paul J. Korshin. Gainsville, Florida: Scholars' Facsimiles and Reprints, 1970.

——. *A True and Faithful Relation of what passed for many years Between Dr. John Dee . . . and some spirits.* London, 1659.

Catherine, Sister. *La vie de Soeur Catherine de Jésus.* Paris, 1628.

Chishull, Edmund. *The Great Danger and Mistake of all New Uninspired Prophecies, Relating to the End of the World, Being a Sermon Preached on Nov. 23rd, 1707.* London, 1708.

Chronica, Ordo Sacerdotis, Acta HN: Three Texts on the Family of Love. Edited with an introduction by Alistair Hamilton. Leiden: Brill, 1988.

Clavis Prophetica: or a Key to the Prophecies of Mons. Marion, and the other Camisars, With some Reflections on the Characters of these New Envoys, and Mons. F.—their Chief Secretary. London, 1707.

Constantinus Africanus. . . . *Opera conquisita undique magno studio.* . . . Basel, 1536.

Craig, John. *Theologiae Christianae Principia Mathematica.* London, 1699.

Cramer, Gabriel, and Jallabert, Jean. *Theses Physico-Mathematice de Gravitate.* Geneva, 1731.

Daniel, le père Gabriel. *Voyage du monde de Descartes.* Paris, 1690. Translated into English by T. Taylor under the title, *A Voyage to the World of Cartesius.* London, 1692. Translated into Latin under the title, *Iter per mundum Cartesii.* Amsterdam, 1694.

——. *Nouvelles difficultés proposées à l'auteur du Voyage de Monde de Descartes.* Paris, 1693.

Defoe, Daniel. *A Review of the State of the British Nation.* Vol. V, no. 12 (April 12, 1708). Facsimile reproduction edited by Arthur W. Secord, under the title *Defoe's Review.* New York: Columbia University Press, 1938.

Descartes, René. *Oeuvres de Descartes.* Edited by Charles Adam and Paul Tannery. 13 vols. Paris: Cerf, 1897–1913. Reprint. Paris: Vrin, 1957–58.

A Dissuasive against Enthusiasm: Wherein the Pretensions of the modern Prophets to Divine Inspiration, and the Power of Working Miracles, are examined and confuted by Scripture and Matter of Fact. London, 1708.

Dort, Synod. *Acta Synodi Nationalis.* . . . *Dordrechti Habitae.* Leiden, Dordrecht, 1620. Translated into English by Thomas Scott under the title, *The Articles of the Synod of Dort.* Philadelphia: Presbyterian Board of Publication, 1856.

Edzardi, S. *Impietas cohortis fanaticae, ex propriis Speneri, Rechenbergii, Petersenii, Thomasii, Arnoldi, Schützii, Böhmeri, aliorumque fanaticorum scriptis.* Hamburg, 1703.

Erasmus, Desiderius. *Annotationes in Novum Testamentum.* In *Opera Omnia.* Vol. 6. Hildesheim: Georg Holms Verlag, 1962. Reproduction of the Leiden, 1705 edition.

Erasmus, Desiderius. *Erasmus' Annotations on the New Testament: Acts—Romans—I and II Corinthians.* Edited by Anne Reeve and M.A. Screech. Studies in the History of Christian Thought, vol. 42. Leiden: Brill, 1990.

Fabricius, Wilhelm. *Observationum et Curationum Chirurgicarum Centuriae Sex.* In *Opera quae extant omnia.* Frankfurt a/M, 1646.

Fatio de Duillier, Nicolas. "De la Cause de la Pesanteur: Mémoire de Nicolas Fatio de Duillier Présenté à la Royal Society le 26 février 1690." Edited by Bernard Gagnebin. *Notes and Records of the Royal Society* 6 (1949): 105–160.

——. "Die Wiederaufgefunde Abhandlung von Fatio de Duillier: De la Cause de la Pesanteur." Edited by K. Bopp. In *Drei Untersuchungen zur Geschichte der Mathematik.* Schriften der Strassburger Wissenschaftlichen Gesellschaft im Heidelberg, Neue Folge, 10 heft. Berlin, Leipzig, 1929.

Fernel, Jean. *De Abditis Rerum Causis Libri Duo.* Paris, 1560; Frankfurt, 1577.

——. *Methodi Medendi Ferneliana, enucleata et controversiarum decisionibus illustrata.* Wittenberg, 1630.

Fienus, Thomas. *De viribus imaginationis tractatus*. Louvain, 1608. Leiden, 1635.

Foreest (Forestus), Pierre de, *Observationum et Curationum Medicinalium, sive Medicinae Theoricae et Practicae Libri XXVIII*. Frankfurt, 1634. In *Observationum et Curationum Medicinalium ac Chirurgicarum Opera Omnia*. Frankfurt, 1660.

Fracastoro, G. *Turrius sive de Intellectione*. In *Opera Omnia*. Venice, 1555.

Franck, Sebastian. *Chronica, Zeyt-büch und geschycht-bibell von anbegyn biss in diss gegenwertig MDXXXI. jar verlengt*. Strasbourg, 1531. Reprint. Darmstadt: Wissenschaftliche Buchgesellschaft, 1969.

Fuschsius, L. *De Sanandis Totius Humani Corporis Malis Libri Quinque*. Lyon, 1546; 1547. Enlarged and corrected edition, Frankfurt, 1567.

Galen. *De Usu Partium*. In *Galeni Opera Omnia*. Edited by C.G. Kühn. Vol. 3. Leipzig, 1822. English translation by M.T. May, under the title, *Galen on the Usefulness of the Parts of the Body*. Ithaca, N.Y.: Cornell University Press, 1968.

———. *De Lociis Affectis*. In *Galeni Opera Omnia*. Edited by C.G. Kühn. Vol. 8. Leipzig, 1824. Translated from the Greek text with explanatory notes by Rudolph E. Seigel, under the title, *On the Affected Parts*. Basel: S. Karger, 1976.

Gerson, Jean. *De Distinctione Verarum Visionum a Falsis*. In *Opera Omnia*. Vol. 1. Antwerp, 1706.

Glanvill, Joseph. *Plus Ultra*. London, 1668. Facsimile edition and introduction by J.I. Cope. Gainesville, Florida: Scholars' Facsimiles and Reprints, 1958.

———. *Philosophia Pia: or, a Discourse of the Religious Temper and Tendencies of the Experimental Philosophy which is profest by the Royal Society*. London, 1671.

———. *Essays on Several Important Subjects in Philosophy and Religion*. London, 1676.

———. "Bensalem, being a Description of a Catholick and Free Spirit both in Religion and Learning." Manuscript in the University of Chicago Library.

Gordonius, Bernard. *Opus, Lilium Medicinae Inscriptum, de morborum propè omnium curatione, septem particulis distributum*. Lyon, 1574.

Guainerius, Antonius. *Practica . . . et Omnia Opera*. Venice, 1517.

Ficino, Marsilio. *Marsilio Ficino, Three Books on Life*. Edited by Carol V. Kaske and John R. Clark. Binghamton, New York: The Renaissance Society of America, 1989.

[Fowler, Edward?] *Remarks upon the Letter to a Lord Concerning Enthusiasm. In a Letter to a Gentleman, Not written in Raillery, Yet in Good Humour*. London: Printed by W.D., for John Wyat, 1708.

Gassendi, Pierre. *Examen Philosophiae Roberti Fluddi Medici in quo et ad illius libros adversus R.P.F. Marinum Mersennum . . . scriptos, respondetur*. 1629. In Gassendi. *Opera Omnia*. Lyon, 1658.

Gerdessen, H.J. *De Enthusiasmo schediasma inaugurale . . . contra fanaticos nov-antiquos*. Wittenberg, 1708.

Heer, Henricus ab. *Observationes Medicae*. Liège, 1630.

Hickes, George. *The Spirit of Enthusiasm Exorcised: in a Sermon Preached before the University of Oxford, on Act-Sunday, July 11, 1680*. First edition, London, 1680. Fourth edition, much enlarged, London, 1709.

[Hoadly, Benjamin]. *A Brief Vindication of the Antient Prophets, from the Imputation and Misrepresentation of such as adhere to our Present Pretenders to Inspiration. In a Letter To Sir Richard Bulkeley*. London, 1709. Republished in Benjamin Hoadly, *Several Tracts*. London, 1715.

Hog, James. *Notes about the Spirit's Operations*. Edinburgh, 1709.

Hoornbeek, Johannes. *Summa Controversiarum Religionis*. First edition, Utrecht 1653; amended and enlarged edition, 1658; Frankfurt a/M, 1697.

Hortensius, Lambertus. *Tumultuum Anabaptistarum liber unus*. Basel, 1548.

Huet, P.-D. *Censura Philosophiae Cartesianae*. Paris, 1689.

[Huet, P.-D.]. *Nouveaux mémoires pour servir à l'histoire du Cartésianisme*. Paris, 1711.

———. *Memoirs of the Life of Peter Daniel Huet, written by himself*. Translated from Latin by John Aikin. Vol. I. London, 1810.

Humfrey, John. *An Account of the French Prophets, And their pretended Inspirations, in Three Letters sent to John Lacy*. London, 1708.

Hunnius, Nikolaus. *Principia theologiae fanaticae, quam Theophrastus Paracelsus genuit, atque Weigelius interpolavit.* Wittenberg, 1619. Edited by Johann Heinrich Feustkings. Dresden and Leipzig, 1704.

Hutchinson, Francis. *A Short View of the Pretended Spirits of Prophecy.* London, 1708.

Jones, William. *An Essay on the First Principles of Natural Philosophy.* Oxford, 1762.

Lapide, Cornelius à. (Cornelis Cornelissen van den Steen). *Commentaria in Pentateuchum Mosis.* Second edition. Antwerp, 1618.

Laurens, André Du. *Discours de la conservation de la vue; des maladies melancholiques, des catarrhes et de la vieillesse.* Paris, 1594. Translated into English by Richard Surphlet under the title *A Discourse of the Preservation of the Sight: of Melancholike Diseases; of Rheumes, and of Old Age.* London, 1599. Reprint. Shakespeare Association Facsimiles, No. 15. London: Oxford University Press, 1938.

Lavater, Ludwig. *De Spectris, Lemuribus et Magnis atque Insolitis Fragoribus, variisque praesagitionibus, quae plerunque obitum hominum, magnas clades, mutationesque Imperiorum praecedunt. Liber Unus.* Geneva, 1570. Second Latin edition, 1580. Translated into English under the title *Of Ghostes and Spirites walking by nyght.* London, 1572, 1596.

Le Sage, George-Louis, (Sr.). *Essai sur les caractères d'une vocation divine.* Amsterdam, 1721; first edition, London, 1708.

Le Sage, George-Louis, (Jr.). "Quelques Fragmens de l'ouvrage projeté par Le Sage sur Les Causes Finales" published by E.S.F. Reverdil. In Prevost. *Notice de la vie et des écrits de George-Louis Le Sage,* pp. 495–560. Original manuscript notes, BPU, Mss. Suppl. 765/1, fols. 1–96.

———. "Lucrèce Newtonien." In *Mémoires de l'Académie Royale des Sciences et Belles-lettres de Berlin* (1784). Reprinted in Pierre Prévost. *Notice de la vie et des écrites de George-Louis Le Sage de Genève,* 561–604. Geneva, 1805.

Leibniz, G.W. *G.W. Leibniz, Philosophische Schriften.* Edited by C.J. Gerhardt. Reprint edition. Hildesheim: Olms Verlag, 1978.

———. *Gottfried Wilhelm Leibniz: Philosophical Papers and Letters.* Edited by Leroy E. Loemker. Chicago: Chicago University Press, 1956.

Lemnius L. *De Occultis Naturae Miraculis.* Antwerp, 1581. English translation under the title *The Secret Miracles of Nature in Four Books.* London, 1658.

Leslie, Charles. *The Snake in the Grass.* London, 1698.

Linden, J.A. Van der, and Mercklin, G.A. *De Scriptis Medicis.* Nuremberg, 1686.

Locke, John. *An Essay Concerning Human Understanding.* Edited by Peter H. Nidditch. Oxford: Clarendon Press, 1975.

———. *An Early Draft of Locke's Essay together with Excerpts from his Journals.* Edited by R.I. Aaron and J. Gibb. Oxford: The Clarendon Press, 1936.

———. *The Correspondence of John Locke.* Edited by E.S. De Beer. Oxford: Oxford University Press, 1979.

Luther, Martin. *D. Martin Luthers Werke: Kritische Gesamtausgabe, Abteiliung Werke.* Weimar, 1883–. Reprint edition, 1964–1968. Abbreviated as *WA* in this book.

———. *D. Martin Luthers Werke: Kritische Gesamtausgabe, Briefwechsel.* 18 Vols. Weimar, 1930–1985. Abbreviated as *WA, Briefwechsel* in this book.

———. *Luther's Works.* Edited by Jaroslav Pelikan and H.T. Lehmann. St. Louis: Concordia Publishing House; Philadelphia: Fortress Press, 1955–1986. Abbreviated as *LW* in this book.

The Magick of Quakerism or, the Chief Mysteries of Quakerism Laid Open. London, 1707.

Maresius, Samuel. [Desmarets, Samuel]. *Antirrheticus; sive Defensio pii zeli pro retinenda recepta in Ecclesiis Reformatis Doctrina, praesertim adversus Chiliastas et Fanaticos; contra Joh. A. Comenii Fanatici zelum amarum, scientia et conscietia destitutum.* Groningen, 1669.

———. *De abusu philosophiae cartesianae in rebus theologicis et fidei.* Groningen, 1670.

Melanchton, Philipp. *Philippi Melanchtonis Opera quae supersunt omnia.* Edited by C.G. Bretscheider and H.E. Bindseil. Halle, 1834–1860. In *Corpus Reformatorum.* Vols. 1–28.

Mesnard, Philippe. *Les faux prophètes convaincus.* London, 1708.

Montalto, P.E. *Archipathologia*. Paris, 1614.
More, Henry. *A Collection of Several Philosophical Writings of Henry More*. London, 1662.
——. [Alazonomastix Philalethes, pseud.] *Observations upon Anthroposophia Theomagica and Anima Magica Abscondita*. Parrhesia [London], 1650.
——. [Anon.] *The Second Lash of Alazonomastix*. Cambridge, 1651. Republished in 1655, 1656.
——. *Enthusiasmus Triumphatus, or a Discourse of the Nature, Causes, Kinds, and Cure, of Enthusiasme*. First published in 1656 as a Preface to the previous text.
——. *An Antidote against Atheisme*. London, 1652.
——. *The Immortality of the Soul*. London, 1659.
——. *An Explanation of the Great Mystery of Godliness*. London, 1660.
——. *Henrici Mori Cantabrigiensis Scriptorum Philosophicorum*. London, 1679.
Morer, Thomas. "A Sermon Concerning Agitations." In *Sermons on Several Occasions*. London, 1708.
Merlat, Elie. *Le moyen de discerner les esprits*. Lausanne, 1689.
Mothe, Claude Grosteste de la. *Caractère des Nouvelles Prophécies en quatre Sermons, Prononcez dans l'Eglise Française de la Savoye*. London, 1708.
[N.N.] *An Account of the Lives and Behaviour of the Three French Prophets, Lately come out of the Cevennes and Languedoc; And of the Proceedings of the Consistory of the Savoy in Relation to them*. London, 1708.
Neumann, Johann Georg. *Synopsis errorum fanaticorum quos Tremuli moderni fovent, disputationibus aliquot academicis exposita*. Wittenberg, 1703.
Newton, Isaac. *Sir Isaac Newton's Mathematical Principles*. Edited by E. Cajori. Berkeley and Los Angeles: University of California Press, 1966.
——. *Opticks; or a Treatise of the Reflections, Refractions, Inflections and Colours of Light*. New York: Dover, 1952, based on the 4th edition, London, 1730.
——. *Isaac Newton's Papers and Letters on Natural Philosophy and Related Documents*. Edited by I.B. Cohen. Cambridge Mass.: Harvard University Press, 1978.
——. *The Correspondence of Isaac Newton*. Edited by H.W. Turnbull et al. 7 Vols. Cambridge: Cambridge University Press, 1959–1977.
——. *Treatise on Revelation*. Ms. Yahuda Ms. 1. National and University Library, Jerusalem.
Nicholson, Henry. *The Falsehood of the New Prophets Manifested with their Corrupt Doctrines and Conversations*. London, 1708.
Observations upon Elias Marion and his Book of Warnings, Lately Published, Proving this Elias to be a false Prophet, and a dangerous Person. London, 1707.
Oldenburg, Henry. *The Correspondence of Henry Oldenburg*. Edited by A.R. Hall and M.S. Hall. Madison: University of Wisconsin Press, 1969.
Parker, Samuel. *Disputationes de Deo et Providentia Divina*. London, 1678.
[Parker, Samuel, Jr.]. *Censura Temporum: The Good or Ill Tendencies of Books, Sermons, Pamphlets, etc. Impartially consider'd, In a dialogue betweeen Eubulus and Sophronius*. London, printed for H. Clements, 1708.
Paulus Aegineta. *Pauli Aeginetae Libri Tertii, Interpretatio Latina Antiqua*. Edited by J.L. Heiberg. Leipzig; G. Teubner, 1912.
——. *Paulos' von Aegina des besten Arztes sieben Bücher*. Translated and edited by I. Berendes. Leiden: Brill, 1914.
——. *Paulus Aegineta*. In *Corpus Medicorum Graecorum*, vol. IX, 1. Edited by J.L. Heiberg. Leipzig: G. Teubner, 1921.
Peucer, Caspar. *Commentarius de Praecipuis Generibus Divinationum*. Wittenberg, 1576.
Pfaff, Ch. M. *Introductio in historiam theologiae literariam*. Tübingen, 1725.
Philadelphus, George [pseud.]. *An Answer to the Right Way of Trying Prophets by F.M. [Francis Moult] . . . as delivered in a Sermon, November 9, 1707*. London, 1708.
Pictet, Bénédict. *Lettre sur ceux qui se croyent inspirés*. Geneva, 1721.
Pitcarnius, Alexander. *Compendiaria et perfacilis Physiologiae Idea, Aristotelicae forte*

conformior . . . Una cum anatome Cartesianismi in qua Cartesii speculationes metaphysicae examini subjiciuntur. London, 1676.

Platter, Felix. *Observationum . . . libri tres*. Basel, 1614.

———. *Praxeos Medicai Tomi tres*. Basel, 1625; first edition, 1602.

Poisson, Nicolas-Joseph. *Commentaire, ou Remarques sur la Méthode de René Descartes*. Vendôme, 1670, 1671. Facsimile edition in the series "The Philosophy of Descartes." Edited by W. Doney. New York and London: Garland, 1987.

Pomponatius, P. *De naturalium effectuum causis sive De incantationibus*. 1567. Reprint. Hildesheim, New York: Georg Olms Verlag, 1970.

———. *Les Causes des merveilles de la nature ou les enchantements*. With an Introduction by H. Busson. Paris, 1930.

Ponce de Santa Cruz, Antonio. *Praelectiones Vallisoletanae, in Librum Magni Hipp. Coi de morbo sacro*. Madrid, 1631.

Psellus, Michael. *De Operatione Deaemonum Dialogus*. Translated into Latin by Gilbert Gaulminus. Paris, 1515. Translated into French by Pierre Moreau under the title, *Traicté par dialogue de l'énergie ou opération des diables*. Paris, 1576.

Rapin, P. *Réflexions sur la philosophie ancienne et moderne, et sur l'usage qu'on doit faire pour la religion*. Paris, 1676; subsequent editions in Rapin's *Oeuvres*. Amsterdam, 1709, 1725. Translated into English under the title *The Whole Critical Works of Mons. Rapin, newly done into English by Several Hands*. London: 1706; 3rd ed., 1731.

Régis, P.S. *Réponse au livre qui a pour titre "P.D. Huetti Censura Philosophiae Cartesianae"*. Paris, 1691.

Reflections on Sir Richard Bulkeley's Answer to Several Treatises. London, 1708.

Reflections upon a Letter concerning Enthusiasm, to my Lord*****. In another Letter to a Lord. London: Printed for H. Clements, 1709.

[Rochon, Ant.]. *Lettre d'un Philosophe à un Cartésien de ses Amis*. Published by le Père Paradies. Paris, 1685.

Rufus of Ephesus. *Oeuvres de Rufus d'Ephèse*. Edited by Ch. Daremberg and Ch. E. Ruelle. Paris: l'Imprimerie Nationale, 1879.

Saxonia, Hercules. *Pantheum Medicinae Selectum, sive Medicinae Practicae Templum, Omnibus Omnium fere Morborum Insultibus Commune, Libris Undecim Distinctum*. Frankfurt, 1603.

———. *De Melancholia Tractatus*. Venice, 1620.

Schoock, Martin. *Admiranda Methodus Novae Philosophiae Renati Descartes*. Utrecht, 1643.

Sennert, Daniel. *Opera Omnia*. Paris, 1641.

———. *Institutionum medicinae libri V*. Wittenberg, 1611. Translated into English under the title *Nine Books of Physick and Chirurgy Written by that Great and Learned Physitian, Dr. Sennertus*. London, 1658.

———. *Medicinae Practicae Lib. I*. Paris, 1628. In Sennert. *Opera Omnia*. Paris, 1641.

Sergeant, John. *The Method to Science*. London, 1696.

———. *Raillery defeated by Cold Reason: or the New Cartesian Method of Arguing and Answering Expos'd. In a letter to all lovers of Science, Candour and Civility*. London, 1699.

[Sergeant, John] J.S. *Non Ultra, or a Letter to a Learned Cartesian*. London, 1698.

Shaftesbury, Anthony Ashley Cooper, third Earl of. *Select Sermons of Dr. Whichcote*. London, 1698.

———. *A Letter Concerning Enthusiasm, to My Lord******. London, 1708.

———. *An Old-Spelling, Critical Edition of Shaftesbury's "Letter Concerning Enthusiasm" and "Sensum communis: An Essay on the Freedom of Wit and Humour"*. Edited by Richard B. Wolf. New York and London: Garland, 1988.

———. [Anon.]. *Several Letters Written by a Noble Lord to a Young Man at the University*. London, 1716.

———. *Characteristicks of Men, Manners, Opinions, Times*. London, 1732; first published edition, 1711.

Smith, John. *Select Discourses*. London, 1672; first published posthumously by John Worthington in 1660. Reprint. Delmar, N.Y.: Scholars' Facsimiles and Reprints, 1979.

Sonntag, Christopher. *Animadversiones centum miscellae in Fanaticismum tam veterem quam recentiorem.* N.p. 1701.

South, Robert. *Sermons Preached Upon Several Occasions.* 7 vols. Oxford: Clarendon Press, 1823. 2 vols. New York, 1870.

Spanheim, Friedrich. *Disputationes Anabaptisticae.* Leiden, 1643–1646.

———. *Diatriba Historica de Origine, Progressu, et Sectis Anabaptistarum.* Published as an appendix to Johann Cloppenburg. *Gangraena Theologicae Anabaptisticae.* Franeker, 1645, 1656. Translated into English under the title, *Englands Warning by Germanies Woe: or An Historicall Narration, of the Originall, Progresse, Tenets, Names and severall Sects of the Anabaptists, in Germany and the Low Countries.* London, 1646.

———. *Dubiorum Evangelicorum.* Geneva: Chouet, 1655.

Spanheim, Friedrich, Jr. *Selectae Controversiae cum Enthusiastici.* In Friedrich Spanheim. *Opera Omnia.* Vol. 3. Leiden, 1703.

Spinckes, Nathaniel. *The New Pretenders to Prophecy Examined, and their Pretences Shewn to be Groundless and False.* London, 1709.

Sprat, Thomas. *The History of the Royal Society of London, for the Improving of Natural Knowledge.* Edited by J.I. Cope and H.W. Jones. St. Louis, Miss.: Washington University Studies, 1958.

Stephens, W. *Sermons on Several Subjects.* Oxford, 1737.

Stillingfleet, Edward. *Origines Sacrae: or a Rational Account of the Grounds of Christian Faith, as to the Truth and Divine Authority of the Scriptures and the matters therein contain'd.* First edition, London, 1662; third edition, corrected and amended, London, 1666.

Stubbe, Henry. *A Censure upon Certain Passages contained in the History of the Royal Society.* Oxford, 1670.

———. *The Plus Ultra Reduced to a Non Plus.* London, 1670.

———. *Campanella Reviv'd or, an Enquiry into the History of the Royal Society, Whether the Virtuosi there do not pursue the Projects of Campanella for the reducing of England into Popery.* London, 1670.

———. *A Reply unto the Letter written to Mr. Henry Stubbe in Defense of the History of the Royal Society.* Oxford, 1671.

———. *The Lord Bacon's Relation of the Sweating-Sickness Examined.* London 1671.

Stumpf, Johann. *Gemeiner loblicher Eydgenoschafft Stetten, Landen und Völckeren Chronickwirdiger thaaten beschreybung.* 2 vols. Zurich, 1548.

Sturm, Johann-Christoph. *De Cartesianis et Cartesianismo Brevis Dissertatio.* Altdorff, 1677.

Swift, Jonathan. *A Tale of a Tub. Written for the Universal Improvement of Mankind.* Fifth edition, London, 1720. In *A Tale of a Tub to which is added The Battle of the Books and the Mechanical Operation of the Spirit by Jonathan Swift.* Edited by A.C. Guthkelch and D. Nichol Smith. Oxford: At the Clarendon Press, 1920.

[Swift, Jonathan]. *A Discourse Concerning the Mechanical Operation of the Spirit. In a Letter to a Friend. A Fragment.* London, 1710. In *A Tale of a Tub.* Edited by A.C. Guthkelch and D. Nichol Smith. Oxford: At the Clarendon Press, 1920.

Tillotson, John. *The Works of Dr. John Tillotson . . . containing four sermons and discourses.* London, 1696.

Trallianus, Alexander. *De Arte Medica Libri Duodecim.* Translated into Latin by J.G. Andernacus. In *Medicae Artis Principale post Hippocratem et Galenum.* Edited by H. Estienne. Paris, 1567.

———. *Alexander von Tralles: Original-Text und Übersetzung, Ein Beitrag zur Geschichte der Medizin.* Translated and edited by T. Puschmann. 2 vols. Vienna, 1878. Reprint. Amsterdam: Hakkert, 1963.

———. *Oeuvres médicales d'Alexandre de Tralles.* Volumes 2–4. Translated and edited by F. Brunet. Paris, 1933.

[Trenchard, John]. *The Natural History of Superstition.* London, 1709.

Turretin, Samuel. *Préservatif contre le fanatisme, ou réfutation des pretendus inspirez des derniers siècles.* Geneva, 1723.

Vergilius, Polydore. *Dialogarum de Prodigiis Libri Tres.* Basel, 1533.

Vernous, Marc. *A Preservative Against the False Prophets of the Times: Or, A Treatise Concerning*

True and False Prophets, With their Characters: Likewise A Letter to Mr. Maximilian Misson, upon the Subject of the Miracles, pretended to be wrought by the French Prophets, and their Adherents. London, 1708.

Voetius, Gisbertus. *Testimonium Academiae Ultraiectinae, et Narratio Historica qua defensae, qua exterminatae novae Philosophiae.* Utrecht, 1643.

Ward, Richard. *The Life of the Learned and Pious Dr. Henry More.* London, 1710. Edited with an introduction by M.F. Howard. London, 1911.

Wharton, Henry. *The Enthusiasm of the Church of Rome demonstrated in some observations upon the life of Ignatius Loyola.* London, 1688.

Whiston, William. *Astronomical Principles of Religion, Natural and Reveal'd.* London, 1717.

Whitfeld, William. *A Discourse of Enthusiasm.* London, 1698.

Wierus, Johann. [Johann Weyer]. *De Praestigiis Daemonum, et Incantationibus, ac Veneficijs, Libri V.* Basel, 1563. Translated into French under the title, *Histoires, disputes et discours des illusions et impostures des diables, des magiciens infâmes, sorcières et empoisonneurs.* Geneva, 1579. Reprint edition, together with the two dialogues by Thomas Erastus on the subject of witches. Paris, 1885.

Willis, Thomas. *Two Discourses Concerning the Soul of Brutes.* In *Dr. Thomas Willis's Practice of physick, being the Whole Works.* Translated by S. Pordage. London, 1684. First published in Latin under the title *De Anima Brutorum.* London, 1672.

Woodward, J. *Remarks on the Modern Prophets, and on Some Arguments Lately published in their Defense.* London, 1708.

Zwingli, Huldreich, *Sämtliche Werke.* Edited by E. Egli et al. Berlin, Leipzig, Zurich, 1905–. In *Corpus Reformatorum.* Vols. 88 ff.

SECONDARY LITERATURE

Aldridge, Alfred Owen. "Shaftesbury and the Deist Manifesto." *Transactions of the American Philosophical Society* 41 (1951): 297–385.

Allen, Michael J.B. *Marsilio Ficino and the Phaedran Charioteer.* Berkeley: University of California Press, 1981.

Anglo, S. "Melancholia and Witchcraft: the debate between Wier, Bodin and Scot." In *Folie et déraison à la Renaissance,* 209–28. Travaux de l'Institut pour l'étude de la Renaissance et d'Humanisme. Brussells, 1973.

Aronson, Samuel. "The Gravitational Theory of George-Louis Le Sage." *The Natural Philosopher* 3 (1964): 51–74.

Ashworth, William B. Jr. "Natural History, Antiquarianism, and the Demise of the Emblematic Cosmos." In *Reappraisals of the Scientific Revolution,* edited by David C. Lindberg and Robert S. Westman, 303–332. Cambridge: Cambridge University Press, 1990.

Babb, L. *Sanity in Bedlam: A Study of Robert Burton's Anatomy of Melancholy.* East Lansing: Michigan State College Press, 1959.

———. *The Elizabethan Malady: A Study of Melancholy in English Literature from 1580 to 1642.* East Lansing: Michigan State College Press, 1951.

Bennett, G.V. "Conflict in the Church." In *Britain after the Glorious Revolution* edited by Geoffrey Holmes, 155–175. 1969. Reprint paperback, London: Macmillan, 1982.

Betts, C.J. *Early Deism in France.* The Hague: Martinus Nijhoff, 1984.

Beyreuther, Erich. *Geschichte des Pietismus.* Stuttgart: J.F. Steinkopf Verlag, 1978.

Bizer, Ernst. "Die reformierten Orthodoxie und der Cartesianismus." *Zeitschrift für Theologie und Kirche* 55 (1958): 306–372.

Blekastad, Milada. *Comenius: Versuch eines Umrisses von Leben, Werk und Schicksal des Jan Amos Komensky.* Oslo: Universitetsforlaget, 1969.

Boas, Marie. *Robert Boyle and Seventeenth-Century Chemistry.* Cambridge: Cambridge University Press, 1958.

Boland, Paschal. *The Concept of Discretio Spirituum in John Gerson's 'De Probatione Spirituum' and 'De Distinctione Verarum Visionum à Falsis'*. Studies in Sacred Theology (Second Series), No. 112. Washington: Catholic University of America, 1959.

Borgeaud, Charles. *Histoire de l'Université de Genève.* Vol. I: *L'Académie de Calvin, 1559–1798.* Geneva: Georg et Co., 1900.

Bossy, John. *The English Catholic Community, 1570–1850.* London: Darton, Longman and Todd, 1975.

Bost, Charles. "Les Prophètes du Languedoc en 1701–1702." *Revue historique* 136 (January–April, 1921): 1–37; 137 (May–June, 1921): 1–31.

———. "Les 'Prophètes des Cévennes' au XVIIIe siècle." *Revue d'histoire et de philosophie religieuse* 5 (1925): 401–430.

Bouillier, F. *Histoire de la philosophie cartésienne.* Paris: Delgrave et Cie., 1868; Geneva: Slatkine Reprints, 1970.

Bourke, Vernon J. "An Illustration of the Attitude of the Early French Jesuits toward Cartesianism." In *Cartesio: nel terzo centenario del "Discoroso del Metodo",* 129–137. A special supplement to vol. 19 of *Rivista di Filosofia Neo-Scolastica* (July 1937).

Bowles, G. "Physical, Human and Divine Attraction in the Life and Thought of George Cheyne." *Annals of Science* 31 (1974): 473–488.

Boylan, Michael. "Henry More and the Spirit of Nature." *Journal of the History of Philosophy* 18 (1980): 395–405.

Braeuer, Siegfried. "Die Vorgeschichte von Luthers 'Ein Brief an die Fürsten zu Sachsen von dem aufrührerischen Geist." *Luthers Jahrbuch* 47 (1980): 40–70.

Braithwaite, William Charles, *The Second Period of Quakerism.* London, 1921.

Brann, Noel L. "The Renaissance Passion of Melancholy: The Paradox of its Cultivation and Resistance." Ph.D. dissertation, Stanford University, 1965.

———. "The Conflict between Reason and Magic in Seventeenth-Century England: A Case Study of the Vaughan-More Debate." *Huntington Library Quarterly* 43 (1980): 103–126.

Brecht, Martin. *Martin Luther. Shaping and Defining the Reformation 1521–1532.* Translated by James L. Schaaf. Minneapolis: Fortress Press, 1990.

Brockliss, L.W.B. *French Higher Education in the Seventeenth and Eighteenth Centuries: A Cultural History.* Oxford: Clarendon Press, 1987.

Brown, Theodore, *The Mechanical Philosophy and the "Animal Oeconomy".* New York: Arno Press, 1981.

Brunet, F. *Oeuvres médicales d'Alexandre de Tralles.* Vol. 1: *Alexandre de Tralles et la Médecine Byzantine.* Paris, 1933.

Brunet, Pierre. *L'Introduction des théories de Newton en France au XVIII siècle.* Paris, 1931; Geneva: Slatkine Reprints, 1970.

Budé, Eugène de. *Vie de Bénédict Pictet, théologien genevois, (1655–1724).* Lausanne: Bridel, 1874.

Burke, Peter. *Popular Culture in Early Modern Europe.* London: Temple Smith, 1978.

Burnham, Frederick B. "The More-Vaughan Controversy: The Revolt against Philosophical Enthusiasm." *Journal of the History of Ideas* 35 (1974): 33–49.

Capp, Bernard S. *The Fifth Monarchy Men.* London: Faber and Faber, 1972.

Centore, F.F. *Robert Hooke's Contribution to Mechanics: A Study in Seventeenth Century Natural Philosophy.* The Hague: Martinus Nijhoff, 1970.

Clasen, Claus-Peter. *Anabaptism. A Social History, 1525–1618. Switzerland, Austria, Moravia, South and Central Germany.* Ithaca, N.Y.: Cornell University Press, 1972.

Clément, L'abbé. "Le Cartésianisme à Vendôme: Le Père Nicolas-Joseph Poisson (1637–1710)." *Bulletin de la Societé archéologique scientifique et littéraire du Vendômois* 37 (1898): 258–275; 38 (1899): 23–46; 164–175.

Cohen, Gustave. *Ecrivains français en Hollande dans la première moitié du XVIIe siècle.* Paris: Champion, 1920.

Cole, John R. *The Olympian Dreams and Youthful Rebellion of René Descartes.* Urbana and Chicago: University of Illinois Press, 1992.

Collinson, Patrick. *The Elizabethan Puritan Movement.* London: Jonathan Cape, 1967.

Cooperman, Bernard. "Eliahu Montalto's 'Suitable and Incontrovertible Propositions' A Seventeenth-Century Anti-Christian Polemic." In *Jewish Thought in the Seventeenth Century*, edited by I. Twersky and B. Septimus, 469–497. Cambridge Mass.: Harvard University Press, 1987.

Cope, Jackson I. " 'The Cupri-Cosmites': Glanvill on Latitudinarian Anti-Enthusiasm." *The Huntington Library Quarterly* 17 (1954): 269–286.

———. *Joseph Glanvill, Anglican Apologist* St. Louis: Washington University Studies, 1956.

Cotton, Charles. "Meric Casaubon, Canon of Canterbury 1628–1671." *Friends of the Canterbury Cathedral* 11 (1938): 51–57.

Cragg, G.R. *From Puritanism to the Age of Reason*. Cambridge: Cambridge University Press, 1950.

Cumont, F. *Oriental Religions in Roman Paganism*. New York: Dover, 1956.

Davis, Natalie Z. *Society and Culture in Early Modern France*. Stanford: Stanford University Press, 1975.

Dayre, J. *Jérôme Cardan (1501–1576) Esquisse biographique*. Grenoble: Allier, 1928.

Debus Allen G., ed. *Science and Education in the Seventeenth Century: The Webster-Ward Debate*. London: Macdonald, New York: Elsevier, 1970.

Delatte, A. "Les conceptions de l'enthousiasme chez les philosophes présocratiques." *L'Antiquité Classique* 3 (May, 1934).

Delumeau, Jean. *Le Catholicisme entre Luther et Voltaire*. "Nouvelle Clio". Paris: P.U.F., 1971.

DePorte, M.V. *Nightmares and Hobbyhorses: Swift, Sterne and Augustan Ideas of Madness*. San Marino, California: The Huntington Library, 1974.

Dewhurst, Kenneth. *Thomas Willis as a Physician*. William Andrews Clark Memorial Library. Los Angeles: University of California Press, 1964.

Dewhurst, Kenneth. *Thomas Willis's Oxford Lectures* Oxford: Sanford Publications, 1980.

Diamond, Craig. "Public Identity in Restoration England: From Prophetic to Economic." Ph.D. diss., Johns Hopkins University, Baltimore, 1982.

Dibon, Paul. *La Philosophie néerlandaise au siècle d'or: L'enseignement philosophique dans les universités à l'époque pré-cartésienne, 1575–1650*. Amsterdam: Elsevier, 1954.

———. "Lettres de S. Desmarets à Claude Saumaise, 1644–1657." *Lias* 1 (1974): 267–269.

Diethelm O., and Heffernan, T.F. "Felix Platter and Psychiatry." *Journal of the History of the Behavioral Sciences* 1 (1965): 10–23.

Dobbs, B.J.T. *The Foundations of Newton's Alchemy: or, 'The Hunting of the Greene Lyon'*. Cambridge: Cambridge University Press, 1975; paperback ed., 1983.

———. *The Janus Faces of Genius: The Role of Alchemy in Newton's Thought*. Cambridge: Cambridge University Press, 1991.

Domson, Charles A. *Nicholas Fatio de Duillier and the Prophets of London*. New York: Arno Press, 1981.

Donovan, D.G. "Robert Burton, Anglican Minister." In *Renaissance Papers*, edited by G.W. Williams, 33–9. The South Eastern Renaissance Conference, 1967.

———. "Robert Burton, 1924–1966" in *Elizabethan Bibliographies*. Supplement 10 (1968): 35–46.

Dunn, John. "The Claim to Freedom of Conscience: Freedom of Speech, Freedom of Thought, Freedom of Worship?" In *From Persecution to Toleration: The Glorious Revolution and Religion in England*, edited by O.P. Grell, J.I. Israel and N. Tyacke, 171–193. Oxford: Clarendon Press, 1991.

Eeg-Olofsson, Leif. *The Conception of the Inner Light in Robert Barclay's Theology: A Case Study in Quakerism*. Studia Theologia Lundensia. Lund: CWK Gleerup, 1954.

Eisenstadt, S.N. ed. *Max Weber on Charisma and Institution Building*. Chicago and London: University of Chicago Press, 1968.

———. "The Axial Age: the Emergence of Transcendental Visions and the Rise of Clerics." *Archives Européennes de Sociologie* 29 (1982): 294–314.

———. "Explorations in the Sociology of Knowledge: The Soteriological Axis in the

Construction of Domains of Knowledge." In *Cultural Traditions and Worlds of Knowlege: Explorations in the Sociology of Knowledge*. Edited by Shmuel N. Eisenstadt and Ilana Friedrich Silber, 1–71. Knowledge and Society: Studies in the Sociology of Culture Past and Present, vol. 7. Greenwich, Connecticut, London, England: JAI press, 1988.

Emerson, Roger L. "Latitudinarianism and the English Deists." In *Deism, Masonry and the Enlightenment. Essays honoring Alfred Owen Aldridge*, edited by J.A. Leo Lemey. Newark: University of Delaware Press, 1987.

Fast, Heinold. *Heinrich Bullinger und die Täufer*. Weierhof, Pfalz: Mennonitischen Geschichtsverein, 1959.

Feingold, Mordechai. *The Mathematicians' Apprenticeship: Science, Universities and Society in England, 1564–1640*. Cambridge: Cambridge University Press, 1984.

Fichtner, G. "Neues zu Leben und Werk von Leonhart Fuchs aus seinen Briefen an Joachim Camerarius I. und II. in der Trew-Sammlung." *Gesnerus* 25 (1968): 65–82.

Figala, Karin and Petzold, Ulrich. "Physics and Poetry: Fatio de Duiller's *Ecloga* on Newton's *Principia*." *Archives Internationale d'Histoire des Sciences* 37 (1987): 316–349.

Fischer-Homberger, Esther. *Das Zirkuläre Irresein*. Zürich, 1968.

———. *Hypochondrie. Melancholie bis Neurose: Krankheiten und Zustandsbilder*. Bern, Stuttgart, Wien: Huber, 1970.

Fix, Andrew C. *Prophecy and Reason: The Dutch Collegiants in the Early Enlightenment*. Princeton: Princeton University Press, 1991.

Flashar, H. *Melancholie und Melancholiker in den Medizinischen Theorien der Antike*. Berlin: De Gruyter, 1966.

Foucault, Michel. *Histoire de la folie à l'âge classique*. 1961. Revised edition, Paris: Galllimard, 1972. English translation by Richard Howard, under the title *Madness and Civilization: A History of Insanity in the Age of Reason*. New York: Vintage Books, 1965.

Fox, R.A. *The Tangled Chain: The Structure of Disorder in the Anatomy of Melancholy*. Berkeley: University of California Press, 1976.

French, Peter J. *John Dee: The World of an Elizabethan Magus*. London: Routledge and Kegan Paul, 1972; paperback edition, 1984.

Friedenwald, H. "Montalto, a Jewish physician at the court of Marie de Medicis and Louis XIII." *Bulletin of the Institute of the History of Medicine* 3 (1935): 129–58.

Funkenstein, Amos. *Theology and the Scientific Imagination from the Middle Ages to the Seventeenth Century*. Princeton: Princeton University Press, 1986.

Gabbey, Alan. "Philosophia Cartesiana Triumphata: Henry More (1646–1671)". In *Problems of Cartesianism*, edited by Thomas M. Lennon, John M. Nichols, and John W. Davis, 171–250. Kingston and Montreal: McGill-Queen's University Press, 1982.

Gagnebin, Bernard. "Un Maniaque de l'introspection révélé par 35.000 cartes à jouer: Georges-Louis Le Sage." In *Mélanges d'histoire du livre et des bibliothèques offerts à M. Frantz Calot*, 145–157. Paris, 1960.

Garcia Archilla, Aurelio A. *The Theology of History and Apologetic Historiography in Heinrich Bullinger*. San Francisco: Mellen Research University Press, 1992.

Gardiner, J.K. "Elizabethan Psychology and Burton's *Anatomy of Melancholy*." *Journal of the History of Ideas* 38 (1977): 373–388.

Georges-Berthier, Auguste. "Le Mécanisme cartésien et la physiologie au XVIIe siècle." *Isis* 2 (1914): 37–89.

———. "Descartes et les Rose-Croix." *Revue de synthèse* 18 (1939): 9–30.

Gerth H.H. and Mills, C. Wright, eds., *From Max Weber: Essays in Sociology*. New York: Oxford University Press, 1946; paperback edition, 1958.

Gibson S. and Needham, F.R.D. "Lists of Burton's library." In *Oxford Bibliographical Society Proceedings and Papers*, edited by F. Madan, vol. I (1922–6), 222–46.

Goldie, Mark. "The Theory of Religious Intolerance in Restoration England." In

From Persecution to Toleration: The Glorious Revolution and Religion in England, edited by O.P. Grell, J.I. Israel and N. Tyacke, 331–368. Oxford: The Clarendon Press, 1991.

Gouhier, Henri. *Les premières pensées de Descartes*. Paris: Vrin, 1958.

Grean, Stanley. *Shaftesbury's Philosophy of Religion and Ethics: A Study in Enthusiasm*. Athens, Ohio: Ohio University Press, 1967.

Grell, O.P., Israel, J.I. and Tyacke, N., eds. *From Persecution to Toleration: The Glorious Revolution and Religion in England*. Oxford: The Clarendon Press, 1991.

Guinsburg, Arlene M. "Henry More, Thomas Vaughan and the Late Renaissance Magical Tradition." *Ambix* 27 (1980): 36–58.

Gunther, Robert W.T. *The Cutler Lectures of Robert Hooke*. Vol. 8 of *Early Science in Oxford*. Oxford: Dawson of Pall Mall, 1931.

Gür, André. "Un Précédent à la Condamnation du 'Contrat Social': L'Affaire Georges-Louis Le Sage (1752)." *Bulletin de la Société d'histoire et d'archéologie de Genève* 14 (1968): 77–94.

Hall, Thomas S. "Descartes' Physiological Method: Position, Principles, Examples." *Journal of the History of Biology* 3 (1970): 53–79.

Hall, A. Rupert and Hall, Marie Boas. "Newton's Theory of Matter." *Isis* 51 (1960): 131–144.

Hamilton, Alistair. *The Family of Love*. Cambridge: Cambridge University Press, 1981.

Hannaway, Owen. *The Chemists and the Word: The Didactic Origins of Chemistry*. Baltimore: Johns Hopkins University Press, 1975.

Harrison, J. *The Library of Isaac Newton*. Cambridge: Cambridge University Press, 1978.

Harth, Phillip. *Swift and Anglican Rationalism: The Religious Background of A Tale of A Tub*. Chicago: Chicago University Press, 1961.

Hatfield, G. "The Senses and the Fleshless Eye: The *Meditations* as Cognitive Exercises". In *Essays on Descartes' Meditations*, edited by Amelie O. Rorty, 45–79. Berkeley and Los Angeles: University of California Press, 1986.

Hay, D. *Polydore Vergil*. Oxford: Clarendon Press, 1952.

Hazard, Paul. *La crise de la conscience européenne* (Paris, 1935), translated into English by L. Lewis May under the title *The European Mind*. London: Hollis and Carter, 1953; Penguin ed. 1964, and subsequent paperback editions.

Heimann, P.M. " 'Nature is a perpetual Worker': Newton's Aether and Eighteenth-Century Natural Philosophy." *Ambix* 20 (1973): 1–8.

Heimann, P.M. "Voluntarism and Immanence: Conceptions of Nature in Eighteenth-Century Thought." *Journal of the History of Ideas* 39 (1978): 271–283.

Heimann, P.M., and McGuire, J.E. "Newtonian Forces and Lockean Powers: Concepts of Matter in Eighteenth-Century Thought." *Historical Studies in the Physical Sciences* 3 (1971): 237–246.

Henry, John. "Occult Qualities and the Experimental Philosophy: Active Principles in Pre-Newtonian Matter Theory." *History of Science* 24 (1986): 333–381.

———. "Henry More *versus* Robert Boyle: The Spirit of Nature and the Nature of Providence." In *Of Mysticism and Mechanism: Tercentenary Studies of Henry More (1614–1687)* edited by Sarah Hutton. Dordrecht: Kluwer, 1989.

Heyd, Michael. *Between Orthodoxy and the Enlightenment: Jean-Robert Chouet and the Introduction of Cartesian Science in the Academy of Geneva*. The Hague, Jerusalem: Martinus Nijhoff, Magnes Press, 1982.

———. "The Reaction to Enthusiasm in the Seventeenth Century: Towards an Integrative Approach." *Journal of Modern History* 53 (1981): 258–280.

———. "The Reaction to Enthusiasm in the Seventeenth Century: From Antistructure to Structure". *Religion* 15 (1985): 279–289.

Hill, Christopher. *The World Turned Upside Down: Radical Ideas During the English Revolution*. New York: Viking Press, 1973.

Holmes, Geoffrey. *The Trial of Doctor Sacheverell*. London: Methuen, 1973.

Hoppen, K. Theodore. *The Common Scientist in the Seventeenth Century: A Study of the Dublin Philosophical Society.* London: Routledge and Kegan Paul, 1970.

Horkheimer, Max, and Adorno, Theodore W. *Dialektik der Aufklärung* (1944). Translated into English by John Cumming, under the title *Dialectic of Enlightenment.* New York: Continuum, 1982.

Horsch, John. "An Inquiry into the Truth of Accusations of Fanaticism and Crime Against the Early Swiss Brethren." *Mennonite Quarterly Review* 8 (1934): 18–31, 73–89.

Howell, W.S. *Logic and Rhetoric in England 1500–1700.* Princeton: Princeton University Press, 1956.

Hunter, Michael. *Science and Society in Restoration England.* Cambridge: Cambridge University Press, 1981.

Hutchinson, Keith. "What Happened to Occult Qualities in the Scientific Revolution?" *Isis* 73 (1982): 233–253.

Hutin, Serge. *Henry More, Essai sur les doctrines théosophiques chez les Platoniciens de Cambridge.* Hildesheim: Olms, 1966.

Isler, Hansruedi. *Thomas Willis 1621–1675, Doctor and Scientist.* New York, London: Haefner, 1968.

Jackson, Stanley W. *Melancholia and Depression: From Hippocratic Times to Modern Times.* New Haven, London: Yale University Press, 1986.

——. "Melancholia and the Waning of the Humoral Theory." *Journal of the History of Medicine and Allied Sciences* 33 (1978): 370–371.

——. "Burton and Psychological Healing." *Journal of the History of Medicine and Allied Sciences* 44 (1989): 160–178.

Jacob, James R. *Robert Boyle and the English Revolution.* New York: Burt Franklin, 1977.

——. *Henry Stubbe, Radical Protestantism and the Early Enlightenment.* Cambridge: Cambridge University Press, 1983.

Jacob, Margaret C. *The Newtonians and the English Revolution: 1689–1720.* Ithaca: Cornell University Press, 1976.

——. *The Radical Enlightenment: Pantheists, Freemasons and Republicans.* London: Allen and Unwin, 1981.

——. "Newton and the French Prophets: New Evidence." *History of Science* 16 (1978): 134–142.

Jacob, James R. and Jacob, Margaret C. "The Anglican Origins of Modern Science: The Metaphysical Foundations of the Whig Constitution." *Isis* 71 (1980): 251–267.

Jaspers, Karl. *Vom Ursprung und Ziel der Geschichte.* Munich: Piper and Co., 1949. Translated into English by Michael Bullock, under the title *The Origin and Goal of History.* New Haven and London: Yale University Press, 1953.

Jobe, J.H. "Medical Theories of Melancholia in the 17th and early 18th Centuries." *Clio Medica* 11 (1976): 217–231.

Jones, R.F. *The Seventeenth Century.* Stanford: Stanford University Press, 1951.

Jordan-Smith, P. *Burton's Anatomy of 'Melancholy' and Burtoniana: A Checklist of a Part of the Collection in Memory of Sarah Bixby Smith (1871–1935).* Oxford: Printed for the Honnold Library, 1959.

——. *Bibliographia Burtoniana: A Study of Robert Burton's Writings.* Stanford: Stanford University Press, 1931.

Joutard, Philippe. *Les Camisards.* Paris: Coll. Archives, 1975.

——. *La légende des Camisards: Une sensibilité au passé.* Paris: Gallimard, 1977.

King, Lester S. *The Philosophy of Medicine: The Early Eighteenth Century.* Cambridge Mass.: Harvard University Press, 1978.

Klibansky, R., Panofsky E., and Saxl, F. *Saturn and Melancholy: Studies in the History of Natural Philosophy, Religion and Art.* New York: Basic Books, 1964.

Knox, R.A. *Enthusiasm: A Chapter in the History of Religion.* Oxford: Oxford University Press, 1950.

Kolakowski, Leszek. *Chrétiens sans église*. Paris: Gallimard, 1969.
Kors, Alan C. and Korshin, Paul J. *Anticipations of the Enlightenment in England, France, and Germany*. Philadelphia: University of Pennsylvania Press, 1987.
Koyré, A. *Mystiques, spirituels, alchimistes du XVI siècle allemand*. Paris: Gallimard, 1971.
Kreiser, B. Robert. *Miracles, Convulsions, and Ecclesiastical Politics in Early Eighteenth-Century Paris*. Princeton: Princeton University Press, 1978.
Kuhn, A.J. "Glory or Gravity: Hutchinson vs. Newton." *Journal of the History of Ideas* 22 (1961): 303–322.
Labrousse, Elisabeth. *Pierre Bayle*. 2 vols. The Hague: Martinus Nijfhoff, 1963, 1964.
Laplanche, François. *L'Evidence de Dieu chrétien. Religion, culture et société dans l'apologétique protestante de la France classique (1576–1670)*. Paris: Association de publication de la faculté de théologie protestante de Strasbourg, 1983.
——. *L'Ecriture, Le Sacré et l'Histoire*. Amsterdam and Maarssen: APA-Holland University Press, 1986.
Laudan, Larry. *Science and Hypothesis*. Dordrecht: Reidel, 1981.
——. "The Medium and its Message: A Study of Some Philosophical Controversies about Ether." In *Conceptions of Ether. Studies in the History of Ether Theories 1740–1900*, edited by G.N. Cantor and M.J.S. Hodge. Cambridge: Cambridge University Press, 1981.
Lenoble, Robert. *Mersenne ou la naissance du mécanisme*. Paris: Vrin, 1943.
Lichtenstein, Aharon. *Henry More: The Rational Theology of a Cambridge Platonist*. Cambridge, Mass.: Harvard University Press, 1962.
Lindberg, David C. and Numbers, Ronald L., eds. *God and Nature: Historical Essays on the Encounter between Christianity and Science*. Berkeley and Los Angeles: University of California Press, 1986.
——. "The Genesis of Kepler's theory of Light: Light Metaphysics from Plotinus to Kepler." *Osiris* 2 (1986): 5–42.
Lindeboom, G.A. *Descartes and Medicine*. Amsterdam: Rodolpi, 1979.
——. *Dutch Medical Biography. A Biographical Dictionary of Dutch Physicians and Surgeons 1475–1975*. Amsterdam: Rodolpi, 1984.
Lloyd, Arnold. *Quaker Social History: 1669–1738*. London: Longmans, 1948.
Locher, Gottfried W. *Zwingli's Thought: New Perspectives*. Studies in the History of Christian Thought, vol. 25. Leiden: Brill, 1981.
Luyendijk-Elshout, Antonie M. "Oeconomia Animalis, Pores and Particles." In *Leiden University in the Seventeenth Century: An Exchange of Learning*, edited by Th.H. Lunsingh Scheurleer and G.H.M. Posthumus Meyjes, 295–307. Leiden: Brill, 1975.
Lyons, B.G. *Voices of Melancholy: Studies in Literary Treatments of Melancholy in Renaissance England*. London: Routledge and Kegan Paul, 1971.
Mandrou, Robert. *Magistrats et sorciers en France au XVIIe siècle*. Paris: Seuil, 1968. Reprint, 1980.
Manuel, Frank E. *Isaac Newton Historian*. Cambridge: Cambridge University Press, 1963.
——. *A Portrait of Isaac Newton*. Cambridge, Mass.: Harvard University Press, 1968. Reprint, London: Frederick Muller, 1980.
——. *The Religion of Isaac Newton*. Oxford: The Clarendon Press, 1974.
——. *The Broken Staff: Judaism through Christian Eyes*. Cambridge Mass.: Harvard University Press: 1992.
Martin, H.-J. *Livre, pouvoirs et société à Paris au XVIIe siècle*. Geneva: Droz, 1969.
McAdoo, H.R. *The Spirit of Anglicanism: A Survey of Anglican Theological Method in the Seventeenth Century*. London: Adams and Charles Black, 1965.
McDonald, Michael. *Mystical Bedlam: Madness, Anxiety, and Healing in Seventeenth-Century England*. Cambridge: Cambridge University Press, 1981.
McGuire, J.E. "Force, Active Principles, and Newton's Invisible Realm." *Ambix* 15 (1968): 154–208.
——. "Boyle's Conception of Nature." *Journal of the History of Ideas* 33 (1972): 523–542.

——. "Neoplatonism and Active Principles: Newton and the *Corpus Hermeticum*." In *Hermeticism and the Scientific Revolution*, 95–142. Los Angeles: William Andrews Clark Memorial Library, 1977.

McGuire, J.E. and Rattansi, P.M. "Newton and the 'Pipes of Pan'." *Notes and Records of the Royal Society of London* 21 (1966): 108–143.

McMullin, Ernan. *Newton on Matter and Activity.* Notre Dame, Indiana: University of Notre Dame Press, 1978.

Mesnard, Pierre. "L'Esprit de la physiologie Cartésienne." *Archives de Philosophie* 13 (1937): 181–220.

Metzger, Hélène. *Attraction universelle et religion naturelle chez quelques commentateurs anglais de Newton.* Philosophie et histoire de la pensée scientifique, IV–VI. Paris: Hermann, 1938.

Midelfort, H.C. Erik. *Witch Hunting in Southwestern Germany, 1562–1648.* Stanford: Stanford University Press, 1972.

Millen, Ron. "The Manifestation of Occult Qualities in the Scientific Revolution." In *Religion, Science and Worldview: Essays in Honor of Richard S. Westfall*, edited by Margaret J. Osler and Paul L. Farber, 185–216. Cambridge: Cambridge University Press, 1985.

Morris, John. "Descartes' Natural Light." *Journal of the History of Philosophy* 11 (1973): 169–187.

Moss, Jean Dietz. *"Godded with God": Hendrick Niclaes and His Family of Love.* Transactions of The American Philosophical Society, vol. 71, part 8. Philadelphia, 1981.

Muchembled, Robert. *Culture populaire et culture des élites dans la France moderne (XVe–XVIIIe siècles). Essai.* Paris: Flammarion, 1978.

Murray, James P. "Charity, Zeal and Spiritual Authority in Britain, 1660–1700." Ph.D. diss., Johns Hopkins University, Baltimore, 1986.

Mühlpfordt, Günther. "Luther und die 'Linken': eine Untersuchung seiner Schwärmer-terminologie." In *Martin Luther: Leben, Werk, Wirkung*, edited by Günther Volger, 325–45. Berlin: Academie Verlag, 1983.

Nauta, D. *Samuel Maresius.* Amsterdam: H.J. Paris, 1935.

Nicolson, Marjorie H. *Conway Letters.* New Haven: Yale University Press, 1930.

——. "The Early Stages of Cartesianism in England." *Studies in Philology* 26 (1929): 356–74.

——. "Christ's College and the Latitude-Men." *Modern Philology* 27 (1929–30): 35–53.

Niebyl, Peter H. "The Non Naturals." *Bulletin of the History of Medicine* 45 (1971): 486–492.

O'Malley, Charles D. *Michael Servetus.* Philadelphia: American Philosophical Society, 1953.

O'Neill, Y. Violé. "The history of the publication of Bernard of Gordon's *Liber de Conservatione Vitae Humanae.*" *Sudhoff Archiv für Geschichte der Medizin und der Naturwissenschaften* 49, no. 3 (September 1965).

Oberman, Heiko A. *Luther: Man between God and the Devil.* Translated by E. Walliser-Schwarzbart. New Haven: Yale University Press, 1989.

Oyer, John S. *Lutheran Reformers against Anabaptists.* The Hague: Martinus Nijhoff, 1964.

Paknadel, F. *"Lettre Concernant L'Enthousiasme* de Shaftesbury." In *L'Enthousiasme dans le monde Anglo-Americain aux XVIIe et XVIIIe siècles*, edited by D. Bulckaen, 109–120. Actes du Colloque tenu à Paris les 20 et 21 octobre 1989.

Perry, Ruth. *The Celebrated Mary Astell: An Early English Feminist.* Chicago: Chicago University Press, 1986.

Pitassi, Maria Cristina. *Le Philosophe et l'écriture: John Locke exégète de Saint Paul.* Cahiers de la Revue de Théologie et de Philosophie, 14 (Geneva, Lausanne, Neuchâtel, 1990).

Popkin, Richard H. *The History of Scepticism from Erasmus to Spinoza.* Berkeley, Los Angeles: University of California Press, 1979.

———. "Newton and Maimonides." In *A Straight Path. Studies in Medieval Philosophy and Culture. Essays in Honor of Arthur Hyman*, edited by Ruth Link-Salinger et al., 216–229. Washington D.C.: Catholic University of America Press, 1988.

———. "Some Further Comments on Newton and Maimonides." In *Essays on the Context, Nature and Influence of Isaac Newton's Theology*, edited by James E. Force and Richard H. Popkin, 1–7. Dordrecht, Boston, London: Kluwer Academic Publishers, 1990.

Prévost, Pierre. *Notice de la vie et des écrits de George-Louis Le Sage de Genève.* Geneva, 1805.

Rabb, Theodore K. *The Struggle for Stability in Early Modern Europe.* New York: Oxford University Press, 1975.

Rand, Benjamin. *The Life, Unpublished Letters, and Philosophical Regimen of Anthony, Earl of Shaftesbury.* London: Macmillan, 1900.

Rather, L.J. "The 'Six Things Non-Natural': A Note on the Origins and Fate of a Doctrine and a Phrase." *Clio Medica* 3 (1968): 337–347.

Rattansi, P.M. "Paracelsus and the Puritan Revolution." *Ambix* 40 (1963): 24–32.

———. "The Helmontian-Galenist Controversy in Restoration England." *Ambix* 21 (1964): 1–23.

Renaker, D. "Robert Burton's palinodes." *Studies in Philology* 76 (1979): 162–81.

Robbins, Caroline. *The Eighteenth Century Commonwealthmen.* Cambridge, Mass: Harvard University Press, 1958.

Rodis-Lewis, Geneviève. *Lettres à Regius.* Bibliothèque des Textes Philosophiques. Paris: Vrin, 1959.

Rood, W. *Comenius and the Low Countries.* Amsterdam: A.L. van Gendt and Co., 1970.

Rosen, George. "Enthusiasm: 'a dark lanthorn of the spirit'." *Bulletin of the History of Medicine* 42 (1968): 393–421.

Rothkopf, A. "Manie und Melancholie bei Aretaios von Kappadokien." *Confinia Psychiatrica* 17 (1974).

Rothkrug, Lionel. *Opposition to Louis XIV: The Political and Social Origins of the French Enlightenment.* Princeton: Princeton University Press, 1965.

Rousseau, G.S. "Mysticism and Millenarianism: 'Immortal Dr. Cheyne'." In *Millenarianism and Messianism in English Literature and Thought 1650–1800*, edited by R.H. Popkin, 81–126. Clark Library Lectures, 1981–1982. Leiden: Brill, 1988.

Ruesche, Franz. "Zur Lehre Descartes' von den 'Lebensgeistern'." *Philosophisches Jahrbuch* 60 (1950): 450–456.

Ruestow, Edward G. *Physics at Seventeenth and Eighteenth Century Leiden: Philosophy and the New Science in the University.* The Hague: Martinus Nijhoff, 1973.

Ryan, John K. "Anthony Legrand (1629–1699): Franciscan and Cartesian." *The New Scholasticism* 9 (1935): 226–250.

Sarton, George. "Lilium Medicinae." In *Medieval Studies in Honor of J.D.M. Ford*, edited by V.T. Holmes and A.J. Denomy. Cambridge, Mass.: Harvard University Press, 1948.

Schwartz, Benjamin, ed. "Wisdom, Revelation and Doubt: Perspectives on the First Millennium B.C." *Daedalus* (Spring, 1975).

Schwartz, Hillel. *Knaves, Fools, Madmen and that Subtile Effluvium: A Study of the Opposition to the French Prophets in England, 1706–1710.* Gainsville: University Presses of Florida, 1978.

———. *The French Prophets: The History of A Millenarian Group in Eighteenth-Century England.* Berkeley, Los Angeles, London: University of California Press, 1980.

Screach, M.A. *Ecstasy and the Praise of Folly.* London: Duckworth, 1980.

———. *Montaigne and Melancholy.* London: Duckworth, 1983.

———. "Good Madness in Christendom." In *The Anatomy of Madness: Essays in the History of Psychiatry*, edited by W.F. Bynum, Roy Porter and Michael Shepard, vol. I, 25–39. London and New York: Tavistock, 1985.

Sebba, Gregor "Adrien Baillet and the Genesis of His *Vie de M. Des-Cartes*." In *Problems of Cartesianism*, edited by Thomas M. Lennon, et al., 9–60. Toronto: University of Toronto Press, 1982.

Secret, François. "G. Postel et les courants prophétiques de la Renaissance." *Studi Francesi*, 3 (1957).

Seigel, Rudolph E. *Galen's System of Physiology and Medicine*. Basel, New York: S. Karger, 1968.

Sena, John F. "Melancholic Madness and the Puritans." *Harvard Theological Review* 66 (1973): 293–309.

Serrurier, Cornelia. *Descartes, l'homme et le penseur*. Paris: P.U.F.; Amsterdam: Editions Français, 1951.

Shapin, Steven, and Schaffer, Simon. *Leviathan and the Air Pump: Hobbes, Boyle and the Experimental Life*. Princeton: Princeton University Press, 1985. Reprint, paperback, 1989.

Shapiro, Barbara. *John Wilkins, 1614–1672*. Berkeley: University of California Press, 1969.

——. *Probability and Certainty in Seventeenth-Century England*. Princeton: Princeton University Press, 1983.

——. "Latitudinarianism and Science." *Past and Present* 40 (1968): 16–41.

Shea, William R. *The Magic of Numbers and Motion: The Scientific Career of René Descartes*. Canton, MA.: Science History Publications U.S.A., 1991.

Simon, I. *Three Restoration Divines: Barrow, South, Tillotson. Selected Sermons*. Paris: Société Les Belles Lettres, 1967.

Simon, J.R. *Robert Burton (1577–1640) et l'Anatomie de la Mélancolie*. Paris: Didier, 1964.

Snyder, David C. "Faith and Reason in Locke's *Essay*." *Journal of the History of Ideas* 47 (1986): 197–213.

Sortais, Gaston. "Le Cartésianisme chez les Jésuites français au XVIIe et au XVIIIe siècle." *Archives de Philosophie* 6, no. 3 (1929): 56–62.

Spiller, Michael R.S. *"Concerning Natural Experimental Philosophie": Meric Casaubon and the Royal Society*. The Hague: Martinus Nijhoff, 1980.

——. "The Idol of the Stove: The Background to Swift's Criticism of Descartes." *Review of English Studies* 25 (1974): 15–24.

Spink, J.S. *French Free Thought from Gassendi to Voltaire*. New York: Greenwood, 1960.

Spoo, Peter. "Enthusiasm." In *Europäische Schlüsselwörter*. Band II: *Kurzmonographien I: Wörter im geistigen und sozialen Raum*, 50–67. Munich: Max Huber Verlag, 1964.

Staudenbaur, C.A. "Platonism, Theosophy, and Immaterialism: Recent Views of the Cambridge Platonists." *Journal of the History of Ideas* 35 (1974): 157–69.

Steck, Karl Gerhard. "Luther und die Schwärmer." *Theologische Studien* 44 (1955).

Stefan, Truman G. "The Social Argument against Enthusiasm (1650–1660)." *Studies in English*, no. 4126. Austin, University of Texas (1944): 39–63.

Steneck, N.H. "Greatrakes the Stroker: The Interpretations of Historians", *Isis* 73 (1982): 161–177.

Stephens, W.P. *The Holy Spirit in the Theology of Martin Bucer*. Cambridge: Cambridge University Press, 1970.

——. *The Theology of Huldrych Zwingli*. Oxford: The Clarendon Press, 1986.

Syfret, R.H. "Some Early Reactions to the Royal Society." *Notes and Records of the Royal Society* 7 (1949–50): 207–258.

Taylor, Charles. *Sources of the Self*. Cambridge Mass.: Harvard University Press, 1989.

Temkin, Owsei. *The Falling Sickness; a History of Epilepsy from the Greeks to the Beginning of Modern Neurology*. Revised edition. Baltimore: Johns Hopkins University Press, 1971.

——. "On Galen's Pneumatology." *Gesnerus* 8 (1950): 180–189.

Thijssen-Schoute, C. Louise. *Nederlands Cartesianisme*. Amsterdam: N.V. Noord-Hollandsche Uitgevers, 1954.

Thomas, Keith. *Religion and the Decline of Magic*. New York: Scribner's, 1971; Penguin University Books, 1973, and subsequent paperback editions.

Thomas, Henry. "The Society of Chymical Physitians, an Echo of the Great Plague of London, 1665." In *Science, Medicine and History: Essays on the Evolution of Scientific Thought and Medical Practice in Honour of Charles Singer*, edited by E. Ashworth Underwood, vol. I, 55–71. Oxford: Oxford University Press, 1953.

Thorndike, Lynn. *A History of Magic and Experimental Science*. 6 vols. New York and London: Columbia University Press, 1923–1941.

Trevor-Roper, H.R. "The European Witch-Craze of the Sixteenth and Seventeenth Centuries." In *The European Witch-Craze of the Sixteenth and Seventeenth Centuries and Other Essays*, 90–192. New York and Evanston: Harper Torchbooks, 1969.

———. "Robert Burton and *The Anatomy of Melancholy*." In *Renaissance Essays*, 239–274. Chicago: University of Chicago Press, 1985.

Tucker, Susie I. *Enthusiasm: A Study in Semantic Change*. Cambridge: Cambridge University Press, 1972.

Turner, Victor. *Dreams, Fields, and Metaphors: Symbolic Action in Human Society*. Ithaca, N.Y.: Cornell U.P., 1974.

Van Der Wall, E.G.E. "De Mystieke Chiliast Petrus Serrarius (1600–1669) en zijn Wereld." Ph.D. diss., University of Leiden, 1987.

Vickers, Brian. *In Defence of Rhetoric*. Oxford: Clarendon Press, 1988.

———. "The Royal Society and English Prose Style: A Reassessment." In *Rhetoric and the Pursuit of Truth: Language Change in the Seventeenth and Eighteenth Centuries*, 1–76. Los Angeles: William Andrews Clark Memorial Library, 1985.

Vidal, Daniel. *Le Malheur et son prophète: Inspirés et sectaires en Languedoc calviniste (1685–1725)*. Paris: Payot, 1983.

Voitle, Robert. *The Third Earl of Shaftesbury. 1671–1713*. Baton Rouge and London: Louisiana State University Press, 1984.

Wade, Ira O. *The Intellectual Origins of the French Enlightenment*. Princeton: Princeton University Press, 1971.

Waite, Gary K. *David Joris and Dutch Anabaptism 1524–1543*. Waterloo, Ontario: Wilfrid Laurier University Press, 1990.

Waldron, J. "Locke: Toleration and the Rationality of Persecution." In *Justifying Toleration: Conceptual and Historical Perspectives*, edited by S. Mendus, 61–86. Cambridge: Cambridge University Press, 1988.

Walker, Daniel P. *Spiritual and Demonic Magic from Ficino to Campanella*. London: Warburg Institute, 1958.

———. *Unclean Spirits: Possession and Exorcism in France and England in the Late Sixteenth and Early Seventeenth Centuries*. London: Scolars Press, 1981.

———. "The Astral Body in Renaissance Medicine", *Journal of the Warburg and Courtauld Institutes* 21 (1958): 119–133.

———. "Medical *Spirits* and God and the Soul." In *Spiritus. IV Colloquio Internazionale del Lessico Intellettuale Europeo*, edited by M. Fattori and M. Bianchi. Rome: Edizioni dell'Ateneo, 1984.

———. "The Cessation of Miracles." In *Hermeticism and the Renaissance*, edited by Ingrid Merkel and Allen G. Debus, 114–124. Washingon D.C.: The Folger Shakespeare Library, 1988.

Wang, Leonard J. "The Life and Works of Adrien Baillet." Ph.D. diss., Columbia University, New York, 1955.

Watson, A. *The Downfall of Cartesianism, 1673–1712*. The Hague: Martinus Nijhoff, 1966.

Weber, Max. *Economy and Society*. Edited by Günther Roth and Claus Wittich. New York: Bedminster Press, 1968.

Webster, Charles, ed. *Samuel Hartlib and the Advancement of Learning*. Cambridge: Cambridge University Press, 1970.

———. *From Paracelsus to Newton: Magic and the Making of Modern Science*. New York: Cambridge University Press, 1982.

Webster, C.M. "Swift and Some Earlier Satirists of Puritan Enthusiasm." *PMLA* 48 (1933): 1141–53.

———. "The Satiric Background of the Attack on the Puritans in Swift's *A Tale of a Tub*." *PMLA* 50 (1935): 210–23.

Westfall, R.S. *Force in Newton's Physics*. London: Macdonald; New York: American Elsevier, 1971.

———. *Never at Rest: A Biography of Isaac Newton*. Cambridge: Cambridge University Press, 1980.

Wilde, C.B. "Hutchinsonianism, Natural Philosophy and Religious Controversy in Eighteenth-Century Britain." *History of Science* 18 (1980): 1–24.

Williams, George H. *The Radical Reformation*. Philadelphia: The Westminster Press, 1962. Revised edition, 1991.

Williamson, George. "The Restoration Revolt against Enthusiasm." *Studies in Philology* 32 (1935): 553–579. Reprinted in Williamson, *Seventeenth Century Contexts*, 202–239. London: Faber and Faber, 1959; Chicago: University of Chicago Press, 1961.

Windhorst, Christof. "Luther and the 'Enthusiasts': Theological Judgements in his Lecture on the First Epistle of St. John (1527)." *Journal of Religious History* 9 (1977): 339–348.

Wittkower, R. "Genius: Individualism in Art and Artists." *Dictionary of the History of Ideas*, vol. 1, 297–312. New York: Scribner's, 1973.

Wood, P.B. "Methodology and Apologetics: Thomas Sprat's *History of the Royal Society*." *British Journal for the History of Science* 13 (1980): 1–26.

Yates, Frances A. *The Rosicrucian Enlightenment*. London: Routledge and Kegan Paul, 1972.

Zehe, Horst. *Die Gravitationstheorie des Nicolas Fatio de Duillier*. Hildesheim: Gerstenberg Verlag, 1980.

INDEX

Compiled with the help of Shlomit Schuster

This Index includes names, topics and major themes mentioned in the text and notes. Authors of secondary literature appear only if mentioned in addition to bibliographical references. Biblical references appear at the end. Names of countries and places are usually not included. The terms "Enthusiasm" (except in relation to other themes), "Enthusiast", "Fanatics", "God", "Inspiration", "Jesus Christ", "Prophecy", "Prophesying", "Protestant", "Revelation", and "Visions" are not included either as they appear throughout the book.

Biblical References

BRILL'S STUDIES IN INTELLECTUAL HISTORY

1. POPKIN, R.H. *Isaac la Peyrère (1596-1676)*. 1987. ISBN 90 04 08157 7
2. THOMSON, A. *Barbary and Enlightenment*. European Attitudes towards the Maghreb in the 18th Century. 1987. ISBN 90 04 08273 5
3. DUHEM, P. *Prémices Philosophiques*. With an Introduction in English by S.L. Jaki. 1987. ISBN 90 04 08117 8
4. OUDEMANS, TH.C.W. & A.P.M.H. LARDINOIS. *Tragic Ambiguity*. Anthropology, Philosophy and Sophocles' *Antigone*. 1987. ISBN 90 04 08417 7
5. FRIEDMAN, J.B. (ed.). *John de Foxton's Liber Cosmographiae (1408)*. An Edition and Codicological Study. 1988. ISBN 90 04 08528 9
6. AKKERMAN, F. & A. J. VANDERJAGT (eds.). *Rodolphus Agricola Phrisius, 1444-1485*. Proceedings of the International Conference at the University of Groningen, 28-30 October 1985. 1988. ISBN 90 04 08599 8
7. CRAIG, W.L. *The Problem of Divine Foreknowledge and Future Contingents from Aristotle to Suarez*. 1988. ISBN 90 04 08516 5
8. STROLL, M. *The Jewish Pope*. Ideology and Politics in the Papal Schism of 1130. 1987. ISBN 90 04 08590 4
9. STANESCO, M. *Jeux d'errance du chevalier médiéval*. Aspects ludiques de la fonction guerrière dans la littérature du Moyen Age flamboyant. 1988. ISBN 90 04 08684 6
10. KATZ, D. *Sabbath and Sectarianism in Seventeenth-Century England*. 1988. ISBN 90 04 08754 0
11. LERMOND, L. *The Form of Man*. Human Essence in Spinoza's *Ethic*. 1988. ISBN 90 04 08829 6
12. JONG, M. DE. *In Samuel's Image*. Early Medieval Child Oblation. (in preparation)
13. PYENSON, L. *Empire of Reason*. Exact Sciences in Indonesia, 1840-1940. 1989. ISBN 90 04 08984 5
14. CURLEY, E. & P.-F. MOREAU (eds.). *Spinoza. Issues and Directions*. The Proceedings of the Chicago Spinoza Conference. 1990. ISBN 90 04 09334 6
15. KAPLAN, Y., H. MÉCHOULAN & R.H. POPKIN (eds.). *Menasseh Ben Israel and His World*. 1989. ISBN 90 04 09114 9
16. BOS, A.P. *Cosmic and Meta-Cosmic Theology in Aristotle's Lost Dialogues*. 1989. ISBN 90 04 09155 6
17. KATZ, D.S. & J.I. ISRAEL (eds.). *Sceptics, Millenarians and Jews*. 1990. ISBN 90 04 09160 2
18. DALES, R.C. *Medieval Discussions of the Eternity of the World*. 1990. ISBN 90 04 09215 3
19. CRAIG, W.L. *Divine Foreknowledge and Human Freedom*. The Coherence of Theism: Omniscience. 1991. ISBN 90 04 09250 1
20. OTTEN, W. *The Anthropology of Johannes Scottus Eriugena*. 1991. ISBN 90 04 09302 8
21. ÅKERMAN, S. *Queen Christina of Sweden and Her Circle*. 1991. ISBN 90 04 09310 9
22. POPKIN, R.H. *The Third Force in Seventeenth-Century Thought*. 1992. ISBN 90 04 09324 9
23. DALES, R.C. & O. ARGERAMI (eds.). *Medieval Latin Texts on the Eternity of the World*. 1990. ISBN 90 04 09376 1
24. STROLL, M. *Symbols as Power*. The Papacy Following the Investiture Contest. 1991. ISBN 90 04 09374 5
25. FARAGO, C.J. *Leonardo da Vinci's 'Paragone'*. A Critical Interpretation with a New Edition of the Text in the *Codex Urbinas*. 1992. ISBN 90 04 09415 6
26. JONES, R. *Learning Arabic in Renaissance Europe*. Forthcoming. ISBN 90 04 09451 2
27. DRIJVERS, J.W. *Helena Augusta*. The Mother of Constantine the Great and the Legend of Her Finding of the True Cross. 1992. ISBN 90 04 09435 0
28. BOUCHER, W.I. *Spinoza in English*. A Bibliography from the Seventeenth-Century to the Present. 1991. ISBN 90 04 09499 7
29. McINTOSH, C. *The Rose Cross and the Age of Reason*. Eighteenth-Century Rosicrucianism in Central Europe and its Relationship to the Enlightenment. 1992. ISBN 90 04 09502 0
30. CRAVEN, K. *Jonathan Swift and the Millennium of Madness*. The Information Age in Swift's *A Tale of a Tub*. 1992. ISBN 90 04 09524 1
31. BERKVENS-STEVELINCK, C., H. BOTS, P.G. HOFTIJZER & O.S. LANKHORST (eds.). *Le Magasin de l'Univers. The Dutch Republic as the Centre of the European Book Trade*. Papers from the Int. Colloquium, Wassenaar, 5-7 July 1990. 1992. ISBN 90 04 09493 8
32. GRIFFIN, JR., M.I.J. *Latitudinarianism in the Seventeenth-Century Church of England*. Annotated by R.H. Popkin. Edited by L. Freedman. 1992. ISBN 90 04 09653 1

33. WES, M.A. *Classics in Russia 1700-1855*. 1992. ISBN 90 04 09664 7
34. BULHOF, I.N. The Relationship between Literature and Science. With a Case Study in Darwin's *The Origin of Species*. 1992. ISBN 90 04 09644 2
35. LAURSEN, J.C. *The Politics of Skepticism in the Ancients, Montaigne, Hume and Kant*. 1992. ISBN 90 04 09459 8
36. COHEN, E. *The Crossroads of Justice*. Law and Culture in Late Medieval France. 1993. ISBN 90 04 09569 1
37. POPKIN, R.H. & A.J. VANDERJAGT (eds.). *Scepticism and Irreligion in the Seventeenth and Eighteenth Centuries*. 1993. ISBN 90 04 09596 9
38. MAZZOCCO, A. *Linguistic Theories in Dante and the Humanists*. 1993. ISBN 90 04 09702 3
39. KROOK, D. *John Sergeant and His Circle*. A Study of Three Seventeenth-Century English Aristotelians. Ed. with an Introduction by B.C. Southgate. 1993. ISBN 90 04 09756 2
40. AKKERMAN, F., G.C. HUISMAN & A.J. VANDERJAGT (eds.). *Wessel Gansfort (1419-1489) and Northern Humanism*. 1993. ISBN 90 04 09857 7
41. COLISH, M.L. *Peter Lombard*. 2 volumes. 1994. ISBN 90 04 09859 3 (Volume 1), ISBN 90 04 09860 7 (Volume 2), ISBN 90 04 09861 5 (Set)
42. VAN STRIEN, C.D. *British Travellers in Holland During the Stuart Period*. Edward Browne and John Locke as Tourists in the United Provinces. 1993. ISBN 90 04 09482 2
43. MACK, P. *Renaissance Argument*. Valla and Agricola in the Traditions of Rhetoric and Dialectic. 1993. ISBN 90 04 09879 8
44. DA COSTA, U. *Examination of Pharisaic Traditions*. Supplemented by SEMUEL DA SILVA's *Treatise on the Immortality of the Soul*. Translation, Notes and Introduction by H.P. Salomon & I.S.D. Sassoon. 1993. ISBN 90 04 09923 9
45. MANNS, J.W. *Reid and His French Disciples*. 1994. ISBN 90 04 09942 5
46. SPRUNGER, K.L. *Trumpets from the Tower*. English Puritan Printing in the Netherlands, 1600-1640. 1994. ISBN 90 04 09935 2
47. RUSSELL, G.A. (ed.). *The 'Arabick' Interest of the Natural Philosophers in Seventeenth-Century England*. 1994. ISBN 90 04 09888 7
48-49. SPRUIT, L. *Species intelligibilis: From Perception to Knowledge*. 2 vols. Volume I: Classical Roots and Medieval Discussions. 1994. ISBN 90 04 09883 6. Volume II: Renaissance Controversies, Later Scholasticism, and the Elimination of the Intelligible Species in Modern Philosophy. 1995. ISBN 90 04 10396 1
50. HYATTE, R. *The Arts of Friendship*. The Idealization of Friendship in Medieval and Early Renaissance Literature. 1994. ISBN 90 04 10018 0
51. CARRÉ, J. (ed.). *The Crisis of Courtesy*. Studies in the Conduct-Book in Britain, 1600-1900. 1994. ISBN 90 04 10005 9
52. BURMAN, T.E. *Religious Polemic and the Intellectual History of the Mozarabs, 1050-1200*. 1994. ISBN 90 04 09910 7
53. HORLICK, A.S. *Patricians, Professors, and Public Schools*. The Origins of Modern Educational Thought in America. 1994. ISBN 90 04 10054 7
54. MacDONALD, A.A., M. LYNCH & I.B. COWAN (eds.). *The Renaissance in Scotland*. Offered to John Durkan. 1994. ISBN 90 04 10097 0
55. VON MARTELS, Z. (ed.). *Travel Fact and Travel Fiction*. Fiction, Literary Tradition, Scholarly Discovery and Observation in Travel Writing. 1994. ISBN 90 04 10112 8
56. PRANGER, M.B. *Bernard of Clairvaux and the Shape of Monastic Thought*. Broken Dreams. 1994. ISBN 90 04 10055 5
57. VAN DEUSEN, N. *Theology and Music at the Early University*. The Case of Robert Grosseteste and Anonymous IV. 1994. ISBN 90 04 10059 8
58. WARNEKE, S. *Images of the Educational Traveller in Early Modern England*. 1994. ISBN 90 04 10126 8
59. BIETENHOLZ, P.G. *Historia and Fabula*. Myths and Legends in Historical Thought from Antiquity to the Modern Age. 1994. ISBN 90 04 10063 6
60. LAURSEN, J.C. (ed.). *New Essays on the Political Thought of the Huguenots of the Refuge*. 1995. ISBN 90 04 09986 7
61. DRIJVERS, J.W. & A.A. MacDONALD (eds.). *Centres of Learning*. Learning and Location in Pre-Modern Europe and the Near East. 1995. ISBN 90 04 10193 4
62. JAUMANN, H. *Critica*. Untersuchungen zur Geschichte der Literaturkritik zwischen Quintilian und Thomasius. 1995. ISBN 90 04 10276 0
63. HEYD, M. *"Be Sober and Reasonable."* The Critique of Enthusiasm in the Seventeenth and Early Eighteenth Centuries. 1995. ISBN 90 04 10118 7
64. OKENFUSS, M.J. *The Rise and Fall of Latin Humanism in Early-Modern Russia*. Pagan Authors, Ukrainians, and the Resiliency of Muscovy. 1995. ISBN 90 04 10331 7
65. DALES, R.C. *The Problem of the Rational Soul in the Thirteenth Century*. 1995. ISBN 90 04 10296 5

DATE DUE

			Printed in USA